Farm Business Management
Successful Decisions in a
Changing Environment

Farm Business Management

Successful Decisions in a Changing Environment

Peter H. Calkins / Dennis D. DiPietre
Iowa State University

Macmillan Publishing Co., Inc.
New York
Collier Macmillan Publishers
London

Macmillan Publishing Co., Inc.
866 Third Avenue, New York, New York 10022

Collier Macmillan Canada, Inc.

Library of Congress Cataloging in Publication Data

Calkins, Peter H.
  Farm business management.

  Includes index.
  1. Farm management—Decision making. 2. Farm
management—United States—Decision making.
I. DiPietre, Dennis D. II. Title.
S561.C254   630'.68   82-6618
ISBN 0-02-318320-9   AACR2

Printing: 1 2 3 4 5 6 7 8   Year: 3 4 5 6 7 8 9 0

ISBN   0-02-318320-9

For

Nancy and Adam

Susan and Jacob

Preface

In writing *Farm Business Management: Successful Decisions in a Changing Environment,* we have tried to provide a unique approach to the study of managing agricultural production. The period between the early 1980s and the year 2000 will see tremendous changes in the environment in which agricultural producers must operate. There will be increasing discussion of laws to limit agricultural pollution and soil erosion. There will be a movement to reduce the use of energy in agricultural production until a cheap alternative to imported petroleum can be found. There will be changes in the dietary preferences of Americans at home and in all probability increased demand for American exports abroad. In this period of change it is important that students graduating from colleges and universities who prepare to enter employment in production agriculture have a clear conception of the essential principles of farm management science. If they become bogged down in details, especially if those details are outdated, the important tools of the science may be missed. The emphasis in college courses in the 1980s should be on the application of consistent tools to a constantly changing production environment.

It is understanding, above all, that is important as students acquire skills as farm managers. Thus, in addition to presenting a how-to book we also address the questions what and why. The format of the book is simple. There are four parts which progress from the clearest vision of how production decisions ought to be made (Part I), through intermediate stages (Parts II and III), to an appreciation of how the farm manager must operate in the complexities of the real world (Part IV). We present a definition of farm management which binds together these major sections of the book.

After an introduction which outlines the objectives and process of farm decision making, we present the **Ideal World** of economic relationships in the absence of risk, uncertainty, and lack of knowledge (Part I). Even students who have had a principles course in economics should be reintroduced to the fundamental production relationships in economics as applied to a farm context both in the long and short run. Chapters

2 and 3 endeavor to do this. Three production relationships are covered. Three methods of solving each are demonstrated in a parallel manner. The three solution methodologies (algebraic, graphical, and longhand) arrive at the same answer, but the graphical method allows the student to solve for an optimum with continuous functions but without the use of the production calculus. This format allows the individual instructor to omit any of the relationships or any of the three solution methodologies, if desired.

Once the ideal world has been presented, we take the students into the realm of imperfect knowledge or budgeting. Thus, Part II is called **Approximating the Real World.** The student will learn in this section the use, meaning and interrelationships between budgets and records. This section progresses through a series of management-oriented questions: what resources are available (inventory), what is the value of the resources and the financial position of the farm (inventory valuation, depreciation, net worth, etc.), what can be done with available resources (enterprise budgets, whole farm plans, linear programming), are the plans efficient (efficiency measures), what adjustments can be made for improving efficiency (partial budgets), are the plans profitable (income statement), and are the plans financially feasible (cash flow budget and credit restraints)? Even though this ordering separates the traditional treatment of financial statements and some records and budgets, its advantage lies in the systematic utilization of these statements and budgets in a logical management process. The traditional treatment of financial statements as a combined package occurs in Chapter 13 when credit acquisition is addressed. Where appropriate, each type of budget demonstrated points the student back to the particular analysis which it approximates in the ideal world of economic principles. Thus the traditional frustration felt by students in relating economic theory to applied analysis is largely resolved.

After the budgeting and the record keeping process is over, there are other aspects of the real world which have to be taken into account. Therefore in Part III, **Improving the Approximation**, the student is introduced to prices, risk, and government programs, how prices may be measured, the trade-offs between risk and profit, and how the farm operator should respond to government programs.

Finally in Part IV, **The Real World**, the student is introduced to further complexities of actual farm and ranch management. In addition to the lack of perfect knowledge and the difficulties which price variation, yield variability, and changing government programs entail, the farm manager must also be able to acquire and manage wisely the four basic factors of production—land, capital, labor and management. We present these in reverse order because we feel that it is easier to acquire management than land and also because an understanding of capital investment and acquisition is necessary to a good understanding of land acquisition.

In Chapter 16 of Part IV, we introduce a chapter on tax management. This is more complete than chapters commonly presented in farm management texts which tend to deal only with income tax management. Tax implications of farming and the way farm managers handle taxes are not only becoming more complex with time, but regulations are themselves in constant flux. Again, the emphasis is on understanding rather than dealing with the code of a particular year. Finally in Chapter 17, the student is introduced to the advantages and disadvantages of various types of farm business organizational structure.

Unique aspects of this text include the systematic progression from the ideal world to the real world, the complete and parallel coverage of economic principles, the clear relationship between economic principles and budgets, the detailed presentation of risk management strategies, the inclusion of a chapter on government programs (which are very important determinants of optimal farming patterns and practices), and the expanded chapter on tax management. Another new aspect of the book is that we introduce the concept of general energy management in Chapter 14 as a supplement to the traditional approach to machinery management.

We hope that most instructors will choose to present all of these chapters in some detail. However, in some curricula there is not enough time or the level of the students' preparation is not adequate to cover some of the advanced material. If this is the case, Part III can be cut short to include only Chapter 9. Because Part III is devoted to fine-tuning of the approximations entailed in budgets, it is obvious that upper level techniques will be presented in these chapters. Not every classroom will be suited for introducing them. If after eliminating Chapters 7, 8 and 10, further shortening of the course is required, it would also be possible to skip over Chapter 2 or to present it in a cursory way for those students who have already had a firm introduction to economic principles.

The structure of each chapter is designed to cause the student to think about the lessons and the principles which can be learned. At the beginning of each chapter, he or she is told what concepts and skills will be presented. At the end there are sections which alert the student to further readings, and a set of questions which help the student and teacher relate the material to the particular agricultural environment in their part of the United States. We also provide quantitative examples where appropriate to give further experience in the application of farm management principles.

Throughout the book we frequently use direct address in communicating with the student. Some may find this style too informal but our experience indicates that students respond well to being addressed in person and that much clarity can be gained from short direct statements which involve the student.

We also recognize the long-standing importance of women in agricultural decision making. A growing proportion of U.S. farms are operated by women, and women have long taken primary responsibility in record-keeping and tax management. However, until the English language develops a less awkward third person pronoun than s/he, we follow the custom of using the masculine pronoun to represent farm managers of both sexes.

We wish to acknowledge the helpful suggestions of many of our colleagues, especially those who reviewed early versions of this manuscript. In particular, we are grateful to Raymond R. Beneke, Chairman of the Economics Department at Iowa State University, for his personal support and encouragement. We are also thankful to our typists, Josanne Niemand and Shelley Murrell.

Constructive comments for improving the text in later editions will be warmly welcomed.

Peter H. Calkins
Dennis D. DiPietre

Ames, Iowa
January, 1983

Contents

Part I

$$\frac{\partial y}{\partial y} Y + \frac{\partial y}{\partial y} P_y - \frac{\partial P_{x_1}}{\partial y} \cdot X_1 - \frac{\partial X_1}{\partial y} \cdot P_{x_1} -$$

$$\frac{\partial P_{x_2}}{\partial y} \cdot X_2 - \frac{\partial X_2}{\partial y} P_{x_2} - \frac{\partial FC}{\partial y} = 0$$

The Ideal World

1

Introduction to Management

It was not very difficult, either, to decide where we should look for a beginning, for I knew already that one begins with the simplest and easiest to know.

Réné DesCartes, Discourse on Method and Meditations

Concepts

In this chapter you will come to understand:

1. The changing environment within which farm decisions must be made.
2. The five components of the management function.
3. The distinctive characteristics of production agriculture compared to non-agricultural businesses.
4. The ideal world framework within which the study of management science will begin.
5. The four classifications of inputs or resources necessary for all productive activity.
6. The definitions of technology, technological progress and appropriate technology.
7. The three fundamental resource allocation questions facing every farm manager.
8. The three solution methodologies which may be employed to solve these fundamental questions.

THE CHANGING ENVIRONMENT

As we enter the last two decades of the twentieth century the challenges to successful farm management are manifold. Adding to a long and traditional list of problems confronting today's farmer, the challenges of dwindling world energy resources, government intervention through changing policy actions, tax laws, and business structure options are calling forth a higher level of understanding and management ability.

3

The subject matter of farm management is evolving along with these changing complexities and increased challenges. Historically, farm management instruction was very general, emphasizing specific agronomic and livestock cultivation techniques. Much, if not all, of this material is now offered in separate courses in agronomy and animal science departments. Farm management courses have become increasingly quantitative, emphasizing decision making techniques, economics, finance, strategies for handling risk and taxes, and the skills necessary to tie technical cultivation practices together into a successful, profitable, and continuing farm business.

The importance of good management is accentuated in a changing environment. Surprising to some, the management function is typically the significant difference between high and low profit farms (Table 1-1). Frequently, high profit farms will earn between eight and nine times greater return to management while utilizing nearly identical values of land, labor, and capital. A study conducted by the division of Agricultural Economics at the University of Wyoming indicated that the top 20 percent of Wyoming cattle ranchers earned three times the income per cattle unit while investing 10 percent less capital per cattle unit than the lowest 20 percent of producers. Such results raise the stakes of good management. Even small farmers frequently control hundreds of thousands of dollars worth of resources. Managing these resources requires analyzing hundreds of pieces of information. This information revolution has led to the growth of a quantitative emphasis in farm management. As agricultural technology advances, microcomputers and hand-held computing devices are rapidly becoming as much a tool of modern farming as tractors, plows, and other farm equipment.

TABLE 1-1.   COMPARISON OF HIGH AND LOW PROFIT IOWA FARMS, 1980

	Low Profit Farms	*High Profit Farms*
Income		
Net farm income	$27,699	$90,898
Resources Used		
Land—total value	$430,199	$455,987
Labor—man/months	14.8	17.4
Machinery and equipment	$38,066	$44,266
Return to management	−$6,815	$50,626
Efficiency of Operations		
Corn yield per acre—bushels	121	133
Livestock return per $100 feed fed	$169	$218
Gross profits per man	$67,962	$108,747
Gross profits per $100 invested	$16	$27

Source: "Selected Readings in Farm Management," (mimeograph), Iowa State University Bookstore Press, Ames, Iowa.

Successful farm management involves the ability to plan, measure and properly choose among the multitude of trade-offs and options available in utilizing resources to accomplish desired goals. However, management ability is not simply a set of equations to be memorized once and for all but a skill of understanding which is possessed in some degree by nearly everyone. This understanding must be flexible, evolve, grow, and be capable of rapid response to the changing environment.

Consistent with these characteristics, the current process of successful farm decision-making can be defined as "the attainment of **farm family goals** by using **economic principles** to formulate and implement **budgets**, adjusted for **risk and government programs**, that combine the **factors of production** within a suitable **tax and business structure**" (Figure 1-1).

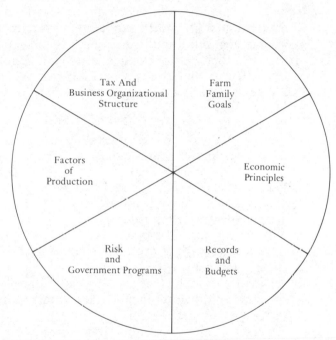

FIGURE 1-1. *The Components of Farm Business Management. While studied separately, each component is essential to a full understanding of management science.*

FUNCTIONS OF MANAGEMENT

The five functions of management necessary to successfully engage in production agriculture are an adaptation of the scientific method, which was first described by the philosopher Descartes in the seventeenth century (Table 1-2). These five functions are:

1. **Formulating goals**—The need to measure trade-offs in farm decisions by evaluating both economic and non-economic factors. The deci-

TABLE 1-2.   THE FIVE FUNCTIONS OF MODERN FARM MANAGEMENT AS
DERIVED FROM THE SCIENTIFIC METHOD OF DESCARTES

Modern Farm Management	*Descartes Scientific Method*
1. Goal formulation	1. Describe what is (hypothesis)
2. Compilation of relevant data	2. Collect and order information
3. Planning activities to achieve goals	3. Test hypothesis
4. Implementation of best plan	4. Accept, reject or reformulate hypothesis
5. Evaluation of results	

Source: Adapted from Descartes, René, *Discourse on Method and Meditions*, translated by L. J.
Lafleur, The Bobbs-Merrill Co., Inc., 1960.

sions which result will largely be a function of the goals of each
individual operator. Stating farm goals and diagnosing problems
which limit goal attainment are very important. There is usually not
one single goal but a multitude of farm and family goals which are
often in conflict. Part of the decision making process is learning how
to evaluate the compromises necessary to accommodate farm and
family goals. It will be useful to review and list some of the possible
goals of farming.

a. Profit maximization. This is the most commonly cited goal in
   other economics courses. Certainly an acceptable level of profit
   must be achieved if you expect to continue in farming, but it is
   not the only possible goal.
b. Farm ownership. Many people are willing to live on less income
   and pay high principal and interest payments if it means eventually owning the farm property.
c. Farm expansion. The family already has a farm but realizes that
   to take advantage of economics of size and compete with already
   large farms, expansion is required.
d. Avoidance of risk. One might want to bridle his rate of expansion or avoid venturing into new enterprises in order to reduce
   the risk of losing the farm.
e. Having an enjoyable standard of living. The farm operator may
   want to spend at least ten hours a week with his family or keep
   out $2,000 per year for travel and entertainment. This money
   could otherwise be reinvested in the farm business. The operator
   may have some specific enterprises that he likes to do (such as
   raise rabbits or turkeys) or may be determined to purchase his
   next tractor with an air-conditioned cab when it is not strictly
   justified.
f. Master Farmer or other production awards. It may be desirable
   to go all out to get the maximum yield even though it is not the
   most profitable level of production.

These are all examples of goals which, in and of themselves, are
quite legitimate. Yet it is easy to see how trying to accomplish all of
them would lead to serious conflicts in decision making. The successful manager accomplishes goals by carefully evaluating each and
implementing them in the way and to the extent which achieves

the highest level of satisfaction. It is important to remember that it is not always the wealthiest manager who achieves the highest level of satisfaction.

2. **Compilation**—The collection of data such as resource inventory, farm production records, and experimental data made available through plant and animal scientists who study physical relationships. All of these help in describing your current situation and projecting future prospects.

3. **Planning**—Stating your objectives and using economic principles and budgets to predict the need for resources and prescribe the production alternative which allocates them most efficiently.

4. **Implementation**—Actually putting the plan to work: buying and feeding out of feeder pigs, the planting, maintaining, and harvesting of crops, etc.

5. **Evaluation**—Going back afterwards and checking to make sure that all of the preceding steps have been effective and accomplished as planned. For example, in the compilation stage the availability of labor may have been underestimated or the yield from crops overestimated. Or in the planning stage, suppose that the poor drainage on a particular field was not taken into account and it turned out to be a wetter than usual spring. Whatever the result, you must realize why things were different than expected in order to plan for the next production period. It is important to know why you did well, whether you could have done better, and what options you have for future periods.

Management Capacity

The concept of management capacity can be defined as **the ability to make and improve decisions over time both efficiently and rapidly.** This ability involves two components. First, there must be knowledge of the five functions of management involved in the decision making process. Second, decisions can be classified by several important characteristics to aid the manager in effectively addressing them:

Imminence. This refers to the lead time a manager has in making or changing a decision before an opportunity is lost or substantially diminished. While many farm decisions are only made once per year (such as planting decisions), the period during the year when the decision must be implemented can be a very few days. The decision as to which variety of a particular crop to plant or which crop should be chosen, when replanting is necessary, requires a timely response during the planting season. Chapter 11 deals with the question of imminence concerning hired labor decisions. Many of these decisions can be anticipated well in advance providing sufficient time to collect information and make an appropriate decision.

Importance. Since decisions on the farm vary as to their importance, a hierarchy of planning is critical to effective decision making. The importance of a decision is generally measured by its potential effect on net income. It should be obvious that the bulk of the manager's efforts should be directed to those decisions offering the greatest possible gains (or losses) in net income. Concentrating on the insignificant problems and questions generally yields insignificant results. Since these relatively insignificant problems usually comprise the majority of farm decisions, the manager must be careful to set aside sufficient time and energy for the important decisions of the farm.

Alternatives. Many farm production activities can be accomplished by a variety of means. The farm manager must carefully evaluate the various alternatives to select those which accomplish farm goals in the most efficient and profitable way. Economic principles, for example, can be a great aid in selecting the least cost mix of inputs necessary to accomplish production activities. Several factors effect the desirability of alternatives. Some of these include farm family goals, manager ability, hired labor availability, and input supply sources, etc.

Frequency. The frequency of decisions varies widely among farm production activities. Generally, livestock require more frequent decisions than cropping activities. A carefully prepared schedule can help reduce the daily efforts involved in feeding and milking decisions, etc. While the daily, repetitive decisions in managing a farm may be relatively insignificant on any particular day, their cumulative effect can be very important.

Revocability. Many farm decisions cannot be easily undone once resources are committed. Because most farm production processes take many weeks or months to complete, once initiated, these processes are very difficult to alter or reverse without considerable cost. Generally there is no market for products partway through a production process (such as corn before ears have formed). Immature livestock can be sold but usually at a large discount. Therefore, it is wise to carefully study farm product production decisions before committing resources. Chapter 5 treats the various budgets farm managers can use to test a decision on paper before costly implementation occurs.

DISTINCTIVE ASPECTS OF PRODUCTION AGRICULTURE

The vocation of farming can no longer be considered just a way of life. Successful farming comes to those who recognize it as a business and prepare themselves in the skills of business management. As a business, farming has problems and challenges both unique to it and similar to other businesses.

Dissimilarities

Unlike other business enterprises, farming depends heavily on biological relationships. Climate, growth potential, disease, and gestation period are only a few of the factors affecting the biological nature of farm products over which the manager has little or no control. Operations cannot be easily speeded up in response to favorable prices or slowed down when prices fall. Combining the same amount of inputs in farm production processes can lead to dramatically different output even within the same production period.

Another problem unique to farming is that the factors of production are not separately supplied. The farm operator is frequently manager and laborer. The family car may double as the business car. Farm credit may be extended on the basis of family credit history and reputation. This creates difficulty when measuring efficiency as the manager attempts to identify which factor of production has been the least efficient. Difficulties in allocation also occur. Machines are guided by labor, which in turn is guided by management. Should you spend more time managing or in labor?

As a rule, fixed costs are higher in agriculture: about 70 percent of total cost in agriculture compared to 30 percent in non-agricultural enterprises. This difference is primarily due to the large investments in land and machinery per unit of output required in farming. Family labor is generally available year round whether it can be utilized or not. In other words, family members represent fixed labor costs. Because there is a relatively slow turnover process in farming (i.e., one cotton crop per year, one and one-half years per calf crops) and large price fluctuations due to the biological character of the output, it is sometimes difficult to cover the fixed costs of production.

Farm work is much less specialized than other business labor. As a farm operator you must to a certain extent be a jack of all trades. For example, throughout the production season, you may be called upon to be at once a production planning expert, plant pathologist, animal nutritionist, and veterinarian. This is one reason why more and more operators are considering partnership and corporations as ways to bring more managers into a single farm operation.

Primarily due to the aforementioned problems, risks in farming are higher than in non-farm business. Two types of risk can be distinguished. Business risk is anything that affects the variability of net farm income. Such things as price change, yield variation, government policy changes, technological change, changes in tax law and shifts in consumers' tastes and preferences combine to increase the risk of wide fluctuations in net income. On the other hand, financial risk is anything which affects the survival of the farm. These risks largely involve farm credit. Both kinds of risk will be explored further in later chapters.

Similarities

There also exist similarities between farming and non-farm businesses. As in other businesses, the success of the farm business depends upon efficiency. Evaluating efficiency necessitates monitoring (in the evaluation stage) how well goals have been met. It should be obvious that carefully kept records are a prerequisite for determining efficiency.

Furthermore, success requires adequate volume. In the early stages of U.S. agriculture, all farms were relatively small and fairly poor. The size of the farm was limited by the number of people who lived on it, and technology was constant. Now, however, larger farms can invest in larger, more efficient machinery, and go farther out on what you will come to know as the long-run average cost curve. The result is that their unit costs of production are lower than for smaller farms. Even when farm prices are low (and they typically do not keep up with increases in prices in the rest of the economy), the larger farmers can make a profit, but the smaller ones may be forced out of business unless their operators become excellent managers and/or seek off-farm employment.

Lastly, the farm business manager must be sensitive to the remainder of the economy. An eye to current events, a sensitivity to changes in consumer tastes, and a knowledge of the non-farm business cycle are examples of some of the information that can give the farmer an extra edge when planning a year in advance in a changing environment.

THE IDEAL WORLD

The journey to the goal of becoming better managers begins in what will seem to some an unlikely place: the ideal world. Implicit in the assumption of the ideal world is that the farm manager has perfect knowledge. This means that such things as the specific purchase price of resources, exactly what prices will be received for output, and precisely how much output can be produced given the combination of inputs used, are known in advance. Such knowledge requires that the farm operator has, among other things, perfectly forecasted all prices that will affect him, all political and social events which can affect those prices (wars, embargoes, changes in consumer tastes, etc.), all disease and pest problems that might occur and of course, the weather. In short, we begin in a risk free environment.

The ideal world environment is both the simplest and most logical starting point. By assuming perfect knowledge, most of the complications of the decision-making process have been eliminated. In this way, the fundamental questions and decision-making rules which will set the stage for entry into the uncertain world of reality can easily be addressed.

Beginning in an ideal world of perfect knowledge is not unique to management science. Almost all scientific inquiry begins in a theoretically perfect environment. For instance, physicists and engineers speak of their ideal world as a vacuum or frictionless environment. The first postulates of theoretical physics were developed in this ideal environment. Gradually adjustments to the theory were made to take into account the drags and frictions of the real world. Ultimately, by beginning with theories and equations developed for the ideal world, and then making appropriate adjustments for the real world in which they lived, scientists were able to do such things as place men on the moon, build great structures and transmit pictures and voices across the globe in fractions of a second.

You should realize that by beginning the study of the management functions in the ideal world, only the environment and the conditions have been established under which the fundamental questions facing the manager can be analyzed. There will remain many questions to be answered, problems to be solved, and decisions to be made. Once the fundamental decision rules necessary to solve these problems have been presented, the appropriate adjustments will be made step by step throughout the rest of the text, to move steadily into the uncertainties and problem-solving challenges of the real world. The discussion begins with the building blocks or factors (inputs) of production.

THE FACTORS OF PRODUCTION

All productive activity on the farm utilizes inputs or factors of production. Economists have grouped the factors of production into four major classifications. These classifications include the location or space utilized for productive activity (**land**), the constructive implementation of the activity over time (**labor**), the tools and energy with which the task is accomplished (**capital**), and the knowledge necessary for planning, directing, evaluating and bearing risk (**management**). Land, labor, capital and management are all necessary in varying quantities to engage in any production on the farm.

Some of these factors may be utilized in fixed quantities in any given year, whereas some may be used in varying amounts as conditions require. For example, in a given production cycle or period (one year for most crops) land is generally considered a fixed factor of production. While additional land can be added in later periods by purchase or rental, the acreage available for utilization in any one period is considered fixed. By contrast, hired labor is usually considered a variable factor of production. This is so because the quantity of labor hired during any given year may vary as the work load on the farm increases and decreases from planting through harvest. As the operator considers the factors of production necessary to accomplish farm goals, the cost of each type of factor will aid in planning the allocation of these resources. The importance of the distinction between fixed and variable factors of production will become apparent when long-run planning is introduced.

PRODUCTION TECHNOLOGY

The proportions and quality of factors used to produce agricultural products is referred to as the technology of production. Consider Figure 1–2. This figure illustrates a general system diagram for agricultural production. Beginning on the left-hand side, notice an enumeration of inputs or resources. These inputs are utilized in a production process to produce various outputs. The center of the diagram is the production process or the technology employed to create useful products from raw materials and other inputs. To the right are listed the various farm products or output which result from combining inputs in a given production process.

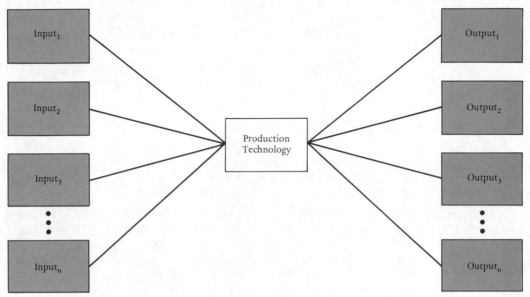

FIGURE 1-2. *A General Diagram of the Process of Production Agriculture.*

The production process or technology of production is not static but has tended to improve over time. This process is known as technological advance or progress. A technological advance results in at least one of three events:

1. The production of more product from the same amount of resources
2. The production of the same amount of product from fewer resources
3. The production of more product from fewer resources

In the last fifty years U.S. agriculture has undergone tremendous advances in technology. These advances flow from several factors including the substitution of machinery for labor, improvements in weed and disease control, introduction of genetically superior crops and livestock, and the increased use of chemical fertilizers. This progression of events can be broadly attributed to the substitution of capital for labor. As a result, U.S. agriculture is now characterized by a relatively high capital/low labor technology when compared to lesser developed countries or even to our own technology some fifty years ago. The direct benefit of this evolution in technology has been tremendous increases in food and fiber output at lower per unit costs.

Probably the most important single reason that U.S. agricultural technology has undergone such rapid advancement is related to factor availability. An abundant supply of natural resources including farm-land, mineral resources and energy has been combined with scientific knowledge through research, development and farmer implementation to achieve startling advances. Many countries throughout the world, because of a lack of suitable factors of production, are characterized by low capital/high labor technologies, with resulting lower output and higher costs. However, given a set of resources or factors of production, it is important that an appropriate technology be utilized so that the greatest possible long-run economic efficiency is achieved. Excessive waste, erosion, and depletion of finite energy resources can then be avoided.

The selection of an appropriate technology for your farm is a personal decision having both regional consequences (profit, erosion, prevention of pollution via runoff, etc.) and global consequences (depletion of world energy reserves, alleviation of world hunger and the maintenance world-wide environmental quality). Although each farm represents a miniscule percent of total world-wide factor demand, the widespread adoption of short-sighted, potentially destructive technologies and land cultivation practices should be avoided. Wise individual stewardship and management of the factors of production by farmers will help to insure the relative abundance which results from a long-run economically appropriate technology.

THE FUNDAMENTAL QUESTIONS

In all of the analyses about to be considered, the attainment of the greatest amount of net income is the common objective. It is important to note the frequent disparity between the solution which gives the greatest gross income and the solution giving the greatest net income (income left over after expenses are paid). Since net income or profit is the money which is truly the farmer's to do with as desired, it is net income that will be maximized.

Maximizing net income is only one of many goals which a farm family may seek. As discussed, some of the other goals may be in conflict with profit or net income maximization. As this occurs, the careful manager will implement that combination of goals which leads to the greatest level of satisfaction. In the following presentation of economic principles it is implied that profit maximization is the only goal (we are after all beginning in the ideal world). In practice, it will be seen that to some extent a variety of goals which conflict with profit maximization can be accomplished simultaneously. Within the constraints these goals impose upon the production activity, suboptimization or achieving the greatest level of profit possible given all farm goals, can be accomplished. For example, if the operator decides to take off weekends or a month each year for vacation, the application of economic principles can still maximize, within the remaining time available for productive activity, whatever net income is still possible.

In general, there are three basic types of economic analysis which capture the broad scope of decisions the farm manager must make regarding the best use of available resources.

1. How much of each input should be applied in order to maximize net return? The shorthand economic term for this question is factor/ product analysis. Within this analysis, the farm manager seeks to discover the utilization level of each input in a production activity that yields the greatest net income. Since many inputs in a single production season are applied at rates directly under management control, this type of problem is frequently encountered and very important. The analysis of this problem in Chapter 2 will be limited to studying one input at a time. Solving for the profit maximizing level of each input simultaneously requires techniques presented in more advanced courses.

Once the decision is made concerning the optimal quantity of each input, the problem of choosing the best mix of inputs to produce a given amount of output will be addressed. This analysis is the second of the three fundamental questions.

2. What is the least-cost combination of inputs necessary to produce a given target level of output? The shorthand economic term for this question is factor/factor analysis. Farm production processes can typically utilize a variety of different inputs to accomplish a given level of production. Because many farm resources can be substituted for one another, it becomes the problem of the farm manager to select that combination or mix of inputs which is suitable to production and least costly.

Just as many different inputs can be used to produce farm products, many different products can be produced from a given set of resources. This introduces the last class of decisions which will be addressed with economic principles. That is, given a set of farm resources:

3. What combination of products should be produced in order to maximize net income? This question is referred to as product/product analysis. Many different production activities complement or supplement each other. Choosing the best rotation of crops or best combination of livestock to produce, given farm resources, is probably the most fundamental decision facing the farm manager. Exploiting complementarity and supplementarity between enterprises and selecting the profit maximizing enterprise combination is vital to achieving the best possible use of limited resources.

DATA REQUIREMENTS

Each of the analyses that have been mentioned will be examined in detail in the following chapters. Addressing each of these fundamental questions will require two types of data. The first is physical or biological data. Because each of the fundamental questions involves analyzing the interaction of living organisms within the production environment, it will be necessary to obtain data from scientists who study these relationships.

The **physical data** for crops can be obtained from agronomists and agricultural engineers. These may include data on how different crops respond to chemical fertilizers or herbicides or how varying levels of sunlight, temperature, moisture, and tillage affect the germination and growth of crops. Agronomists at universities and private agencies all over the world study, experiment, and collect data on how food and fiber crops respond to various production environments.

Animal scientists can provide necessary physical data for analyzing livestock activities. These may include data on feed conversion, genetic improvements, gestation and reproduction traits or how different livestock respond to their various production environments. Physical data from crop and animal scientists is vital to solving the many resource allocation questions facing the farm manager. However, physical data alone cannot answer any of the fundamental resource allocation questions.

The other type of data necessary to solve the fundamental questions is **economic data**. These data are principally composed of input costs and output prices. Planning decisions are frequently made up to a year or more in advance of product sales. Because of this, it is important to collect the best possible estimates or forecasts of these costs and prices during the time they are relevant to the decision-making process. This frequently involves forecasting the costs and prices for future periods when inputs will be purchased or products sold. Economic data can be obtained from agricultural economists and others who closely monitor the agricultural markets and forecast price changes within the sector.

By combining the physical and economic data within the framework of economic principles, each of the three broad types of economic analyses previously mentioned can be solved.

TECHNIQUES FOR SOLVING THE FUNDAMENTAL QUESTIONS

Three different techniques can be employed to solve the fundamental questions facing the farm manager. Each method requires both physical and economic data to arrive at a solution. Each is related to the other two solution methods, and each has its own advantages and disadvantages. By approaching each problem from three slightly different angles, the logic of the decision-making process should become apparent. Before beginning to address the fundamental questions within the ideal world environment, these three solution techniques will be described.

The first solution technique is the **algebraic method**. This method is based upon a simple decision rule: never pay more for something than you can expect to receive in return. Utilizing this commonsense rule of economics, you will discover that the physical data in each analysis can be used to generate trade-off rates. These trade-off rates will describe in physical units how inputs can be traded for output or other inputs, and how outputs can be traded for one another. The economic data can then be used to generate trade-offs in the form of price ratios describing the relative value of inputs, outputs, and their combinations. The solution to each of the analyses will occur at the point where the physical trade-off data and the economic trade-off data are equal.

The speed of solving with this technique is its greatest advantage. Although elementary algebra is required to develop the decision rule, once obtained, it can be used to solve problems in a very short time. Because of its speed and simplicity, this method can be used very profitably in the planning stage when it may be desirable to consider several different prices for each input and output.

The second solution technique which will be employed is the **graphical method**. This method is really just a graphical translation of the algebraic method. You will discover that physical data, when graphed, produce a curve. The slope of the curve over various ranges is the physical trade-off rate employed in the algebraic method. The economic trade-off data can then be used to construct straight-line price relationships or ratios. It will become apparent that optimization occurs in each class of problems at the point of tangency between the physical data (curve) and economic data (straight line).

The real advantage of the graphical method is that when the complete physical relationship is known, this method can demonstrate where profits are maximized without the production calculus. This can be important when a high level of precision is needed. The disadvantage is that the method requires careful plotting of points, which can be difficult for those with little patience.

The last method to be considered is the traditional or **longhand method**. This method using only basic arithmetic, involves the computing of costs and/or returns from all the possible combinations under consideration. This method is demonstrated primarily as a verification of the other two methods. The biggest disadvantage to this method is the tremendous number of individual calculations required. These calculations require more time and increase the chance of human error. However, when carefully performed, the longhand method results in the same solution as the other two methods.

SUMMARY

In this chapter the changing environment within which farm production takes place were introduced. These changes include increases in the variability of prices and government policy actions, increases in the value of farm assets, and the growth in quantitative methods needed to analyze resource allocation questions.

The five functions of management were discussed as a modern adaptation of the scientific method necessary to improve management capacity. The formulation of goals as the first step in management function was covered in some detail. The remaining functions will be emphasized in detail throughout the rest of the text.

The similarities and differences in farm businesses compared to non-farm businesses were discussed. The distinctive aspects of production agriculture greatly increase the risk of farming as a business enterprise.

The ideal world was introduced as the environment within which the management science will be initially explored. This risk-free environment is characterized by perfect knowledge, enabling the student to consider the fundamental resource allocation questions facing the farm business manager without the attendant complexities of the real world.

The four major classes of inputs necessary to farm production—land, labor, capital and management—were described. The proportions and qualities of these factors determine the production technology. While U.S. agriculture is currently characterized by a high capital/low labor technology it is most important that, given the resources available to agriculture, an appropriate technology be employed.

The three fundamental resource allocation questions facing farm managers were presented. There are three methods by which the fundamental questions regarding resource allocation can be solved: algebraic, graphical and longhand. The advantages and disadvantages of each were discussed.

DISCUSSION QUESTIONS

1. Identify ways in which the changing environment in agriculture has affected farming in your area.
2. Discuss how farm and family goals might come into conflict on a farm and what steps might be taken to resolve these conflicts.
3. What is the scientific method and how can it help farm managers in attaining farm and family goals?
4. What steps can be taken to improve your management capacity?
5. An alternative classification of the factors of production might be space, time, energy and knowledge. Discuss how several farm inputs might fit into this classification.
6. What are some of the ways in which the current technology employed in your region could be adjusted to make it a more appropriate technology from the standpoint of preserving the environment?
7. Discuss why it is important to maximize net income rather than gross (or total) income when planning resource allocation.

SUGGESTED READINGS

Duft, Kenneth D. *Principles of Management in Agribusiness*, Chapter 2. Reston, Va.: Reston Publishing Co., 1979.

Harsh, Stephen B., Larry J. Connor and Gerald D. Schwab. *Managing the Farm Business*, Chapters 1, 2, 16. Englewood Cliffs, N.J.: Prentice-Hall, Inc., 1981.

Herbst, J. H. *Farm Management, Principles, Budgets, Plans*, Fourth Revised Edition, Chapter 1. Champaign, Il: Stipes Publishing Company, 1980.

Luening, Robert A. and William P. Mortenson. *The Farm Management Handbook*, 5th edition, Chapters 1–4. Danville, Il: The Interstate Printers and Publishers Inc., 1979.

Osburn, Donald D., Kenneth C. Schneeburger. *Modern Agricultural Management*, Chapter 1. Reston, Va.: Reston Publishing Co., 1978.

Paarlberg, Don. *Farm and Food Policy, Issues of the 1980's*, Chapter 1, 2, 11, 16. Lincoln Ne: University of Nebraska Press, 1980.

Schertz, Lyle P. and others. *Another Revolution in U.S. Farming?*. Washington, D.C.: U.S. Department of Agriculture, 1979.

2

The Best Combinations of Inputs and Outputs

In the beginning it was hoped that the discussion could be made nontechnical. Very quickly it became apparent that such a procedure, while possible, would involve a manuscript many times the present size.

Paul Samuelson, Foundations of Economic Analysis

Concepts

In this chapter you will come to understand:

1. The importance of selecting the optimal quantity of each input.
2. The importance of selecting the least cost mix of inputs.
3. The importance of selecting the best mix of farm enterprises.
4. The physical restraint properties limiting farm production processes.
5. The stages of production and the commonsense decisions about production which can be drawn from them.
6. The complementary, supplementary and competitive interactions of output combinations.

Tools

You will also gain the following skills:

1. How to solve for the profit maximizing level of input using the algebraic, graphical, and longhand methods.
2. How to solve for the least cost combination of inputs to produce a target level of output using the three solution methods.
3. How to solve for the profit maximizing combination of output to produce using the three solution methods.

HOW MUCH OF EACH INPUT SHOULD BE APPLIED TO MAXIMIZE NET INCOME?

As you learned in Chapter 1, once the goals of a manager have been formulated, the next steps are compiling data and planning the activities necessary to achieve those goals. The use of economic principles becomes of paramount importance to wise decision-making in these activities. Consistent with the definition of farm management, attention will be focused on discovering what these economic principles are and how they can help the operator achieve farm goals (Figure 2-1).

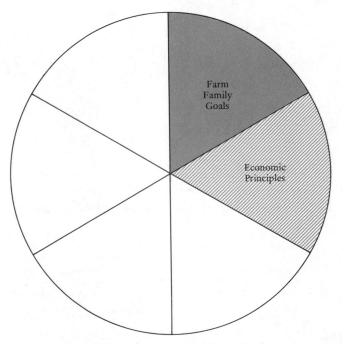

FIGURE 2-1. The Components of Farm Business Management. Adding economic principles to farm family goals.

FACTOR/PRODUCT ANALYSIS

The study of resource allocation begins by examining the first of the three types of economic analysis mentioned in Chapter 1. This analysis involves deciding how much of each input should be used in a production process in order to maximize net returns. The shorthand term for this is the factor/product relationship. This is an important relationship because the level of many inputs used in a production process is under the direct control of the manager. How much herbicide should be applied to soybeans, how much labor should be employed this year or how many acre-inches of irrigation should be applied to the vegetable crop are all examples of input use questions which the farm manager must decide. Economic principles can be used in making these decisions and to assure the greatest possible net income.

How Much Output Results from Each Combination of Inputs?

As an aid in discussing the problem of finding the optimal amount of each input to apply, the concept of a production function is necessary. A production function is simply a formulation of how various amounts of resources, combined in a production process, produce various amounts of output. With the aid of the production function, the manager is able to predict how much output can be obtained from every possible combination of inputs. Figure 2-2 should aid you in grasping this concept. The approach to the factor-product problem will involve assuming a fixed and appropriate technology, and that all resources or inputs are used in fixed amounts except the one input under consideration. By varying the amount of this one input, in its combination with the other fixed inputs, the effect on output can be discovered. Mathematicians have a special way of characterizing this formulation. The general form of the production function in the factor/product case can be written as follows:

$$Y = f(X_1 \mid \overline{X}_2, \overline{X}_3, \overline{X}_4, \ldots \ldots \overline{X}_n),$$

where Y is the output being produced, X_1 is the input that can be varied and the X's with bars over them are the fixed inputs. The f indicates output is a function of inputs used. The line between X_1 and the other inputs is simply a way of dividing the variable input from its fixed com-

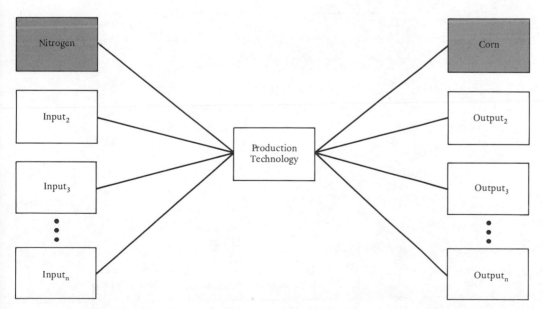

FIGURE 2-2. *The Production Flow Diagram for the Factor/Product Case.*

panions. It may help to rewrite this general equation in terms of a real world example. A production function for corn might look like this:

Corn output = f(nitrogen | seed, herbicide, gasoline, . . . tractor hours),

and would be read in the following manner: "corn output is a function of the level of nitrogen applied to fixed levels of seed, herbicide utilized, gasoline consumed, ... , and tractor hours." In this example, nitrogen is the input which can be varied when combined with fixed amounts of all the other inputs necessary in corn production. As the amount of nitrogen is varied, the amount of corn produced changes.

Recall that the data for each of the economic analysis has a physical component and an economic component. With this in mind, consider Table 2-1. The first two columns show the physical data obtained from agronomists, describing the amount of corn produced per acre when specific levels of nitrogen were applied. Agronomists have conducted the experiment so that every factor (except the level of nitrogen) was exactly the same for each acre. Given the complete production function, a graph can be constructed showing the relationship of corn output per acre to the amount of nitrogen applied. Figure 2-3 is the graph of this total production function for corn. Nitrogen is on the horizontal axis

TABLE 2-1.   PHYSICAL DATA OF CORN OUTPUT AT VARIOUS LEVELS OF NITROGEN APPLICATION

Nitrogen Units X_1	Corn Output In Bushels TPP	Bushels MPP	Bushels APP
0	0		—
		32	
1	32		32
		41	
2	73		36.5
		37	
3	110		36.7
		19	
4	129		32.3
		7	
5	136		27.2
		4	
6	140		23.3
		-3	
7	137		19.6
		-8	
8	129		16.1

Source: J. R. Webb, Department of Agronomy. "Economics of Nitrogen Fertilizer for Corn," *Selected Readings in Farm Management*, (mimeograph). Iowa State University Bookstore Press, Ames, Iowa.

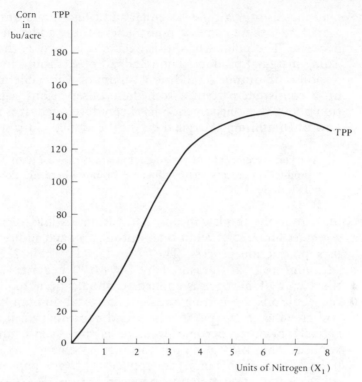

FIGURE 2-3. *The Graph of the Complete Production Function for Corn with Nitrogen as the Variable Input.*

and the Total Physical Product (*TPP*) of corn produced is shown on the vertical axis.

Several important relationships can be drawn from this graph of the physical data. Beginning with no nitrogen applied, note that no corn output results. When the first unit of nitrogen is applied, output (*TPP*) rises from zero to 32 bushels. This is a change in output equal to 32 bushels. When the second unit of nitrogen is applied, *TPP* jumps to 73 bushels which represents a change of 41 bushels. From this observation, it can be seen that equal additional applications of nitrogen will not necessarily produce an equal additional amount of output. For the sake of comparison, a column of data has been developed in Table 2-1 to describe how much additional output is gained by adding each additional unit of nitrogen. This type of data is called the Marginal Physical Product (*MPP*) and is calculated as follows:

$$MPP = \frac{\Delta TPP}{\Delta X_1} \text{ (the symbol } \Delta \text{ stands for "the change in").}$$

Column three in Table 2-1 shows the *MPP* between each level of nitrogen applied.

It is clear from examining the *MPP* that, while additions to output may increase for a time (as equal additional units of the variable input are added), there comes a point where these additions to *TPP* begin to decrease. The point where this occurs is known as the point of diminishing marginal product. Thousands of observations by scientists on the response of output to additional units of a variable input have turned up a consistent pattern. From these observations, a law or generalization about this phenomenon has been developed. It is referred to as the Law of Diminishing Marginal Physical Product and is stated like this:

> As equal increments of a variable input are combined with other fixed inputs in a production process, there will come a point where **additions** to total output will decline.

Stated simply, this law means that it is impossible to continually receive a greater amount of additional output for each additional unit of input in a production process. The corn data in Table 2-1 shows that the additions to *TPP* (measured by the *MPP*) begin to decline when the third unit of nitrogen is applied. It should be noted that even though the additions are getting smaller, the total amount of the product is still growing at this point. This trend continues until additions to *TPP* actually begin to become negative as the seventh unit of nitrogen is applied. The *MPP* is simply the rate of change in *TPP* as additional units of the variable input are applied. The *MPP* approximates the slope of the production function between various levels of nitrogen application.

Along with studying the additions to *TPP* as increases in nitrogen are applied, it is useful to know the average amount of output generated at each level of input use. This data is called the Average Physical Product (*APP*) and is calculated as follows:

$$APP = \frac{TPP}{X_1}.$$

Column four of Table 2-1 shows the *APP* of nitrogen for corn in the experiment. For example, the *APP* of three units of nitrogen is:

APP = 110 bushels of corn/3 units of *N* = 36.7 bushels of corn/unit of *N*.

This means that on the average, 36.7 bushels of corn were produced for each unit of nitrogen applied at this level.

The Stages of Production

With the aid of the physical data alone, some commonsense conclusions can be reached regarding how much nitrogen to apply to corn. In general, it would be foolish to stop applying nitrogen as long as the average output per unit of nitrogen (*APP*) is increasing. Referring to the *APP* column in Table 2-1, this means that at least three units of nitrogen should be applied. It would likewise be foolish to continue adding nitrogen when the *TPP* is falling. Again, referring to Table 2-1, this means that the seventh unit of nitrogen should not be considered because *TPP* actually declines by three bushels! Based on these observations, economists frequently divide the production function into three distinct stages. Figure 2-4 shows the stages of production and the relationship among *TPP*, *MPP*, and *APP* in each of the stages. Stage I of the production function begins at the zero level of input use and continues until *APP* is at a maximum. Stage II begins here and continues until *TPP* has reached a maximum. After this point, *TPP* is declining, which signals that Stage III has begun.

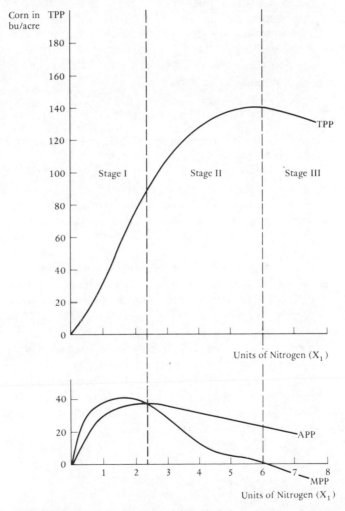

FIGURE 2-4. The Graph of TPP, APP and MPP with the
Stages of Production.

It should now be obvious that the ideal level of nitrogen application will fall somewhere in Stage II. Economists refer to this stage as the *rational stage of production*. The physical data have been important in that they have helped to zero in on the optimal level of input use. In order to find the level of nitrogen within Stage II which maximizes net income, the economic data must now be considered.

The Economic Data: What are the Costs and Returns?

The economic data in the factor/product analysis are based upon two prices. These are the price (or cost) of the inputs used (P_{x_i}) and the price of each unit of output produced (P_y). Consider first the cost associated with input use.

There are actually two types of costs which make up the Total Costs (*TC*) of using inputs. The first of these is the cost of inputs whose level the farmer can control. These costs are known as Variable Costs. Within a production activity, the Variable Costs will change as the level of output changes. In the example, nitrogen is the only Variable Cost of production. The Total Variable Cost (*TVC*) at each level of input use can be calculated as follows:

$$TVC = P_{x_1} \cdot X_1,$$

that is, the price of each unit of the variable input times the amount of the input being utilized.

The other costs referred to as part of the Total Cost of production result from using those inputs whose levels are fixed. These costs are appropriately referred to as the Fixed Costs of production. As the name implies, Fixed Costs do not change as the level of output varies. Examples of Fixed Costs include depreciation, machinery insurance and property taxes. There is no single formula for calculating the Fixed Costs of production; however, the methods for estimating these will be discussed in later chapters. Total Fixed Cost (*TFC*) is the sum of all Fixed Costs. Total Cost (*TC*) is the sum of *TFC* and *TVC* at each level of input use.

With the aid of the *TVC* calculation, an item of data can be developed which will aid in solving for the optimal level of input use. First, it is important to the analysis to know how much each additional level of nitrogen application costs. This piece of information is known as the Marginal Input Cost (*MIC*). In general, the *MIC* describes how much *TVC* increases as each additional unit of the variable input is added. The calculation of *MIC* is as follows:

$$MIC = \frac{\Delta TVC}{\Delta X_1}.$$

For the purpose of the example, assume that each unit of nitrogen costs $15.00 and that Total Fixed Cost is $110 per acre. Table 2–2 shows *TVC*, *TFC*, *TC* and *MIC* for each level of nitrogen.

You will note from Table 2–2 that *MIC* is simply equal to the cost of one unit of the variable input (nitrogen). This is true at **each** level of nitrogen applied.

TABLE 2-2. THE PHYSICAL AND ECONOMIC DATA

	The Physical Data				*The Economic Data*			
Nitrogen X_1	Corn Output Y bu.	MPP bu.	APP bu.	TVC $	TFC $	TC $	MIC $	VMP $
0	0		—	0	110	110		
		32					15	80.00
1	32		32	15	110	125		
		41					15	102.50
2	73		36.5	30	110	140		
		37					15	92.50
3	110		36.7	45	110	155		
		19					15	47.50
4	129		32.3	60	110	170		
		7					15	17.50
5	136		27.2	75	110	185		
		4					15	10.00
6	140		23.3	90	110	200		
		-3					15	-7.50
7	137		19.6	105	110	215		
		-8					15	-20.00
8	129		16.1	120	110	230		

Note: TFC = $110.00
P_y = $2.50/bushel
P_x = $15.00/unit

The other price which makes up the economic data is P_y, the price of the output being produced. From this price, an item of data can be developed which describes the value of additional output which is produced as each unit of the variable input is added. This is called the Value of the Marginal Product (*VMP*) and is calculated as follows:

$$VMP = MPP \cdot P_y.$$

Because the *MPP* describes the additional physical units (in the example: bushels) produced as each unit of the variable input is added, we simply multiply this by the price of the output to calculate its value. Table 2-2 contains the *VMP* for each unit of nitrogen applied. The graph of the *VMP* (downward sloping portion) is the individual farmer's demand curve for the variable input (See Figure 2-5). With the calculation of the *VMP*, there is now sufficient information to solve for the optimal level of input use.

Optimizing: Solving for the Best Level of Input Use

There are three methods which can be employed to solve each of the economic decisions in this Chapter. These techniques are the algebraic method, the graphical method, and the longhand method.

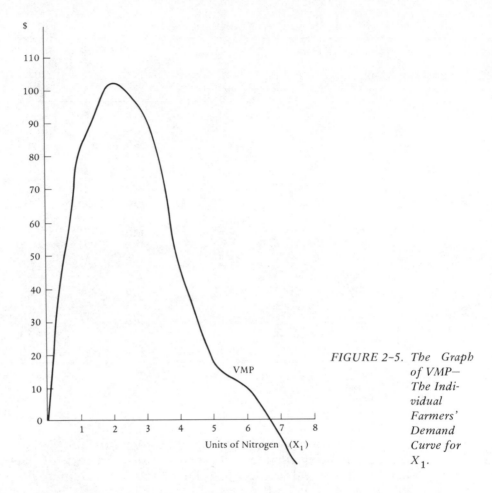

FIGURE 2-5. *The Graph of VMP— The Individual Farmers' Demand Curve for X_1.*

The Algebraic Method

There is a very simple rule behind the algebraic method of solving the types of problems associated with input use decisions. The farm manager should keep increasing the level of a variable input until the cost of an additional unit (*MIC*) is just equal to the value of the additions to output that result (*VMP*). If the complete production function is known it may not always be practical to do this. For instance, when solving for the ideal level of nitrogen on corn for your farm, it may turn out to be 5.384756 units per acre. Achieving this kind of precision would be impractical. Economists refer to this as the problem of "lumpy" inputs. When faced with the problem just mentioned, an operator may want to limit the solutions possible to five or six practical levels of nitrogen. When only a portion of the possible solutions are considered it is frequently not possible to exactly equate the *MIC* and the *VMP*. In such a case, the manager should only continue adding the variable input as long as the return received from each additional unit is greater than the cost of that unit. In general, this means that the optimal level of input use will occur where the *VMP* is as close as possible to but still greater than the *MIC*.

From the rationale that has just been stated, a simple algebraic rule can be developed which will solve the problem. Recalling that *MIC* is equal to the price of a unit of input, the decision rule in the algebraic method is that maximum net income results when:

$$VMP = P_{x_1}.$$

Breaking down the *VMP* to its component parts gives:

$$MPP \cdot P_y = P_{x_1}.$$

Dividing both sides by the price of the output (P_y) gives:

$$MPP = \frac{P_{x_1}}{P_y}.$$

In the example, the price of Nitrogen (P_{x_1}) is \$15 per unit. Assuming that the price of corn (P_y) is \$2.50 per bushel, it is possible to solve for the profit maximizing level of nitrogen use. Given the rule above and the price information, the level of nitrogen which maximizes net income will result where:

$$MPP = \frac{\$15.00}{\$2.50} = 6.$$

Referring to Table 2-2, and scanning down the columns containing Levels of Nitrogen (X_1) and the *MPP*, you will see that five units of nitrogen is optimal for any price ratio between seven and four. Since a price ratio of six falls within this range, the level of nitrogen which maximizes net income is five units. Note from Table 2-2 that the *VMP* resulting from applying the fifth unit of nitrogen is \$17.50 and the cost of the fifth unit is \$15.00. That is, it would cost \$15.00 to apply the fifth unit and \$17.50 worth of additional corn would result. If the sixth unit of nitrogen were applied, it would cost an additional \$15.00 (*MIC*) but only \$10.00 worth of additional output (*VMP*) would result. Therefore, given these prices and the levels of nitrogen we consider practical to apply, five units of nitrogen is the solution.

The real advantage of the algebraic method is that the prices of the input and output can be changed and the new optimum solved for immediately. This is very valuable in the planning stage when the exact prices to be paid for inputs or received for outputs are not known. Various combinations of prices can be considered to see how sensitive the optimal solution is to changes in price. For instance, if the manager were relatively sure that nitrogen would cost \$15.00 per unit, he could solve for the price of corn which would justify adding the sixth unit. This can be done from the decision rule as follows.

Given that the maximum net income occurs where:

$$MPP = \frac{P_{x_1}}{P_y},$$

and knowing the *MPP* between the fifth and sixth unit is four bushels,

$$4 \text{ bushels} = \frac{\$15.00}{P_y}.$$

Rearranging gives:

$$P_y = \frac{\$15.00}{4 \text{ bushels}}.$$

Solving gives:

$$P_y = \$3.75/\text{bushel}.$$

In order to justify adding the sixth unit of nitrogen, the farm operator must expect to receive at least \$3.75 per bushel for corn. The value of this simple formula in the planning process should now be obvious.

The Graphical Method

Another solution technique for solving this problem is the graphical method. Whatever method you choose to employ, when only a limited number of input levels are considered, each level is optimal for several price ratios. It is sometimes useful to know the input level which maximizes net income for each price ratio. In the case of limited data, an approximation of the complete production function can be made by fitting a curve to available points. This technique often allows the manager to consider points between the discrete levels given. The graphical method can achieve this precision without listing the tremendous number of observations in a complete production function.

In the graphical method of solving, the algebraic decision rule can be employed as a starting point. Recall that this rule is:

$$MPP = \frac{P_{x_1}}{P_y} \text{ at the point of maximum profits.}$$

You will also remember that the calculated *MPP* approximates the slope of the production function between two successive levels of input use. Therefore, the optimal level of input use can be found where the slope of the complete production function is just equal to the price ratio. From the initial assignment of prices for nitrogen and corn, the price ratio developed was equal to six (P_{x_1} = \$15 and P_y = \$2.50).

Because the production function is not linear (a straight line) the slope is different at each point along it. Locating the point on the production function where its slope is equal to six is not difficult. On the graph of the production function, simply construct a line of slope equal to six and carefully shift it out until it is just tangent (touching one point only) to the production function. This technique is demonstrated in Figure 2-6, where the smooth *TPP* curve suggests that the complete production function has been approximated. If a straight line is drawn from this point of tangency down to the horizontal axis, it intersects this axis at the location of the level of nitrogen which maximizes net income for a price ratio equal to six. Note that the optimal level of nitrogen using the graphical method results in a solution somewhere between the fifth and sixth units of nitrogen. The sensitivity of the solution can be tested by changing the prices and constructing new

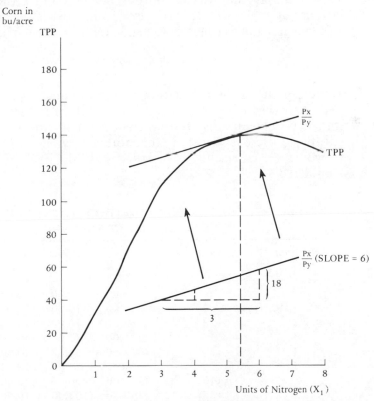

FIGURE 2-6. *The Graphical Solution of the Factor/Product Analysis.*

lines. Where these new lines (representing different price combinations for input and output) are tangent to the production function, the new optimal level of nitrogen is determined by again drawing a straight line from the point of tangency down to the horizontal axis.

The Longhand Method

Finally, consider the longhand method for solving the problem. This method is probably the traditional one used by many of your parents and grandparents. It can achieve the same solution but it is time consuming. Because of the number of calculations required, this method is subject to an increased chance of error, however, only basic arithmetic is required.

The longhand method begins by calculating Total Revenue (TR) and Total Cost (TC) for each level of input specified. Once these figures are calculated, TC is subtracted from TR to produce Net Revenue (NR). The level of input use where NR is the greatest is the optimal level.

Total Revenue can be calculated as

$$TR = P_y \cdot TPP.$$

This is simply the price of output per unit times the Total Physical Product at each level of input use. Total Cost is the sum of TVC and TFC at each input level. Net Revenue (NR) is calculated as

$$NR = TR - (TFC + TVC).$$

Table 2-3 shows the calculation of NR at each level of nitrogen specified. As expected, NR is maximized at the fifth level of nitrogen. It should be obvious that testing the sensitivity of the solution by substituting different prices in this formula would be time consuming. It would be especially so if every possible level of input use were considered.

TABLE 2-3. THE LONGHAND METHOD—TOTAL REVENUE,
TOTAL COST AND NET REVENUE

Nitrogen X_1	Corn Output Y bu.	TR $	−	(TVC $	+	TFC) $	=	NR $
0	0	(0.00	− (	0.00	+	110.00)	=	−110.00
1	32	(80.00	− (	15.00	+	110.00)	=	−45.00
2	73	(182.50	− (	30.00	+	110.00)	=	42.50
3	110	(275.00	− (	45.00	+	110.00)	=	120.00
4	129	(322.50	− (	60.00	+	110.00)	=	152.50
5	136	(340.00	− (	75.00	+	110.00)	=	155.00[1]
6	140	(350.00	− (	90.00	+	110.00)	=	150.00
7	137	(342.50	− (105.00		+	110.00)	=	127.50
8	129	(322.50	− (120.00		+	110.00)	=	92.50

[1]Optimal level of nitrogen use.

WHAT IS THE LEAST COST COMBINATION OF INPUTS TO PRODUCE A TARGET LEVEL OF OUTPUT?

Most production activities on the farm can be accomplished with a wide variety of different input combinations. For instance, in many crop production activities, additional cultivation may substitute for herbicide application. Corn and soybean meal can be used in varying combinations in a livestock feed formula to produce gain. Hand labor for picking tomatoes can be substituted for mechanical picking machines. The farm manager must decide, based on physical and economic data, just what combination (if any) will produce the output desired at minimum cost. The shorthand term for this type of economic decision is factor/factor analysis.

THE ISOQUANT: WHICH COMBINATIONS OF INPUTS PRODUCE THE SAME AMOUNT OF OUTPUT?

Just as in the case of deciding the best level of each input to use, the production function will be used as an aid in solving this problem. The mathematical representation of the production function for a factor/factor problem looks much like the one for the factor/product case. The only differences are that the amounts of two inputs are allowed to vary in combination with other fixed inputs to produce a **fixed** amount of output. Figure 2-7 illustrates this idea. The formulation of the production function for a factor/factor analysis looks like this:

$$\overline{Y} = f(X_1, X_2 \mid \overline{X}_3, \overline{X}_4, \overline{X}_5, \ldots \overline{X}_n),$$

where $\overline{Y}$ is the target level of output to be produced, X_1 and X_2 are the variable inputs and $\overline{X}_3$ through $\overline{X}_n$ are the fixed levels of the other inputs used in the production process. Again, it may help to rewrite this general equation in terms of a real world example. A typical production function for 100 pounds of gain on hogs where corn and soybean meal are used in varying combinations as part of the protein requirement of the ration might look like this:

$$\begin{array}{c} \text{100 lbs. of gain} \\ \text{on hogs} \end{array} = f(\text{corn, soybean meal} \mid \text{salt, calcium, vitamin mix,} \ldots \text{wheat}).$$

This production function is read: "One hundred pounds of gain on hogs can be achieved as a function of some combination of corn and soybean meal combined with a fixed amount of salt, calcium, vitamin mix . . . and wheat." In this example, corn and soybean meal are substitutes. This fact allows these two inputs, over a certain range, to be mixed in various combinations and added to the other ingredients in the ration to achieve one hundred pounds of gain on a group of hogs.

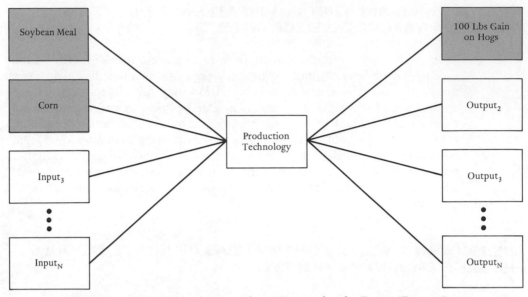

FIGURE 2-7. *The Production Flow Diagram for the Factor/Factor Case.*

The important point to remember is that as corn is substituted for soybean meal in the ration, the amount of output produced does not change. With this in mind, consider Table 2-4. The first two columns show the physical data, obtained from animal scientists that describe some of the combinations of corn and soybean meal, which when added to other feed inputs, produce one hundred pounds of gain on hogs.

A graph of the complete physical data is presented in Figure 2-8. Pounds of soybean meal are measured on the vertical axis and pounds of corn on the horizontal axis. The curve, in this case representing the tradeoff of corn for soybean meal in a hog ration, is called an isoquant.

TABLE 2-4.   VARIOUS QUANTITIES OF SOYBEAN MEAL AND CORN THAT PRODUCE 100 POUNDS OF GAIN ON HOGS

Ration	Soybean Meal	△Soybean Meal	Corn	△Corn	MRS
1	60 lbs.		160 lbs.		
		-10 lbs.		+15 lbs.	.67
2	50 lbs.		175 lbs.		
		-10 lbs.		+25 lbs.	.40
3	40 lbs.		200 lbs.		
		-10 lbs.		+35 lbs..	.29
4	30 lbs.		235 lbs.		
		-10 lbs.		+50 lbs.	.20
5	20 lbs.		285 lbs.		
		-10 lbs.		+75 lbs.	.13
6	10 lbs.		360 lbs.		

Hypothetical Data

The term isoquant comes from two root words: **iso** meaning equal and **quant** meaning quantity. The isoquant is simply a curve (in this case) showing all the combinations of two inputs in a production process that produce an equal quantity of output.

By examining the physical tradeoff data for the two variable inputs in this example, it will become clear that once again a physical restraint property exists similar to the law of diminishing marginal product in the factor/product case. Referring to Table 2–4, for ration #1, when 60 pounds of soybean meal are used, 160 pounds of corn are required. If, as in ration #2, the soybean meal is reduced by 10 pounds, the additional amount of corn needed is 15 pounds. However, moving to ration #3, reducing soybean meal by another 10 pounds requires 25 additional pounds of corn to substitute for this equal additional reduction in soybean meal. Similarly, as successive ten-pound quantities of soybean meal are withdrawn from the ration, greater and greater amounts of corn must be added. This phenomenon relates to the lack of perfect substitutability of these two inputs in providing the nutrients necessary to produce growth in hogs. Very few inputs are perfect sub-

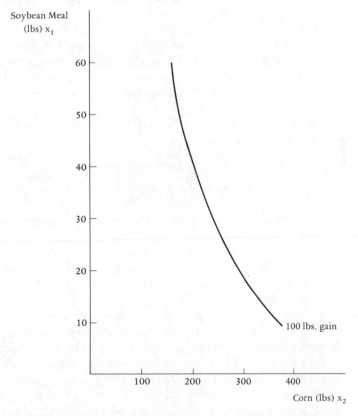

FIGURE 2–8. *The Isoquant—A Picture of the Physical Data Describing the Trade-Off of Corn and Soybean Meal in a Ratio to Produce 100 lbs. of Gain on Hogs.*

stitutes for one another. The Law of Diminishing Marginal Factor Sub-stitution describes this phenomenon:

> When two inputs are substituted for one another in a production process to produce a given level of output, increasing amounts of the first input must be added to replace equal additional reductions of the second input.

In the case of biological production processes common to farming, this law or generalization is related to the way living organisms (hogs, tobacco, tomatoes, etc.) metabolize or utilize various inputs to produce growth. The isoquant in Figure 2-8 depicts this physical restraint property for all combinations of corn and soybeans which achieve 100 pounds of gain on hogs.

It would be very useful to develop an item of data which describes the tradeoff of inputs over various ranges along the isoquant. Econo-mists call this piece of information the Marginal Rate of Substitution (*MRS*) and it is calculated as follows:

$$MRS = \frac{\Delta \text{ in the saved input}}{\Delta \text{ in the added input}} = \frac{\Delta X_1}{\Delta X_2}.$$

In the example, soybean meal is X_1, and corn is X_2. The *MRS* is cal-culated between each pair of successive rations in Table 2-4 and describes the number of pounds of soybean meal that can be withdrawn from the feed formula for each pound of corn added. For example, moving from ration #1 to ration #2, the change in soybean meal is −10 pounds and the change in (or additional) corn needed to offset this reduction is 15 pounds. The *MRS* between ration #1 and ration #2 is calculated as follows:

$$MRS = \frac{\Delta \text{ in the saved input}}{\Delta \text{ in the added input}} = \frac{-10 \text{ lbs.}}{15 \text{ lbs.}} = 0.67 \text{ lbs.}$$

(Although the *MRS* is actually a negative number, the sign is dropped by convention.)

This result means that two-thirds of a pound of soybean meal can be withdrawn from the ration for each pound of corn that is added. Note that this particular tradeoff rate is not constant but only exists between ration #1 and #2.

Because the *MRS* is the rate of change of one input for the other, you should recognize it to be an approximation of the slope of the isoquant between adjacent input combinations. The final column in Table 2-4 shows the *MRS* between each pair of successive rations listed. It is clear from this column of data that less and less soybean meal can be with-drawn for each pound of corn added as the rations become more heavily composed of corn. With the aid of the physical data, the tradeoff in terms of physical units has been demonstrated. In order to solve for the minimum cost ration in the example presented, the economic data must now be introduced.

The Economic Data: What are the Costs and Returns?

In the case of the factor/factor analysis, the economic data which will be critical to solving for the minimum cost combination of inputs are the prices of the variable inputs. Since the amount of output being produced is fixed, the returns from that output are constant. Therefore, given a fixed level of return, the relevant question becomes how to achieve this fixed return with the least possible cost.

The cost associated with input use consists of two components. The first is the Total Variable Cost (*TVC*). This cost is the sum of the costs which are incurred by utilizing specific combinations of the variable inputs. This costs varies among alternative combinations of the variable inputs and can be calculated as follows:

$$TVC = (P_{x_1} \cdot X_1 + P_{x_2} \cdot X_2).$$

The other cost of producing output is for those inputs used in fixed amounts. Just as in the case of the factor/product analysis, the Total Cost (*TC*) of production is the sum of Total Variable Cost (*TVC*) and Total Fixed Cost (*TFC*). Because the variable costs of production are within the control of the farm manager, it is necessary to solve for the minimum cost combination of these variable inputs.

Optimizing: Solving for the Best Combination of Input Use

Beginning with the algebraic method, recall the commonsense rule behind this approach. In the factor/factor case, this rule is that one variable input should be substituted for the other until the cost of adding an extra unit of the first input is just equal to the savings obtained by decreasing the second input. There are actually an infinite number of combinations of corn and soybean meal which achieve the desired weight gain of 100 pounds. If only a limited number of these combinations (in this case, six different rations) are under consideration, the farm manager should continue substituting one input for the other as long as the savings from reducing one input is greater than the cost of adding the additional amount of the other input.

From this rationale, the algebraic rule which solves for the minimum cost combination of inputs can be developed. Continue substituting X_2 for X_1 until:

$$P_{x_1} \cdot \Delta X_1 \quad = \quad P_{x_2} \cdot \Delta X_2.$$

$$\text{additional savings} \quad \text{additional costs}$$

Dividing both sides by ΔX_2 and cancelling gives:

$$\frac{P_{x_1} \cdot \Delta X_1}{\Delta X_2} = P_{x_2}.$$

Dividing both sides by P_{x_1} and cancelling gives:

$$\frac{\Delta X_1}{\Delta X_2} = \frac{P_{x_2}}{P_{x_1}}.$$

The left-hand side of this equation is the *MRS*. The rule for solving this type of problem with the algebraic method is to locate the *MRS* which is just equal to the inverse ratio of the prices. That is, cost minimization occurs where:

$$\frac{\Delta \text{ saved input}}{\Delta \text{ added input}} = \frac{\text{price of the added input}}{\text{price of the saved input}},$$

which in our shorthand notation is where:

$$MRS = \frac{P_{x_2}}{P_{x_1}},$$

and in the example is where:

$$\frac{\Delta \text{ soybean meal}}{\Delta \text{ corn}} = \frac{\text{price of corn}}{\text{price of soybean meal}}$$

Note that if the two fractions in this equality are cross-multiplied, the resulting equality is:

(price of soybean mean) (Δ soybean meal) = (price of corn) (Δ corn).

           additional savings   additional cost

Assume, for example, that the price of corn is 5¢ per pound and the price of soybean meal is 8¢ per pound. The solution to this problem using the algebraic method occurs where:

$$MRS = \frac{\$.05}{\$.08} = .625.$$

Referring to Table 2-4, notice that ration #2 is optimal for any price ratio between .67 and .40. Since the price ratio of .625 falls between these, the cost minimizing ration is #2. If only the rations specified are to be considered it may not be possible to equate the *MRS* and the inverted price ratio.

The simplicity of the algebraic method can be demonstrated by changing the prices of the inputs and immediately solving for the new solution. For example, assume the price of soybean meal rises to 12¢ per pound and corn falls to 4¢ per pound. Applying the algebraic method, select a ration where:

$$MRS = \frac{\$.04}{\$.12} = .33.$$

In this case, the cost minimizing ration would be #3 which is optimal for any price ratio between .40 and .29 (see Table 2-4). Since from the first set of prices, soybean meal went up by 4¢ per pound and the corn price fell by 1¢ per pound, the new cost-minimizing ration would be expected to be more heavily weighted with corn. This is exactly what happens in moving from ration #2 to ration #3.

The Graphical Method

Because the *MRS* describes the rate of change in one input for the other it can be used as a basis for solving this problem graphically. Because the isoquant in this example depicts a biological relationship, it takes on the shape of a curve. This means that the actual slope of the isoquant is different at each point along it. The Marginal Rates of Substitution which are given in Table 2-4 are an approximation of the slope of the isoquant between each pair of successive rations specified. Using the algebraic decision rule as a starting point, and the complete physical relationship, you can graphically locate the combination of corn and soybean meal which minimizes cost for each price ratio. First, it is necessary to construct a line which has a slope equal to the inverse ratio of prices of the inputs.* This line is referred to as an isocost line because each point along it depicts the physical units of the two inputs whose combined total cost is the same.

Once the isocost line is constructed, it is simply shifted out parallel to itself until it just touches (is tangent to) the isoquant at one point. Figure 2-9 shows the tangency of the isoquant and isocost line in the example. Note that the solution falls between ration #2 and ration #3 when the complete production relationship is considered.

In order to examine the effect on the solution of a change in input prices, simply construct new isocost lines with slopes equal to the new price ratios and locate the tangencies.

Longhand Method

The longhand method or traditional method of solving this problem is rather simple but involves many calculations. The task involves calculating the Net Revenue associated with each ration and choosing the one which produces the greatest Net Revenue. Remember that the formula for Net Revenue is Total Revenue minus Total Cost. Since

---

Recall that the MRS is mathematically a negative number. This is so because the numerator is always negative reflecting the amount of a given input withdrawn from the production activity. By convention, this negative sign is dropped and the MRS is referred to by its absolute value. However, when using the graphical method, it becomes important to draw the isocost line with a slope equal to the negative ratio of prices in order to locate a tangency with the isoquant.

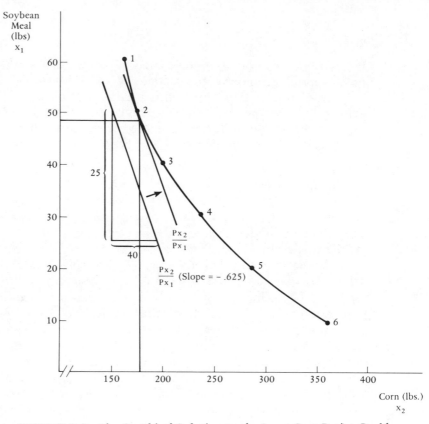

FIGURE 2-9. The Graphical Solution to the Least Cost Ration Problem.

the Total Revenue in this type of problem is fixed (i.e., 100 pounds of gain multiplied by market price), the Net Revenue will be greatest where the Total Cost is the least.

Table 2-5 shows the calculation of Total Cost for each ration specified. You will note that the solution is ration #2, the same as in the algebraic method. Given the prices we have assigned, Total Cost is minimized (therefore, Net Revenue is maximized) at ration #2.

TABLE 2-5.   THE LONGHAND SOLUTION TO THE LEAST COST RATION PROBLEM

Ration	Soybean Meal	Corn	$(X_1 \cdot P_{x_1}) + (X_2 \cdot P_{x_2}) = TC$
1	60 lbs.	160 lbs.	$(60 \times \$.08) + (160 \times \$.05) = 12.80$
2	50 lbs.	175 lbs.	$(50 \times \$.08) + (175 \times \$.05) = 12.75$[1]
3	40 lbs.	200 lbs.	$(40 \times \$.08) + (200 \times \$.05) = 13.20$
4	30 lbs.	235 lbs.	$(30 \times \$.08) + (235 \times \$.05) = 14.15$
5	20 lbs.	285 lbs.	$(20 \times \$.08) + (285 \times \$.05) = 15.85$
6	10 lbs.	360 lbs.	$(10 \times \$.08) + (360 \times \$.05) = 18.80$

[1]Optimal input combination.

WHICH COMBINATION OF ENTERPRISES RESULTS IN THE GREATEST INCOME?

Perhaps the most fundamental decision which must be made by the farm manager is what to produce. Frequently this decision will be dictated by the region of the country in which the farm is located or by the unique characteristics of each farm. Most areas of the country have a distinct advantage in the production of some agricultural products (see Figure 2–10). However, this advantage usually extends to a set of production possibilities rather than dictating a single crop or livestock activity.

Frequently, among the set of production possibilities, there will be some crop or livestock activities that will complement one another. For example, corn following soybeans in a rotation needs less nitrogen applied due to the beneficial nitrogen fixation properties of soybeans. Other examples of complementary activities include bee-keeping and apple production and grazing cattle over corn stubble. Given the possi-

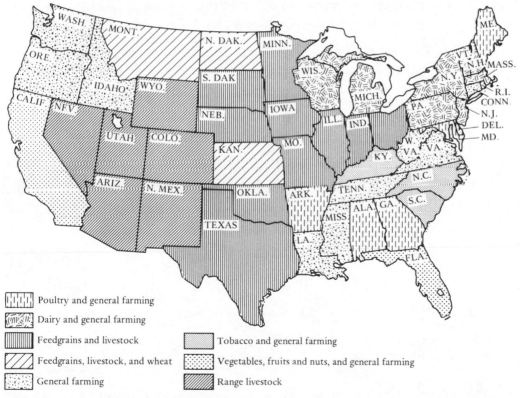

Poultry and general farming

Dairy and general farming

Feedgrains and livestock

Feedgrains, livestock, and wheat

General farming

Tobacco and general farming

Vegetables, fruits and nuts, and general farming

Range livestock

FIGURE 2–10. *"Types of Agricultural Enterprises by Cash Receipts Received by Farmers and Ranchers," Crop and Livestock Producing Areas in the United States. (From* Agricultural Economics and Agricultural Business *by Cramer and Jensen. Reprinted by permission of the Publisher, © 1979 by J. Wiley and Sons, Inc., New York.)*

ble enterprises which can be successfully undertaken, it is important to select that combination which yields the greatest income. This type of analysis is referred to as the product/product problem.

THE PRODUCTION POSSIBILITIES FRONTIER: WHAT COMBINATIONS OF PRODUCT ARE POSSIBLE GIVEN THE AVAILABLE RESOURCES?

Given a fixed value of resources on the farm, the production function in the product/product case describes the various quantities of products which can be produced. The mathematical formulation of the production function for the product/product case can be represented as follows:

$$Y_1, Y_2 = f(\overline{X_1, X_2, X_3, \ldots, X_n}).$$

From this formulation it should be noted that we are now considering varying the amounts of two different products which could be produced while holding constant the value of inputs used. Notice that all of the X's (which stand for inputs) have a single bar over them. This indicates that a fixed total amount of inputs are used in the production of Y_1 and Y_2.

Y_1 and Y_2 are the quantities or combinations of two products which can be produced from this given set of resources. Figure 2-11 should aid you in grasping this concept.

As a further aid in understanding the idea of the production function, consider a real world example involving a rotation choice of corn and

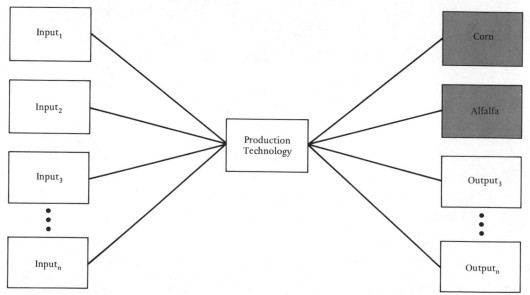

FIGURE 2-11. The Production Flow Diagram for the Product/Product Case.

alfalfa. The various combinations of corn and alfalfa which might be produced from a given value of inputs could be represented in the following manner:

$$\text{Corn, Alfalfa} = f(\overline{\text{Farm Resources}}).$$

This production function indicates that various combinations, or rotations of corn and alfalfa can be produced as a function of a fixed set of farm resources. Deciding which rotation results in the greatest net income is the problem. In order to gain additional understanding of the interaction of products it is necessary to consult agricultural scientists. The physical data for several rotations of corn and alfalfa are given in Table 2-6. Alfalfa is a legume, which means that among other characteristics, this crop imparts nitrogen to the soil by means of bacteria present in its root nodules. Because corn requires a relatively large amount of nitrogen in order to produce well, the alfalfa will tend to increase the amount of corn produced by fixing additional nitrogen in the soil. This effect can be observed in Table 2-6.

Along with each rotation, Table 2-6 lists the rotation-acre yields of corn and alfalfa which result. Rotation #1 is simply continuous corn. When continuous corn is produced, approximately 4,000 pounds of yield results per rotation-acre. Rotation #2 is 3/4 corn and 1/4 alfalfa. Note that when alfalfa is introduced, the rotation acre yield of corn increases. This is due to the additional nitrogen supplied by the alfalfa. This type of relationship only exists over a rather narrow range. When successively increasing quantities of alfalfa are introduced, the rotation-acre yield of corn begins to drop.

The physical tradeoff relationship between corn and alfalfa can be measured by constructing an item of data known as the Marginal Rate

TABLE 2-6. THE PHYSICAL DATA FOR SIX DIFFERENT ROTATIONS OF CORN (C) AND ALFALFA (A)

	Yield per Rotation Acre			
Rotation	Corn	△Corn	Alfalfa	△Alfalfa
1 (C)	4000 lbs.		0 lbs.	
		+300		+1000
2 (CCCA)	4300 lbs.		1000 lbs.	
		−100		+1000
3 (CCA)	4200 lbs.		2000 lbs.	
		−900		+1600
4 (CA)	3300 lbs.		3600 lbs.	
		−1100		+700
5 (CAA)	2200 lbs.		4300 lbs.	
		−2200		+1000
6 (A)	0 lbs.		5300 lbs.	

Hypothetical Data

of Transformation. This piece of information describes the number of pounds of corn which must be given up to gain one additional pound of alfalfa. The general formula for the *MRT* is:

$$MRT = \frac{\Delta \text{ in the reduced product}}{\Delta \text{ in the gained product}} = \frac{\Delta Y_1}{\Delta Y_2}.$$

Table 2–7 contains the Marginal Rates of Transformation between each rotation. As you may have guessed, the *MRT* will be used in the algebraic method to solve for the profit maximizing output combination.

Consider Figure 2–12, a graph of the complete production relationship of corn and alfalfa. If you have taken an introductory economics course you should recognize this curved biological relationship as the **production possibilities frontier**. Each point along this curve traces out a combination of corn and alfalfa which could be produced by fully employing a given fixed amount of farm resources. Points (such as point **z**) outside the curve are not attainable with present technology unless additional resources are employed. Points inside the curve (such as point **x**) are feasible but represent underemploying or wasting the farm resources.

From this graph of the physical data some commonsense conclusions can be drawn regarding the best use of farm resources. First of all, even though all points within and on the curve are possible output combinations, only those combinations which are **on** the curve should be considered in order to assure that the resources are being fully employed. Second, consider the three areas outlined on a typical hypothetical production possibilities curve shown in Figure 2–13. Beginning on the left hand side at the Y_1 intercept (point **a**), this point indicates a production plan producing only product Y_1. Moving out along the curve to point **b** by adding an additional product (Y_2) to the production activities

TABLE 2–7. VARIOUS ROTATIONS OF CORN AND ALFALFA WITH YIELDS PER ROTATION ACRE AND MARGINAL RATES OF TRANSFORMATION

Rotation	Yield per Rotation Acre		$MRT = \dfrac{\Delta \, Corn}{\Delta \, Alfalfa}$
	Corn	*Alfalfa*	
1 (C)	4000 lbs.	0 lbs.	
			.3 complementary
2 (CCCA)	4300 lbs.	1000 lbs.	
			.1
3 (CCA)	4200 lbs.	2000 lbs.	
			.56
4 (CA)	3300 lbs.	3600 lbs.	
			1.57
5 (CAA)	2200 lbs.	4300 lbs.	
			2.2
6 (A)	0 lbs.	5300 lbs.	

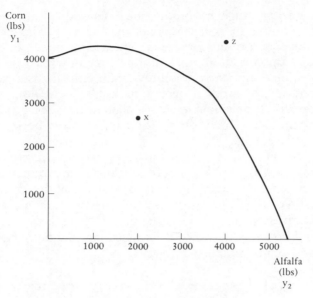

FIGURE 2-12. The Production Possibility Frontier—
The Graph of the Physical Data.

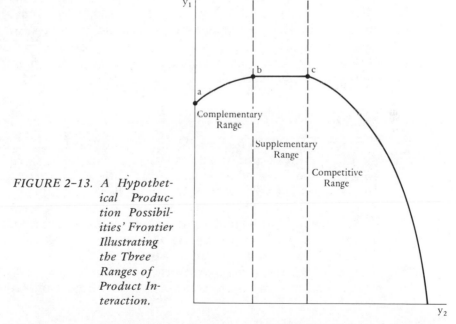

FIGURE 2-13. A Hypothet-
ical Produc-
tion Possibil-
ities' Frontier
Illustrating
the Three
Ranges of
Product In-
teraction.

increases the production of Y_1. The range over which increasing the amount of one product results in the increase of another is known as the **complementary range of production**. This range in our example is where the added nitrogen from the alfalfa boosts the rotation-acre output of corn even though the rotation mix of corn is reduced. Moving from point **b** to point **c**, the increase in Y_2 produced does not add to or reduce the amount of Y_1 produced. This range is known as the **supple-**

mentary range of production. Beyond point **c**, any equal additional increase in Y_2 is accompanied by a larger and larger reduction in Y_1. This range of production, where increasing one product requires reducing the amount of another product, is known as the **competitive range of production.** Since it is only upon entering the competitive range that any loss of product occurs, it should be obvious that any complementary or supplementary range that exists should be fully exploited. The optimal product combination will always be somewhere in the competitive range.

As with all of the production relationships studied so far, a physical restraint property exists for the product/product analysis. This physical restraint property becomes operative in the competitive range where larger and larger quantities of one product must be forgone for each additional unit of the other product which is gained. This phenomenon is known as the Law of Diminishing Marginal Product Transformation and can be stated as follows:

> As a fixed set of resources is gradually shifted from the production of one product to another, there will come a point where equal additions of the first product result in larger and larger reductions of the second product.

This physical restraint property in farming is the result of the way different living organisms interact with one another in the production environment. Trading one product for another in the competitive range results in gaining some of one product and losing some of another. Deciding where to stop exchanging one product for another requires the use of economic data.

The Economic Data: What Are the Costs and Returns?

The economic data in the product/product analysis consist of two prices. These two prices are the price of each of the products under consideration. Since the resource base with which these products can be produced is fixed (in terms of value) the relevant question becomes: which combination of these two products results in the greatest amount of net income? Net income is that income which is left over after all the expenses are paid. Since the cost of resources used is the same (fixed) for any combination of products produced on the production possibilities curve, the problem is locating that combination of products whose combined value results in the greatest amount of income.

Optimizing: Solving for the Best Combination of Products

The Algebraic Method

The three solution methodologies used in the preceding sections will be employed. Let us begin with the algebraic method, and apply the commonsense rule which supports it. First, continue to transfer resources from the production of one product to the other until the value of the product given up is just equal to the value of the other product which is gained. If only a limited number of product combinations are under consideration, then you should continue transferring resources out of the production of one product and into the production of the other as long as the value of the product gained is greater than the value of the product which is forgone.

From this rationale, a simple algebraic rule can be developed. Continue transferring resources away from one product and into the production of another until

$$P_{Y_1} \cdot \Delta Y_1 \qquad\qquad = \qquad\qquad P_{Y_2} \cdot \Delta Y_2.$$

value of the product given up   value of the product gained

Dividing both sides by ΔY_2 and cancelling gives:

$$\frac{P_{Y_1} \cdot \Delta Y_1}{\Delta Y_2} = P_{Y_2}.$$

Dividing both sides by P_{Y_1} and cancelling gives:

$$\frac{\Delta Y_1}{\Delta Y_2} = \frac{P_{Y_2}}{P_{Y_1}}.$$

The lefthand side of this equation is the physical tradeoff rate or Marginal Rate of Transformation.[1] It may help to rewrite this equality in terms of its components. In ordinary language this profit maximizing condition is:

$$\frac{\Delta \text{ product given up}}{\Delta \text{ product gained}} = \frac{\text{Price of the product gained}}{\text{Price of the product given up}}.$$

$$MRT \qquad\qquad\qquad \text{Inverse Price Ratio}$$

In order to solve for the rotation which gives the greatest amount of net income, the value of the inverse price ratio must be calculated. Referring back to the algebraic decision rule, the *MRT* is equal to this inverse price ratio at the profit maximizing rotation.

Assume that corn currently sells for 6¢/pound and alfalfa hay is worth 3¢/pound as a livestock feed. Expect to find the profit maximizing rotation of corn and alfalfa where:

$$MRT = \frac{\$.03}{\$.06} = .5.$$

Scanning down the columns containing the rotations and the Marginal Rates of Transformation in Table 2-7, note that rotation #3 is optimal for all price ratios between .10 and .56. Therefore rotation #3 results in the greatest net income given the prices assumed.

The speed with which this type of problem can be solved using the algebraic method is its biggest advantage.

Now consider a different set of prices for corn and alfalfa in order to test if the optimal rotation changes. This can be accomplished very quickly with the algebraic method. For instance, assume you wish to check for the optimal rotation if corn price remains at 6¢/pound but alfalfa increases in value to 4¢/pound. Before solving this it should be intuitively obvious that if the value of one product rises in relation to another, more of it should be produced. Given these new prices it would be expected that the new profit maximizing rotation be more heavily weighted with alfalfa. Solving with new prices gives:

$$MRT = \frac{\$.04}{\$.06} = .667.$$

Scanning the column of Marginal Rates of Substitution in Table 2–7 notice that rotation #4 is optimal for price ratios between .56 and 1.57. Rotation #4 is approximately one half corn and one half alfalfa, compared to the first solution of rotation #3 which is roughly two-thirds corn and one-third alfalfa. The rising value of alfalfa relative to corn in the second solution verifies our intuition that a rotation more heavily weighted to alfalfa is now the optimum.

The stability of the solution is generally related to the number of rotations we specify. In general, the fewer rotations considered, the greater the change in relative prices of products necessary to alter the optimal solution.

The Graphical Method

Recall that the graph of the physical data produced the production possibilities frontier. The rate of change or slope of this curved physical relationship between rotations is approximated by the *MRT*. Since we know from the algebraic method that the optimal combination of products (or rotation) occurs where the *MRT* is equal to the inverse price ratio, construct a line equal in slope to the ratio of prices and move it out until it is just tangent to the graph of physical data.* Figure 2–14 illustrates the construction of the price line (assuming the first set of prices, i.e., corn = $.06/pound and alfalfa = $.03/pound) and the location of the tangency yielding the optimal solution.

The price line which has been constructed in Figure 2–13 has a special

---

As in the case of the isoquant and the MRS, the MRT is actually a negative number. Its sign is dropped by convention. That is, the MRT is referred to by its absolute value rather than its arithmetic value. This distinction is important to remember when you construct the price line (iso-revenue line) because it must be constructed as a negative price ratio to find a tangency with the production possibilities frontier.

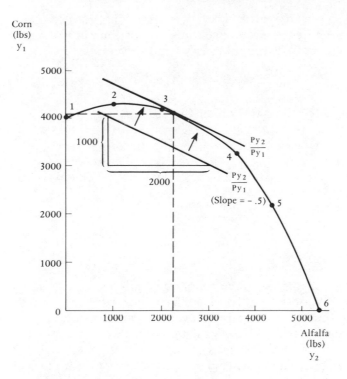

FIGURE 2-14. *The Graphical Solution to the Product/ Product Problem.*

name and an interesting characteristic. It is called an **iso-revenue line** (Remember, iso means equal.) and has the following property. Every point along the iso-revenue line traces out a unique combination of corn and alfalfa (in this example) whose combined value is equal. As you move this line out to a tangency with the production possibilities frontier the total value represented by the iso-revenue line increases. Since the point of tangency represents the greatest distance this line can be moved out (away from the origin) while still touching the production possibilities frontier, that point is the unique combination of corn and alfalfa which generates the greatest total revenue. Because the cost associated with each rotation is the same (i.e., the cost of the fully employed resources) net income is greatest in this case where total income is greatest.

In order to solve this problem graphically, when it is desirable to consider several output prices, you simply redraw the iso-revenue line consistent with the price combinations you wish to consider. Each new iso-revenue line is moved out parallel to itself to discover the new tangency point that traces out the new optimal solutions.

The Longhand Method
The longhand method involves calculating the Total Revenue (*TR*) achieved by each rotation and then simply choosing that rotation which

produces the greatest Total Revenue. This rotation will by necessity maximize net revenue since the total costs are equal among rotations.

In the product/product case, Total Revenue is:

$$TR = (P_{Y_1} \cdot Y_1) + (P_{Y_2} \cdot Y_2).$$

Table 2-8 shows the calculation of *TR* for each of the six rotations (assuming the original set of prices). As in the case of the algebraic method, when a limited number of rotations are considered, rotation #3 proves to be optimal. When the complete relationship was considered using the graphical technique, a rotation mix between #2 and #3 was found to be best.

SUMMARY

In this chapter the three economic analyses which can aid in achieving the best allocation of resources have been presented.

The first type of analysis involves planning how much of each input should be used to maximize net income. Since the levels of many inputs are under direct management control, the factor/product analysis is crucial in deciding how much of each should be applied. Considering all inputs simultaneously requires techniques presented in advanced farm management courses. However, even without these techniques, improving net income by adjusting the levels of two or three key inputs individually can be very valuable.

Secondly, many different inputs can be substituted for one another in agricultural production processes. Since not all inputs cost the same, the wise manager must be skilled at achieving the least cost mix of inputs to accomplish a given level of output. The relative prices of sub-

TABLE 2-8.   THE LONGHAND SOLUTION TO THE PRODUCT/PRODUCT PROBLEM

	Yield per Rotation Acre (lbs)		$(P_{Y_1} \cdot Y_1) + (P_{Y_2} \cdot Y_2) = TR$
Rotation	Corn	Alfalfa	
1 (C)	4000	0	$(.06 \cdot 4000) + (.03 \cdot 0) = \$240$
2 (CCCA)	4300	1000	$(.06 \cdot 4300) + (.03 \cdot 1000) = \$288$
3 (CCA)	4200	2000	$(.06 \cdot 4200) + (.03 \cdot 2000) = \$312$[1]
4 (CA)	3300	3600	$(.06 \cdot 3300) + (.03 \cdot 3600) = \$306$
5 (CAA)	2200	4300	$(.06 \cdot 2200) + (.03 \cdot 4300) = \$261$
6 (A)	0	5300	$(.06 \cdot 0) + (.03 \cdot 5300) = \$159$

Note: Price of corn = 6¢/pound
       Price of alfalfa = 3¢/pound

[1]Optimal product mix.

stitutes in a production activity will tend to vary over time so that the appropriate (least-cost) mix of factors may change frequently. The factor/factor analysis was demonstrated as the principle behind substituting factors in a production process to achieve the least cost combination.

Choosing that combination of products which best utilizes a given set of resources is fundamental to good farm management. Most farms can produce many different products. Frequently however, climate, custom, geography and personal taste will narrow this choice to a small set of activities.

The product/product analysis demonstrates the rationale behind choosing that set of production enterprises which maximizes net income. This mix of products is subject to changes as the value of the products change in the market place. Thus, the optimal choice of products is not a one time decision but must be continually evaluated as market prices change.

All three analyses require both physical and economic data. The solution to each was demonstrated with an algebraic, graphical and longhand technique. Planning for resource allocation continues in the next chapter, where production costs are introduced. These costs add a new dimension to the decision making process.

PROBLEMS AND DISCUSSION QUESTIONS

1. The following table lists physical data for the application of nitrogen to corn. Complete the table. Total fixed costs are $125.

Nitrogen 40 lb/unit	TPP	MPP	APP	TVC	TFC	TC	MIC	VMP
0	0							
1	35							
2	76							
3	106							
4	127							
5	135							
6	140							
7	139							
8	127							

   a. Solve for the profit maximizing level of input use if N is $17/unit and corn is $3/bushel.
   b. Solve again with another method to verify your result.
   c. Where do diminishing marginal returns set in (at what input level)?
   d. Change nitrogen to $23/unit and corn price to $2.75/bushel. Is there a new optimum? If so, what level of input use is now best?
   e. At what input levels do Stage I, Stage II, and Stage III begin?

2. The following table shows a tradeoff between corn and *SBOM* in a ration to produce 180 lbs. of gain on feeder pigs.

Ration	Corn	SBOM	Output (lbs. of gain)	MRS
1	675	0	180 lbs.	_____
2	575	25	180 lbs.	_____
3	475	75	180 lbs.	_____
4	375	150	180 lbs.	_____
5	275	275	180 lbs.	_____
6	175	415	180 lbs.	_____

  a. Graph and label the isoquant.
  b. If corn is 4.5¢/lb. ($2.52/bushel) and *SBOM* is 7¢/lb., which ration is optimal? (Solve by algebraic method.)
  c. If *SBOM* goes to 15¢/lb. and corn rises to 5¢/lb., what is the new optimal ration? (Solve by graphical technique.)
  d. Does this change in ration seem rational? Why?

3. You have been spraying Treflan and Sencor to control weeds in soybeans, however, many weeds remain. In order to get yields up to 40 bu./acre, the chemical representative suggests the following combinations of hired labor for pulling weeds by hand and Basagran (a chemical herbicide).

Option	Basagran (gal/acre)	Labor (hrs/acre)	Output/Acre	MRS
1	.35	0	40 bu.	_____
2	.245	1	40 bu.	_____
3	.1575	2	40 bu.	_____
4	.0875	3	40 bu.	_____
5	.035	4	40 bu.	_____
6	.0	5	40 bu.	_____

  a. Which option is best if Basagran costs $71/gallon (including application) and teenagers will walk the beans for $3.25/hour?
  b. Which option is best if Basagran goes on sale at $60.70/gallon (including application) and teenagers demand $4.25/hour this year?

4. Given the following data on possible corn/soybean rotations, calculate the most profitable combination when corn is 6¢/lb. and soybeans are 19¢/lb.

Rotation	Corn (lbs.)	Soybeans (lbs.)	MRT
1	5000	0	_____
2	5200	400	_____
3	4600	800	_____
4	3600	1200	_____
5	2400	1600	_____
6	0	2000	_____

    a. What is the most profitable rotation?

    b. Interpret in two sentences or less the *MRT* you calculated between the 3rd and 4th rotations.

    c. If corn stays at 6¢/lb. and soybeans fall to 17¢/lb., what is the new optimum?

    d. A graph of this physical data produces a _____ .

5. Explain why the border point between Stage II and Stage III (i.e., the point where *TPP* is at a maximum) must be considered in Stage II (the "rational" stage of production) in a factor/product problem.

6. What products in your area have a complementary or supplementary interaction?

SUGGESTED READINGS

Buse, Rueben C., and Daniel W. Bromley. *Applied Economics, Resource Allocation in Rural America*, 2nd edition. Ames, Iowa: Iowa State University Press, 1975.

Castle, Emery N., Manning Becker and Frederick J. Smith. *Farm Business Management*, 2nd edition, Chapter 2. New York: Macmillan Publishing Co., Inc., 1972.

Halcrow, Harold G. *Economics of Agriculture*, Chapter 2. New York: McGraw-Hill Book Company, 1980.

Harsh, Stephen B., Larry J. Conner and Gerald D. Schwab. *Managing the Farm Business*, Chapter 3. Englewood Cliffs, New Jersey: Prentice-Hall, Inc., 1981.

Osburn, Donald D., and Kenneth Schneeburger. *Modern Agricultural Management*, Chapter 2. Reston, Virginia. Reston Publishing Company, 1978.

Snodgrass, Milton M., and L. T. Wallace. *Agriculture, Economics and Resource Management*, 2nd edition, Chapters 11, 12, and 13. Englewood Cliffs, New Jersey: Prentice-Hall, Inc., 1980.

3

Equimarginal Returns and Production Costs—Added Dimensions in Decision Making

.... for in the field of economic and political philosophy there are not many who are influenced by new theories after they are twenty five to thirty years of age, ...

John Maynard Keynes, The General Theory

Concepts

In this chapter you will come to understand:

1. How to allocate one or more resources to one or more products over the whole farm.
2. The difference between the short run and long run periods for resource allocation purposes.
3. How a farm manager can decide whether or not to continue producing indefinitely, to produce only during the current period, or to shut down production.
4. How to discover if increasing the size of the farm will lower per unit costs or if the farm is already too big.

Tools

You will also gain the following skills:

1. How to allocate resources to farm investments under conditions of limited and unlimited capital.

2. How to solve for the profit maximizing level of output to produce.

Chapter 2 provided a great deal of insight into the three production decisions facing the farm manager: how much of each input should be applied, which combination of inputs produces a target amount of output at least cost and which combination of enterprises maximizes net returns. Most of the effort in these analyses has been centered on input use questions. That is, with the exception of the product/product case, the approach has been to vary the level of input(s) used and measure the response in net income. This approach has two important limitations.

1. The manager can really only concentrate on one, or at most two, variable inputs.
2. The manager knows nothing about the impact of fixed costs or whether or not a product should be produced at all on a long-term basis.

EQUIMARGINAL RETURNS

The first limitation may be addressed by examining how the farm manager, in a given production period, determines the best allocation of one or more inputs over one or more products for the whole farm. To understand the problem more clearly, one may start by looking at a single input. As an example, consider operating capital as an input which can be applied to the production of hogs, crops or milk. First assume that an unlimited amount of capital is available.

Table 3-1 lists the gross returns which could be realized by investing $1000 increments in each of the three activities. Reading across the first

TABLE 3-1. HYPOTHETICAL INVESTMENT OPPORTUNITIES REQUIRING $1,000 OF CAPITAL

Investment	Gross Returns From Hogs	Gross Returns From Crops	Gross Returns From Dairy
	($)	($)	($)
1	1500	1800	1200
2	1450	1700	1200
3	1400	1600	1200
4	1350	1450	1100
5	1250	1300	1050
6	1150	1100	1000
7	1050	1000	900
8	900	900	800
Total Gross Returns From All Eight Investments	10,050	10,850	8,450

row, a thousand dollars invested in hogs returns $1,500 in gross revenue. The same thousand dollars invested in crops or dairy results in $1,800 and $1,200, respectively. The column totals describe the total gross revenue which would be obtained if all eight investment possibilities were taken in each alternative. Notice that in each case, the total gross returns are greater than the total required investment when all opportunities are taken.

Consider, however, what might happen if each thousand dollar investment was individually examined and only those investments which returned a profit were undertaken. This approach is identical to the solution rationale employed in Chapter 2, which was to keep investing until the additional returns were just equal to the additional costs. If achieving this optimum was not possible because of limited investment capital, the farm operator would continue investing as long as the returns were greater than the cost for the last unit invested.

In the case of unlimited investment capital, seven units would be allocated to hogs, seven units to crops and six units to dairy. The remaining opportunities are rejected as they do not return a profit on the margin. The reader can demonstrate that greater **net** returns result from using this approach than from simply investing in all possible alternatives even though total revenue exceeds total cost.

When investments are allocated across competing alternatives a concept emerges which is known as the **opportunity cost** of investment. Opportunity cost is the gross return that could have been realized by applying a given input in its next best alternative. From this table, notice that if the first thousand dollar increment was allocated to crops, the next best alternative for that investment would have been in hog production. Therefore, the opportunity cost of placing the first thousand dollars in crops is the $1,500 in gross returns which are foregone by rejecting the hog alternative.

Frequently, the farm manager has insufficient capital to invest in every possible alternative available. This situation gives rise to the rationale of allocating scarce inputs to their most profitable use. When only limited capital is available, the farm manager must examine each increment of investment and allocate it to the alternative yielding the greatest returns.

Assume that only $6,000 of capital were available, at no interest cost. Allocating each thousand dollars to the activity producing the greatest returns would result in placing the first three investments in crop activities, the fourth and fifth in hogs[1], and the sixth in crops. The final result is $4,000 invested in cropping activities, $2,000 in hog production and no additional investment in dairy. Allocating each increment of total investment to the highest return assures the farm manager that the greatest amount of net income will result. This process is called the

---

[1] *The fifth investment can be placed in hogs or crops since both yield $1,450 in gross returns. Whichever is chosen, the sixth unit would go to the other, leaving the final result unchanged.*

equimarginal returns principle. Where capital is unlimited and resources perfectly divisible, the returns from the last unit invested in each alternative should be equal.

Consider Figure 3-1, a graph of the Value of the Marginal Product of capital for the crop activities in Table 3.1. Assuming a 15 percent interest rate per year, the horizontal line labeled P_k is the marginal input cost of capital. The intersection of the cost of capital and the Value of the Marginal Product curve indicates the optimal amount of capital that should be invested in the cropping activity. Ideally, where perfect information is available for each set of investments, the farm manager should employ inputs up to the point where the price of the input is equal to the value of returns on the margin for each investment.

The graph illustrates the lumpiness of inputs described in Chapter 2. Because it is frequently difficult to borrow very small sums of money, the manager may be required to round credit needs to the nearest thousand dollars. Therefore, a step function occurs, as in Figure 3-1. In choosing whether to invest either $5,000 or $6,000 in crop production, you should notice that even though a portion of this investment has a marginal return greater than the price of capital, the investment as a whole does not. Therefore, only continue increasing the investment of an input until the point where its marginal return is just equal to its cost. If this equality cannot be achieved or seems to fall between two discrete levels of input use, always drop back to where the marginal return is greater than input cost.

Now that allocation of one input has been considered, the process of equimarginal investment analysis can be generalized to cover all inputs

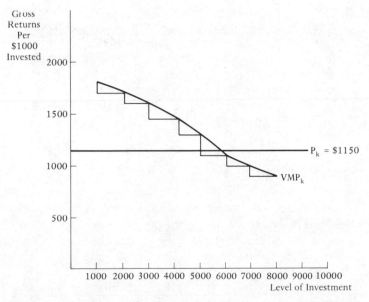

FIGURE 3-1. *The Value of the Marginal Product of Cropping Activities in Table 3-1.*

and all products. The rule appears somewhat imposing in algebraic form but is really only common sense. Consider the following equation:

$$\frac{VMP_{x_1}, Y_1}{P_{x_1}} = \frac{VMP_{x_2}, Y_1}{P_{x_2}} = \frac{VMP_{x_1}, Y_2}{P_{x_1}} = \frac{VMP_{x_2}, Y_2}{P_{x_2}}.$$

The equation is read as follows: "the Value of the Marginal Product of X_1 in the production of Y_1 divided by the price of X_1 is equal to the Value of the Marginal Product of X_2 in the production of Y_1 divided by the price of X_2," . . . etc. In this equation, two outputs and two inputs are considered. If the two outputs (Y_1, Y_2) are corn and soybeans and the two inputs (X_1, X_2) are a herbicide and a fertilizer, this equation can be interpreted as follows: the increase in the value of corn generated by applying the last unit of herbicide divided by the price of herbicide should equal the increase in the value of corn generated by applying the last unit of fertilizer to corn divided by the price of fertilizer. If one fraction were greater than the other, more resources could be profitably applied in that element of the equation. Further, these two fractions on the left should be equal to the value of the increases in soybeans generated by putting the last unit of herbicide there divided by its price, which in turn should be equal to the value of the increase in soybeans generated by putting the last unit of fertilizer on soybeans divided by the price of fertilizer. If the soybean values are greater than the corn values, resources should be shifted from corn to soybeans.

The decision rule in the ideal world for all products and all inputs on the farm is that the value of the marginal product divided by the respective input prices should all be equal across all products. In the ideal world with perfect divisibility of inputs and unlimited capital, all of these fractions would equal 1 where whole farm profits are maximized. In the real world where lumpy inputs and limited capital are facts of life, the operator should consider individually all possible investments and allocate inputs on a marginal basis to the activities which give the greatest marginal return. If all of the limited capital on the farm were allocated by this process, the best possible level and mix of inputs and outputs would result.

PRODUCTION COSTS

The second limitation to studying resource allocation from the input side is the lack of information necessary to judge whether long-term production should be taking place. Instead of varying an input and looking at the effect on net income, one can vary output and observe the effects in production costs. Doing so gives insight into whether the production of each particular enterprise should be shutdown, carried out in the short run only, or produced on a continuous basis. Before approaching this analysis, it is important that a distinction be made between the long run and the short run. These terms refer to periods of time over which planning and implementation activities can be undertaken.

Economists usually refer to the **short run** as one production season. Of course, one production season can vary from a few months to a few years for some crops, but it is usually twelve months or less for most crops produced in the United States. A production season or short-run period for livestock can also vary from a few weeks for broilers up to two years for some aspects of cattle production. A distinguishing characteristic of the short run is that the levels of some inputs are fixed. Usually, land, machinery, family labor and buildings are considered fixed in the short run. The use of these inputs in the production process must be limited to the amount on hand.

In the **long run** by contrast, all inputs are variable. Land can be added to the production process by rental, lease or purchase. Additional capital equipment can be acquired and new buildings constructed. Family labor can increase or decrease in the long run. By definition, the long-run time period is a time horizon beyond one production season.

Up to this point only short run decisions facing the farm manager have been addressed and those decisions have been approached from the input side. Attention will now be turned to decisions regarding the optimal amount of output to produce, beginning with the short run case.

Figure 3–2 is a graph of Total Cost, Total Variable Cost and Total Fixed Cost from an example involving the optimal level of calf production. The data appears in Table 3–2. This example demonstrates a way to establish the best number of stocker cattle to produce on 100 acres of pasture. In Figure 3.2, costs are now measured on the vertical axis and physical **output** on the horizontal axis. The Total Fixed Cost curve is horizontal because total fixed costs are the same at any level of output. The Total Cost curve and Total Variable Cost curve are upward sloping to the right, indicating that as additional cattle are produced, total variable cost, and therefore total costs, rise. Because total cost is equal to the sum of total fixed cost and total variable cost, the difference between total cost and total variable cost at each level of output is simply the amount of total fixed cost.

Also recall from the analysis done in Chapter 2 that the wise farm manager is not concerned so much with total cost as with Marginal Input Cost and the Value of the Marginal Product when choosing optimal input levels. These marginal figures refer to the additions to total cost and the additions to total revenue, respectively, from adding one more unit of the variable input to the production process. To analyze production costs, it is necessary to examine what additions to total cost result from producing an additional unit of output rather than from adding an additional unit of input. Therefore, an item of data is needed which measures this cost. The Marginal Cost (*MC*) of production,

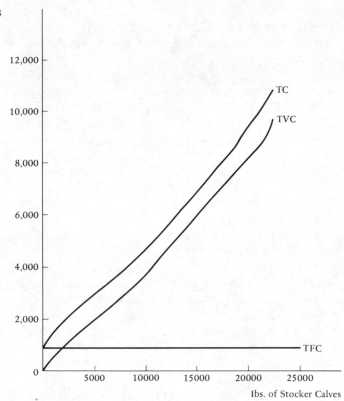

FIGURE 3-2.   *TVD, TFC, and TC Curves for Various Levels of Stocker Calf Production.*

TABLE 3-2.   DATA DESCRIBING THE COSTS ASSOCIATED WITH VARIOUS LEVELS OF CALF PRODUCTION ON 100 ACRES OF PERMANENT PASTURE

Cow-calf Pairs	TPP	MPP	TVC	TFC	TC	AVC	AFC	ATC	MC	MR
10	4000		1600	850	2450	.40	.21	.61		
		400							.40	.55
20	8000		3200	850	4050	.40	.11	.51		
		425							.38	.55
30	12250		4800	850	5650	.39	.07	.46		
		375							.43	.55
40	16000		6400	850	7250	.40	.05	.45		
		360							.44	.55
50	19600		8000	850	8850	.41	.04	.45		
		270							.59	.55
60	22300		9600	850	10450	.43	.04	.47		

Hypothetical data

defined as the additions to Total Cost resulting from producing an additional unit of output, can be calculated as follows:

$$\text{Marginal Cost} = \frac{\Delta \text{ Total Cost}}{\Delta \text{ output}}.$$

Marginal Cost (*MC*) is equal to the change in Total Cost divided by the change in output. Figure 3–3 graphs the Marginal Cost as additional units of output are produced. Notice that Marginal Cost is a U-shaped curve. That is, it begins at some level of cost, declines over a range, reaches a low point, and then begins to rise. This means that over the range where Marginal Cost is decreasing, additional units of output can be produced at smaller and smaller per unit costs. This range does not continue indefinitely. At the point where Marginal Cost begins to rise, the cost of producing each additional unit of output also rises. The question now becomes, "How much output should be produced?" Since Marginal Cost describes how much each additional unit of output costs, a corresponding figure is needed which describes how much each additional unit output is worth in the market place.

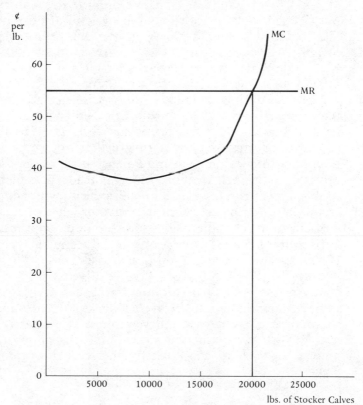

FIGURE 3–3. *MC and MR Indicating the Most Profitable Level of Stocker Calf Production.*

The value of output is measured by its price on a per unit base. The item of data which can be calculated to indicate this value is referred to as Marginal Revenue (*MR*). Marginal Revenue is calculated as follows:

$$\text{Marginal Revenue} = \frac{\Delta \text{ Total Revenue}}{\Delta \text{ output}},$$

or the change in Total Revenue divided by the change in output. In Figure 3.3 Marginal Revenue has also been graphed, indicating an output price of 55¢/lb. You should note that the graph of Marginal Revenue for a typical farmer in perfectly competitive agricultural markets is a horizontal line. This indicates that the market price is not affected by the production of an individual farmer.

Our decision is to continue increasing production as long as the Marginal Revenue is greater than the Marginal Cost. The optimal level of output occurs where the additional costs (*MC*) are just equal to the additional revenue (*MR*) gained from the last unit produced. This point can be found graphically where the Marginal Revenue curve intersects Marginal Cost (Figure 3-3). Therefore, the decision rule from the output side is that the profit maximizing level of output will occur where Marginal Cost is equal to Marginal Revenue. Notice in Figure 3-3 that Marginal Revenue crosses Marginal Cost at 20,000 pounds (approx. 51 head). When the expected price of stocker calves is 55¢/pound, 20,000 pounds will be the profit maximizing level of production.

When the optimal amount of output is calculated, there is no guarantee that this level will produce profits, only that it is the best possible level of output given the prices and costs associated with a particular production function. This is to say that by producing at the optimal level of output you may be minimizing losses as opposed to maximizing profits. Additional analysis, which is made possible by studying this problem from the output side, will indicate whether this optimal level of output does in fact result in profits or whether it is the best possible loss situation. A third possibility is to shut down if losses are excessive.

To gain insight into this problem and aid in analyzing profitability, it is necessary to calculate additional cost figures. These figures are: the Average Total Cost (*ATC*), Average Fixed Cost (*AFC*), and Average Variable Cost (*AVC*) of production. The average costs of production indicate how much, on the average, each unit of output costs in terms of total cost, fixed cost and variable cost, respectively. The way the average costs of production are calculated is simply to divide the total amount of each type of cost by the level of output being produced. Thus:

$$\text{Average Variable Cost} = \frac{TVC}{Y},$$

$$\text{Average Fixed Cost} = \frac{TFC}{Y},$$

$$\text{Average Total Cost} = \frac{TC}{Y} = AVC + AFC.$$

Figure 3–4 shows a graph of these three average cost relationships. Note that Average Variable Cost and Average Total Cost are U-shaped curves, again indicating that as the level of output increases, these costs decline until they reach a low point and then begin to rise. Average Fixed Cost steadily declines throughout the entire range of Stages I and II, but rises in Stage III. This is so in Stages I and II because Total Fixed Costs are spread over more and more units of output. Since Total Fixed Costs do not change, this number on the average becomes smaller as more units of output are produced.

Figure 3–5 shows typical Average Cost curves with a Marginal Cost and some Marginal Revenue curves superimposed upon them. With these relationships one can determine whether a production activity should be continued in the long run, operated only in the short run, or

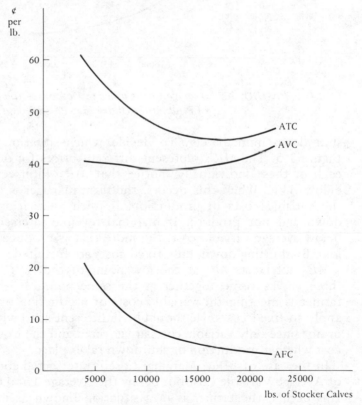

FIGURE 3–4. *The AVC, AFC, and ATC Relationships Associated with Stocker Calf Production.*

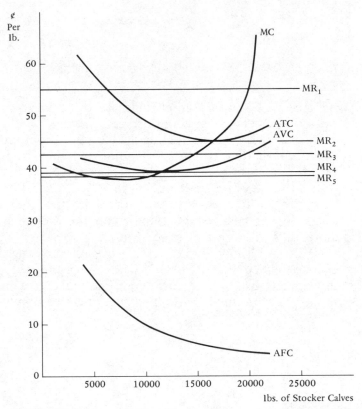

FIGURE 3–5. *Average Cost Curves to Determine the Profitability*
of Production Under Five Possible Output Prices.

shut down immediately. To decide which situation applies, refer to Figure 3–5. The *MR*'s represent different prices for output. Examining each of these individually, notice that MR_5 intersects *MC* at a point below *AVC*. When this occurs, the farm manager is not able to cover the variable costs of production. In such a situation he should shut down and not produce. If marginal revenue intersects marginal cost below average variable cost, the more that is produced, the greater the loss. By shutting down, only fixed costs are forfeited.

MR_4 intersects *MC* at the low point of the *AVC* curve so that all three curves come together at the same point. In this situation, the farmer is meeting the variable costs of production but has nothing to apply to fixed costs. He should be indifferent as to whether to produce or not since only variable costs are covered and the loss is equal to fixed cost whether production or shutdown takes place.

In the case of MR_3, Marginal Cost is intersected above the low point of Average Variable Cost but below the Average Total Cost curve. When this occurs, the farmer is in a situation known as loss minimization. That is, all the variable costs are being covered and some contribution is being made to fixed costs but not all fixed costs are being covered.

Therefore, the farmer should produce in the short run (for the next production season) and hope that prices improve. However, should the price received be equal to price MR_3, no profit will accrue but losses will be at a minimum. Shutdown in this case would result in a loss of fixed costs (greater than the loss involved with production).

MR_2 intersects Marginal Cost at the point where Average Total Cost is at a minimum. In this situation, the farmer is meeting all of the total costs of production and, therefore, making a normal profit. Recall from Chapter 2 that there are four factors of production used in any production activity on the farm. These are land, labor, capital and management. If the farmer is meeting the total costs of production, then each of these four factors of production will be receiving its fair return. The return to land is called **rent**. The return to labor is called **wages**. The return to capital is called **interest**. These terms apply even if the farmer uses his own land, labor, and capital. The return to management is called **profit**. These are the four costs of using factors of production. If the total costs of production are being met, there is a fair return to each of the factors of production including management, that return is profit. When all costs are met, the farmer should continue producing in the long run.

Finally, notice that MR_1 passes through Marginal Cost at a point above Average Total Cost. This point indicates that the farmer is not only earning revenue to cover all the variable and fixed costs of production but is receiving an amount over and above all costs. This latter is referred to as excess or **economic profits**. When this situation occurs, it should only be present for a short-run period of time. As excess profits are available for any production activity, they cause entry by other farmers and entrepreneurs seeking to capture some of these profits. As more producers enter the industry, more of the product will be produced and, all things being equal, a downward pressure on price will result.

The Marginal Cost curve above Average Variable Cost is referred to as the individual farmer's short-run supply curve for output. This short-run supply curve traces the output levels the individual farmer should be willing to produce at each level of price. The horizontal summation of the Marginal Cost curves for each individual farmer traces the total short-run supply curve for each individual commodity. This curve is referred to as the market supply curve.

FARM ANALYSIS IN THE LONG RUN

You should recall that all of the factors of production are variable in the long run. In the long run the farm manager can increase or decrease the level of each factor of production. This means that land, buildings, machinery, operator labor, etc., can be added to increase farm size.

Likewise, the level of each factor of production currently used can be reduced or disinvested in the long run as conditions require.

There are certain similarities and relationships which exist between short and long-run analysis. The production cost problem just presented from the short-run side will now be used to consider what changes might be indicated for the long run. Applying the principles of short-run analysis to the stocker cattle example, the marginal cost was set equal to the marginal revenue to discover the optimal level of calf production. This is the short-run optimal level of production. We would now like to examine whether increasing the size of the operation would be profitable. In order to increase the capacity of the farm to produce stocker steers, additional pasture land would need to be acquired. The farm manager is faced with the decision as to whether the current fixed inputs allow the farm enough capacity to produce a long-run optimal level of production.

To understand better the concept of long run you may view it in one of two ways:

1. Down the road in the concrete sense of comparing the costs in Table 3-1 with those of farmers producing 100, 200 or 300 head today on neighboring farms.
2. Down the road in the abstract sense in which you imagine where your own farm will be five, ten or fifteen years from now. Should you be producing 100, 200 or 300 head or still producing 50 head?

Additional understanding can be gained by plotting (under current technology) the average total costs and marginal costs of the 60 head capacity operation depicted in Table 3-1. The graph appears in Figure 3-6. If data were available from neighboring farms which are physically down the road, a comparison of their costs would give the farm manager additional insight as to the costs of other operations producing the same product. Each operation has its own short-run Average Total Cost curve. By connecting all these short-run Average Total Cost curves together, the long-run Average Total Cost curve can be drawn. The long-run Average Total Cost curve ($LRAC$) resembles an envelope formed from all the short-run Average Total Cost curves. It is also called the planning curve because it shows the different sizes of operation that could be implemented in the long-run when all resources are variable. Notice that the long-run Average Total Cost curve is more gently sloped than the short-run cost curves. This is so because of the greater flexibility available in modifying the size of the operation in the long run. Just as in the case of each short-run Average Total Cost curve, the long-run Average Total Cost curve is U-shaped. A region exists over which costs per pound of stocker calves produced are declining. Eventually, these costs increase because of the law of diminishing marginal physical product. Up until the point where the long-run Average Cost curve

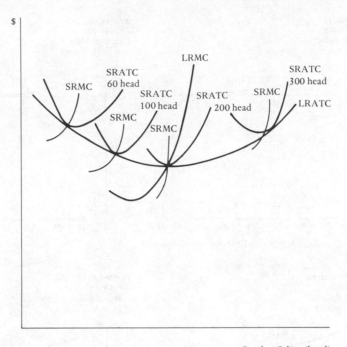

FIGURE 3-6. *The SRATC for Various Levels of Stocker Calf Production and the LRATC for the Industry.*

reaches a minimum, economies of size are available. That is, the bigger the operation, all things being equal, the less it will cost on a per unit basis to produce output. After the low point of the long-run Average Total Cost curve, diseconomies of size will result. The bigger the operation becomes beyond this point the larger the costs per unit of output become.

Studies conducted by the *USDA* for U.S. field crops indicate the most medium sized crop farms (gross income between $41,000–$76,000) are able to fully exploit available economies of size. Figure 3–7 illustrates *LRAC* (Long-Run Average Cost) curves for different crop farms throughout the nation. As the *LRAC* curve approaches the $1.00 line, all factors of production are earning a fair return. By imputing the rate of return on the most efficient farms as a cost to all farm size categories, a $1.00 cost per dollar of gross income occurs at the most efficient size and a higher cost results for other farm sizes. Expanding size beyond this most efficient point doesn't seem to affect per unit costs, indicating that the *LRAC* curve has a long flat range at the low point.

Economies of size in crop production are primarily related to the efficiencies of larger machinery (technology) and the fully employed operator/laborer. Small farmers can overcome some of the problems related to size by custom hiring machine work when the purchase of large more efficient machinery is unjustified (Chapter 14). Some other

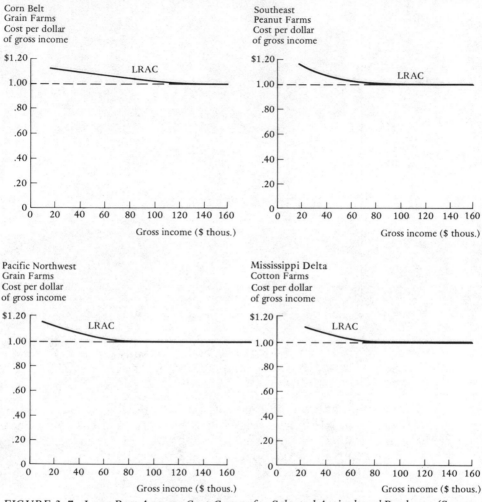

FIGURE 3-7. *Long Run Average Cost Curves for Selected Agricultural Products. (Source: Miller, T.A., G.E. Rodewald and R.G. McElroy, "Economies of Size in U.S. Field Crop Farming," United States Department of Agriculture, AER #472, July, 1981.*

options for small scale farmers include performing custom work when excess machinery capacity exists and seeking off farm employment when labor requirements of the farm are low.

It should be pointed out that size is not the only determinant of efficiency. Technologies employed along with the rate of technological adaptation, management ability and resource productivity have been found to account for a wide range of incomes within each size of farm.

In general, it pays to increase the size of an operation up to the low point of the *LRAC*. In Figure 3-6 this would be up to 200 head, because lower and lower costs can be achieved given a certain price per pound for calves. The farmer producing 60 head will equate his Marginal Costs and his Marginal Revenue. The farm manager producing 300 head will equate his Marginal Cost with Marginal Revenue. Since we have already discovered that the Marginal Cost curves always intersect Average Cost at their lowest point, there is also a Long–Run Marginal Cost curve (*LRMC*). At the long-run optimal production level, *SRMC* = *SATC* = *LRAC* = *LRMC*.

Thinking of the *LRAC* (road) in the concrete sense of a neighbor's operation in the present, the farm manager can be fairly sure that the *LRAC* does indeed have this U-shape. But, thinking of it in the abstract sense of his own operation somewhere down the road, he cannot be completely sure that the optimal size today will stay the same ten to fifteen years from now. This is so because of two important factors:

1. Change in Input Prices. These are things such as gasoline prices and the prices of grain, feed, veterinary services, etc. They almost always can be expected to increase over time. However, each of these may not increase at the same rate. The effect that this will have on the *LRAC* is to drive it upward. All farmers with similar technology will be affected just about equally.

2. Change in Technology. This may involve genetic improvements in cattle such as multiple births. The use of new hybrid crops, multiple cropping, enhancement of photosynthetic efficiency (increased yield) and the development of bioregulators to enhance ripening and extend shelf-life are some of the technological advancements expected in crop production. The impact of changes in technology on the *LRAC* will be to shift it down and outward to the right. Changes associated with technology tend to benefit the larger-scale operator. In Figure 3–6 the larger producer already has a higher margin between *SATC* and the marginal revenue curve. Technical change will favor him even more. However, long-run prices of output do not affect the long-run Average Total Cost curve. No matter what prices are, larger-scale producers will get greater profits or sustain smaller losses per hundredweight. These do not affect the optimal size of the farm unless, for instance, there is a whole-scale consumer revolt against red meats (which is very unlikely) and it becomes unprofitable for anyone to produce.

You would expect that in the long-run all farms will gravitate towards the best size if technology remains constant. However, the problems of entry such as land acquisition, capital acquisition, corporate taxation, investment credit limits, financial risk, the types of commodities that are eligible for crop insurance and price support programs, pollution control programs, and the relative ease with which larger farmers can obtain credit, all work against small farmers moving out along their long-run Average Total Cost curve trying to reach the minimum cost size. When technology changes, larger farmers usually have a head start in adoption. An actual example from the cattle industry in Iowa demonstrates these facts. The graph in Figure 3–8 shows how techno-

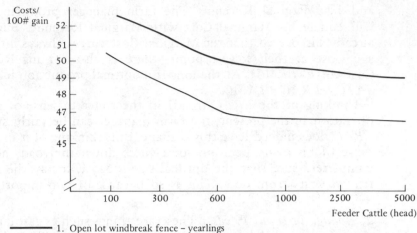

1. Open lot windbreak fence – yearlings
2. Cold confinement pit – field spread – yearlings

FIGURE 3-8. Short-Run Total Costs per 100 lb. Gain on Fat Cattle Produced in Iowa. (Source: Department of Animal Science, Iowa State University, Ames, Iowa.)

logical change has benefited larger operators. Work at Iowa State University has shown that for cattle feedlots, which have shown a tremendous increase in numbers handled over the last 25 years, costs have become lower and lower over time due to technological change. It used to be that 25 head per feedlot was a typical operating size in Iowa. Now, it appears that the lowest per unit costs occur somewhere near 5,000 head.

SUMMARY

In this chapter, several added dimensions to the problem of resource allocation in the ideal world were introduced. The process of allocation known as equimarginal returns is a method by which the farm manager can assure that all inputs used in production are properly allocated. In the case of capital scarcity, where only a limited number of profitable opportunities can be exploited, this process assures that the greatest possible income is achieved.

Approaching resource allocation from the output side was also demonstrated as a method by which the manager can explore the questions of profitability and long-run planning. The distinction between the long run and short run was demonstrated and the long-run Average Total Cost curve was developed as a planning tool. Economies and diseconomies of size were discovered via the use of the long-run Average Total Cost curve as a basis for planning optimal farm size.

SAMPLE PROBLEMS

1.

TPP	TFC	TVC	TC	AFC	AVC	ATC	MC
7	100	176	_____	14.29	25.14	39.43	39
8	100	220	_____	12.50	27.50	_____	_____
9	100	280	380	11.11	31.11	42.22	60
10	100	345	_____	_____	_____	44.50	65

   a. Fill in the blanks in the table above.
   b. At what level of output would you produce, if the price of output was:
      1. $39 _____
      2. $61 _____
      3. $64.95 _____
   c. Are you making excess profits if you produce where price of output is equal to $60? Yes _____ No _____

2. Match the descriptions below to the situation they dictate by placing the correct letter in the blank provided.
   a. $MR = ATC$ at optimum   _____ excess profits
   b. $MR < AVC$ at optimum   _____ normal profits
   c. $MR > ATC$ at optimum   _____ indifferent as to production
   d. $MR = AVC$ at optimum   _____ stop producing
   e. $ATC > MR > AVC$ at optimum   _____ loss minimization

3. Below is a comparison of costs and returns for adding nitrogen (N) to corn, using additional fuel for tilling, applying additional phosphorous (P), and applying additional potassium (K). Gross returns per $1000 invested are shown in the table.

Capital Invested ($)	N	P	K	fuel
1st 1000	2050	1900	1850	2400
2nd 1000	1750	1450	1300	2150
3rd 1000	1100	1050	800	1600
4th 1000	900	700	650	1150
5th 1000	600	500	500	750

   a. If unlimited capital were available at no opportunity cost, how much should be invested in each alternative?
      N $_____   P $_____   K $_____   fuel $_____
   b. If unlimited capital were available at 17% interest, how much should be invested in each alternative?
      N $_____   P $_____   K $_____   fuel $_____
   c. How much should be invested if only $7000 is available at no interest cost?
      N $_____   P $_____   K $_____   fuel $_____

4. At the long-run optimal level of output
   a. economies of size are possible
   b. *LRAFC* is at a minimum
   c. *LRATC* is at a minimum
   d. total costs are at their lowest
   e. none of the above

5. If *AVC* is $15, *TVC* is $165 and *TFC* are $110. Then *ATC* must be
   a. $125
   b. $265
   c. $55
   d. $25
   e. insufficient information to calculate

6. Normal profits result when:
   a. *MR* is above *MC* at the optimum
   b. *AFC* is above *AVC* at the optimum
   c. *ATC* is just being met at the optimum
   d. *MR* is above *ATC* at the optimum
   e. These never occur in farming

7. *ATC* includes a fair return to:
   a. land, labor, machinery, and equipment
   b. land, labor, capital and net worth
   c. labor, capital, land and management
   d. management, variable inputs, capital and land
   e. none of the above

SUGGESTED READINGS

Buse, Rueben C., and Daniel W. Bromley. *Applied Economics, Resource Allocation in Rural America*, 2nd edition, Ames, Iowa: Iowa State University Press, 1975.

Castle, Emery N., Manning Becker and Frederick J. Smith. *Farm Business Management*, 2nd edition, Chapter 2. New York: MacMillan Publishing Co., Inc., 1972.

Halcrow, Harold G. *Economics of Agriculture*, Chapter 2. New York: McGraw-Hill Book Company, 1980.

Harsh, Stephen B., Larry J. Conner and Gerald D. Schwab. *Managing the Farm Business*. Chapter 3. Englewood Cliffs, New Jersey: Prentice–Hall, Inc., 1981.

Kay, Ronald D. *Farm Management, Planning, Control, and Implementation*, Chapter 3. New York, New York: McGraw-Hill Book Company, 1981.

Osburn, Donald D., and Kenneth Schneeburger. *Modern Agricultural Management*, Chapter 2. Reston, Virginia: Reston Publishing Company, 1978.

Snodgrass, Milton M., and L. T. Wallace. *Agriculture, Economics and Resource Management*, 2nd edition, Chapters 11, 12, and 13. Englewood Cliffs, New Jersey: Prentice–Hall, Inc., 1980.

Part II

Approximating
the Real World

4

The Role of Budgets, Records and Planning

It is a capital mistake to theorize before
one has data. Insensibly one begins to twist
facts to suit theories, instead of theories
to suit facts.

Sherlock Holmes

Concepts

In this chapter you will come to understand:

1. The budgeting process as a method by which resources can be rationally allocated under conditions of imperfect knowledge.
2. The uses of budgeting in exploring the allocation of resources.
3. The common steps involved in constructing all budgets.
4. The importance of record keeping in the farm business.
5. The components of record keeping systems to assess past performance, calculate net income, and take stock of available resources.
6. The valuing process for the farm inventory.
7. The financial statement which provides management information regarding total farm assets and the ownership claims upon them.

Tools

You will also gain the following skills:

1. How to account for and value farm inventory items.
2. How to calculate depreciation expense and the adjustments that must be made under a variety of circumstances.
3. How to construct the net worth statement.
4. How to measure farm liquidity, solvency, and leverage.

So far, we have discussed the proper use of economic principles to find the most profitable use of production factors. This discussion has taken place in the framework of the Ideal World or risk-free environment. If all the information were available so that production functions and physical relationships could be perfectly predicted, as well as an exact future prediction of prices, then the text could stop right here. For any given resource base on any particular farm, the maximization of profits would be a simple matter.

Unfortunately, experimental data on test plots at universities throughout the United States and in fact throughout the world, can never perfectly predict the yields you can expect on your farm. Likewise, even though sophisticated price prediction models are constructed and operated by agricultural economists throughout the world, the particular prices faced when you buy inputs or sell your crops cannot be perfectly anticipated. There is tremendous variability in all of the basic information needed to plan for resource allocation. Prices faced by farmers have a great deal of seasonal, cyclical, business and random movements. There is genetic variability in livestock and crops. The weather, of course, is extremely variable. All of these factors affect the proper allocation of resources.

At this point it is necessary to concentrate on how to make a rational assessment of what prices and yields to expect, so that in the presence of incomplete knowledge, appropriate economic plans can be made. This process is called budgeting. Budgeting is the major activity involved in the planning function of management. Furthermore, budgeting facilitates the evaluation function wherein the farm manager compares actual performance with predicted performance as a means to identify and correct misallocations. Consistent with our definition of farm management, budgets and record keeping are now introduced (Figure 4–1). Budgeting is **a systematic approach to organizing data to make accurate decisions on costs and returns under conditions of incomplete knowledge**. This is our first step out of the ideal world of complete knowledge, into the real world of incomplete knowledge in which we live.

There are several kinds of budgets which can be constructed to aid the farm manager in planning the allocation of resources. These budgets will be covered in detail in the next two chapters. An introduction to the role of each major type of budget follows.

THE ROLE OF BUDGETS

Budgets approximate the analysis done in Chapter 2 where complete knowledge was assumed. For instance, **enterprise budgets** are a substitute for complete knowledge of the factor/product relationship. These budgets look at physical inputs and outputs and assign a value to them. Output expressed as yield per acre, pigs weaned per litter, percent calves weaned per cow bred, dairy income per 10,000 pounds of milk, egg income per hen, average daily gain in feeder animals, and net returns

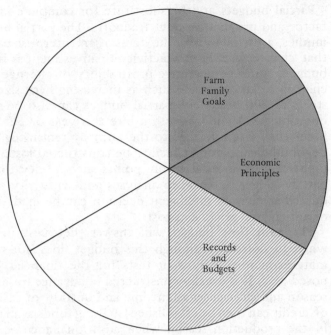

FIGURE 4-1. *The Components of Farm Business Management. Adding records and budgets.*

per acre are some examples of the units upon which enterprise budgets are constructed. After this is accomplished a rate of return or net return per unit of enterprise can be calculated. The first step in constructing these budgets is a well-kept set of records. The enterprise budgets will be the individual building blocks for a complete farm plan.

Whole farm budgets can be constructed using enterprise budgets to facilitate an analysis of the entire productive activity taking place on the farm. Whole farm budgeting is an approximation of the product/product relationship. Every piece of information available can go into them. The whole farm budget looks at the most profitable enterprise budgets and combines them into the most likely five or ten total farm plans. With the aid of these budgets, all income and all expenses of a particular organization of a farm can be anticipated.

The whole farm budget attempts to maximize net farm income while living within the resource requirements of the farm. Other nonincome goals of the farmer can also be incorporated. The whole farm budget is not constructed on a year-by-year basis but only constructed every three or four years or when major changes are anticipated. Yields per acre, livestock income per $100 feed fed, and other efficiency measures can be developed to aid the farmer in finetuning the analysis to increase profitability and efficiency over time. After checking these indices, alternative whole farm plans can be constructed so that net farm income can grow over time and weak points in the ongoing operation can be isolated and improved.

Partial budgets are the substitute for complete knowledge of factor-factor and product/product tradeoffs. The partial budget is, as its name implies, a partial look at the items of an enterprise or a complete budget that change when a new activity or investment is implemented. These budgets study comparative profitability of alternative small (marginal) changes in an enterprise such as increasing herd size from 100 head of steers to 200 head. The partial budget can also be used to decide such questions as: should I custom hire this year or purchase my own combine? shall I add acreage to the farm by renting or leasing? or should a new building or storage facility be constructed instead of relying totally on storage at local assembly points such as elevators? With the aid of partial budgets, breakeven analyses and sensitivity analyses can be conducted so that an intelligent decision can be made under a wide range of anticipated prices and costs.

The **cash flow budget** will answer the question of how much and when to borrow. Although this budget does not specifically approximate economic analysis, it tests for the financial feasibility of a proposed plan. It is usually constructed in advance for an entire production season and anticipates all income and outflow of cash. Appropriate lines of credit can then be established, making funds available at critical times in the production season when additional income may be necessary. Since the timing of cash inflows and outflows are notoriously incongruous in farming, this type of budgeting is an absolute necessity.

Before examining each one of these budgets in detail in the chapters which follow, several common characteristics of all budgets can be noted.

1. All budgeting is closely related to the ideal world analysis of economic principles. The factor/product, factor/factor, and product/product relationships each have a corresponding budget or budgets which allow the types of questions these analyses address to be dealt with in a situation of incomplete knowledge.
2. Budgets are particularly adapted to asking larger either/or type questions: should you have more or less livestock, should you add bigger and more efficient machinery, what rotation should you use this year, should you own the combine or custom hire.
3. Common steps in budgeting are:
   a. Identifying the relevant production alternatives. Only those production alternatives which the farm manager would consider implementing are budgeted. All possible combinations of livestock and cropping activities can be examined with the budgeting process. Once these have been systematically constructed and organized, the appropriate combination and level of implementation of each activity can be pursued.
   b. Collecting cost and returns data. The budgeting process is only as good as the data which go into it. Predictions of costs and returns require careful planning and consultation with experts who follow

cost and return movements over time. Such information is available through extension services and other farm service organizations throughout your area.

c. Organization to make decisions in a useable format. All budgets should be a simple and consistent set of plans necessary to implement the activities the farm manager desires to undertake.

4. The purposes or advantages of budgeting include:

a. Budgets are a nearly costless way of considering alternatives before committing resources. It is important that the farm manager have a clear concept of what costs, machinery, equipment and other inputs will be necessary to undertake an activity, and what returns can be expected. It is much better to succeed or fail on paper before the activity is undertaken than to commit resources and take a wait-and-see approach.

b. Budgeting usually enforces the inclusion of all costs and returns, death losses, and a margin for unexpected expenses. If you only lean over the fence and speak to neighbors regarding how their particular activities have turned out, you may get less than the full picture. By carefully organizing all data necessary to properly evaluate a decision, many overlooked items of costs and returns can be specified and the correct outcome of an activity can be predicted.

c. Budgeting forces the planning function and the evaluation function. You should remember that five functions of management were examined in Chapter 1. One of the most frequently neglected is the evaluation function or the correction process. By keeping records and planning ahead through budgeting, the evaluation function is properly implemented and forced upon the manager. Last year's performance is clearly laid out, along with the predictions from the budgets which were made in advance of implementation. To the extent that the activities did not turn out as expected, the farm manager can carefully examine the result and make the necessary changes to improve profits.

d. Budgeting is a very important input to obtaining credit. Walking into a banker's office with a complete set of records and budgets to support a claim for funds will place you in a much stronger position than someone who has just scratched out a few ideas on the back of an envelope. With extremely volatile interest rates and shortages of funds available to farmers, financial institutions are requiring greater and greater evidence that the money lent to individuals will be eventually returned. The budgeting process can aid in demonstrating this to a lending institution.

Some of the records necessary to properly undertake the budgeting process will now be examined. We begin with records because past performance is perhaps the best indicator, not only of future performance, but also of the possibility of improvement. The management process uses records and budgets to pose a series of important questions. These questions are guideposts in a step-by-step approach to planning the resource allocation under conditions of incomplete knowledge.

THE ROLE OF RECORDS

It is important to note that record keeping is the absolute prerequisite for effective budgeting. Record keeping provides:

1. A Baseline of Data and a Format for Budgeting.   In fact, budgets are nothing more or less than forward records. Budgets are an anticipation of what records will contain once the production season is over.

2. Information on Current Levels of Efficiency.   Properly–kept yearly records allow the farm manager to compare progress made on his farm with farms in his immediate area, in his state and in his region of the country. Several different ways to measure efficiency will be presented in a later chapter. But, for now, it should be realized that well-kept records for an individual farm are the best source of effective planning for the future.

3. A Way to Meet Legal Obligations.   Current law requires that records be kept to establish tax obligations of the farm. Depending on the accounting system employed, legal requirements are very specific regarding the information content of the record system. The mere estimation of inventory and income is not sufficient to satisfy this requirement.

4. A View of Available Resources.   Records should contain a listing or inventory of the productive factors available for employment in farm activities. Deciding what to produce requires a knowledge of the resources available to apply to each production process.

RECORDS TO ASSESS PAST PERFORMANCE

As indicated, past performance is a clue to future performance. A well–kept set of production records can pinpoint for the manager both production potential and areas needing improvement.

The record system chosen by an individual farmer should provide only that information which can aid in the planning and accounting process. Tremendous detail is not required. Record keeping systems should be tailored to the individual enterprises and management practices present on each farm. There is no single perfect format that can be applied in every case. However, the following guidelines and minimum standards are applicable to almost all systems.

Crop Records

Crop records provide information on input use, output result and any other factors which make a significant impact on performance. Records should be kept on each major soil type and productivity characteristic of the farm. Levels of such major inputs as fertilizer, herbicide and seed per acre should be recorded, along with resulting yields. This and other useful information is summarized below. The actual format of the record is unimportant as long as it is clear, consistent and usable.

1. Acquisition and Type.   A record should be made regarding the particular hybrid or variety of crop planted. A notation as to whether the seed was purchased or produced on the farm is also important. Differing varieties perform differently on certain soil types or under different weather conditions. It is necessary to discover which varieties do best on a given set of soil, cultivation practices, and weather conditions.

2. Input Rates.   Usually it is sufficient to list only a few of the most important inputs used and their rates of application. Items such as fertilizer levels, herbicide application and seed density are important to record. Another important variable to record is tillage method and cultivation practice. Many crops respond favorably to minimum tillage and cultivation practices while others require a great deal of preparation and maintenance in order to produce well. The operator should also note whether or not the field was custom harvested. Timeliness factors and skill of the operator are important inputs affecting output performance.

3. Output Results.   The level of inputs applied will largely dictate output performance. Keeping careful records of historical yield will facilitate predicting future yield. If the crop is sold there is no problem obtaining yield information. However, if stored, an approximation of yield may be necessary. Various formulas are available to estimate crop volume kept in storage facilities (Table 4–1). An agricultural engineering extension person can provide additional techniques for this estimation.

4. Environment.   The production environment is actually reflected in input use rates, but additional variables will prove helpful. Field identification and characteristics are part of the information necessary to properly identify the growing environment. The Soil Conservation Service (SCS) can provide information via soil maps to aid the operator in identifying soil types and configurations as well as erosion potential on various sections of the farm. Weather conditions can be noted, especially if usual circumstances were present. Unusually high or low yields may be attributable to abnormally good or poor weather. A brief notation of unusual weather is usually sufficient to avoid adjusting input rates and/or eliminate overly optimistic or pessimistic future production forecasts.

5. Other Unusual Circumstances.   Certain years may bring particularly troublesome pest infestation. As an example, the Mediterranean Fruit Fly infestation in California in 1981 threatened major fruit and vegetable production areas. Many times infestations occur in regular cycles or may be enhanced by peculiar weather conditions. Careful examina-

TABLE 4–1. ESTIMATING GRAIN AND ROUGHAGE VOLUMES

1. Shelled corn, soybeans, and other grains (bushels)

   Round bin: diameter ✕ diameter ✕ average
   depth   ✕ .628 (all in feet)

   Rectangular bin: length   ✕ width   ✕ average
   depth   ✕ .8 (all in feet)

2. Ear corn (bushels)

   Round crib: distance around crib   ✕ diameter
   ✕ depth ✕ .1 (all in feet)

   Rectangular crib: length ✕ width ✕ depth ✕ .1 (all in feet)

3. Hay (tons):   length ✕ width ✕ height ÷ 500 (all in feet)

4. Straw (tons):   length ✕ width ✕ height ÷ 1000 (all in feet)

5. Corn silage (tons at 65% moisture):[1]

   Upright silo

| | *diameter (feet)* | | | | |
height (ft)	*18*	*20*	*22*	*24*	*30*
40	202	249	300	356	557
50	227	342	416	439	771
60	361	445	538	638	1000
70				790	1235
80				949	1478

   Bunker silo (tons per feet of length)

| *bottom width* | *depth* | | | | |
(feet)	*8*	*10*	*12*	*16*	*20*
20	3.5	4.5	5.5		
30	5.0	6.5	7.9	10.9	
40	6.6	8.5	10.3	14.1	18.0
50	8.2	10.5	12.7	17.3	22.0
60		12.5	15.1	20.5	26.0
70			17.5	23.7	30.0
80			19.9	26.9	34.0
100				33.3	42.0

[1] For haylage at 50% moisture multiply by .715.

Source: Cooperative Extension Service,
    PM 417-b, Selecting and Locating Silage Storage.
    Iowa State University, Ames, IA

tion of crops and consultation with extension entomologists may be required. Unusually late or early planting or pruning may also be noteworthy as yields can be affected independent of input use levels.

Livestock Records

The same basic categories applied to cropping records provide the components of a well kept and useful livestock performance record.

1. Acquisition and Type. Records should be kept on the source of livestock and their breed or genetic type. Not only can this information be used to predict yield, it can also serve to trace disease problems infiltrating the stock. Records should identify the source of each animal or flock, distinguishing whether they were produced on the farm or purchased from off-farm sources.

2. Input Rates. Of paramount importance is the quantity and quality of feed. These can be difficult to measure for individual animals but records should be kept on lots, pens, or similar groups if individual consumption is impractical to measure. Growth rates and gain performance can be calculated when feed information is known. Several feed conversion indices to evaluate efficiency will be examined in the next chapter. All of these require accurate data on inputs to assure useful and accurate comparisons. Other important inputs which should be recorded include veterinary services (vaccination, artificial insemination, castration, etc.) and vitamin and other supplements, etc. to feed inputs.

3. Output Results. Careful accounting of gain is the other component necessary to evaluate feed and gain efficiency. Animals should at least be weighed upon purchase and at disposal. The difference will indicate farm production. Output records also include breeding performance. Purebred producers will usually record the performance of individual animals in detail. Commercial producers may need to know only the breeding performance of a group of stock. Mortality records or death loss should also be recorded. Disease prevention can be facilitated and productive efficiency measured. Cause of death should be recorded where possible. Improving calving percent or pigs weaned per litter can be traced historically where careful attention to death loss is noted.

4. Environment. The production environment will frequently be as great a factor in performance as feed inputs used. Records should indicate whether animals were produced in open environments or housed in production buildings. Overcrowding in broiler houses or feedlots may reduce yields due to aggression and disease proliferation. However, underutilization of available facilities also presents economic problems. Unusual weather conditions can be noted for animals raised in an open environment. Extreme heat, cold or drought can frequently lead to poor gains or high death losses. A simple notation of these unusual circumstances can aid the manager in correctly attributing causation and indicate the appropriate corrective action.

5. Other Unusual Circumstances. Records can indicate unusual pest or disease problems present during a production period. As with crops, many pest and disease problems occur cyclically in livestock. Identifying these problems in records will aid in avoiding the misplacement of blame for poor performance or gain. Unusually traumatic transportation over long distance either to or from market should be noted. Shock due to handling or injury in moving livestock to different locations on the farm can be briefly noted. Recording any other atypical circumstance that may affect gain or performance will aid in improving management.

Examples of crop and livestock record-keeping formats appear in Figures 4–2 and 4–3. Records to assess past performance aid the operator in predicting future results and improving management practices via the evaluation function. Correctly attributing causation of good or poor

ROTATED CROP RECORDS

FIELD NO. _____ SOIL _____
ACRES _____ CHARACTERISTICS _____

YIELD	CROP	UNIT	Per Acre	TOTAL	VARIETY AND RATE	FERTILIZER APPLIED	CHEMICALS APPLIED	COMMENTS

FIELD NO. _____ SOIL _____
ACRES _____ CHARACTERISTICS _____

CROP PRODUCTION SUMMARY

				RENTED LAND							WHOLE FARM			
					LANDLORD SHARE			OPERATOR SHARE						
	YIELD	PRODUC-TION	AMOUNT		%	QTY.	AMOUNT	QTY.	AMOUNT		ACRES	YIELD	PRODUC-TION	AMOUNT
1														
2														
3														
4														
5														
6														
7														
8														
9														
10														

FIGURE 4–2. Sample Format for a Crop Production Record-Keeping System. (Source: James, S.C., and Larry Trede, Midwest Farm Account Book, *Agricultural Experiment Station, Iowa State University, Ames, Iowa, 1967.)*

BREEDING RECORD

Individual animals may be identified or a number of animals may be grouped by breeding date. The breeding date may be a specific day or extend over several weeks.

The comments column is for recording unusual information such as birth difficulties, disease, and weather.

	NAME OR NUMBER	DATE BRED	DATE DUE	SIRE	DATE BORN	NO. BORN	NO. WEANED	WEANING WEIGHT	COMMENTS
1									
2									
3									
4									
5									
6									
7									
8									

MORTALITY RECORD

The dollar value of death loss should be calculated on the basis of production costs including purchase cost. This information may be useful for filing insurance claims and calculating business loss for tax purposes.
Include in the "cause of death" column information which will help in interpreting the death record and guide preventative measures.

	DATE	LIVESTOCK CLASS or DESCRIPTION	NO. DIED*	WEIGHT or AGE	AMOUNT**	CAUSE OF DEATH
1					$	
2						
3						
4						
5						
6						
7						
8						

LIVESTOCK FEEDING RECORD

These pages are for recording the total feed fed to one enterprise. Lines are provided for weekly summaries or a representative day in a week. Any method which will measure the total feed fed is acceptable.

Day, Week or Month	No. Animals	Pasture				Corn Shelled	Ground Ear Corn			Hay		
		Field	Days	Field	Days							

FIGURE 4–3. *Sample Format for a Livestock Production Record-Keeping System. (Source: James, S.C., and Larry Trede,* Midwest Farm Account Book, *Agricultural Experiment Station, Iowa State University, Ames, Iowa, 1967.)*

performance is a prerequisite to adjusting management techniques. Establishing efficiency indices to compare performance over production periods also requires carefully kept records. However, these factors are only part of the function of records in the farm business.

RECORDS TO ASSESS INCOME AND EXPENSES

The governmental system under which we live requires that individuals pay taxes on income-producing activities. Normally, income taxes are charged to the net income in a farming operation. A record of total receipts received and total expenses used in generating those receipts must therefore be recorded. The Internal Revenue Service (IRS) of the United States government requires that farmers keep records in sufficient detail to demonstrate the net income received from farming. While the IRS does not prescribe any particular kind of record keeping system, it does require that an accurate record showing income, deductions, credits and other matters must be maintained. A record system which can do little more than approximate income is not adequate.

The type of record keeping system which a farm operator adopts to measure receipts and expenses should be tailored to the particular accounting system that the manager uses. These receipt and expense records can be used to generate the income statement which will be discussed in Chapter 6. Whichever method is employed, it should be capable of establishing the net income and tax burden of the farm. When the income statement is presented in Chapter 6, the various accounting methods which are available for farmers to use will also be discussed. At this time, it is only necessary to demonstrate the components of a system which can accurately record receipts and expenses of the farm business.

The primary account which records the receipts and expenses of the farm business is called a **cash journal**. Entries in the cash journal are recorded chronologically in a manner very similar to the records kept for checkbook balances. After each entry has been made, whether it is a receipt or an expense, a new cash balance is calculated. Normally the entry in the cash journal will reflect whether the receipt or expense was generated through the livestock or cropping enterprises or whether these items originated from the purchase or sale of capital goods. Expenditures associated with non-farm or family activities are also recorded in the cash journal. Since the entries in the cash journal are recorded by the date they occur, it may be difficult to analyze individual activities of the farm business over time. A typical cash journal format appears in Figure 4-4.

To calculate the total sales associated with livestock or crops, or to establish the total expenses of each activity on the farm, the farm manager must categorize the various entries in the cash journal according to the activities associated with them. Since a single check may be written to cover a variety of items, the cash journal may not give sufficient detail to properly allocate receipts and expenses. An account which separates the various receipts and expenses according to enterprise is therefore generally indicated. This account is referred to as the **cash flow summary** account. In the cash flow summary account, several individual accounts for all the production activities, capital purchases,

CASH JOURNAL

	EXPENSES					POST REFERENCE		
	NON-FARM		FARM			FARM		NON-FARM
	CASH	ACCT. PAY	CASH	ACCT. PAY		ACCOUNT		ACCOUNT
1	$	$	$	$				
2								
3								
4								
5								
6								
7								
8								
9								

FIGURE 4–4. *Sample Cash Journal.* (*Source:* James, S.C., and Larry Trede, Midwest Farm Account Book, *Agricultural Experiment Station, Iowa State University, Ames, Iowa, 1967.*)

family living expenses, etc., are segregated. This two-part set of accounts, the cash journal and cash flow summary account, provides the farmer with sufficient detail to calculate the tax burden of the farm and construct the income statement. The actual detail of the accounting system can be constructed and amended over time according to the individual needs of the producer. A sample format for the cash flow summary statement appears in Figure 4–5.

RECORDS TO ASSESS AVAILABLE RESOURCES

Before a profitable and efficient allocation of resources can take place, the farm manager must be aware of what resources are available. Frequently, the resources which are available to the farm manager will dictate what options for productive activity exist. Taking inventory is the manager's first step in discovering which resources are available for farm use and which products are available to generate farm income.

Taking inventory consists of two basic functions: the physical count and valuation. Physical count is the process of describing and listing all productive resources and farm assets. Valuation of the farm inventory involves placing a dollar value on each of the elements in the physical count records.

Depending upon the method of accounting which the farm manager uses, taking inventory may involve a legal obligation. The Internal Revenue Service requires that if the farmer is using the accrual method of accounting (see Chapter 6), a complete record of inventory must be maintained. This record must show an actual count or measurement of all productive assets on the farm and all products which have been produced or purchased. This record must also show the quantity and quality

MONTHLY CASH FLOW SUMMARY

	This summary traces the flow of cash into and out of the business on a monthly basis. It serves as a check against bank statement totals. Also, it will provide information useful in planning future credit needs.		JAN.	FEB.	MAR.	APR.
1	CASH INCOME:		xxx	xxx	xxx	xxx
2	Feeder livestock sales					
3	Livestock product sales					
4	Crop sales					
5	Other farm receipts					
6	Total Operating Farm Income					
7	Breeding livestock sales					
8	Machinery and equipment sales					
9	Other capital sales:					
10	Total Capital Sales					
11	Total Farm Receipts					
12	Non-farm Cash Income					
13	TOTAL CASH INCOME - all sources					
14	CASH EXPENDITURES:		xxx	xxx	xxx	xxx
15	Feeder livestock purchases					
16	Feed purchases					
17	Livestock expenses					
18	Crop expenses					
19	Machinery hire - crops, livestock					
20	Machinery and equipment repair					
21	Fuel and lubricants expense					
22	Building and improvements repair					
23	Hired labor expense					
24	General business expenses					
25	Taxes, insurance, rent, etc.					
26	Other cash expenses:					
27	Total Cash Farm Expenses					
28	Breeding livestock purchases					
29	Machinery and equipment purchases					
30	Building and improvement purchases					
31	Other capital investments:					
32	Total Capital Expenditures					
33	Total Farm Expenditures					
34	Non-farm cash expenditures					
35	TOTAL CASH EXPENDITURES					
36	Net cash difference					
37	Prin. & int. payments on prior loans					
38	Cash difference - loan payments					
39	CASH POSITION ($)					
40	New loans					
41	Prin. & interest payments on new loans					
42	MONTHLY CASH BALANCE					

FIGURE 4–5A. Sample Monthly Cash Flow Summary Account, (Source: James, S.C., and Larry Trede, Midwest Farm Account Book, *Agricultural Experiment Station, Iowa State University, Ames, Iowa, 1967.)*

of inventory items and method by which these factors have been valued. The inventory must include all unsold items at the end of the tax year, whether raised or purchased as long as they are being held for sale.

All livestock must be inventoried, including hogs, cattle, sheep, poultry, etc. This listing of livestock must include livestock held for breeding, dairy, draft, sales, or sporting purposes whether raised or purchased. All harvested farm products which are held for sale, feed or seed must also be inventoried. All supplies, unless very small amounts are on hand, must also be included in the farm inventory. As a general rule, crops which are growing in the field do not require an inventory calculation. However, once they are harvested and held for storage, the amount, quality, and estimated value must be accounted for.

The Physical Count

Taking inventory first involves the physical count, which is the means by which the quantity and quality of all items in the farm inventory are accounted for and recorded. It is very important to measure inventory items in their commonly used units. Establishing values is thus facilitated. As an example, accounting for grains in the physical count should be done by bushels (or hundredweights in the case of certain crops such as rice). Bales are a common unit of measurement for hay and cotton. Hundredweight is the common unit of measurement for most livestock. The farmer can use gallons for fuel and other liquids and any meaningful quantity measurement upon which a price can be easily placed.

When taking the physical count for inventory purposes, like items should be grouped according to their use in the farm business. As an example, farm machinery could be grouped by purpose or use. All equipment used in the cropping operation should be kept separate from that which is used for livestock. Sometimes it may be desirable to separate machinery into powered and nonpowered categories under each of the use characteristics.

Crops should be grouped and divided by type and expected use. Crops primarily intended for farm use might be kept separate from those crops which are primarily intended for sale. Livestock can be grouped by type, age and purpose and further subdivided by quality characteristic, or genetic background. The important point is to make divisions and classifications which are meaningful to the farmer for management purposes. A sample record system for the farm inventory appears in Figure 4–5b.

Valuing the Farm Inventory

There are several methods which can be used to value the inventory once the physical count has been completed. The most common methods are market cost, net market price, farm production cost, cost minus depreciation, and cost minus depletion. Each of these will be examined separately.

1. Market Cost Method. This method of valuing the inventory is particularly suited for items which will be used within one production period. Examples include feed, seed, fertilizer, and agricultural chemicals. Some feeder livestock which will be kept for a short period of time can also be valued by this method. The method involves placing a value on the item equal to its price in the market place at the time when it was purchased. Since the item is not anticipated to be in the farm inventory for more than one production period, it is not likely that substantial increases or decreases in value will occur. Therefore, the market price is probably the best estimate of true value. The cost of site preparation or installation required for items which must be transported to the farm may be added to the purchase price to establish the market cost value of each item.

LAND INVENTORY

Prices for land can be shown by land quality of individual tracts or for the total farm. Values may be arrived at from comparative sales, capitalization or based upon general values published by the Agricultural Experiment Station or Cooperative Extensive Service. Land values need not be retabulated annually. Capital gains should not be added to the annual income statement.

OWNED LAND (excluding buildings)

ACRES	DESCRIPTION	USE	VALUE PER ACRE	TOTAL VALUE
			$	$
	TOTALS (show average value per acre)		$	$
Capital gain (loss over value shown in previous year's inventory			$	$

RENTED LAND (including buildings rented)

	TOTALS (show average value per acre)		$	$

Legal descriptions:

NON-FEED DROPS AND SUPPLIES INVENTORY

QUANTITY	PRICE	19___ VALUE	QUANTITY	PRICE	19___ VALUE	QUANTITY	PRICE	19___ VALUE
	$	$		$	$		$	$

FEED CROP INVENTORY

Supplies include fuel, fetilizer, twine, etc.

QUANTITY	PRICE	19___ VALUE	QUANTITY	PRICE	19___ VALUE	QUANTITY	PRICE	19___ VALUE
	$	$		$	$		$	$

FIGURE 4–5b. Sample Inventory Record Account. (Source: James, S.C., and Larry Trede, Midwest Farm Account Book, *Agricultural Experimental Station, Iowa State University, Ames, Iowa, 1967.)*

2. Net Market Price.   The net market price valuing of inventory is particularly suited to those items which will be taken from the farm for sale or disposal. The net market price is calculated as the market price received less any transportation, handling, or sales expenses which are

POULTRY INVENTORY

DESCRIPTION	NO.		PRICE	19____ VALUE	NO.		PRICE	19____ VALUE
			$	$			$	$

SHEEP INVENTORY

Entries are for the end of each year. See tax regulations for valuing livestock and be consistent from year to year. Live-stock on depreciation will be recorded in this section and also be shown on the depreciation schedule.

Value at their undepreciated balance.

DESCRIPTION	NO.	TOTAL WEIGHT	PRICE	19____ VALUE	NO.	TOTAL WEIGHT	PRICE	19____ VALUE
			$	$			$	$

OTHER LIVESTOCK INVENTORY

NO.	TOTAL WEIGHT	PRICE	19____ VALUE	NO.	TOTAL WEIGHT	PRICE	19____ VALUE	NO.	TOTAL WEIGHT	PRICE	19____ VALUE
		$	$			$	$			$	

incurred in order to dispose of the item. Examples of inventory items which can be valued under net market price are market livestock and farm produced crops. The net market price method establishes the value of an item at its net sales price to the farm.

3. Cost or Market, Whichever is Lower. Under this method of valuing inventory, the actual cost of producing or purchasing the item is compared to its current market value and the lower of the two values is taken as the value to be used in inventory. The current cost of replacing an item in inventory is its current market value for comparable quality and grade in the quantities that the farm manager usually purchases. Farm tools, replacement parts and some supplies are items commonly valued by this method. This method is closely allied to the conservative principles used by accountants in general. It has a major flaw in that it probably values items too conservatively in times of inflation and not conservatively enough when items are undergoing depreciation or when the general price level in the economy has fallen.

4. Farm Production Cost Method. The farm production cost method of valuing assets is closely related to the unit livestock price method described by the Internal Revenue Service. Under this method, primarily livestock are given a value estimated by their production cost. It can be very difficult at times to place a value on a particular animal being

BEEF CATTLE INVENTORY - BREEDING AND FEEDING

Entries are for the end of each year. See tax regulations for valuing livestock and be consistent from year to year. Livestock on depreciation will not be recorded in this section but will be shown on the depreciation schedule.

Values for livestock on depreciation should be the undepreciated balances.

NO.	TOTAL WEIGHT	PRICE	19___ VALUE	NO.	TOTAL WEIGHT	PRICE	19___ VALUE	NO.	TOTAL WEIGHT	PRICE	19___ VALUE
						$	$			$	$

DAIRY INVENTORY

DESCRIPTION	NO.	TOTAL WEIGHT	PRICE	19___ VALUE	NO.	TOTAL WEIGHT	PRICE	19___ VALUE
			$	$			$	$
BREEDING STOCK TOTAL			xxx	$			xxx	$
FEEDER STOCK TOTAL			xxx	$			xxx	$
TOTAL FARM			xxx	$			xxx	$

raised for market sale. For example, feeder pigs may be purchased at forty pounds and grown out to approximately half of anticipated market weight. If the farmer takes inventory at this point and attempts to value these animals it may be difficult to establish a market price for animals which are not ready for market. This method has been established in order to facilitate valuing items which are partway through the production process. The rationale is to estimate value as the purchase price plus any additional costs that have been put into the animal since its purchase. Livestock must be grouped or classified according to kind and age and a standard unit price used within each class or group. Breeding stock is also particularly suited to this method of valuation.

Standing crops can also be valued by the farm production cost method. Since crops which are growing in the field have a large amount of risk associated with them, a conservative estimate of their value should be used. After planting and before harvest the costs necessary to establish the crop in the field and maintain it, (e.g., cultivation, etc.) are used to value these assets. Standing crops which are near harvest can be valued at their estimated yield multiplied by an expected market price.

However, adjustment must be made for the uncertainty of harvest as well as harvesting, marketing and transportation costs.

5. Cost Minus Depreciation Method. This method is primarily used to evaluate investment properties that provide a flow of services to the business for a period greater than one production season. Items which undergo a decrease in value over this period will normally be on the farmer's depreciation schedule. Such items include machinery, large equipment, wells, tiling, fencing, etc. A book value can be established each year by subtracting the current year's depreciation expense from the undepreciated balance. For example, a combine may last ten to fifteen years. Its book value will diminish over time as it undergoes wear and obsolescence. Its value for inventory purposes can be established at its original cost minus this accumulated depreciation. The value of the asset at the beginning of the accounting period less the depreciation expense occurring during the current year establishes the book value.

6. Cost Minus Depletion. This method of valuing inventory is a special method used to account for the value of items such as timber stands, mineral deposits, etc. The value of the asset will be diminished as harvest or displacement of the resource takes place. The original value of the stock less the accumulated value of depletion is used to value such resources for inventory purposes.

Depreciation Techniques

Some items in the farm inventory will be used by the farm manager over several production seasons. Many of these items depreciate or decline in value over time due to wear and tear and obsolescence. From the points of view of both inventory management, where the farmer is trying to value each item in inventory, and tax management, where expenses offset income to determine net taxable income, depreciation becomes important.

Machinery, buildings, equipment and some livestock that will be serving the farm production processes for more than one year usually depreciate. The cost of the item must be spread out over its useful life so that only a portion of the cost can be deducted as expense in any one year. Several depreciation techniques have been developed by the Internal Revenue Service for use by farmers. Each method has its own particular advantages and disadvantages. It is important to realize that the amount of depreciation expense accounted to an item during an accounting period may differ from the business valuation of an asset. This problem arises due to the different motives and logic of sound business practice and tax regulations.

Whichever method you use, it is important to keep good records on depreciable property because the Internal Revenue Service may require you to demonstrate that you have complied with tax laws. They recommend that a simple system be used that avoids complicated adjustments and change. As a general rule, three conditions must be met for property to be depreciable.

1. It must be used in the farm business. A car or pickup truck which is used strictly for family business cannot be depreciated as it is not a part of the farm production process.
2. The item or asset must have a definite and determined useful life greater than one year. The IRS has some restrictions on useful life calculations which will be discussed.
3. The item must undergo actual loss in value over time. That is, the item must wear out or become obsolete. This eliminates land from the items which may be depreciated because the flow of value from land should, with proper care, continue indefinitely.

Generally the new cost of the item is used to determine its original value. However, if there is a trade-in or if the property is a gift or an inheritance, the cost or value may not be easily determined. In this case, the IRS substitutes an approximation of value called the **basis** in place of cost. When a trade-in occurs, the undepreciated value of the asset traded in plus the additional cash paid determines the basis for the new item. This amount will be equal to cost only if the trade-in value received is equal to the undepreciated or book value of the trade-in.

Depreciation for an item begins when it is first placed into service on the farm or production process, not necessarily on the purchase date. However, once an item has been purchased, transported to the farm, and placed in a state of readiness or availability for its particular use, that date can be considered the acquisition date for depreciation purposes.

In the case of livestock, immature animals do not undergo depreciation. That is, you must wait until an animal reaches an age where it can actually be used to produce income for the farm. Feeder animals are not as a rule depreciable assets. Likewise, an orchard or vineyard or any income producing activity which has not currently reached a level of maturity where it can produce income is not depreciable. When the orchard or vineyard reaches an income producing stage, the plants can then undergo depreciation for IRS purposes.

For depreciable property placed in service after 1980, you must calculate depreciation expense under the new Accelerated Cost Recovery System (ACRS) implemented by the IRS in 1981. Items placed in service prior to 1981 require different treatment. Both the new ACRS and the traditional methods of calculating depreciation will be covered, beginning with the new treatment.

In general, under the ACRS, all depreciable property must be assigned a recovery period. Table 4.2 describes the recovery periods and the types of depreciable assets which qualify for each. Note that most farm machinery and equipment are "5-year property." Buildings and certain farm structures and improvements are normally "15-year property." Each recovery period has a set of associated percentages which also appear in Table 4–2. These percentages will change after 1984. You should consult the Farmers Tax Guide after 1984 for appropriate rates.

TABLE 4–2. RECOVERY PERIODS AND RATES[1] OF ANNUAL DEPRECIATION EXPENSE UNDER THE ACCELERATED COST RECOVERY SYSTEM

1. **3-year property.** This class includes personal property with a short useful life, such as automobiles and light-duty trucks. Also included are breeding hogs, race horses more than 2 years old when you place them in service, and any other horses that are more than 12 years old when you place them in service.

2. **5-year property.** This class includes personal property that is not 3-year property. It includes most equipment, single purpose livestock and horticultural structures, and livestock that are not 3-year property.

3. **10-year property.** This class includes certain real property such as manufactured homes, (including mobile homes).

4. **15-year real property.** This class includes all real property, such as farm buildings, and most land improvements other than any designated as 5-year or 10-year property.

3-year property	
1st year	25%
2nd year	38%
3rd year	37%
5-year property	
1st year	15%
2nd year	22%
3rd through 5th year	21%
10-year property	
1st year	8%
2nd year	14%
3rd year	12%
4th through 6th year	10%
7th through 10th year	9%

[1]These rates will change for assets placed in service after 1984.
Source: "Farmers Tax Guide," Publication 225, Department of the Treasury, Internal Revenue Service, 1981.

The recovery periods are standardized and do not necessarily reflect the useful life of the assets which can be classified in each. As a general rule, the recovery periods for eligible assets are shorter than their actual useful life. This results in an accelerated write-off of cost. An accelerated method of depreciation is any method which accounts for the cost of an asset more rapidly than the asset loses value. Accelerated cost recovery has great advantages to farmers with high taxable incomes, as depreciation expense offsets taxable income. Alternative methods are available for farmers with low incomes who do not need this fast write-off. These methods will be discussed below.

To calculate the depreciation expense allowed in each year, you simply multiply the purchase price (or "unadjusted" basis) by the percentage indicated. Table 4–3 shows an example involving the calculation of depreciation expense for a tractor purchased in 1981 at a cost of $25,000.

Although the ACRS is a greatly simplified means of computing depre-

TABLE 4-3.   ACRS DEPRECIATION FOR A TRACTOR COSTING $25,000.00

Year	Purchase Price	X	Applicable Percent	=	Depreciation Expense	Book Value End of Yr.
1	$25,000	X	.15	=	$3,750	$21,250
2	25,000	X	.22	=	$5,500	$15,750
3	25,000	X	.21	=	$5,250	$10,500
4	25,000	X	.21	=	$5,250	$ 5,250
5	25,000	X	.21	=	$5,250	0

ciation expense, some special rules apply. First, even if the tractor was purchased and placed into service for only part of the first taxable year, the entire first year depreciation expense can be taken. This rule applies to part-year ownership of any length in the first year. This rule does not apply to "15-year" property which must be prorated by the number of months in use during the first year. Secondly, if the tractor was sold during the five-year period, no depreciation expense would be allowed for the last part-year of ownership. An exception to this rule is again made for "15-year" property such as farm buildings, where an amount of part-year depreciation is allowable in the last year of ownership. Consult the Farmers Tax Guide for additional information.

An alternative method to the regular ACRS system is to use the straightline method of depreciation (to be discussed in the next section) and make deductions over a longer period of time. The Farmers Tax Guide lists the optional recovery periods available under this method.

When using the ACRS to calculate depreciation, some additional special rules apply. First, you must use the same recovery period for all property in the same class placed in service during the same year except for "15-year" property. That is, all "5-year" property placed in service during a taxable year must be treated the same in terms of depreciation calculation. You may, however, elect different methods for similar machinery and equipment not placed in service during the same year. Secondly, components of farm buildings such as farrowing crates must be treated in the same way as the building itself. If an alternate method is used for the building, it must also be used for any added components, etc.

Property placed in service prior to 1981 cannot qualify for the ACRS. You also may not use the ACRS for personal property placed in service after 1980 if any of the following three conditions applies:

1. You or a party related to you owned the property in 1980.
2. You leased the property to anyone who owned or used it in 1980.
3. You acquire the property from its 1980 owner, but the person who operates the property does not change.

In such a case, the traditional methods of depreciation must be used. A discussion of the major traditional methods for depreciating property will now be undertaken.

In determining depreciation expense in any one given year, two important calculations are necessary. The first calculation is determining useful life. This calculation is unnecessary for assets which qualify for ACRS treatment where recovery periods substitute for useful life estimates. In general, the useful life of an asset is your best estimate of how long an item will provide a flow of services to the farm business. It is over this time that the cost or basis of an asset must be prorated. The IRS lists several factors which affect the useful life of an asset including how often it is used in the farm business, whether it was new or used when it was acquired, the topography and climate in which it will be used, and how old it was when it was purchased. In general, consistency is required by the IRS so that similar property, while it may vary in its use from one person to another, should have a similar useful life. A great deal of latitude is given in determining useful life, but excessive overestimates or underestimates should be avoided.

The second important calculation in determining depreciable value is the salvage value of an asset. Although the new ACRS eliminates the need to estimate salvage value, in the traditional treatment, salvage value is simply your best estimate of the value of the item when it is no longer useful in the farm production process. Salvage value is a function of how long any particular operator uses the property. Also involved is whether the operator usually disposes of the property while it is still useful to others or whether it is operated until it is no longer useful. In general, the IRS has established a guideline whereby ten percent of the new cost or basis of the property may be deducted from your actual estimate of salvage value. In effect, more of the total value of the machine or depreciable asset can be depreciated as an expense over time. If this substraction results in a value less than zero, it must be set equal to zero so that as a maximum, only the full value or cost of the item can be depreciated. If the so called ten percent rule is taken advantage of, it is required that the asset have a useful life of at least three years.

Several methods of depreciation can be used by the farm operator to value farm assets which are not eligible for ACRS treatment. Each method differs in the speed with which it depreciates the purchase price or basis of an asset. The IRS only requires a test of reasonableness as to the method selected. Some of the methods depreciate an asset very rapidly in the first years of its useful life and then level off to smaller and smaller amounts as the asset reaches the end of its useful life. Other methods depreciate an asset at an equal rate over time. In general, none of the following methods will allow as fast a write off of expense as the ACRS.

1. The Straight-line Method. This method is probably the easiest method of depreciation to calculate. If no complications exist, a single calculation can provide the farmer with the yearly depreciation for the entire life of the asset. Under this method, the amount of depreciation expense taken each year of the asset's life does not change. The formula for calculating depreciation expense under the straight line method of depreciation is as follows:

$$\text{Current depreciation expense} = \frac{\text{Cost or basis} - \text{salvage value}}{\text{useful years of life}}.$$

You should notice that the rate of depreciation or the amount of depreciation which can be taken each year on an asset is equal to one divided by the useful years of life. If an asset has a five-year expected useful life, one-fifth or twenty percent of its value could be deducted each year as a measure of its decline in value.

Once the depreciation expense has been calculated, it is subtracted from the cost or basis to establish the book value of the asset going into its second year of life. In the second year, the depreciation expense is likewise calculated and subtracted from the undepreciated balance to establish the book value going into year three. This process continues until the salvage value has been reached. If the effective date of purchase and implementation for depreciation purposes is the first of the year, then each year's value of depreciation expense under the straight line method will be equal and the undepreciated balance at the end of the useful life will equal the salvage value.

The straight line method of depreciation has a disadvantage in that for farmers having a high level of taxable income, a relatively small amount of depreciation expense is generated using this method during the first years of useful life. However, for farmers who are just beginning or for farmers who anticipate a low level of income during the next few years, gradually rising over time, this methods preserves depreciation expense for those later years when it can be used more effectively in tax reduction. Such farmers may elect to use the straightline method even for assets which qualify for ACRS treatment. However, assets which qualify for ACRS treatment and are depreciated under the alternative straightline technique must use useful life estimates provided by the IRS.

2. The Declining Balance Method.   The declining balance method of depreciation is more complicated than the straight line method in that a different value of depreciation expense must be calculated for each year of useful life. This method causes much of the depreciation expense to occur early during the life of the asset and then diminish to smaller amounts in later years. Items such as machinery and equipment are frequently depreciated using the declining balance method since the real decline in machinery value frequently matches the pattern of allowable expense under the declining balance method. The formula for calculating depreciation by this method is as follows:

Current depreciation expense = undepreciated balance × depreciation rate.

This method requires that you first establish a rate of depreciation. As a maximum, up to two times the straight line rate can be used. That is, if the straight line rate is $1 \div 5$, (i.e., a useful life of five years) up to twice this amount or forty percent could be used as the depreciation rate under certain conditions.

To calculate the depreciation expense in each year, this depreciation rate is multiplied by the undepreciated balance (cost or basis in the first year). The first year's depreciation expense is subtracted from the cost or basis to establish the undepreciated balance going into year two. This beginning balance in year two is then again multiplied by the depreciation rate, in the example 40 percent, to calculate the depreciation allowable for the second year. This process is continued throughout the entire useful life of the asset or until salvage value has been reached.

However, one word of caution should be noted. This method does not guarantee that salvage value will automatically be reached at the end of useful life. Indeed, if there is no salvage value at all, this method will not fully account for the total cost of the item. Frequently farmers change to the straight line method after two to four years under the declining balance method to capture all of the depreciation expense which is allowable. If, however, there is a salvage value, it is possible that in the last year of useful life, the calculated depreciation may, if fully taken, push the undepreciated balance below salvage value. Caution should be exercised because, if this occurs, only that amount which brings the undepreciated value down to salvage value may be deducted.

If twice the straight line is used as the depreciation rate, this method is referred to as the double-declining balance method. Any factor equal to the straight line rate and up to but not greater than twice the straight line rate can be used, but restrictions apply. The advantage to this method is that it results in the greatest possible depreciation rate in the early years of asset ownership. To qualify for the double declining balance method of depreciation, the IRS requires that the asset be purchased new and have a useful life of at least three years. You should consult the Farmer's Tax Guide, published annually by the Internal Revenue Service, to make sure that you are properly conforming to current tax law regarding this method.

3. The Sum of the Year's Digits Method. This method of determining depreciation expense is also an accelerated method of depreciation. That is, it allows more of the value of the asset to be depreciated earlier in its life than under the straight line method of depreciation. This method is also rather complicated in that the depreciation expense changes each year and must be calculated for each year. The formula for calculating the depreciation expense under this method is as follows:

Current depreciation expense = (cost or basis – salvage) $\times$ depreciation rate.

The depreciation rate is calculated as follows: the number of years of useful life of an asset are added together so that if an asset has a useful life of five years, $1 + 2 + 3 + 4 + 5 = 15$. This sum is divided into the number of years of useful life remaining in the asset to establish the depreciation rate or that fraction of cost that can be deducted in the current year. As an example, if an asset has a useful life of five years, 5/15 of its value may be deducted in the first year, 4/15 in the second year, 3/15 in the third year, 2/15 in the fourth year, and 1/15 in the last year of useful life. These fractions are multiplied by cost or basis minus salvage to determine the depreciation expense for each year. Since the sum of these factors is equal to one, this method results in depreciating the entire amount of eligible expense and the attainment of salvage value in the last year is guaranteed. Unlike the declining balance method, where the manager must be careful not to depreciate the item below salvage value, no adjustment is necessary with the sum of the year's digits method. The graph in Figure 4–6 shows the relative rates of depreciation under each method including the ACRS when they are applied to an asset of equal value.

Some additional restrictions on depreciation are that once a method has been established for a particular asset, consent of the IRS is required before the method can be changed. This restriction applies in all cases except when the farmer is switching from the declining balance method to the straight line method in order to capture all of the expense which is eligible. To change depreciation methods the appropriate petition must be filed and permission granted. Secondly, it is important to keep

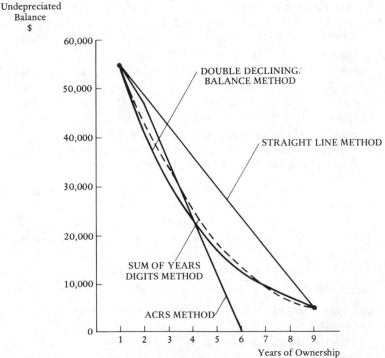

FIGURE 4–6. *Relative Rates of Depreciation Under the Straight Line,*
Sum of Years Digits, Declining Balance, and ACRS
Methods.

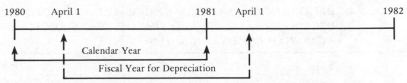

FIGURE 4–7. *The Fiscal Year Adjustment for Depreciating an Asset Purchased on April 1, 1980 under the Straight Line and Sum of Years Digits Methods.*

careful records of depreciation, as mentioned, because depreciation can only be taken in the year in which it is eligible. If you neglect to take eligible depreciation, it cannot be added to the current year or future year's eligible expenses.

Adjusting Depreciation for Part Year Ownership

Unlike the ACRS, where a full years depreciation can be taken for assets purchased and placed into service for only part of a year, depreciation expense under the traditional methods must be prorated by the amount of the first year the asset is actually owned or ready for use. This also applies to part year ownership of "15-year" property. To obtain the first year expense under part-year ownership, calculate the regular first year depreciation expense allowable under the method of choice. The amount is then multiplied by the fraction of the year that the asset has been owned. If the purchase date was April 1, the asset will only have been owned for three-fourths of the year. Therefore, only three-fourths of the regular depreciation which is calculated by the various formulas can be taken during the first year. The other one-fourth which is not allowable in this first year is picked up in the first fourth of year two. In year two, this portion is added to three-fourths of the depreciation which would have been allowed in year two to calculate the entire second year's eligible expense. This process continues throughout the rest of the asset's useful life. The depreciation year is shifted forward off the calendar or taxable year by the fraction of the first year the asset is owned. Figure 4–7 may help you in grasping this concept. An exception is the declining balance method where the part year depreciation is subtracted from cost or basis to establish the undepreciated balance for year two. The depreciation rate is then applied to this balance to calculate depreciation in the second year. If an asset is purchased on April 1, only three-fourths of the regular depreciation can be written off in the first taxable year. Part year adjustments for "15-year" property are provided by the IRS. A comprehensive example appears in Table 4–4.

THE NET WORTH STATEMENT

Once the inventory has been valued, it is important to monitor the financial progress of the business on an ongoing basis. The changing values of the inventory and changing values of the productive resources

TABLE 4–4. DEPRECIATION EXPENSE UNDER THE STRAIGHT LINE, DOUBLE DECLINING BALANCE AND SUM OF YEARS' DIGITS METHODS AND ACRS WITH PART-YEAR ADJUSTMENTS

Purchase: $55,000 combine
Purchase Date: 1/1/81
Salvage Value: $5,000
Useful Life: 8 years

Year	Straight Line	Double Declining Balance	Sum of Years' Digits	"5-Year" Property ACRS
1981	6,250	13,750	11,111	8,250
1982	6,250	10,313	9,722	12,100
1983	6,250	7,734	8,333	11,550
1984	6,250	5,801	6,944	11,550
1985	6,250	4,351	5,556	11,550
1986	6,250	3,262	4,167	0
1987	6,250	2,447	2,778	0
1988	6,250	1,836	1,389	0
TOTAL	50,000	49,494	50,000	55,000
Unrecovered Cost	0	506	0	0
Assuming Purchase Date of 4/1/81:				
1981	4,688	10,313	8,333	8,250
1982	6,250	11,172	10,069	12,100

on the farm can provide important management information. The value of the inventory, other assets, and ownership claims upon them are recorded in the net worth statement. The **net worth statement** is a financial statement sometimes referred to as a balance sheet which lists all of the assets on the farm and the claims against them. An asset is a productive or income-earning resource held for use or sale in the farm business.

The net worth statement is normally constructed at the end of the accounting period—the length of time over which the productive activities engaged in on the farm undergo one complete cycle. For most farms, the accounting period is one year. Often the accounting period corresponds to the calendar year so that it begins on January 1 and ends December 31. However, this can be changed to begin on any month of the year if it is more convenient to do so. Frequently, accounting periods are adjusted to begin coinciding with leasing arrangements, contractual obligations, or major sales of crops or livestock. When the accounting period does not begin with the calendar year, it is referred to as a **fiscal year.**

The net worth statement, constructed at the end of the accounting period, gives a picture of the financial position of the business at that point in time. Once a comprehensive inventory has been taken, the net worth statement is easily constructed. It is only necessary at the end of each accounting period to take into account those items which have changed over the production season and to revise this material by constructing an updated inventory and net worth statement.

The net worth statement is a listing of all assets, all liabilities, and owner's equity or net worth. A fundamental accounting equation balances the net worth statement. Total assets are always equal to the sum of total liabilities and net worth. Total assets once valued, measure the total value of all productive resources and output on the farm; liabilities and net worth measure ownership claims against those assets. Therefore, the total value of assets will always be equal to the claims against them, whether they originate from bankers and others outside the business (liabilities) or whether they involve owner's equity (net worth).

Assets are frequently divided into three major categories based on the time period over which they will be used up or disposed of.

These are:

1. Short-term Assets. Short-term assets are those resources or products on the farm which are expected to be used up or sold in the next accounting or production period. Such items include feed, seed, fertilizer, any livestock which will be market-ready in this year, and stored grain. Also, in this category is any cash on hand, prepaid expenses, or accounts receivable which are expected to be paid to the business in the current year. These assets are sometimes referred to as current assets or near cash since they can usually be converted into cash rapidly, without much loss in value, in order to pay short-term debt.

2. Intermediate Assets. Intermediate assets are those assets used in the production of crops or livestock for several production seasons. Intermediate assets largely include machinery, equipment items, tools and breeding livestock. Some temporary buildings are also considered intermediate assets. Most intermediate assets are depreciable items and generally have a life of between two to ten years.

3. Long-term Assets. Long term assets are those assets which have a productive life expectancy greater than ten years. Such assets include permanent buildings and improvements such as tiling, fencing, ponds, and land.

Table 4–5 shows a typical net worth statement for a farm business over a two-year period of time. Note that a subtotal for each of the classifications of assets and liabilities is calculated along with the totals. This will facilitate important financial analysis using the items of data in the net worth statement. Corresponding to the assets are claims on ownership called liabilities. Liabilities are also divided into the same three categories as assets.

1. Short-term Liabilities. Short-term liabilities are those claims on the business which will become due during the next production period. Such short-term debt as charge accounts, debts at the local feed store

TABLE 4–5. A TYPICAL NET WORTH STATEMENT FOR A FARM PRODUCING LIVESTOCK AND CROPS FOR THE YEARS 1981 AND 1982

Net Worth Statement

Current Assets	1981	1982
Cash on hand	$ 2,500	$ 1,200
Accounts receivable	1,500	500
Feed crops	14,000	22,000
Nonfeed crops	27,000	32,000
Seeds and supplies	6,000	7,500
Feeder livestock		
Swine	10,000	14,000
Beef cattle	$ 23,000	$ 20,000
Total Current Assets	$ 84,000	$ 97,200
Intermediate Assets		
Powered machinery	$ 84,500	$ 69,500
Crop machinery	16,000	14,000
Livestock equipment	7,000	6,000
Breeding stock		
Swine	4,500	4,000
Beef Cattle	12,000	14,000
Total Intermediate Assets	$124,000	$107,500
Long-Term Assets		
Land	$425,000	$425,000
Buildings	47,000	47,000
Improvements	26,000	22,000
Total Long-term Assets	$498,000	$494,000
Total Assets	$706,000	$698,700

Current Liabilities	1981	1982
Accounts Payable		
Coop account	$ 3,500	$ 1,500
Diamond Hardware	550	0
PCA operating note	32,000	35,000
Benton Bank	12,000	12,000
Interest payable	2,600	2,500
Zees Machinery, Inc	5,000	5,000
Taylor Finance	$ 2,500	$ 2,500
Total Current Liabilities	$ 58,150	$ 58,500
Intermediate Liabilities		
Notes Payable		
Zees Machinery, Inc.	$ 57,500	$ 52,500
Taylor Finance	7,500	5,000
Total Intermediate Liabilities	$ 65,000	$ 57,500
Long-term Liabilities		
Mortgage (Benton Bank)	$300,000	$288,000
Total Long-Term Liabilities	$300,000	$288,000
Total Liabilities	$423,150	$404,000
Net Worth	$282,850	$294,700
Total Liabilities and Net Worth	$706,000	$698,700

or elevator, short-term notes at a bank or financial institution, and farm operating notes from production credit associations fall into this category. Also, any portion of longer-term debt which is due during the next production season is included in short-term liabilities. For instance, a mortgage payment which is part of a long-term liability but is due in the next period is considered a short-term liability. Likewise, during its last year of life, a mortgage is considered a short-term liability.

2. Intermediate Liabilities. Intermediate liabilities are those claims against the business which will be paid over a period from two to ten years. These liabilities include notes and other obligations to purchase machinery, equipment, breeding livestock, etc., and any debt which has been undertaken in order to purchase intermediate assets, provided, of course that it will be amortized over a period greater than one year.

3. Long-term Liabilities. Long-term liabilities are those claims upon the assets which will be paid over a period greater than ten years. Normally this category includes mortgages and any long-term debt associated with permanent improvements on the farm.

Frequently it is difficult to determine the exact classification of a liability or an asset. Sometimes assets seem to fall between current and intermediate or between intermediate and long-term. When a precise distinction between the classes of assets cannot be drawn, convention can be adopted as long as consistent application of the principle is used throughout time.

Analyzing the Net Worth Statement

As a general financial principle, each category of debt or liability should be originally matched to the type of asset upon which it is undertaken. It is best to finance short-term assets with short-term liabilities so that the debt associated with an asset does not outlive the useful life of the asset. As an example, it would be unwise to pay for a period of several years for an item which will be completely used up during one production season. Likewise, it is best to match long-term debt to those assets which will provide a long-term flow of services to the farm operation. Not many farmers could finance land purchases over a short-run period of time. From a practical financial point of view, the length of the debt should correspond to the length of the useful life of the asset to which it is matched.

For most farmers the sum of total liabilities will not equal the sum of total assets. Notice in Table 4–5 for 1981 that the sum of total liabilities is $423,150 and the sum of total assets is $706,000. Therefore, the value of all productive assets exceeds the claims upon them by outsiders. The residual or remaining amount is that value of total assets which are owned by the farm operator. This amount is referred to as **net worth** or **equity** and in this example is equal to $282,850 in 1981. The change in equity over time can be monitored and several financial ratios or means of analysis applied to evaluate the financial progress of the business. Some of these include:

1. Measuring Liquidity. **Liquidity** is the ability of the farm manager to meet short term debt as it becomes due. One of the principal criteria by which liquidity can be measured is the ratio of current or short-term assets to short-term liabilities. Since short-term assets can generally be quickly converted to cash as a means to pay short-term debt, a ratio of short-term assets to short-term liabilities generates a figure which can be used to interpret the liquidity of the farm business. The interpretation of this ratio, frequently referred to as the **current ratio**, is the number of dollars of current assets which are available per dollar of current liability. You will notice in Table 4–6 that a figure in 1981 of 1.44 indicates that $1.44 of short term assets are available for each dollar of short term debt. A figure of 2 for the current ratio is frequently considered safe by most lending institutions. The current ratio should never be allowed to fall below 1. Being able to meet short term debt as it becomes due is very important for the farmer in establishing a good credit reputation and assures the willingness of input suppliers to do business with the operator in the long run.

2. Measuring Solvency. The **solvency** of a business refers to its ability to remain viable over an extended period of time. Not only must a farmer be able to meet short term debt as it becomes due but because many obligations of the business extend beyond the current period, such as notes for machinery, and equipment and mortgages, many lending institutions are interested in a prediction of the farm's health several years down the road. A measure of solvency frequently used is net worth divided by total assets. The ratio of net worth to total assets is interpreted as the number of cents of equity per dollar of assets managed by the farm operator. You will notice from Table 4–6 in 1981 that the solvency ratio of 0.40 indicates that the farmer's equity is 40 cents per dollar of assets managed. As equity in the assets trans-

TABLE 4–6. MEASURING FARM LIQUIDITY, SOLVENCY AND LEVERAGE UTILIZING THE NET WORTH STATEMENT

	1981	*1982*
Liquidity Measure		
short-term assets/short term liabilities	$\dfrac{\$84,000}{\$58,150} = 1.44$	$\dfrac{\$97,200}{\$58,500} = 1.66$
Solvency Measure		
net worth/total assets	$\dfrac{\$282,850}{\$706,000} = 0.40$	$\dfrac{\$294,700}{\$698,700} = 0.42$
Leverage Measure		
total liabilities/net worth	$\dfrac{\$423,150}{\$282,850} = 1.50$	$\dfrac{\$404,000}{\$294,700} = 1.37$

fers to the farmer by the reduction of debt, greater stability and solvency generally results. While it is not usually wise for this ratio to approach one, indicating that the farmer is using no debt at all, a figure of 0.5 or greater is considered very safe. Many lenders will refuse to permit borrowing which forces this ratio below 0.3. Although reducing debt and increasing ownership are many times primary goals of the farm operator, it is frequently impossible to engage in farming without incurring some amount of debt.

3. Measuring Leverage.   Additional measures of solvency which can be calculated from the net worth statement to evaluate the extent to which a farm manager has used credit available to him, are known as measures of **leverage.** These are called leverage ratios because you can think of debt as a lever with which you can move great weights or accomplish tasks which under your own power (or with your own money) you would be unable to do. Sometimes moving a rock or stump from the field cannot be accomplished with your hands but can be accomplished by placing a lever underneath it and pushing. Likewise, in the financial world, using only your own resources may not be the most effective way to accomplish farm goals. By using credit, additional leverage can be gained to accomplish activities or expand existing enterprises.

A measure of leverage which can give an idea of the extent to which the farm manager has used available credit is total liabilities divided by net worth. Since net worth represents the equity collateral of the business, this ratio shows the total dollars of debt utilized per dollar of ownership equity (the "debt:equity" ratio). A ratio value of one to one or less is generally considered safe. However, remember the extent to which debt must be utilized by young farmers or beginning farmers is generally quite high. Any of the ratios discussed can vary from the norm by some distance and still be acceptable.

The net worth statement is an indispensible financial record, not only for these kinds of analysis, but also for obtaining credit. In Chapter 13, the net worth statement will be combined with the income statement and cash flow budget to demonstrate the package of financial and planning analysis required by many farm lending institutions in order to extend credit.

SUMMARY

This chapter has demonstrated that records are the prerequisite of effective budgeting. The proper construction of useful budgets is possible using data collected from previous production years. Budgets are simply forward records, that is, we predict what our records will eventually contain with the use of budgets. To the extent that the budgets do not predict the future, the evaluation function can be undertaken to discover where the plan deviated from the projected result. Weak points and areas needing improvement can then be examined and effectively changed.

Budgeting is the substitute for the complete knowledge of economic principles assumed in the second chapter. In Chapter 4 the first steps have been taken away from the Ideal World into the real world of every-day farm decision making. The budgeting process will aid in planning the resource allocation under conditions of imperfect knowledge. The common steps in budgeting have been examined and the purposes and uses of budgets have been demonstrated.

Once the goals of the farm manager have been decided upon, it is necessary to assess what resources are available to accomplish those goals. In this chapter the records necessary to evaluate performance, account for income and expenses, and construct the inventory have been introduced.

The first step in constructing the inventory is the physical count, whereby the farm manager lists and describes all income–producing resources. Once the physical count is complete, it is necessary to value inventory items.

Different resources require different valuation methods. Several of these methods have been discussed. Depreciation techniques are used to value those farm assets which are used in the production process over a period of years. Assets which undergo decline in value to the production process through obsolescence or wear have been considered. Further discussion of the tax management involved with depreciation appears in Chapter 16.

The net worth statement can be constructed once the inventory is complete. The net worth statement is a valuable financial snapshot of the business at a specific point in time. It can yield various measures of liquidity, solvency and leverage and also demonstrate to the farm manager whether progress is being made toward ownership and control of the farm's productive resources. Comparison of net worth statements over time is a valuable management tool.

Now that the manager has discovered what resources are available to use in farm production activities, the next step is to plan the allocation of those resources through the various budgeting techniques which are available.

SAMPLE PROBLEMS

1. Assume you purchase a combine for $75,000 on April 1. Determine the yearly depreciation (recovery) for the life of the machine using the ACRS technique.

2. Given the abbreviated Net Worth Statement that follows, answer the questions.

Short term assets	$ 30,000	Short term liabilities	$ 14,000
Intermediate assets	$100,000	Intermediate liabilities	$ 58,000
Long-term assets	$500,000	Long-term liabilities	$280,000

     a. Net worth is $ _____

     b. Calculate a measure of farm liquidity and place the number in the blank provided.

        Liquidity _____

     c. Calculate a measure of farm solvency and leverage and place the numbers in the appropriate blanks.

        Solvency _____   Leverage _____

     d. Is the farmer 'over-leveraged'?

3. In problem 1 above, calculate the annual depreciation expense under the straight line, double declining balance and sum of years digits methods assuming a 10 year useful life and a salvage value of $8000.

     a. Compare these to the ACRS depreciation calculated in problem 1.

     b. Which method was simplest to calculate?

     c. Which method gives the fastest write-off in the first three years?

SUGGESTED READINGS

Edwards, William and Alan M. Charlson. *Your Financial Statement.* FM-1791, Cooperative Extension Service, Iowa State University. Ames, Iowa, 1980.

Farmer's Tax Guide, 1981. Washington, D.C: Internal Revenue Service, Department of Treasury, 1981.

Harsh, Stephen B., Larry J. Connor and Gerald D. Schwab. *Managing the Farm Business*, Chapter 5. Englewood Cliffs, N.J: Prentice–Hall, Inc., 1981.

Herbst, J. H. *Farm Management Principles, Budgets, Plans*, fourth revised edition, Chapter 11. Champaign, Il: Stipes Publishing Company, 1980.

James, S. C. and E. Stoneberg. *Farm Accounting and Business Analysis*, Chapters 1–5. Ames, Iowa: Iowa State University Press, 1974.

James, S. C. and Larry Trede. *Midwest Farm Account Book*. Department of Economics, Agricultural and Home Economics Experiment Station, Iowa State University. Ames, Iowa. 1967.

Osburn, D. D. and K. C. Schneeberger. *Modern Agriculture Management*, Chapters 4–6, 10. Reston, Virginia: Reston Publishing Company, Inc., 1978.

5

Budgets and Tools to Plan the Allocation of Resources

For everything you must have a plan.

Napoleon

Concepts

In this chapter you will come to understand:

1. The use and limitations of enterprise budgets in estimating factor/product relationships.
2. The use and limitations of whole farm budgets and linear programming in planning the entire productive activity: a product/product relationship.
3. Linear programming as a method to solve for the least cost mix of inputs necessary to produce a given level of output: a factor/factor relationship.
4. The technical feasibility and profitability criteria used in the whole farm budgeting process.
5. Efficiency measurements as ways to evaluate the performance of the farm over time.
6. Partial budgeting as a method to fine tune the whole farm plan and improve efficiency and profitability: factor/factor and product/product relationships.
7. Breakeven analysis as a special form of partial budgeting.

Tools

You will also gain the following skills:

1. How to estimate and construct enterprise and rotation budgets.
2. How to construct a whole farm plan from enterprise budgets, block budgets, and the grid of comparisons.

3. How to solve a graphical linear programming problem by approximating a production possibilities curve and constructing an iso-revenue line.
4. How to calculate and interpret efficiency measures for the farm.
5. How to construct a partial budget to make decisions regarding alternative small changes in the whole farm plan.
6. How to calculate breakeven formulas for crops, livestock, machinery, and buildings.

WHAT CAN BE ACCOMPLISHED WITH AVAILABLE RESOURCES?

After the farm inventory and valuing process, the farm operator must decide how best to use what is available. Skillfully allocating resources to productive activity under conditions of incomplete knowledge requires the budgeting process. This chapter will first present enterprise budgets as the building blocks for other types of budgeting. Then it will show how whole farm plans and linear programming can help the manager identify the most profitable-feasible plan. Finally, it will show how efficiency measures help identify weak points and partial budgets help correct them.

ENTERPRISE BUDGETS

The enterprise budget represents an estimate of the combination of inputs that can achieve the optimal level of output per unit of enterprise. As such, the enterprise budget is the real world approximation of the factor/product analysis in economic principles.

Uses of the enterprise budget include:

1. Comparing Product Specific Alternatives. Enterprise budgets can be used to compare various levels of input use and various combinations of output per unit of resource. They can be constructed for a particular crop or livestock enterprise or for various combinations of crops ("rotation" budgets).

2. Building Complete Budgets. Enterprise budgets also serve as the basic building blocks for complete farm planning. Once the individual enterprises have been planned through the use of the enterprise budget, combinations of these budgets can be put together to obtain the complete picture of the farm production plan.

3. Building Linear Programming Models. With the advent of the microcomputer and various linear programming packages available through extension services and private organizations, the farm manager can, in a very short time, analyze a large number of production alternatives for both technical feasibility and profitability. Where a given level of resources must be allocated to achieve the best possible income, linear programming techniques become very valuable. Access to these techniques is becoming much easier. Within the assumptions that they require, extremely valuable information can be gained concerning the allocation of resources.

The enterprise budget really represents a single point on the production function. The stars in Figure 5–1 are individual enterprise budgets which can be constructed in an attempt to discover the profit maximizing level to use of each input. Because the production function and price ratio line are unknown, they are sketched in with dotted lines. Even if data covering ten to fifteen years were available on a particular crop or livestock activity, this information would not be sufficient to indicate exactly where a typical farmer's production function would lie under future conditions. The stars in Figure 5–1, are really guesses at where the operator believes the tangency of the price line to the production function is located for each input level.

The operator should experiment on the farm to determine whether a more profitable point on the production function can be obtained. Examples of experimentation include no-till farming as opposed to conventional tillage and the use of more or less nitrogen or herbicide inputs. Similarly, with livestock there may be more than one budget per enterprise. In a cow-calf operation, the output is stocker steers. An enterprise budget can be constructed for calving in fall or spring or for creep feeding or other options.

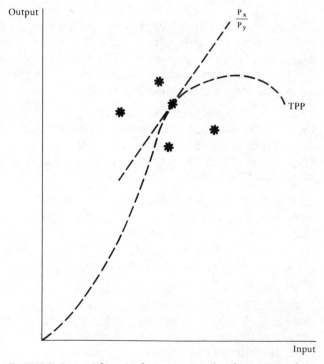

FIGURE 5–1. *The Unknown Production Function and Price Ratio Line with Projected Optimal Resource Use Points (Enterprise Budgets).*

Enterprise budgets can be set up in a number of ways. The method chosen should be adapted to give the farm manager the best possible information. Normally the enterprise budget is based on a common unit. In grain and forage crop production the unit is usually an acre. In cattle, it could be a cow-calf pair or an individual feeder steer or heifer. In hogs, it is typically a sow and her litters or a feeder pig. For milk production, it is typically 10,000 pounds of milk.

Whichever way budgets are set up, they have some common characteristics. The budget usually begins with a gross returns section. This involves an estimate of yield times an expected price per unit. Next comes a section of variable costs which should be broken down into preharvest and harvest sections for crops, grain or forage. The last section lists the fixed costs of production.

Gross returns minus variable costs (these are also called direct costs) indicate to the farmer what is called the gross margin or the returns above variable costs. Once fixed costs are subtracted, a net return to operator labor, management and land results. Some farm managers include a section for opportunity costs such as the opportunity cost of farm operator labor and land. Once these are subtracted, a return to management remains.

Table 5-1 shows enterprise budgets for several crop and livestock activities throughout the nation. For example, in the Arkansas rice budget, the expected yield per acre times the expected price yields gross receipts of $450/acre. Preharvest variable costs including items such as seed, insect control, herbicide, machinery variable costs, and interest on the operating capital amount to $213.20. Harvest costs, again including machinery variable costs, tractor costs, hauling costs, drying costs, and labor, amount to $57.19. The fixed costs of ownership are roughly assigned to each enterprise. While not included in the initial stages of farm planning, fixed costs are included for completeness. Here they are associated with machinery, tractors, and irrigation machinery, totaling $98.66 per acre.

Fixed costs can be estimated with two handy rules of thumb, depending upon whether the items are buildings or equipment. The fixed costs of machinery can be remembered by a handy device called DITIS. DITIS stands for depreciation, interest, taxes, insurance, and shelter. These are the machinery and equipment costs which are expected to be fixed in the production season. It is best to calculate these five components independently and sum them. Alternatively, they can be roughly estimated at 23 percent of new cost. A mnemonic device for the fixed costs associated with buildings is the DIRTI 5. The DIRTI 5 include depreciation, interest, repairs, taxes, and insurance. While, again, it is best to measure them separately, these costs can be estimated at 15 percent of new cost. Notice that repairs are a fixed cost of buildings. This is so because repairs are typically carried out in a systematic way unrelated to use. The barn, for instance, may need to be painted every five years whether there is hay stored in it or not. Repairs are a variable cost of machinery and equipment.

TABLE 5.1a. ENTERPRISE BUDGET FOR RICE PRODUCTION ON CLAY SOILS IN THE NORTH DELTA REGION OF ARKANSAS, 1980

	Unit	Price or Cost/unit	Quantity	Value or Cost	Your Estimate
Gross receipts from production					
Rice	cwt.	9.00	50.00	450.00	
Total				450.00	
Variable costs					
Preharvest					
Rice seed	cwt.	22.00	1.40	30.80	
Laser survey	acre.	2.50	1.00	2.50	
Potash	lb.	0.12	60.00	7.20	
N (urea source)	lb.	0.20	120.00	24.00	
Cust fert ap-air	cwt.	2.75	3.02	8.30	
Propanil	lb.	2.63	4.00	10.52	
Custom prop app	acre	3.50	1.00	3.50	
Ordram 10 G	lb.	0.45	30.00	13.50	
Custom Ordram ap	acre	2.50	1.00	2.50	
2,4,5-T	qt.	5.50	1.00	5.50	
Cust phenoxy app	acre	4.50	1.00	4.50	
Machinery	acre	3.54	1.00	3.54	
Tractors	acre	18.87	1.00	18.87	
Irrigation machinery	acre	32.30	1.00	32.30	
Labor (mach and trac)	hour	3.56	1.73	6.16	
Labor (irrigation)	hour	3.83	7.98	30.56	
Interest on op. cap.	dol.	0.14	63.95	8.95	
Subtotal, preharvest				$213.20	
Harvest					
Custom hauling	cwt.	0.15	55.00	8.25	
Custom drying	cwt.	0.63	55.00	34.65	
Machinery	acre	7.85	1.00	7.85	
Tractors	acre	3.67	1.00	3.67	
Labor (mach and trac)	hour	3.56	0.78	2.77	
Subtotal, harvest				$ 57.19	
Total variable costs				$270.39	
Income above variable costs				$179.61	
Fixed Costs					
Preharvest					
Machinery	acre	7.40	1.00	7.40	
Tractors	acre	10.72	1.00	10.72	
Irrigation machinery	acre	15.96	1.00	15.96	
Harvest					
Machinery	acre	21.85	1.00	21.85	
Tractors	acre	2.06	1.00	2.06	
Overhead labor	acre	40.67	1.00	40.67	
Total fixed costs				$ 98.66	
Total costs				$369.05	
Net returns above specified costs				$ 80.95	

Source: Arkansas Experiment Station, Cooperative Extension Service,
Special Report 81, University of Arkansas, Fayetteville, Arkansas, 1980.

TABLE 5–1b. ENTERPRISE BUDGET FOR SOUTHWEST IDAHO POTATO PRODUCTION

	Unit	Price or Cost/unit	Quantity	Value or Cost	Your Estimate
Gross receipts from production					
Potatoes	cwt.	5.00	300.00	1500.00	
Total				1500.00	
Variable costs					
Preharvest					
Seed potatoes	cwt.	4.50	20.00	90.00	
Nitrogen	lb.	0.25	200.00	50.00	
Phosphate	lb.	0.26	180.00	46.80	
Potash	lb.	0.20	100.00	20.00	
Apply fertilizer	acre	3.75	1.67	6.26	
Sidedress	acre	6.25	1.00	6.25	
Terr-O-Cyde 30D	gal.	11.00	30.00	330.00	
Sencor	lb.	9.10	1.00	9.10	
Monitor	qt.	11.50	2.00	23.00	
Manzate	lb.	2.00	6.00	12.00	
Water assessment	acre	30.00	1.00	30.00	
Potato storage	cwt.	0.40	300.00	120.00	
Machinery	acre	30.63	1.00	30.63	
Tractors	acre	19.97	1.00	19.97	
Irrigation mach.	acre	1.08	1.00	1.08	
Labor (tractor & machinery)	hour	4.25	4.49	19.08	
Labor (irrigation)	hour	3.75	4.80	18.00	
Other labor	hour	3.75	2.00	7.50	
Interest on Op. Cap.			3.53	43.74	
Subtotal, Pre-harvest		12.39		883.41	
Harvest					
Machinery	acre	35.05	1.00	35.05	
Tractors	acre	10.82	1.00	10.82	
Labor (tractor & machinery)	hour	4.25	3.53	15.00	
Subtotal, Harvest				60.87	
Total variable costs				$944.28	
Income above variable costs				$555.72	
Fixed Costs					
Machinery	acre	118.35	1.00	118.35	
Tractors	acre	45.91	1.00	45.91	
Irrigation machinery	acre	17.40	1.00	17.40	
Taxes (land, water)	acre	6.50	1.00	6.50	
Return/land invest.	acre	0.08	2000.00	160.00	
Overhead	acre	30.97	1.00	30.97	
Total fixed costs				379.13	
Management	dol.	0.05	1500.00	75.00	
Total costs				$1323.41	
Net returns above specified costs				$ 101.59	

Source: Idaho Experiment Station, University of Idaho, College of Agriculture, Moscow, Idaho.

TABLE 5–1c. ENTERPRISE BUDGET FOR RED RASPBERRY PRODUCTION, YEARS 3-10

	Unit	Price or Cost/unit	Quantity	Value or Cost	Your Estimate
Gross receipts from production					
Raspberries	ton	1200.00	4.00	$4800.00	
Total				4800.00	
Variable costs					
Preharvest					
Hand prune	hr.	4.00	10.00	40.00	
Custom subsoil	acre	7.50	1.00	7.50	
40" disk drill rent	acre	1.50	1.00	1.50	
Rye seed	lbs.	0.17	30.00	5.10	
Tie canes	hr.	4.00	30.00	120.00	
Baler twine	bale	55.00	0.30	16.50	
Lime-sulfur	gal.	5.75	6.00	34.50	
Top canes	hr.	4.00	6.00	24.00	
Hoe shoots	hr.	4.00	8.00	32.00	
Simazine 80%WP	lbs.	3.25	1.67	5.43	
Paraquat	pt.	5.86	1.33	7.79	
Dinoseb	qt.	3.27	1.00	3.27	
Superior spray oil	gal.	2.95	0.50	1.47	
Diazinon 50%WP	lbs.	4.05	2.00	8.10	
Benlate 50%WP	lbs.	10.45	1.50	15.67	
Fert. 10-20-10	lbs.	0.12	600.00	72.00	
Overhead	dol.	0.05	2039.95	102.00	
Captan	lbs.	2.23	10.00	22.30	
Train canes	hr.	4.00	4.00	16.00	
Machinery repair	acre	6.34	1.00	6.34	
Tractor fuel, lube repair	acre	3.12	1.00	3.12	
Irrigation elec & repair	acre	38.48	1.00	38.48	
Labor (trac & mach)	hour	6.00	16.87	101.22	
Labor (irrigation)	hour	4.00	1.69	6.76	
Int. on Op. Cap.	dol.	0.12	237.13	28.46	
Subtotal, preharvest				$ 719.51	
Harvest costs					
Hand pick	tons	300.00	4.00	1200.00	
Machinery	acre	110.47	1.00	110.47	
Labor (trac. & mach)	hour	6.00	19.20	115.20	
Total variable costs				$2,145.18	
Total above variable costs				$2,654.82	
Fixed costs					
Machinery	acre	275.48	1.00	275.48	
Tractors	acre	92.24	1.00	92.24	
Irrigation machinery	acre	85.78	1.00	85.78	
Taxes (land)	acre	100.00	1.00	100.00	
Prorated Est. cost	acre	3341.86	0.20	668.37	
Land (net rent)	acre	0.12	4000.00	480.00	
Total fixed costs				$1,701.87	
Total costs				$3,847.05	
Net returns above specified costs				$ 952.95	

Source: **Washington Experiment Station, Washington State University, Pullman, Washington.**

TABLE 5–1d. ENTERPRISE BUDGET FOR TOBACCO (14 ACRE OPERATION) SOUTH CAROLINA

	Unit	Price or Cost/unit	Quantity	Value or Cost	Your Estimate
Gross receipts from production					
Tobacco	lbs.	1.77	2100.00	$3717.00	
Total				$3717.00	
Variable costs					
Preharvest					
PB Seed	oz.	31.50	0.17	5.36	
PB 12-6-6-(sprd)	cwt.	8.75	0.50	4.38	
PB 16-0-0	cwt.	9.20	0.05	0.46	
PB Fumigant(CST)	acre	26.00	1.00	26.00	
PB Insecticide	lbs.	0.95	0.75	0.71	
PB Fungicide	oz.	0.98	0.67	0.65	
PB Straw	acre	0.80	1.00	0.80	
PB Labor	hr.	3.65	5.00	18.25	
6-12-18 (spread)	cwt.	12.35	7.00	86.45	
15-0-14	cwt.	11.55	2.50	28.87	
Herbicide	qt.	16.95	1.00	16.95	
Nem.-Syst.Insect	gal.	37.20	1.50	55.80	
Fungicide	qt.	31.25	1.00	31.25	
Insecticide	qt.	6.20	3.00	18.60	
Cont. Sucker Cont	gal.	8.25	4.00	33.00	
Syst. Sucker Cont	gal.	8.25	1.50	12.38	
Crop insurance	hdrd	2.40	20.40	48.96	
Topping labor	hr.	3.65	10.00	36.50	
Machinery	acre	32.34	1.00	32.34	
Tractors	acre	47.07	1.00	47.07	
Interest Op. Cap.	dol.	0.14	221.76	31.05	
Subtotal, Preharvest				$ 535.83	
Harvest costs					
Diesel fuel	gal.	1.25	400.00	500.00	
Warehs & storage	acre	185.85	1.00	185.85	
Barn Elec & repair	acre	22.50	1.00	22.50	
Barn labor	hr.	3.65	65.00	237.25	
Machinery	acre	78.43	1.00	78.43	
Tractors	acre	65.81	1.00	65.81	
Labor, tract & mach	hour	4.00	131.18	524.72	
Subtotal, Harvest				$1,614.56	
Total variable costs				$2,150.39	
Total above variable costs				$1,566.61	
Fixed costs					
Machinery	acre	95.66	1.00	95.66	
Tractors	acrc	86.15	1.00	86.15	
Conv. barn	acre	93.00	1.00	93.00	
Total fixed costs				$ 274.81	
Total costs				$2,425.20	
Net returns above specified costs				$1,291.80	

Source: South Carolina Experiment Station, Cooperative Extension Service, Clemson University, Clemson, South Carolina, 1982.

TABLE 5–1e.   ENTERPRISE BUDGET FOR SOW AND MARKET HOGS (12 PIGS RAISED), MISSOURI, 1981

	Unit	Price or Cost/unit	Quantity	Value or Cost	Your Estimate
Gross receipts from production					
Sow	cwt.	48.00	2	96.00	
Hogs	cwt.	56.00	26.45	1481.00	
Total				$1577.00	
Variable costs					
Grain	bu.	3.40	180.00	612.00	
Protein, salt & minerals	lb.	.13	2200.00	286.00	
Creep feed	lb.	.18	350.00	63.00	
Machinery	litter	50.00	1.00	50.00	
Vet & Medicine	litter	26.00	1.00	26.00	
Other services[1]	litter	50.00	1.00	50.00	
Utilities	litter	26.00	1.00	26.00	
Breeding charge[2]	sow	20.00	1.00	20.00	
Operating interest[3]	sow	40.00	1.00	40.00	
Total variable costs				$1173.00	
Income above variable costs				404.00	
Fixed costs					
Labor	hr.	4.00	28.00	112.00	
Breeding herd investment	litter	175.00	1.00	175.00	
Total fixed costs				287.00	
Total costs				$1460.00	
Net returns above specified costs				$ 117.00	

[1]Includes marketing cost, advertising, bedding, etc.

[2]Fourteen percent interest on average investment.

[3]Breeding costs include boar depreciation, infertility, etc., feed included in budget.

Source: Planning Livestock Systems," *Missouri Farm Planning Handbook,* Part III, University of Missouri, Columbia, Missouri.

Finally note that the total costs have been summed to $369.05. This figure has been subtracted from gross returns to yield net returns above specified costs of $80.95 per acre.

Sensitivity Analysis

The farm manager should check how this enterprise budget would change if some of the key assumptions that went into it were changed. This process is called sensitivity analysis. **Sensitivity analysis** may be defined as the process of changing the yield and price estimates of a budget to determine the range over which the result is the same (insensitive). If reasonably good weather could raise yields to 55 hundredweight per acre, the enterprise budget may be reformulated using a higher

TABLE 5–1f. ENTERPRISE BUDGET FOR DAIRY HERD REPLACEMENTS, KANSAS, 1980

	Unit	Price or Cost/unit	Quantity	Value or Cost	Your Estimate
Gross receipts from production					
Spring heifer	head	1200.00	0.90	1080.00	
New breeder cull	head	495.00	0.10	49.50	
Death loss (10% of calf cost)				−20.00	
Total				$1109.50	
Variable costs					
Calf cost	animal	200.00	1.00	200.00	
Milk replacer	cwt.	40.00	0.50	20.00	
Calf starter	cwt.	12.00	3.00	36.00	
Grain	cwt.	5.60	15.55	87.08	
Protein	cwt.	13.00	3.35	43.55	
Hay equiv.	ton	75.00	3.91	293.25	
Pasture	mo.	14.00	3.00	42.00	
Salt & minerals	cwt.	5.00	0.80	4.00	
Breeding	animal	10.00	1.00	10.00	
Veterinary	animal	4.50	1.00	4.50	
Machinery & equip.	animal	8.00	1.00	8.00	
Repairs	animal	3.50	1.00	3.50	
Interest (13%/2 yr)	animal	63.32	1.00	63.32	
Total variable costs				$815.20	
Income above variable costs				294.30	
Fixed costs					
Building, equip.	animal	13.33	1.00	13.33	
Int. on Bldg (6%)	animal			6.00	
Taxes, insr.	animal			1.00	
Total fixed costs				$ 20.33	
Total costs				$835.53	
Net returns above specified costs				$273.97	

Source: **Kansas State University Farm Management Guides, MF-399, Cooperative Extension Service, Kansas State University, Manhattan, Kansas, 1980.**

estimate of yield. Different prices can also be placed in the budget to test for various expected outcomes.

It is very important to make the best estimates possible for yield and price. These data can come from six major sources:

1. Extension Service Bulletins. Each state has a farm extension service operated through its landgrant university. Frequently, extension service personnel also construct enterprise budgets for different areas of the state. Data on all crops and livestock raised in a particular area are usually available, along with histories of yields, production costs, and expected rates of gain.

2. Private Service Institutions. In recent years many private institutions have emerged which devote their time to estimating yields and prices for various crops. A subscription to their newsletter usually provides the farm operator with this information.

3. Popular Press. Examples include farm magazines and journals. Usually however, the popular press magazines rely on university and government publications and tend not to give as complete information as the extension service. Also, individual farmers may be led to false conclusions from a particular success story which is not representative in the popular press. Therefore, it is safer to go to the source of the data itself.

4. The USDA. The USDA publishes many estimates of farm production costs and yields. These estimates are a valuable source of historical data on farm operations. However, it may be difficult to find a publication suited to your particular region because these are frequently compiled as averages of large regions of the country.

5. Feed Companies. Blank budgets and suggested rations can be obtained from these sources as livestock budgeting aids.

6. The Farmer's Personal Records. These of course are the best possible set of data and should be developed by each operator. Since they are the actual historical results of the farmer's own operation, they provide the best estimate of what future results will be.

Some managers find it useful to construct weighted enterprise budgets for the different rotations they are considering. The **rotation budget** is constructed by weighting each entry in an underlying crop's enterprise budget by its importance in the rotation. Several abbreviated corn-soybean rotations are illustrated in Table 5–2. The unit of measurement is a rotation acre. These budgets require a separate enterprise budget for each crop in the rotation and are of limited usefulness unless each of the component crops is grown in the rotation each year. However,

TABLE 5–2. ABBREVIATED ROTATION ENTERPRISE BUDGETS FOR VARIOUS CORN AND SOYBEAN ROTATIONS

	Corn (C)	Soybeans (S)	Rotations		
			CCCS	CCS	CS
Gross receipts	$420.00	$280.00	$385.00	$373.80	$350.00
Preharvest variable costs	112.00	68.00	101.00	97.48	90.00
Harvest variable costs	24.00	9.00	20.25	19.05	16.50
Fixed costs	197.00	147.00	184.50	180.50	172.00
Returns above specified costs	$ 87.00	$ 56.00	$ 79.25	$ 76.77	$ 71.50

Source: **Estimated Costs of Crop Production in Iowa—1981, FM-1712, Cooperative Extension Service, Ames, Iowa, 1981.**

they can provide quick estimates of crop earnings and expenses for the entire production plan.

Enterprise budgets are reformulated each year as part of the planning process. Because the technical (input use) components change slowly over time, it may only be necessary to reforecast output and input prices with only minor changes in input use levels.

After each enterprise has been budgeted, these unit forecasts can be assembled into the whole farm plan.

WHOLE FARM BUDGETS

Whenever major changes in the organization of the farm are anticipated, the **whole farm budget** should be constructed. Many farms will routinely assemble a whole farm budget every two to four years just to make sure that enterprises selected for the entire farm are still the most profitable given the current prices, technology, weather cycles, and experience of the operator. Rarely is there enough time to develop more than five to ten alternative plans at one time. But it is important to construct the whole farm plan periodically to assure the farm manager that the most efficient use of resources and the most profitable opportunities for the farm are being exploited. In intervening years, partial budgets can be used to fine-tune and improve the current whole farm plan.

Whole farm budgets relate to finding that mix of enterprises which 1) is on the production possibilities frontier and 2) is the most profitable point given expected prices. This first criterion is referred to as **technical feasibility**. It is important to be on the production possibilities frontier, as demonstrated in Chapter 2. To be inside or outside of this frontier means either that we are not using resources in the best possible manner or we do not have adequate resources to implement the plan under consideration. Since the exact representation of the production possibilities frontier is not possible for each individual farm, it is important to test for the feasibility of a set of enterprises by budgeting.

The second criterion for choosing the most profitable point given expected prices is called **profitability**. Even if a plan comes very close to being on the production possibilities frontier it is important to locate that point, among several possible options, which is the most profitable. Figure 5–2 illustrates some of the product/product relationships which might be considered and the possible outcomes of whole farm planning. The whole farm budget differs from economic principles involved in the product-product relationship in that the production possibilities frontier is unknown for most individual farmers' soil types and available resources.

There are at least six situations in which a whole farm budget should be undertaken.

1. The purchase of a new farm. When a new farm is purchased or a sizeable addition to the present farm is acquired, the most profitable and feasible mix of enterprise opportunities need to be explored. The

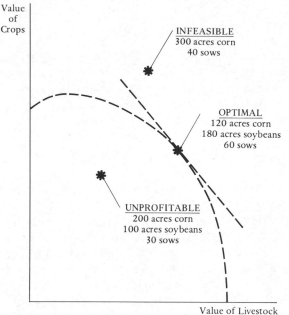

FIGURE 5-2. *Possible Outcomes of Whole Farm Planning.*

Value of Crops

INFEASIBLE
300 acres corn
40 sows

OPTIMAL
120 acres corn
180 acres soybeans
60 sows

UNPROFITABLE
200 acres corn
100 acres soybeans
30 sows

Value of Livestock

whole farm budget will indicate whether certain machinery components and available labor and resources will be able to accomplish production activity on this new acreage.

2. Adding or expanding livestock or cropping activities. It is particularly important to construct a whole farm plan if expanding a cropping or livestock activity necessitates investment in additional buildings or feeding facilities.

3. Change in tenure. The landlord and tenant must usually agree not only on the types of production activities which will be implemented on the rented or leased acreage but also on which groups of enterprises will yield the greatest amount of net farm income (Chapter 15). The whole farm plan helps in estimating a fair division of costs and returns.

4. Changes in government programs. If the government, for instance, were to guarantee the price of a commodity at 90 percent parity, or if regulations for set-aside and commodity storage change, the profitability of all the activities on the farm may be affected.

5. Major changes in demand or supply. Rapidly evolving changes in consumer tastes or the availability of factors of production (such as energy) many times will dictate that the product mix of individual farms should be changed. Recent changes in consumer demand for red meats and products containing nitrites have resulted in major shifts in the demand for these products. The farmer must be ready to change the mix of inputs used and outputs produced in response to these current events. Changes in energy resources have indicated that limited till or no-till operations for preparing the land prior to production may be more profitable.

6. Sudden changes in the farm labor supply. Illness, or more happily marriage, may drastically alter the amount of labor available on the farm. A major change in fixed labor supply would be sufficient reason to initiate a whole farm budget to determine how the other resources on the farm could be more effectively combined.

In general, the whole farm plan is the farmer's best approximation of whether the particular combination of enterprises proposed is both technically feasible and economically profitable. There are four important steps in constructing the whole farm plan:

1. State objectives. You should remember from Chapter 1 that one of the first and most important things a farm manager can do is to formulate clearly the objectives of the farm. Profit maximization may not be the sole objective. Leisure time, farm ownership, farm growth, and individual personal likes and dislikes may dictate that mix of production practices and enterprises which best accomplishes farm goals. It has been discovered that many objectives are in conflict, particularly when income maximization vies with leisure activities and other nonproductive goals. Such conflicts reduce the amount of management and labor available to the farm operation.

2. Inventory resources. Chapter 4 showed that, to make informed decisions, the farm manager must know what resources are available. Knowledge of resource availability and constraints will help the farm manager avoid violating the criterion of feasibility. Four resources must be inventoried:

   a. Land. Is the land rented or owned? How many acres are available? What type of land is available in terms of slope, yield potential, fertility requirements, etc.? Soil considerations for each field should be separately assessed and any particular drainage problem or productivity characteristics should be noted and taken into account.

   b. Labor. How much operator and family labor, permanent hired labor, or seasonal hired labor is available? Knowing the total amount of labor available is not sufficient. The whole farm budget should look at each month to make sure that seasonal peak labor requirements for a given production plan can be accomplished. Although 4,000 hours of labor may be available for the entire year, it may be discovered that the bulk of it may be required in only two or three production months. Therefore labor shortages can arise annually or seasonally.

   c. Capital. It is important to know machinery availability to help schedule the production activities. Suitable field days for local conditions should be estimated for key machinery use periods such as planting and harvest. The choice of tillage systems and harvesting methods is important. The buildings and facilities available for production purposes must also be known. Efficient use of such facilities may require that the farm manager implement an activity such as farrowing within narrow time limits.

Otherwise, under-utilization or over-utilization of facilities may result. Available credit is another component of capital. By having a complete farm budget and cash flow budget, a farmer enhances his chances of obtaining a line of credit necessary to accomplish his farm goals.

d. Management. Inventorying management skills and management goals ensure the farm operator that no production activity which is beyond the abilities or interest of the operator to manage properly will enter the whole farm plan. A particular operator may be well-skilled at certain crop and livestock activities and not at others. The time and cost of improving management skill can be taken into account. However, only those activities which the farm manager is reasonably equipped to handle should be considered in the whole farm plan. It is up to management to orchestrate the entire farm plan.

3. Plan the dominant and secondary enterprises. The dominant enterprice on a particular farm will largely be dictated by the region of the country in which the farm is located. The dominant enterprise will usually be that activity in which a particular region has a comparative advantage. Comparative advantage simply means that the product can be produced for trade with relatively greater efficiency than in other regions of the country. Farmers in that region will produce that product and trade it to other regions where different crops or livestock activities have a comparative advantage. Farmers in Florida typically have a comparative advantage in the production of citrus fruits and many vegetables. Farmers in California enjoy a comparative advantage in fruits, certain nuts, vegetables, and grapes. Farmers in the Midwest will typically have a comparative advantage in dairy products, row and forage crops.

Planning the dominant enterprise involves the construction of enterprise budgets for each crop or livestock activity. In the case of crops which can be rotated, rotation enterprise budgets are also needed. Enterprise budgets for the particular stages in the production of livestock should also be developed. For example, separate budgets can be developed in hog production for farrowing and for feeder pig to fat hog processes. In cattle production, separate budgets can be developed for cow-calf pairs, backgrounding steers, and feedlot production of fat cattle.

When preparing enterprise budgets for inclusion in the whole farm plan, the farm manager must forecast input rates, output results and and their prices. Since whole farm planning is not usually undertaken every year, these forecasts represent expectations for a two to four year period. Input rates pose the smallest problem because these technical factors tend to change slowly over time. Output results and especially prices tend to be much more variable from year to year and present complex forecasting problems. Expected output can be estimated from records, taking into account any cyclical patterns in weather, etc., which are likely to occur over the planning interval. **Planning prices** should be used to estimate expected input costs and revenue. Planning prices represent the farmer's best guess as to the prevailing or most likely (model) price over the planning interval. Information from extension economists and sources previously mentioned, along with the operators experience, can be used to forecast planning prices. Many farmers anticipate input costs and output prices from the previous year's results. This is generally **not** the best method due to the constantly changing factors which determine prices.

Keeping in mind the resource restraints noted in his inventory, the farmer should try to implement the most profitable enterprise budgets up until the point where a resource restraint is encountered. At that time, different activities can be considered which do not require the use of the resource which has been fully utilized. The secondary enterprises usually enter in at this point. These activities involve other commodities the farm manager is considering producing which have not already been planned. A proper mix of dominant and secondary types of enterprises will ensure the farm manager that, within his resource restraints, all productive resources available have been employed as fully possible.

By selecting the most profitable enterprises first, the farm manager can make a first approximation of the most profitable set of enterprises. However, this particular method will not guarantee profit maximization. All activities must be considered simultaneously. This requires the use of more advanced techniques such as linear programming.

4. Compare all plans for feasibility and profitability and select the most profitable, feasible plan. This should be the best approximation of the plan closest to the production possibility curve at the points of tangency of the price lines. Once this process is complete, the farm manager can calculate measures of efficiency and construct a cash flow budget to determine whether the timing of cash inflows and outflows will result in a financially feasible plan.

Constructing the Whole Farm Plan: An Example

In Table 5-3, there is a list of enterprise budgets for six different types of enterprises: three crop and three livestock alternatives. The farm manager based the selection of these enterprises on the particular resources, management skills and capital available to his farm. Several other enterprises were considered but eliminated.

Remember that the first step in constructing a whole farm plan is to state the objectives. In this example, the objective will be to maximize returns above variable cost. Total labor available (operator and family labor) is 3600 hours per year. The farmer has 300 acres of land and sufficient capital to execute any of the six enterprise budgets under consideration. To make a first approximation, assume the farm manager

TABLE 5–3. SIX ENTERPRISE BUDGETS INCLUDING LABOR REQUIREMENTS FOR DEVELOPING A WHOLE FARM PLAN

	Rotations[1]			Livestock[2]		
	C	*CCCSS*	*CCOMM*	*FP*	*PF*	*FF*
Unit	acre	rotation acre	rotation acre	litter	head	litter
Gross receipts	$300	$325	$240	$350	$90	$700
Total variable costs	190	150	120	250	70	500
Gross margin	$110	$175	$120	$100	$20	$200
Corn supplied/acre	100 bu.	62 bu.	45 bu.	—	—	—
Corn required/unit	—	—	—	50 bu.	13.8 bu.	142 bu.
Labor requirements[3] Bi-monthly						
Jan-Feb	0	0	0	1.5	0.1	2
Mar-Apr	1.7	1.3	1	1.5	0.1	2
May-Jun	1	0.7	1	1.5	0.1	2
Jul-Aug	0.7	0.3	1	1.5	0.1	2
Sep-Oct	2	1.4	1	1.5	0.1	2
Nov-Dec	1.7	1.3	0.7	1.5	0.1	2

[1] C = corn, CCCSS = corn-corn-corn-soybeans-soybeans, and CCOMM = corn-corn-oats-meadow-meadow.

[2] FP = farrow-to-feeder pig, PF = feeder pig-to-fat hog, and FF = farrow-to-fat hog.

[3] The livestock labor requirements have been adjusted allowing them to be multiplied by annual capacity to calculate bi-monthly labor requirements.

is unwilling to hire additional seasonal labor or to purchase corn for feed in the marketplace.

From the enterprise budgets in Table 5–3, block budgets can be constructed (Table 5–4). A **block budget** is obtained by multiplying each item in the enterprise budget (which is on a per unit basis) by the amount of resource available to accomplish that activity. Since 300 acres are available for cropping activities, each element of the crop enterprise budgets is multiplied by 300. In this way, the total returns, total variable cost, and the total amount of labor and all other inputs necessary to accomplish each enterprise are calculated. The same is done for the livestock activities. For each livestock enterprise budget, the total number of head which can be produced with available buildings and facilities is multiplied by each element in the enterprise budget.

The block budget figures can now be assembled into a grid to simultaneously compare individual combinations of crop and livestock activities (Table 5–5). By forming a grid, a farm manager can quickly discover which combinations are not feasible due to limited resources, and which combinations of enterprises produce the greatest amount of net income.

The grid in Table 5–5 is such a combination of all the block budgets which have been constructed from the six enterprise budgets. You should notice that labor is a constraining factor in four of the combinations. Continuous corn combined with any of the livestock options

TABLE 5-4. BLOCK BUDGETS DEVELOPED FROM THE ENTERPRISE
BUDGETS OF TABLE 5-3.

Block Budgets for Cropping Rotations Specified

Resource Limitations: 300 acres
600 hours labor/2 month period

	C	CCCSS	CCOMM
1. Total Gross Margin	$33,000	$52,500	$36,000
2. Total Corn Produced	30,000 bu.	18,600 bu.	13,500 bu.
3. Sept-Oct Labor[1]	600 hrs.	420 hrs.	300 hrs.

Block Budgets for Livestock Activities Specified

Resource Limitations: 20 litters/2 month period
1,000 head of fat hogs/year
600 hours labor/2 month period

	FP	PF	FF
1. Total Gross Margin	12,000	20,000	24,000
2. Total Corn Consumed	6,000 bu.	13,800 bu.	17,040 bu.
3. Sept-Oct Labor	180 hrs.	100 hrs.	240 hrs.

[1]Sept-Oct is the most constraining labor period due to harvest labor requirements.
Therefore, only this period needs to be tested for the labor feasibility criterion.

results in utilization of too much labor as does the corn-soybean rotation and the farrow-to-finish livestock combination.

When the farrow-to-finish or feeder pig-to-finish livestock activity is
combined with the corn-oats-meadow rotation, feed produced is a
constraint. This is so because the corn-oats-meadow rotation does not
provide sufficient feed to produce the finished hogs. Among those
combinations which are feasible, the single most profitable is the corn-
soybean cropping pattern combined with the feeder pig-to-finish livestock activity where $74,500 worth of net income is produced.

The grid shows that some options are infeasible while others are
feasible but not most profitable. To demonstrate how this procedure
in budgeting relates to the economic theory embodied in the production possibilities frontier, consider Figure 5-3. This graph demonstrates
a production possibilities frontier constructed from the crop and livestock alternatives in Table 5-5. On the vertical axis the value of cropping
activities is represented. Along the horizontal axis the value of livestock
combinations has been constructed. The production possibilities curve
does not extend to the livestock axis because no grain would result and
therefore no livestock could be produced under the initial assumption
of no purchased feed.

The graph suggests that further analysis is required. For instance it
might be reasonable to relax the constraints involving labor and corn.

TABLE 5–5. GRID APPROACH TO DISCOVERING THE MOST PROFITABLE AND FEASIBLE WHOLE FARM PLAN

	Livestock			
	FP	PF	FF	No Livestock
C	33,000 +12,000 $45,000	33,000 +20,000 $53,000	33,000 +24,000 $57,000	33,000 + 0 $33,000
	available labor exceeded	available labor exceeded	available labor exceeded	
	52,500 +12,000 $64,500	52,500 +20,000 $74,500	52,500 +24,000 $76,500	52,500 + 0 $52,500
CCCSS		Most Profitable Feasible Plan	available labor exceeded	
CCOMM	36,000 +12,000 $48,000	36,000 +20,000 $56,000	36,000 +24,000 $60,000	36,000 + 0 $36,000
	insufficient corn produced	insufficient corn produced	insufficient corn produced	

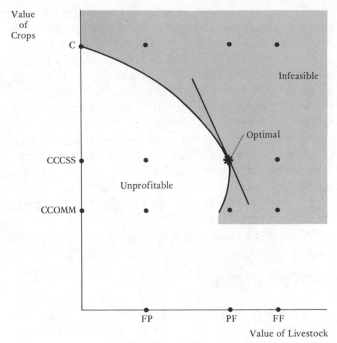

FIGURE 5-3. *The Production Possibilities Frontier Illustrating the Possible Outcomes of Whole Farm Planning.*

By hiring additional seasonal labor or purchasing corn for feed, it may be possible to raise net income. It may also be desirable to use some of the on-farm labor for work in town or for custom farm work so that a crop combination which uses less labor might be chosen.

Sensitivity analyses can also be performed. The prices and yields estimated in the enterprise budgets can be varied to measure the range over which the most profitable and feasible option is still the best. Corn price per bushel might be changed from $3.00 to $3.25 or market prices for finished hogs might be changed from $45/cwt. to $40/cwt. Yield might be changed on corn from 100 bushels per acre to 110 bushels per acre, or pigs weaned per litter might change from six to eight if there is some reason to suspect that death loss might diminish.

The whole farm plan budgeting process has some shortcomings of which the producer should be aware:

1. This budgeting process assumes a linear relationship between output and input when diminishing returns are actually more likely. The possibility of economies or diseconomies of size is ignored when linear relationships are considered.

2. The block budgeting process in the whole farm plan does not consider complementary relationships. If a combination of crop and livestock activities actually results in an increase in yield for one or both, this increase has been lost or does not enter consideration with this budgeting technique.

3. There are serious problems in estimating yields and prices. Sensitivity analyses must be performed. This is especially true if a new farm, new enterprise, or different technology is under consideration. However, even if yield estimates can be accurately projected, price variability due to the commodity cycle, business cycle, trend, and seasonal forms of price movement must be considered.[1] Even though hedging via the futures market or taking an expected five-year average of price may reduce income and price variability over time, the actual prices in a given year are not easily predicted. At this stage, sensitivity analysis is the best the farm operator can do to make an accounting for risk.

4. Many farms may have a much more complicated set of enterprise possibilities and combinations than have been shown in this example. In such a case, the farm operator may have to rely upon more sophisticated techniques requiring micro- and mini-computers or linear programming which is able to handle a large number of activities simultaneously.

LINEAR PROGRAMMING

An alternative form of budgeting to whole farm planning is linear programming. Like all other forms of budgeting, linear programming assumes that perfect knowledge of the production function, isoquant or production possibilities curve does not exist. Unlike other forms of budgeting, it allows the farm manager to systematically sample the range of all possible alternatives, given what knowledge is available, and determine the single best alternative. The knowledge constraint is thus minimized. There are two areas in which linear programming is commonly used in agricultural decision making:

1. Whole farm budgeting, a product-product relationship.
2. Cost minimization, a factor-factor relationship.

The process of whole farm budgeting allows the farm operator to search for a point where the price and physical relationships are just tangent. Linear programming, by contrast, allows the farm manager to construct an angular relationship approximating more systematically the true curvilinear relationship of the factor/factor and product/product analyses. Moreover, high-speed computers facilitate the search through all feasible points to find the most profitable one.

Linear programming as a planning technique was developed by G. B. Danzig to enhance efficiency in military planning during World War II. It is currently the major tool for making economic decisions in the Soviet Union, and other centrally-planned socialist economies where the governments are reluctant to let the profit incentive work through the market to allocate resources. The example which will be presented in this section is a graphic example of linear programming, a technique commonly used in agricultural extension to demonstrate the underlying

[1] *Chapter 9 will describe ways to handle price variability.*

principles of linear programming. This example gives a basis for solving simple optimizing situations involved in farm planning. Once this is accomplished, generalizing to all resources and products is not difficult.

As you have seen, traditional budgeting aggregates enterprise budgets into a set of two or more complete farm budgets to compare the total level of returns over direct and indirect costs. However, this approach to the product-product relationship cannot demonstrate the superior crop and livestock patterns without a great deal of experimentation. Even then, the farm operator is not sure that the single best use of on-farm resources given the present level of technology and prices has been achieved. Linear programming, by contrast, sifts through all possible combinations of enterprises which are feasible, given the resource constraints on the farm, and selects the optimal crop and livestock combination under the specified set of conditions.

The steps in solving a resource allocation problem with linear programming are similar to whole farm budgeting:

1. Inventory resources. It is essential that the total resource inventory be available so that the program can consider the utilization of each resource.

2. Develop enterprise budgets (Table 5-6). For purposes of simplicity, the only resources which will be considered are land, capital, and labor (divided into May and November labor, which correspond to planting and harvest). The data in Table 5-7 show the number of bushels of each crop which can be produced if all of each individual resource is used in each enterprise. These are the results of block budgeting. The total numbers of bushels resulting from fully utilizing each resource form the intercepts of the resource restraint lines. Once these intercepts are plotted, a straight line is drawn between them (Figure 5-4). Each point on these lines represent a combination of corn and soybeans which fully employs the specific resource for which each line is drawn.

The resource restraint lines form a production possibilities frontier, also shown in Figure 5.4. Notice that this frontier is angular.

3. Just as in the product-product example in economic principles, a price ratio line must be constructed based on the relative values of the

TABLE 5-6. ENTERPRISE BUDGETS FOR LINEAR PROGRAMMING EXAMPLE

Enterprise Budgets	*Corn (Y_1)*	*Soybeans (Y_2)*
Gross receipts	$400	$245
Total variable costs	204	113
Gross margin	$196	$132
Resource Requirements		
Acres (X_1)	1	1
Capital (X_2)	$204	$113
May labor (X_3)	0.42 hrs.	0.30 hrs.
November labor (X_4)	0.50 hrs.	0 hrs.

TABLE 5-7. BLOCK BUDGETS FOR LINEAR PROGRAM-MING EXAMPLE

Resource Restraints	Corn (Y_1)	Soybeans (Y_2)
Land (X_1)	400 acres	400 acres
Capital (X_2)	$61,000	$61,000
May labor (X_3)	150 hrs.	150 hrs.
November labor (X_4)	150 hrs.	150 hrs.
Production Possibilities		
Land restraining	400 acres	400 acres
Capital restraining	299 acres	540 acres
May labor restraining	357 acres	500 acres
November labor restraining	300 acres	no restraint

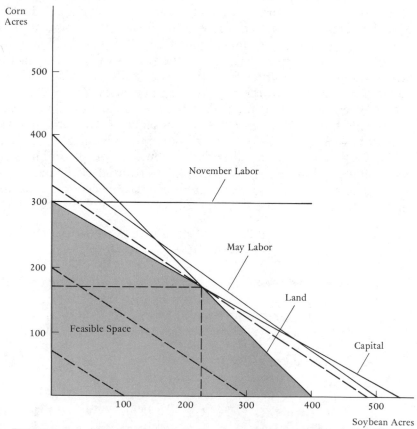

FIGURE 5-4. *The Graphical Solution to the Linear Programming Problem.*

two products. The gross margin of an acre of both corn and soybeans parallel each other. You will notice that three of these lines have been drawn parallel to each other. As more of each crop is produced, the lines move out in value upward and toward the right. Each point on these price lines gives a combination of corn and soybeans whose total value is the same. Where the price ratio line is just tangent to the angular production possibilities frontier, the optimal solution results. The solution is feasible because it is tangent to the frontier and production is taking place within the resource restraints. It is the most profitable because, as you move the price ratio line farther from the origin, the total value of the crop combination represented increases.

Sensitivity analyses can be easily performed with linear programming. Each line depicting a particular restraint can be relaxed or moved out. If additional labor becomes available, or if an additional amount of land or capital is available the appropriate resource restraint line can be moved out accordingly and a new solution discovered. The price line, constructed on the relative net values of an acre of corn and soybeans, can be changed as various prices of these crops are considered.

The use of linear programming as a budgeting tool relates to economic principles in that the construction of overlapping resource restraint lines approximates a production possibilities frontier. Also, the price line used to find the tangency with the production possibility frontier is constructed in a similar fashion to that done in the product-product relationship. The only difference is that the line is defined as the net value of each crop, with prices and unprogrammed costs implicit. The linear programming technique can be considered a form of the graphical solution presented in Chapter 2.

If additional resource constraints or activities (in terms of production, sales, or purchases) are to be considered, the graphical technique becomes very clumsy and difficult to solve. A high-speed computer, using the algebraic technique, can solve for a matrix of simultaneous equations, at a very high speed. The objective function and resource restraint conditions are specified in Table 5–8 to show how these data might be constructed to facilitate a solution by a computer. The enhancement

TABLE 5–8. THE MATHEMATICAL SPECIFICATIONS OF THE LINEAR PROGRAMMING PROBLEM

Objective function to be maximized:

$$= \$196Y_1 + \$132Y_2$$

Subject to:

$$Y_1 + Y_2 \leq 400X_1 \text{ (land)}$$

$$204Y_1 + 113Y_2 \leq 61{,}000X_2 \text{ (capital)}$$

$$0.42Y_1 + 0.30Y_2 \leq 150X_3 \text{ (May labor)}$$

$$0.50Y_1 + 0Y_2 \leq 150X_4 \text{ (November labor)}$$

available in linear programming techniques allows us to define more specific activities. Thus, instead of having a corn budget that lumps all activities together, a budget can be constructed first which produces corn, then sells corn as feed, or stores it, or buys it, and so on. Other activities which allow for the hiring of additional labor or obtaining additional resources can also be specified.

Sensitivity analyses can be performed very efficiently with the computer. Output prices can be varied by 10 cent increments for corn and soybeans, or the labor available in any given month can be varied, to test the stability of the enterprise pattern initially deemed optimal. The matrix of simultaneous equations is solved by the computer in basically the same way as the block budget grid is solved for a whole farm budget.

Linear programming as a whole farm budgeting tool has problems which must be understood. Some of these problems are similar to those in whole farm budgeting:

1. The linear programming technique does not take into account economies of size or diminishing marginal returns. Separate enterprises are linear and additive in this type of technique. This is different from the relationships which we have observed in the section on economic principles, where the true biological relationships were discovered to be curvilinear. In other words, it is assumed that the cost per acre of growing one acre of corn are the same as the costs per acre of growing 500 acres. This is a distortion. However, all other forms of complete budgeting examined so far share this problem.

2. The linear programming technique does not allow the user to account for risk. This is because the solution is often based on price information of a given year without considering the variance in expected returns. Other forms of budgeting also suffer from this drawback. Chapter 8 will discuss quadratic programming, which attempts to overcome this problem.

3. Unless numerous management constraints are introduced into the matrix, the linear programming solution tends to over-specialize. Solutions of linear programming model may indicate that the entire farm should be grown to a single crop. This may lead to risk susceptibility in terms of pests, erosion, or market over-specialization.

4. The technique is designed to maximize income and may leave out other objectives or goals of the farmer unless they are carefully and artistically built in. For example, as with whole farm budgeting, the amount of labor available can be reduced by the time needed for leisure.

5. Unless the programmer is very careful to include a breakdown of the various resources according to their productive characteristics, the results may be unrealistic. The program must differentiate land with low spots or poor drainage from well drained land. Also, if there is a great difference between the capability and experience or quality of labor, separate rows should be established in the matrix to account for this differing productivity. This makes linear programming essentially

an art. The more time spent defining the true and important differences between resources and activities, the more reliable the results. A typical farm may have between 100 and 200 enterprise activities and almost as many row constraints when fully specified.

6. Finally, linear programming can be a high cost method in terms of both computer time and trained manpower. Nevertheless the opportunity costs of management time for a good farm operator, if he must work through a series of eight or ten whole farm budgets by hand, can be quite high. University extension services and certain private firms offer linear programming services at reduced cost. For instance, a budgeting program may be run for customers of a particular machinery dealer. Since this technique is only likely to be employed every three or four years, the true cost on a per year basis may be more reasonable.

Despite the shortcomings of linear programming, it can be a very powerful and useful tool. However, like any tool, it can be misused and must be constructed to reflect the goals of the farm manager and the specific peculiarities of each individual farm.

Linear programming also has great usefulness in analyzing factor-factor relationships, such as the least cost ration for livestock. Since many different feed components may go into a ration, several possible mixes can be considered. Constraints can be placed in the linear programming matrix so that minimal amounts of vitamins and minerals will always enter the solution. Since the prices of feed components change frequently, a well-constructed linear programming model which considers all possible feed inputs can be run several times during the year to keep the ration at least cost.

FARM EFFICIENCY ANALYSIS

Budgeting is the third of five functions of management. When the farm budgeting process is over and the most profitable mix of enterprises and resource combinations has been found, the next step is implementing those activities. Finally, after the production season is over, the farm manager has a responsibility to evaluate the results and adjust the allocation of resources accordingly. The best laid plans of the farm manager may not have produced the results hoped for. In such a case, the evaluation process attempts to determine which factors might be adjusted, if any, to move the farm closer to attaining the stated goals. This process is facilitated by measuring the efficiency of the factors of production in producing farm income.

Various efficiency measures have been developed to aid the farm manager in evaluating farm progress. Different sets of efficiency measures are applied to cropping activities than to livestock activities. Several factors can be measured. The goal of the evaluation process is to first discover where results have deviated from proposed plans and then to identify the causative agents. This may be a difficult process. However, it can be facilitated by a carefully kept set of records.

Chapter 1 presented a brief table showing the relationship between high and low profit farms in Iowa. Higher gross value of crops per rotated acre on high profit farms reflects the higher yields on better managed farms. Lower power and machinery costs per rotated acre show that better farmers use machinery more efficiently and may be taking advantage of the economies of size in their operations through greater specialization. Higher livestock returns per hundred dollars feed fed reflect partly the greater efficiency of certain livestock, and partly the fact that high-profit farmers have chosen to feed hogs, cattle and other livestock through better managed programs. Rotated acres per man are higher on high-profit farms, suggesting that economies of size contribute to more efficient operation and a lower cost per acre. Gross profits per man are almost double on high-profit farms. It has become apparent after many years of study that the same top ten percent of farmers remain in the top ten percent year after year. The farmer in a low profit situation can use the budgeting to develop the kind of indices necessary to facilitate the evaluation process so that performance can improve over time.

The efficiency evaluation of the farm can proceed at several levels. But ordinarily there are two standards of comparison. First, the farm manager can compare this year's performance to historical performance on the farm. Sufficient information must be available from past performance to compare the progress of the farm over time. This is not always possible.

In cases where a new farm is purchased or acreage or facilities are added unlike those already on the farm, the manager must rely on a comparison with other farms in the area. This is the second type of comparison possible. It may be useful to study county, township, and statewide averages to compare relative efficiency of the farm to that of other farms in the immediate area. Because one particular farm may differ substantially from the surrounding region, the larger the area upon which the comparison is made, the less reliable are the results. Therefore, county or township averages are a better source of comparative data than statewide averages.

Most efficiency measures have characteristics in common. Some measure output per unit of resource (Table 5–9), others gauge cost per unit of resource or cost per unit of output. These types of efficiency measures, in a broad sense, allow the farm manager to estimate his place on the long run Average Total Cost curve. The lower the per unit cost of production, the closer to the optimal size and efficiency the farm is likely to be.

Evaluating Farm Efficiency Ratios

Once appropriate ratios for the productive activities on the farm have been calculated, the comparison process begins. In comparing efficiency measures over time for an individual farm, the farm manager hopes to see improvement. He can also detect persistent weak points in the farm operation which show little progress or possible deterioration. Several important factors should be understood regarding the interpretation of measures of performance efficiency.

First, no single ratio is adequate to properly evaluate farm efficiency. An appropriate set of ratios which evaluate output per unit of resource and cost per unit of resource should be employed. Remember that both physical and economic data are necessary to properly evaluate the allocation of resources. If only output per unit of resource measures are used, no reference to costs of production is obtained. Therefore, ever increasing output per unit of resource may be falsely viewed as a good sign when in actuality it may mean that excess production is taking place. Only when a resource is costless should it be used to produce the maximum amount of output possible. Therefore, measures of cost per unit of resource should also be included.

Second, caution should be exercised in evaluating labor productivity ratios, since labor is only as productive as the level of technology to which it is applied. Therefore, on farms with low investments in capital, low labor productivity ratios may not necessarily be a bad sign. Improvements in the level of technology or capital on the farm may yield higher labor productivity ratios.

Third, in livestock efficiency measures, it is important to note that two factors are involved: the price and the quantity of feeds fed. Both are needed to measure total feed costs. The farm manager should calculate separate efficiency factors on quantity per animal unit and on value of feed per animal unit. He then can determine whether high feed costs per unit of gain are due to poor gain performance by the animals or simply to rising prices of feed inputs. Corrective action will be different under each circumstance.

Fourth, because whole farm planning or linear programming to allocate resources on the farm is undertaken only every few years, the farm manager must be able to monitor selected key weak points on the farm in the intervening years to improve farm efficiency. Careful selection and consistent application of appropriate efficiency measures are the first steps in determining where opportunity for improvement lies. Then, a special form of budgeting called partial budgeting can take place to correct individual areas in the whole farm plan.

PARTIAL BUDGETING

Partial budgeting is the process whereby the complete farm plan can be fine-tuned in the period before the next whole farm plan is undertaken. The partial budget is a rough form of marginal analysis related to the factor-factor and product-product analyses of economic principles. It is used to compare the current position on an unknown isoquant or

TABLE 5–9. SELECTED EFFICIENCY MEASURES BY FARM PRODUCTION ACTIVITY

Calf and Stocker Cattle Production

Production Efficiency
  Cow-bull ratio
  Percentage replacement heifers
  Percentage of calves weaned
  Average weaning weight
  Weight weaned per cow
  Lbs. of concentrate/100 lbs. production
  Lbs. of roughage/100 lbs. production
  Acres of pasture per cow

Income Efficiency
  Gross income per cow
  Net income per cow
  Return over all feed fed
  Return over marketable feed
  Returns per $100 feed fed
  Feed cost per 100 lbs. produced
  Total cost per 100 lbs. produced
  Net income per $1 expense
  Gross income per $1 expense
  Returns to labor and management
  Returns to capital
  Returns to capital per $1 invested

Death Loss
  Percent cow loss
  Percent calf loss

Crop Production

Production Efficiency
  Yield per acre

Income Efficiency
  Net income per acre
  Net income per unit of production
  Fertilizer and chemical cost/acre
  Machinery cost per acre
  Net income per $1 expense
  Gross profits per $1 expense
  Returns to labor and management
  Returns to capital
  Returns to capital per $1 invested

Dairy and Milk Production

Production Efficiency
  Breeding efficiency
  Milk produced per cow

Fat Cattle and Sheep Production

Production Efficiency
  Average days in feedlot
  Rate of gain per day
  Lbs. of cencentrate/lb. of gain
  Lbs. of total feed fed/lb. of gain

Income Efficiency
  Returns over feed cost
  Returns per $100 feed fed
  Feed cost/100 lbs. produced
  Total cost per 100 lbs. produced
  Net income per $1 expense
  Gross income per $1 expense
  Returns to labor and management
  Returns to capital
  Returns to capital per $1 invested

Death Loss
  Percent death loss

Poultry and Egg Production

Production Efficiency
  Dozen eggs produced per hen
  Feed per dozen eggs
  Feed per hen

Income Efficiency
  Gross income per hen
  Net income per hen
  Returns over feed fed
  Returns per $100 feed fed
  Feed cost per dozen eggs produced
  Total cost per dozen eggs produced
  Net income per $1 expense
  Returns to labor and management
  Returns to capital
  Returns to capital per $1 invested

Death Loss
  Percent death loss

Swine Production

Production Efficiency
  Breeding to farrowing ratio
  Pigs weaned per sow bred
  Pigs weaned per sow farrowed
  Lbs. of pork per sow farrowed
  Lbs. of feed fed/lb. of pork produced

Dairy and Milk Production

Meat produced per cow
Concentrates fed/100 lb. of milk produced
Roughage fed/100 lb. of milk produced
Acres of pasture per cow

Income Efficiency

Gross income per cow
Net income per cow
Returns over feed cost
Returns per $100 feed fed
Feed cost/100 lb. milk produced
Total cost/100 lb. milk produced
Gross income per $1 expense
Returns to labor and management
Returns to capital
Return to capital per $1 invested

Death Loss

Percent cow loss

Swine Production

Income Efficiency

Gross income per sow farrowed
Gross income per hog marketed
Returns over feed cost
Returns per $100 feed fed
Feed costs per 100 lbs. produced
Total cost per 100 lbs. produced
Net income per $1 expense
Gross income per $1 expense
Net income per sow farrowed
Return to labor and management
Return to capital
Return to capital per $1 invested

Death Loss

Percent to weaning loss
Percent to weaning and maturity loss
Percent sow loss

production possibilities frontier with some other point. Figure 5–5 should help you in grasping this concept.

In the case of the isoquant, suppose that corn production is taking place using some combination of tillage and herbicide to control weeds. Point **a** on the isoquant represents conventional cultivation. The farm manager may wish to consider going to a no-till or limited cultivation practice using more herbicide (point **b**). Even though the exact shape of the isoquant is not known, the partial budget can determine whether moving from point **a** to point **b** will increase farm income.

In the case of the product-product example in Figure 5–5 suppose that various combinations of cropping enterprises and livestock enterprises are being produced. Point **a** on the production possibilities frontier indicates the current combination of crops and livestock, point **b** a combination with more livestock. Partial budgeting can indicate whether a shift from **a** to **b** will increase farm income. The partial budget can also be used in factor-product problems where the addition of some input over current levels is being contemplated. A test can be made with the partial budget to determine if the increased use of a single input, for instance, nitrogen for corn, will yield greater net farm income.

Constructing the Partial Budget: An Example

There are four steps involved in the construction of a partial budget. These steps will be outlined first in a feedlot example (Table 5–10) and then applied to an irrigation example.

The first step in constructing a partial budget is to state the proposed

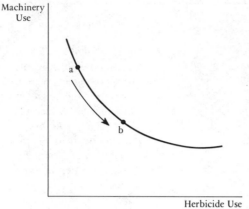

FIGURE 5-5. Graphical Representation of Partial Budgeting Options.

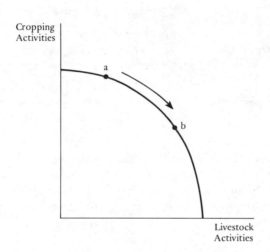

alternative. In this case, the farm manager is considering adding a hundred steers to a feedlot operation. The current operation involves feeding out one hundred steers. The partial budget will test whether doubling the size of the activity will yield greater net farm income.

Step two is to collect data on all aspects of the business that will be affected by the change. Table 5-10 lists the changes which are expected to occur if a hundred additional steers are added to the feedlot. Several points should be noticed. First, any building or equipment necessary to implement the proposed change should be accounted for in terms of a single year's cost rather than the entire purchase price. In the example, you will notice that a $6,000 building is necessary but only the ownership or fixed costs (DIRTI 5) of the building are charged to the budget. In the case of the feeding equipment necessary, the purchase price is $2,000 and the estimate of fixed costs is 23 percent (DITIS). Also note that only the interest cost associated with the operating capital necessary to purchase and grow out the steers has been charged to the enter-

TABLE 5–10. PROJECTED CHANGES FROM ADDING 100 STEERS TO FEEDLOT OPERATION

		Type/Change[1]
Building ($6,000 $\times$ .15)	$900	IC
Feeding equipment ($2,000 $\times$ .23)	$460	IC
Market at 1,100 lbs. ($60/cwt.)	$660/hd.	IR
Purchase steers at 600 lbs. ($70/cwt.)	$420/hd.	IC
Feed		
Corn	70/hd.	IC
Supplement	$25/hd.	IC
Hay	$12/hd.	IC
Labor on new stock (8 hrs./hd. at $4/hr.)	$32/hd.	IC
Labor savings on original stock (2 hrs./hd. at $4/hr.)	$8/hd.	DC
Interest on operating capital	$20/hd.	IC
Veterinary	$7/hd.	IC
Miscellaneous	$5/hd.	IC
Marketing cost	$7/hd.	IC
Death loss	3%	DR

[1]IR = increased return, DC = decreased cost, IC = increased cost, DR = decreased return.

prise. Any principal which must be paid back is not an expense of the operation. Therefore, only the cost of borrowing money (interest expense) is attributed to the partial budget when liability capital is used. If the farmer does not use borrowed funds to purchase necessary inputs an opportunity interest cost should still be charged to the activity for operating inputs.

The third step in estimating the partial budget is to classify the types of change. There are four possible classifications for each change that may occur. The change will either represent an **increased return** (IR), a **decreased cost** (DC), an **increased cost** (IC), or a **decreased return** (DR). In Table 5–10, the farm manager has classified each change according to one of the four outcomes which are possible. An increased return is any return which the farm manager expects to receive over and above present receipts if the proposed alternative is implemented. A decreased cost is a reduction in the current level of cost. An increased cost is an extra cost which must be paid if the proposed change is adopted. A decreased return is a reduction in expected returns.

Notice that the labor requirements do not simply double when the herd size is doubled. Ten hours per head is the current intensity of labor required when one hundred head are produced. If an extra hundred head is added to the feedlot operation, the average hours per head on the entire two hundred fall to eight hours. This is a result of the economies of size which were demonstrated in Chapter 3. The economy which is gained in labor by adding another hundred head involves a two-hour per head reduction in labor costs for the original hundred head but an increased labor requirement of eight hours per head for the second hundred.

The fourth step is to set up the budget (Table 5-11). Notice that all of the items which represent increases in revenue or decreased costs appear on the right hand side of the budget, while all items representing a decrease in return or an increase in cost appear on the left. Each side of the budget is added up to calculate net change in farm income.

The partial budget should be as complete as possible. All items which are expected to change once a new activity or a change in an activity is implemented must be specified. The budget is only as good as the information which goes into it. Notice, however, that no accounting for risk has been made in the partial budget. In this case, the risk associated with changes in cattle price may lead the farm manager to be skeptical about increasing herd size even though the net change in income is positive. One of the ways that risk can be accounted for in a partial budget is to build in a risk premium charge on the lefthand side. This can be done by estimating an income margin for risk which will satisfy the farm manager. The level of the risk premium will depend upon the farmer's estimation of the degree of price variability for each element in the budget. The livestock purchase and sales prices will account primarily for much of the risk in this particular example. You will notice that a $3,000 risk premium would still result in a positive change in net income if the 100 head are added.

TABLE 5–11. PARTIAL BUDGET FOR ADDING 100 HEAD OF STEERS

Increased costs		*Increased returns*	
Building	$ 900	Market 100 steers at 1,100 lbs.	
Equipment	460	($60/cwt.)	$66,000
Purchase 100 steers at 600 lbs.			
($70/cwt.)	42,000		
Feed			
Corn	7,000		
Supplement	2,500		
Hay	1,200		
Labor (8 hours/head at $4/hour)	3,200		
Interest on operating capital	2,000		
Veterinary	700		
Miscellaneous	500		
Marketing cost	700		

Decreased returns		*Decreased costs*	
Death loss at 3% of total additional output ($66,000 × .03)	1,980	Labor on original 100 head (2 hours/ head at $4/hour)	800
A. Total annual additional costs and reduced returns	$63,140	B. Total annual additional returns and reduced costs	$66,800
			$63,140
	Net change in income (B minus A)		+$ 3,660

A second method for adjusting the partial budget to account for risk simply involves respecifying the budget inserting minimum expected prices for output produced and maximum costs for inputs specified. The budget can then be recalculated to see whether the proposed change remains profitable under the worst of expected conditions. The particular change in net farm income which is budgeted using this format may be carried out across two or more accounting periods. All of the proposed costs may occur in one period and the estimated returns may accrue in the next accounting period. Therefore, care should be exercised from a tax management point of view when the partial budget is used to predict the profitability of a proposed alternative.

As an example of using the partial budget to evaluate a change in production practices, consider the case of a farmer in northern Florida who is interested in employing irrigation techniques for corn production. Table 5–12 lists the fixed and variable costs for a 140-acre center pivot irrigation system.

TABLE 5–12. FIXED AND VARIABLE COSTS FOR A 140 ACRE CENTER PIVOT IRRIGATION SYSTEM, NORTHERN FLORIDA, 1978[*]

Item	System 140 Acre	Well 12' X 300'	Pump Submerged	Engine 150 hp	Generator 10 KW	Total
New cost	31,771.00	5,750.00	7,938.00	8,000.00	1,250.00	54,709.00
Average cost[a]	17,474.05	2,875.00	4,365.90	4,400.00	687.50	—
Years life	15	20	15	12	12	—
Deprec[b]	1,906.26	287.50	476.28	600.00	93.75	3,363.79
Interest[c]	1,485.29	244.38	371.10	374.00	58.44	2,533.21
Insurance[d]	333.91	60.43	83.43	84.08	13.14	574.99
Taxes[e]	237.30	39.04	59.29	59.75	9.34	404.72
Repairs[f]	158.85	28.75	39.69	40.00	6.25	273.54
Total annual[g]	4,121.61	660.10	1,029.79	1,157.83	180.92	7,150.25

Operating cost for applying one inch of water at one application with a 140-acre center pivot system, northern Florida, 1978.

Fuel	$1.37
Grease and oil	.38
Labor	.04
Misc. overhead (10%)	.18
Interest on above for 6 months	.08
Total Operating costs/acre	$2.05

[*]Cost in dollars
[a]New cost + salvage value divided by 2.
[b]New cost – salvage value divided by years life.
[c]Average cost X 8.5%.
[d]$10.51 (per thousand (new cost).
[e]Average cost X .01358.
[f]New cost X .5%
[g]Sum of depreciation, interest, insurance, taxes and repairs

Source: Westberry, George O., *Partial Budgeting,* Staff paper 130, University of Florida, Gainesville, Florida, 1979.

The system is to be applied to 160 acres, of which 140 will be effectively irrigated. Corn yield is expected to double from 75 bushels to 150 bushels per acre on irrigated ground. This results in an average yield of 140 bushels per acre on the entire quarter section. Variable costs per acre increase by $37.86 as a result of the increased seed and fertilizer rates, as well as the costs of operating the irrigation equipment. Table 5–13 demonstrates the partial budgeting framework for analyzing this alternative. Note that under the expected changes a $10,000 increase in annual net income results. Additional questions to consider before adoption include: 1) is adequate water available to support this level of irrigation? 2) is management skill and available labor sufficient to operate the system? and 3) are appropriate financing and cash flow available to handle an investment of this size?

Partial budgets can be used to study a variety of proposed alternatives to adjust resource allocation for greater profits. Some of these alternatives include different cropping patterns, livestock facilities, tillage systems, purchase or rental of larger or smaller machinery or capital items, the construction of buildings, and the acquisition of land.

Breakeven Analysis

The simplest form of partial budgeting to fine-tune the allocation of resources is known as breakeven analysis. Breakeven analysis calculates the minimum benefit required from an activity in order to justify making the change. There are special formulas for breakeven analysis, depending upon the farm activity being analyzed. Breakeven analysis can

TABLE 5–13.   PARTIAL BUDGET FOR 140 ACRE CENTER PIVOT IRRIGATION SYSTEM

Increased costs		*Increased returns*	
Seed 3 lbs/acre	$ 336	140 bu./a X 2.25/bu.	
Fertilizer 3.5 cwt./acre	2,040	X 160 acre	$50,400
Nitrogen 25 lbs/acre	960		
Combine Variable costs			
$1.60/acre	297.60		
Irrigation cost	2,134.40		
Interest on operating capital			
$1.81/acre	289.60		
Fixed Costs (See Table 5.12)	7,150.25		

Decreased returns		*Decreased costs*	
Revenue from unirrigated corn	27,000		
160 acres X $168.75			0
(75 bu. @ $2.25/bu.)			

A. Total annual additional costs and reduced returns	$40,207.85	B. Total annual additional returns and reduced costs	$50,400
		Net change in income (B minus A)	+$10,192.15

be conducted for either short-run decisions regarding crops and livestock or long-run decisions regarding buildings.

Crops

Agricultural crop production is unique in that as the season progresses, a greater and greater proportion of costs become committed. Once the planting decision has been made and implemented, and various cultivation practices have been accomplished to maintain the crop, these costs are considered **sunk**. In the planning stage, the costs of planting and cultivation are considered variable costs of production. But, once they have been undertaken, they become part of the sunk costs. There may arise a situation in crop production when the farm manager wishes to decide part way through the season whether the activity should be completed. For example, poor weather or insect pests can sharply diminish the expected yield late in the season. To help evaluate whether such production processes should be completed, the enterprise budgets for crops in the first part of this chapter divided variable costs into two categories: preharvest and harvest.

Assume that a July drought has occurred and the farm manager estimates that only 20 bushels per acre of corn will result. What breakeven price must be expected for these 20 bushels to justify the harvest? The following formula can be used:

$$\text{Breakeven price} = \frac{\text{variable costs remaining}}{\text{estimated yield}} .$$

Using the enterprise budget constructed in advance, the manager discovers that variable costs remaining include harvest, hauling, and drying costs of $41.68. The estimated yield of 20 bushels per acre yields the breakeven price $2.08 per bushel. The manager must compare this price to expected market prices. Any price equal to or above the breakeven price will result in a decision to harvest.

This formula can be adjusted to calculate the breakeven yield necessary to justify harvest. The breakeven yield formula is:

$$\text{Breakeven yield} = \frac{\text{variable costs remaining}}{\text{estimated price}} .$$

If the harvest is near and the price of output can be estimated accurately, this formula allows the farm manager to calculate the minimum yield necessary to justify the harvest. Using the same figures from the enterprise budget, assume that the farm manager feels that $2.75 will be the price for corn harvested. Placing these figures in the breakeven formula results in a breakeven yield equal to 15 bu./acre. This figure is interpreted as the minimum yield necessary to justify harvest given the estimated price per bushel. The manager must then estimate the expected actual yield to decide whether or not to harvest.

Livestock

Breakeven formulas can also be calculated for livestock activities. In contrast to the crop formulas, the livestock breakeven price often is computed before production begins. The breakeven price per hundredweight for livestock can be calculated as follows:

$$\text{Breakeven price/cwt.} = \frac{\text{total production and marketing costs}}{\text{selling weight (cwt.)}}.$$

In the case of hog production, assume that the total cost including feeder pig costs, corn, supplement, labor, buildings, veterinary and medical, and marketing costs are \$95.00 per market-ready animal. If market weight is 220 pounds, the minimum price necessary to break even is:

$$\$95.00 \div 2.2 = \$43.18/\text{cwt.}$$

This formula can be particularly useful if the farm manager wishes to evaluate the sale of livestock which are not market-ready. Such a sale may be required if illness or some other factor requires the liquidation of the herd. The total cost to date would be divided by the expected weight of the animals at the point in the production process where their sale is contemplated. The breakeven price can then be compared to a market quote to see whether or not a breakeven situation will result.

It is important to carefully assess the future price of livestock when calculating the breakeven formula. Even with confinement operations for hogs, there is still seasonal fluctuation in expected prices (Chapter 7). If the breakeven formula is calculated before production begins, the pork producer must make a careful assessment of prices near the expected sales date. Table 5–14 compares the breakeven records of hogs and other forms of livestock in the Midwest over a recent ten year period.

Machinery

There are two forms of breakeven analysis for machinery: maximum price which can be paid and minimum acreage over which the machine

TABLE 5–14. RELATIVE PROFITABILITY OF LIVESTOCK ENTER-
PRISES

Profit Odds	Farrow to Finish Hogs	Fed Cattle	Dairy	Beef Cows
High Return	40%	50%	20%	20%
Average return	40%	20%	50%	50%
Breakeven	10%	0%	20%	10%
Loss	10%	20%	10%	20%
Serious loss	0%	10%	0%	0%

Source: "Relative Profitability of Livestock Enterprises" from *Modern Agriculture Management* by Osburn/Scheeberger is used by permission of the Publisher. Copyright © 1978 by Reston Publishing Company, Reston, VA.

must be used. The formula to calculate the breakeven price for a machine is as follows:

$$\text{Breakeven price} = \frac{\text{total savings per year}}{\% \text{ DITIS}}.$$

Total savings per year is the end product of partial budgeting. Notice that the denominator in this fraction is the percent of ownership costs in a given year. Recall that one estimated percentage for DITIS is 23 percent. Total savings per year can be calculated by setting up a partial budget to compare machinery purchase with current methods which may include custom hire.

Consider the example of a sweet corn picker which shows a savings of $40 per acre in harvest labor and other costs. This sweet corn picker will be utilized over 160 acres. Total savings per year are calculated as:

$$\$40 \times 160 \text{ acres} = \$6,400.$$

The breakeven price becomes:

$$\$6,400 \div .23 = \$27,826.$$

This represents the maximum price which could be paid for this picker in order to break even. This formula is particularly useful when machinery purchase is contemplated. The farm manager can establish a breakeven price and use it to negotiate with the machinery dealer when price discussion takes place.

The second machinery question involves the minimum area over which a machine must be used in order to make the investment worthwhile or profitable. The formula for calculating breakeven acreage per year is:

$$\text{Breakeven area} = \frac{\text{Total Fixed Costs (i.e. DITIS)}}{\text{custom charge/acre} - \text{variable costs of operating/acre}}.$$

Use of this formula is shown at the top of Figure 5–6. Notice that for the combine in this example, approximately 600 acres are necessary to justify the purchase of this machine given its purchase price. This same analysis can be carried out graphically. In Figure 5–6 the intersection of the declining average total cost curve for combine ownership with the custom hire rate determines the breakeven acreage. Notice that at any level of acreage beyond the breakeven rate, the average total costs of ownership per acre are less than the custom costs per acre.

Buildings and Land

A similar form of breakeven analysis can take place for buildings. Frequently the question arises as to how much the farm manager can afford to invest in a building given the annual costs of purchase and maintenance.

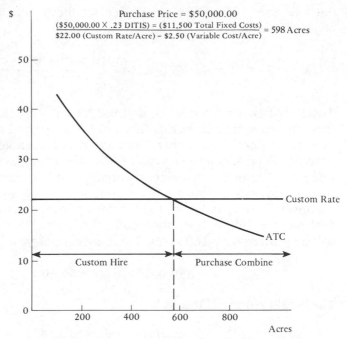

FIGURE 5–6. Breakeven Analysis Using the Mathematical and Graphical Approach.

The formula for calculating the breakeven cost of the building is equal to:

$$\text{Breakeven building cost} = \frac{\text{annual contribution to income}}{\% \text{ DIRTI 5}}.$$

If the estimated annual contribution to income of the building is $1,800, and DIRTI 5 are assumed to equal 15 percent, then the initial breakeven building cost is equal to $12,000.

There is also a breakeven formula for land purchase. Because of the additional techniques and assumptions involved in evaluating land purchase, it is necessary to put off discussion of this formula until Chapter 12.

SUMMARY

This chapter has presented the various budgets and tools necessary to plan the efficient allocation of farm resources. Once the farm manager knows what resources are available and what they are worth to the farm, the selection of enterprise mix becomes the next important step. In this chapter, the enterprise budget, whole farm budget, and linear programming techniques have been examined as ways to analyze what activities are possible for the farm. The criteria of profitability and technical feasibility have been introduced and considered.

Enterprise budgets are building blocks for more complete farm plans such as the whole farm budget or linear programming analysis. Whole farm plans, unlike enterprise budgets, are not typically constructed each production season. The whole farm plan or budget is a means by which the farmer can assure that the current plan is both feasible and the most profitable. When resources are added to the farm, or when any major change takes place, such as the introduction of new technology, a whole farm budget should be constructed. The advantages and disadvantages of whole farm planning were considered.

Linear programming techniques allow the farm manager to consider simultaneously a large number of different alternatives through the use of computers and to attempt to discover the optimal use of resources. A graphical solution to a linear programming problem was presented.

Once the farm manager has selected the most profitable and feasible set of enterprises to produce through whole farm budgeting, he can use partial budgeting to adjust this allocation in the years between the construction of whole farm plans. Partial budgeting is an approximation of the factor-factor and product-product relationship in economic principles. Only those items which change when a proposed alternative is implemented are considered. Breakeven analysis is the simplest form of partial budgeting.

SAMPLE PROBLEMS

1. Given the following enterprise budgets, calculate the rotation budgets below.

Gross Receipts	$325	$240
TVC	195	101
Gross Margin	130	139

   a. Corn-soybeans rotation
      Gross receipts $_____
      TVC $_____
      Gross Margin $_____
   b. Corn-corn-corn-soybean rotation
      Gross receipts $_____
      TVC $_____
      Gross Margin $_____

2. Given the six enterprise budgets and information provided, construct a whole farm plan using the grid approach. Indicate which outcomes are feasible or infeasible and which one is both feasible and most profitable.

   Information:
      Land: 300 acres of crop land available
      Labor: 350 hours available/month

Assumptions:

a. no hired labor available
b. cropping activity must supply corn needed for livestock (no corn to be purchased)
c. facilities allow 125 litters/year or 1,000 head of feeder to fat hog animals

Enterprise Budgets:

	CS	CCS	CCOMM	*farrow to pig*	*pig to fat hog*	*farrow to finish*
	(acre)	(acre)	(acre)	(litter)	(head)	(litter)
Gross receipts	325	300	220	350	100	750
TVC	165	185	110	250	70	525
Gross margin	160	115	110	100	30	215
Corn supplied	80 bu.	100 bu.	45 bu.	—	—	—
Corn demanded	—	—	—	60 bu.	18 bu.	150 bu.
Labor required:						
April–May	1.7	1.3	1.0	1.5	0.1	2.0
Sept–Oct	2.0	1.4	1.0	1.5	0.1	2.0

3. Given the following linear programming constraints, answer the questions which follow.

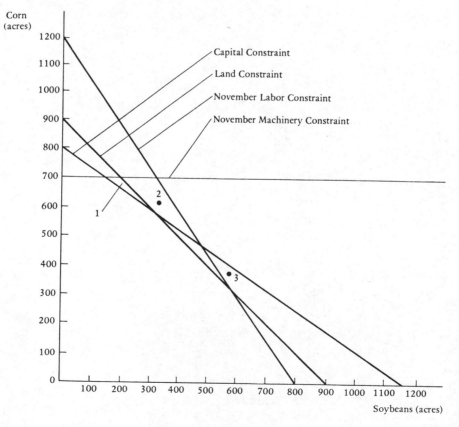

a. List the constraints which are violated by a combination of corn and soybeans at points:

          <u> 1 </u>   <u> 2 </u>   <u> 3 </u>

b. If the gross margins for corn and soybeans from the enterprise budgets were $80 and $100 respectively, what is the best rotation (in terms of acres) that should be employed?

4. You are thinking of buying an electric feed mix mill to grind 410 tons of feed. Current custom charges for grinding are $3.75 a ton. By operating your own mill, you would have to invest $5000 in the electric mix mill, feed house, holding bin and motor. Fixed costs would average 23% of new cost. Electricity, repairs and other variable costs are $.75 per ton. You would also have a net increase in labor input of 30 minutes per ton. You can earn $5.00 per hour in town.

   a. Set up a partial budget to determine whether or not you should buy the mill.
   b. How would your answer change under each of the following conditions:
      1. You had no alternative use for your labor.
      2. You received a ten percent reduction in purchase price through an investment tax credit.
   c. Under the original conditions of the partial budget above, what is the break-even price you should pay for the machine?

5. It is September, and you are concerned about corn yield because late frosts have delayed planting. You have put in $106 worth of seed, chemicals and other preharvest costs. Your land charge is $101 and other fixed costs are $7/acre. Harvest, drying, and hauling costs will total $45/acre.

   a. If you expect a yield of 50 bushels per acre, what is the breakeven price for a bushel of corn?
   b. If you are sure of getting $2.20 per bushel, what is the breakeven yield you must achieve per acre?

SUGGESTED READINGS

Beneke, R. and Winterboer. *Linear Programming Applications to Agriculture.* Ames, Iowa: Iowa State University Press, 1973.

Castle, E. N., M. H. Becker, and F. J. Smith. *Farm Business Management*, second edition, Chapters 9, 11, 12, 13. Reston, Virginia: Reston Publishing Company, Inc., 1972.

Harsh, Stephen B., Larry J. Connor and Gerald Schwab. *Managing the Farm Business*, Chapters 9, 10. Englewood Cliffs, N.J.: Prentice-Hall, Inc., 1981.

Herbst, J. H. *Farm Management, Principles, Budgets, Plans*, fourth revised edition, Chapter 4. Chicago, Il: Stipes Publishing Company, 1980.

Luening, R. A. and W. P. Mortenson. *The Farm Management Handbook*, sixth edition, Chapters 15, 16, 17. Danville, Il: The Interstate Printers and Publishers, Inc., 1972.

Osborn, D. D. and Kenneth Schneeberger. *Modern Agricultural Management*, Chapters 9, 11, 12, 13. Reston, Virginia: Reston Publishing Company, Inc., 1978.

Assessing Financial Feasibility and Measuring Income Performance

It is better to have little, and with it virtue,
than a large income and no right to it.

Proverbs 16:8

Concepts

In this chapter you will come to understand:

1. The budgeting process to evaluate the financial feasibility of the whole farm plan.
2. The two major methods of accounting for farm receipts and expenses.
3. The income statement as a means to measuring the actual income and expense performance of a whole farm plan.

Tools

You will also gain the following skills:

1. How to construct a cash flow budget to estimate the timing of cash inflows and outflows.
2. How to make seasonal and annual adjustments in the whole farm plan to better match the inflows and outflows of cash.
3. How to approximate a line of credit, when necessary, to purchase required inputs.
4. How to account for receipts and expenses under the accrual and cash methods of accounting.
5. How to construct the income statement.

   6. How to distribute adjusted net farm income to the factors of production by two methods to see whether the factors have earned a fair return.

   Chapter 5 presented various means by which the farm manager can plan the most efficient allocation of resources. The whole farm budgeting process helped identify the most profitable and feasible set of production activities. The criterion of technical feasibility located the plan either on or within the production possibilities frontier. However, the discussion of feasibility in whole farm budgeting related to only technical feasibility. That is, production combinations were judged feasible because enough resources were available to accomplish them. Implicit in the production possibilities frontier is that sufficient credit or other liquid capital is available to purchase the necessary resources to accomplish the given alternatives. This chapter will discuss the **financial feasibility** of obtaining the resources necessary to implement the plan.

   Because the returns and expenses in a given farm production process are likely to occur at different times in the production year, the farm manager must be able to decide whether the inflow of cash from productive activities will be sufficient to meet the total expenses of production. Not only must the annual totals be in line, the seasonal timing of the inflows must provide sufficient cash to purchase the inputs necessary when production takes place. When inflows of cash are not timed properly, a line of credit must be established to ensure that funds are available to purchase inputs prior to their use. The **cash flow budget** is a means by which the farm manager can assess the timing of cash inflows and outflows and estimate the line of credit needed (if any) to implement a given production plan.

   Like all other types of budgets, the cash flow budget is calculated in advance of the production year. It is an estimate of all cash receipts and cash expenditures expected during the production season. It can be constructed monthly, bi-monthly, or quarterly. Frequently, for cropping activities which will be produced and harvested over one production season, a quarterly cash flow budget is sufficient. In the case of livestock activities to be produced on a continuous basis with sales and expenses occurring during each month in the production season, a monthly or bi-monthly cash flow budget should be constructed. The cash flow budget includes not only farm income and expense estimates, but also includes nonfarm cash income and family living expenses. The cash flow budget does not estimate net income or profitability, but only the timing of inflows and outflows.

   There are five important reasons to construct a cash flow budget[1] :

   1. Before a cash flow budget can be constructed the farm manager must have a thorough farm plan. Therefore, as a prerequisite to estimating cash inflows and outflows, the farm manager must undertake the whole farm budgeting process. By thoroughly planning the activities to

---

[1] *The following discussion of cash flow budgeting is adapted from: Cash Flow Publication FM-1525, Cooperative Extension Service, Iowa State University Ames, Iowa. Revised, 1980.*

be carried out on the farm, a basis for estimating cash outflows and inflows is available.

2. The cash flow budget tests the farm plan to evaluate whether enough cash income will be generated to meet cash needs. While the cash flow budget does not specifically test profitability, it can project not only whether total cash inflow will be sufficient to meet total cash outflow, but also whether the timing of inflows and outflows will be compatible.

3. When the timing of inflows and outflows is not compatible, the cash flow budget projects the farm operator's need for a line of credit. When cash operating expenses exceed inflows of cash, the cash flow budget indicates when borrowing will be necessary to meet farm expenses. This budget is also a means by which the farm operator can plan the repayment of current, intermediate or long-term loans.

4. A carefully constructed cash flow budget can help the farm manager control finances. By comparing the budget to actual cash flows when they occur, the manager can a) spot developing problems due to an unexpected drop in income or unplanned expenses, and b) spot opportunities to save or invest funds when net cash flow is higher than expected.

5. The cash flow budget is an indispensible aid in communicating credit needs to agricultural lending institutions. If the farm operator can demonstrate the amount of estimated credit needed and further demonstrate the ability to repay these funds, establishing a line of credit becomes much easier.

TWELVE STEPS TO CONSTRUCTING A CASH FLOW BUDGET

Developing a cash flow budget is not difficult if a step-by-step approach is followed. The following guidelines are an example of a step-by-step approach developed by the Iowa State University extension service for estimating cash inflows and outflows over a given production season. The example presented is for a farm producing both livestock and crops.

1. Construct a whole farm plan. As stated, before an estimation of cash inflows and outflows can take place, a plan must be developed. A livestock and crop production plan for the entire year should be on hand before the construction of the cash flow budget is undertaken.

2. Inventory farm resources and products. The farm inventory should be available before a cash flow budget is attempted. The inventory will provide information regarding which inputs must be purchased to accomplish farm goals. It can also provide information regarding livestock currently on hand and the volume of crops stored. Both of these factors will be important in estimating income and expenses. Since the inventory is required to construct the whole farm plan, there should be no problem concerning the availability of inventory information.

3. Estimate feed requirements. The feed requirements necessary to undertake the proposed livestock program should be estimated.

Actual feed records from previous years can be used as an estimate if the livestock program for this year is not significantly different. Adjustments should be made if livestock will only complete part of a feeding program during the budget year. For example, a steer calf placed on feed during November and expected to be sold the following September would have completed about 20 percent of the feeding program by January 1. If the cash flow budget is constructed on a calendar year basis, adjustments for animals which will only complete a portion of the feeding program should be made.

4. Estimate feed and non-feed crop production. The farm operator should estimate the total feed grains to be produced on the farm and the production of all other crops. He should be careful to subtract grain which must be delivered to a landlord under a crop share lease. Once feed supply and requirements are estimated, adjustments in the livestock program under the whole farm plan may be necessary. The amount of grain expected to be on hand at the end of the year should be at least enough to provide a feed supply until the next crop is harvested, unless the operator plans to buy additional feed before the next crop is available. Purchasing feed may be necessary if the livestock enterprise is large in comparison to the farm's feed production capability. Many swine operations in the southern part of the U.S. are of this nature.

5. Estimate livestock sales. An estimate of livestock sales should be based on proposed production and marketing plans.

    a. Begin with livestock on hand and add to that any livestock to be produced during the year. The farm operator should exclude animals to be carried over to the next year or to be used at home. Female animals which will be held back for breeding purposes should also be subtracted, while the sales of cull breeding stock should be added.

    b. Estimate livestock product sales. Items such as milk, eggs, wool, etc., are part of total livestock sales. Careful estimates of these items should be included.

    c. Once the quantity of livestock and livestock products are estimated, estimate appropriate prices. These short-run prices may be different than the planning prices used in the whole farm budget since more information is usually available to use in formulating next year's price expectations compared to forecasting prices over a two to four year period. The price estimates should be based on the best possible forecast available. As you will learn in Chapter 7, it is important to reflect expected seasonal price patterns in these estimates. In the case of hogs, for example, a seasonal price peak usually occurs late in the summer months. During October through December when slaughter levels are high, seasonal prices tend to be the lowest. If the cash flow budget is constructed on a quarterly or bi-monthly basis, the prices used in livestock sales should reflect these seasonal price movements. When estimating prices, it is best to stay on the conservative side. If the projected plan will be profitable under a conservative estimate of price, it can only be better if price expectations are exceeded. Some producers find it helpful to prepare two or three cash flow budgets reflecting different price levels for the different products they sell. This is one way to adjust cash flow budget for price risk.

6. Plan the sales of nonfeed crops and excess feed.
   a. Crops on hand at the beginning of the year should be added to that portion of the crops harvested this year which the farm manager intends to sell.
   b. The farm operator should plan the timing of crop sales and excess feed according to a market strategy (Chapter 9). Since prices for crops are usually lowest during periods of harvest, it may be advantageous, where storage facilities are available, to hold crops for a period of time to avoid this seasonal low.
   c. Once the total volume of nonfeed crops and excess feed has been estimated, a price forecast must be obtained using the same general guidelines as for livestock. The cash flow budget may provide information necessary to revise marketing plans in order to avoid seasonal lows in crop prices. After the total quantities of crops and excess feed have been determined, these are multiplied by expected prices and transferred to the budget form.

7. Estimate other income. Other cash farm income should be included in the cash flow budget. Such income may include government payments, custom work income, income from off-farm work including spouse's income, and any interest, dividends or other returns on off-farm investments. Many times the previous year's additional cash income can be used as a guideline in estimating these other sources of income.

8. Estimate feed and livestock purchases. As mentioned, it may not be possible for the farm to produce sufficient feed to carry out the livestock program. Purchases of corn, supplements, and hay required for livestock production should be included. Livestock purchases include both replacement breeding stock, such as boars, and feeder animals. The full cost of feeder livestock should be included. If credit is necessary for the purchase of feeder livestock, it will be accounted for later in the cash-flow analysis section.

9. Project crop expenses and other farm and family living expenditures.
   a. The previous year's expenditures should serve as a good guide. These should be adjusted for any unusual circumstances or changes in the whole farm plan. Increases in cost due to inflation can be built in. Items to be accounted for here include machinery and equipment repair, gas, fuel, and oil. Family living expenses should include the cost of operating and maintaining the family car, utilities, food expenses, clothing allowance, etc. Non-feed livestock expenses, building repairs, and other farm expenses should also be accounted for. Hired labor

expense can be calculated based on anticipated needs. Fertilizer, seed, insecticide, herbicides, lime and other crop expenses can be estimated from the previous year's expenditures. If cropping plans will be different in the current period, a detailed field-by-field production plan, which should be included in the whole farm budget, can be used to estimate these expenses.

b. Expenses may arise to the farm business as a result of contracts, agreements or legal obligations. These can be estimated directly from the contract terms unless increased rates are expected. Some examples of these items include taxes on real estate and personal property, insurance (such as property and liability insurance), cash rents and life insurance. An estimate of income tax due should also be included along with social security payments. These figures can be estimated from last year's income tax return and adjusted once the current year's tax returns have been completed.

c. The farm manager should use his best judgment, to allocate all expenses of the farm to the appropriate period of the year. Some expenses, such as machine hire, part-time labor, fertilizer, and other crop expenses will mainly occur during certain seasons of the year. Remember to plan to include these for the period during which they will be purchased rather than used. Some expenses will typically be spread out throughout the year but may have definite seasonal peaks. Gas, fuel, oil, machinery and equipment repair and utilities are examples of these. Other expenses may be relatively stable throughout the year, such as the expenses associated with operating the family automobile, and certain livestock and living expenses.

10. Consider capital purchases. The cash flow budget should reflect the anticipated purchase of machinery, equipment, additional breeding stock or land. Major machinery expenses, such as tractor overhaul or new tires, can be included here. The construction or improvement of farm buildings should also be included. If a trade of farm machinery is anticipated, only the cash difference needs to be accounted for. It may be necessary for the farm manager to complete the cash flow budget without considering capital purchases to test whether these expenditures will be feasible. If only a portion of the capital purchase, such as downpayment, will be paid during the current year, only this amount needs to be included. The financed portion of the purchase does not represent a cash flow during the budget period.

11. Summarize debt repayment. At this stage, only those debts which have been acquired prior to the current year should be included. Much of this information can be taken from the net worth statement and can be summarized in the cash flow budget. Calculate interest due at the time the payment will be made. The net worth statement will only reflect interest accrued up to the date of that statement.

12. Determine net cash flow. The previous steps set the stage for determining net cash flow. To do so:
    a. Total the projected income for the year and for each sub-annual period upon which the cash flow budget is constructed. The sum of total inflows for each period should equal the total projected inflow for the year.
    b. Total the projected expenditures for the year and for each sub-annual period. The sum of total cash outflows for each period should equal the projected yearly total cash outflow.
    c. Subtract total expenditures from total income to determine net cash flow. This should be done for each sub-annual period for which the cash flow budget has been constructed.

ANALYZING THE CASH FLOW BUDGET

Remember that the cash flow budget only indicates whether the farm business will produce enough cash income to meet expected cash demands. It does not estimate net income or profit. Net farm income which is a measure of profitability, includes noncash items such as depreciation, changes in crop and livestock inventories, etc., and can be very favorable even when net cash flow is negative. A sample format for a cash flow budget appears in Table 6-1.

The first step in analyzing the cash flow budget is to add cash on hand at the beginning of the period to net cash flow. When total projected net cash flow for the year is negative, the following **annual adjustments** can be made.

1. Sell more current assets (crops and livestock). The sale of current assets can provide the necessary cash to meet expenses but care should be exercised. Reducing inventories may solve a cash flow squeeze this year but can result in more severe problems next year.
2. Finance capital expenditures with credit rather than with cash, or postpone them until another year.
3. Try to reduce the size of intermediate and long-term debt payments by lengthening the repayment period or adding a balloon payment to the last period.
4. Convert short-term debt to intermediate or long-term debt by refinancing. Again, care should be undertaken to avoid violating a financial principle already discussed. Lenders prefer that the debt period associated with a particular asset not be longer than the useful life of the asset. Nevertheless, in the short run it may be necessary to go against this principle.
5. Reduce nonfarm expenditures or increase nonfarm income. Certain nonfarm or family expenditures can be postponed or reduced. The farm manager may also find it necessary to secure off-farm employment, where possible, to supplement cash inflow.

TABLE 6-1. CASH FLOW BUDGET

CASH FLOW BUDGET FOR 19＿＿＿＿   NAME＿＿＿＿＿＿＿＿＿＿＿＿＿   PREPARED＿＿＿＿＿

	Total Projected	Jan.-Feb.	March-April	May-June	July-August	Sept.-Oct.	Nov.-Dec.
INCOME (from all sources)							
Livestock sales	$	$	$	$		$	$
Livestock product sales							
Crop sales—grain (table 4)							
—other							
Government payments							
Machine work income							
Other income							
TOTAL INFLOW	$	$	$	$	$	$	$

162

EXPENDITURES

	$	$	$	$	$	$	$	$
Feed—Commercial (table 5)								
Feed—grain (table 5)								
Livestock purchases								
New purchases—mach.								
other								
Labor								
Mach. & Equip. repair								
Gas, fuel, oil								
Machine hire								
Auto, operating								
Utilities								
Other crop expense								
Livestock expense								
Building repairs								
Taxes—R.E. & P.P.								
Insurance								
Rent								
Other farm expense								
Life insurance								
Living expenses								
Income tax state								
and S.S. federal								
Debt payment due (table 1)								
Interest due (table 1)								
TOTAL OUTFLOW	$	$	$	$	$	$	$	$

Use First Column or Last Year's totals as a Guideline

163

TABLE 6-1. (continued)

NET CASH FLOW (+ or −)

	$	$	$	$	$	$	$

SUMMARY OF CREDIT NEEDS FOR 19___

	Total Projected	Jan.-Feb.	March-April	May-June	July-August	Sept.-Oct.	Nov.-Dec.
CASH TRANSACTIONS							
a) Beginning cash balance							
b) Net cash flow (+ or −)							
c) New borrowing							
d) New loan repayment—principal							
e) —interest							
Cash balance, end of period (a + b + c − d − e)	$	$	$	$	$	$	$
a) Balance, beginning of period							
b) New borrowing							
c) Debt repayment							
Balance, end of period (a + b − c)	$	$	$	$	$	$	$

164

TABLE 6-1a. SUMMARY OF DEBT PAYMENTS DUE THIS YEAR FROM FINANCIAL STATEMENTS

To whom	Principal Payments Due This Year	Interest	Month Due
Current—Notes	$	$	
—Accounts			
TOTAL CURRENTS DUE THIS YEAR	$	$	
Intermediates			
TOTAL INTERMEDIATES DUE THIS YEAR	$	$	
Long Terms			
TOTAL LONG TERMS DUE THIS YEAR	$	$	
TOTAL DUE THIS YEAR	$	$	

TABLE 6–1b. DETERMINING FEED REQUIRED

	No.	Bu. corn equiv*	Total bu. corn equiv*	Lbs. suppl.	Total lbs. suppl.
Dairy cows		117		500	
Beef cows		–		80	
Steer calves fed		64		225	
Yearlings fed		50		155	
Heifer calves fed		45		170	
Litters of pigs, market weight		107		1200	
Feeder pigs purchased 40#		10		100	
TOTAL FEED REQUIRED					

*Total corn equivalent to be harvested

TABLE 6–1c. GRAIN PRODUCTION, PROJECTED YEAR

	Acres	Yld.	Total Prod	Tenant Share
Corn				
Silage				
Oats				

6. Sell intermediate or long-term assets. The projected whole farm plan may have phased out a certain activity which has been undertaken in the past. Any equipment or machinery no longer necessary can be liquidated to provide a positive cash flow. Unused land can also be sold, if necessary to meet expected cash outlays.

Even when the yearly net cash flow is positive, sizeable deficits can occur in certain periods. These will be reflected in the cash flow budget. These deficits stem from the seasonal nature of expenditures in farming and the tendency to sell large quantities of products at one time. However, many types of enterprises, such as dairy, produce a more continuous cash flow. Along with annual adjustments, **seasonal adjustments** can be made when projected net cash flow is positive for the whole year but negative for some period. These include:

1. Shift the timing of some sales. The market strategy for crop and livestock sales can be adjusted to reduce seasonal deficits.

TABLE 6–1d. SUMMARY OF CORN EQUIVALENT REQUIREMENTS

On hand now*	bu.
To be harvested this year* (Table 6–1c)	
TOTAL AVAILABLE	bu.
Corn eqv. required for feed	
Expected on hand, end of year*	
TOTAL ACCOUNTED FOR	bu.
Excess for sale or deficit to be purch.	bu.

*Total corn equivalent to be harvested

TABLE 6–1e. SUMMARY OF FEED PURCHASES ANTICIPATED

Supplement	lbs.	(a) $	per cwt.	= $
Corn*	bu.	(a) $	per bushel	= $

*Includes corn and grain sorghum harvested as grain, plus corn in silage at 5 bushels per ton, plus oats with 2 bushels equal to a bushel of corn.

Table 6–1 and Parts 6–1a through 6–1e were prepared by E. G. Stoneberg, extension economist, and Michael Boehlje, professor of economics. Cooperative Extension Service, Iowa State University, Ames, Iowa 50011.

2. Shift the timing of some expenditures. Many times it is not necessary to purchase and pay for farm inputs until they are actually needed. Many suppliers allow a 30 day period after billing before adding finance charges to purchases. However, this practice is being discontinued due to the high interest charges faced by farm supply firms. Although off-season purchase of inputs at bargain prices can result in savings, purchasing inputs just before their anticipated use can help to adjust the timing of some expenditures.

3. Increase short-term borrowing in periods with negative cash flows and project repayment in periods with positive cash flows. It is important to add the interest charges to these payments.

4. Delay the due date of fixed debt payments to periods of positive net cash flow. Often times the cash flow budget can provide a basis to negotiate the payment of fixed debts to agricultural lenders. The timing of a mortgage payment or a payment for an intermediate asset can be adjusted to occur during periods when cash flows are positive.

Frequently, the farm manager will also want to plan for a minimum cash balance of around $1,000 at the end of each period. This can be accomplished when seasonal net cash flow is negative by including this extra $1,000 in the required borrowings for that period. An alternative solution would be to adjust the sale of crops or livestock to assure that this minimum balance is maintained in each period under consideration.

Some farmers operate with a line of credit from their lender with a maximum borrowing limit. This is probably the most efficient way to take advantage of credit. Instead of borrowing funds in fixed amounts, the farm manager, with the aid of a cash flow budget, can establish a maximum borrowing limit with his banker in advance of the production season. When actual cash outflow exceeds inflow, he need only go to the bank and withdraw the necessary money to pay farm expenses. In this manner, interest charges are held to a minimum, and only the amount necessary to cover the seasonal deficit is borrowed. The cash flow budget can help the farm manager negotiate the maximum borrowing limit under a line of credit.

The cash flow budget should be reviewed from time to time during the production year. Prices and costs may turn out to be different from projected estimates. Production plans may also have changed. Monthly bank statements and cancelled checks are a good source of cash flow information. This information can be used to prepare the cash flow summary statement. This statement can be compared with the original budget to estimate how well it had projected actual cash inflows and outflows. Making this comparison is an important part of the evaluation function and helps the farm manager anticipate changes in cash and credit needs in future periods. Cash flow budgeting is an important part of sound financial management of the business. Developing a cash flow budget for the first time may not be easy but will assure the farm manager that the financial feasibility of the whole farm plan will not be violated.

ASSESSING INCOME

Once the farm manager has decided which mix of enterprises is most profitable and both technically and financially feasible, the next step is to implement those enterprises. When planning the optimal mix of crop and livestock activities through the enterprise and whole farm budgeting process, we calculated an approximation of the income produced. But in a formal sense, the actual flow of income and expenses from the farm that occurs from implementing the proposed activity are summarized on a financial statement known as the **income statement**.

The income statement shows the income and expense performance of a business over time. The period of time upon which an income statement is constructed is usually one production year. However, the income statement can be constructed to correspond to the calendar year, fiscal year, or whatever period of time the farm manager selects to use. Frequently, livestock managers find that preparing the income statement on a bi-monthly basis gives more information on the income performance of the business necessary to analyze management practices. The income statement is the farmer's tool for establishing the tax burden of the farm and analyzing the income efficiency of resource allocation.

From a tax point of view, the Internal Revenue Service requires that the farmer maintain an accurate record of income and expenses. The basic components of a record keeping system necessary to do this were demonstrated in Chapter 4. The IRS has suggested that the system be uncomplicated and consistent over time, yet detailed enough to go beyond a simple estimation of income. To facilitate the construction of the income statement, the farmer must keep accurate records on revenues generated and expenses incurred.

Typically, the farm manager will select one of two accounting systems by which the expense and revenue accounts are to be recorded. Under certain circumstances the Internal Revenue Service may require one of these methods be adopted over the other. The two methods are the **cash method** and the **accrual method** of accounting.

THE CASH METHOD OF ACCOUNTING

The cash method of accounting is by far the most popular and simpler method of recording receipts and expenses, as only the actual flows of cash in and out of the business are recorded. These flows are recorded during the accounting period in which they take place. A sale of crops or livestock is recorded only when the actual cash is received for the goods which have been tendered. Likewise, a purchase of inputs necessary to generate farm income is recorded at the time the payment is made. Both in sales and purchase transactions, the actual exchange of goods may take place at a different time than the exchange of cash. When these times differ, the entry is made when the actual or constructive receipt of cash takes place, not when the goods are transferred.

Most farmers use a single entry system of accounting. Each income and outflow of cash is recorded in the cash journal as it occurs. This single entry system of accounting demonstrated in Chapter 4 is consistent with the cash method of accounting.

There are some peculiarities which should be noted when using the cash method of accounting. Changes in the value of inventory items are not recorded under the cash method of accounting. Any change in the value of inventory items becomes evident only when the item is sold or disposed of. Fixed noncash costs are likewise not recorded under the cash method.

The cash method of accounting is the most flexible method from a tax management point of view since income can be postponed by this method and expenses hastened (or vice versa). By doing so, the farm manager can cause expenses and receipts to occur in different taxable years than when the actual transfer of the physical item takes place. This may be advantageous in evening out the tax burden over time. Further, unsold livestock, crops and other farm products avoid income tax as they pass to the estate of heirs at the death of the farmer.

THE ACCRUAL METHOD

Under the accrual method of accounting, transactions are recorded when the sales or purchase agreement is made, goods are tendered, and consideration demanded, whether or not any cash changes hands. The accrual method of accounting is considered by accountants and business analysts to be the most accurate method for analyzing the farm business. Under the accrual method, income is attributed to the period in which it is earned rather than received. For instance, if a farmer is growing corn, harvests it, and places it in storage on the farm, it is recorded as a receipt even though it has not yet been sold. A tax obligation is incurred on the stored grain. Expenses are likewise accounted for in the period during which they were incurred instead of when they were paid. As this implies, a careful accounting for the value of inventory is required under the accrual method of accounting. Increases and decreases in the value of inventory cause income and expenses to occur even though no actual cash changes hands. Likewise, under the accrual method of accounting, fixed costs and other noncash costs such as depreciation expense are recorded in the accounts. These noncash expenses can be used to reduce the tax burden of the farm under either method but they reduce calculated profits under the accrual method. A new tax-payer has the choice both of accounting method (cash or accrual) and reporting period (calendar year of fiscal year). Permission is required to change these once the original choice has been made. Whichever method is employed, it should be consistently and accurately applied. Frequently, because of the advantages inherent in both systems, many farmers choose to keep a double set of books or a hybrid method involving both cash and accrual concepts when permissible tax practices and good business management practices are divergent.

The type of income statement generated depends upon which system of accounting the farmer selects to use. Because the accrual method of accounting is most complete, the remainder of the discussion in this chapter will assume that the accrual method is employed. The basic components of the income statement under either method of accounting are largely the same, but some important differences will be noted.

CONSTRUCTING THE INCOME STATEMENT

All income statements have three basic parts: a list of farm earnings or revenues, a list of farm expenses, and a calculation of net income. Net income is simply the difference between revenues and expenses.

The actual accounting of all sources of revenue generated by production activity on the farm is the first part of the income statement. Sources of revenue include crop sales, livestock sales, capital sales, and other earnings. These other earnings may be wages received from custom work or interest on farm investments. In the farm revenue accounts, a listing of all crop, livestock, and capital sales, along with all other earnings, should be carefully recorded. Since these have been grouped together in the cash flow summary statement, posting them to the income statement in consolidated form is facilitated. In the accrual income statement, receipts will also include any increase in inventory of livestock, crops or supplies and farm products used in the home. These items are not generally recorded in the cash method income statement. The change in inventory value for crops or livestock can be calculated with the following general formula:

Beginning Inventory + purchases + production – sales – farm use – death loss or spoilage = closing inventory.

The actual outflow of cash and the incurring of debts to produce farm income are recorded as expenses. These typically include crop and livestock production expenses, capital expenses, and noncash expenses. Again, the individual transactions involved in purchasing farm inputs are generally kept in a detailed expense account. These expenses are then consolidated into major categories and placed in the income statement. Fixed expenses may include taxes, insurance, interest or rent. Noncash expenses recorded on the accrual income statement include any decrease in inventory and all depreciation expense. The typical entries in an accrual income statement appear in Table 6–2.

Once the total amount of revenue and expense have been posted to the income statement, net income can be determined. The total of cash and noncash expenses is called total business debits. The total of cash and noncash receipts is called total business credits. Total business credits less total business debits is equal to net farm income. A typical income statement constructed using the accrual method of accounting appears in Table 6–3.

Net farm income measures a return to unpaid factors of production. These unpaid factors of production include family and operator labor, a return to the management function, and a return to equity capital. All other items have been paid a return for their use in the business. Market prices have been charged for operating expenses and fixed cash expenses. Depreciation has been charged for machinery and buildings, and interest has been charged for liability capital used in the business.

Net farm income is similar to net income used for tax purposes. However, because of the capital gains treatment of certain sales and other differences in accounting for expenses and revenues under the tax code, the net income for tax purposes must be separately determined. Gross profits are another measure of income useful in calculating efficiency measures. Gross profits measure the total value of farm-produced crops and livestock (Table 6–2).

TABLE 6-2. ENTRIES IN AN ACCRUAL INCOME STATEMENT

Debits	*Credits*
Cash Expenses	*Cash Income*
Operating	Livestock sales
Livestock expense	Livestock product sales
Crop expense including fertilizer	Crop sales
Machinery and equipment repair	Machine hire
Improvements, repair, maintenance	Misc. receipts (gov't., refunds, dividends, etc.
Fuel, oil, grease	Machinery and improvements, profit or loss
Hired labor	from sale
Farm utilities	
Misc. farm (dues, literature, office, etc.)	*Noncash Income*
	Inventory increase: livestock, crops, supplies
Feed: grain and hay purchased	Farm products used in the home
Livestock purchased	*Total Cash-Flow Farm Income*
Poultry	Cash income plus undepreciated value of
Hogs	machinery, equipment and improvements
Cattle	sold, new loans, and outstanding balance
Other	of accounts
Fixed expenses	
Taxes	*Income Measures*
Insurance	
Interest	*Gross Profit*
Rent	Total business credits minus inventory
	decreases: crops, supplies, livestock, live-
Noncash Expenses	stock purchases; and feed purchases
Depreciation	
Machinery and equipment	*Net Farm Income*
Buildings and improvements	
Inventory decrease: livestock, crops, supplies	Total business credits minus total business
	debits
Total Business Debits	
Cash expenses plus noncash expenses	*Net Cash-Flow Income*
	Total cash farm income minus total cash
Total Cash Expenditures	expenditures
Cash expenses plus cash paid out for capital	
purchases, principal payments on loans,	
and beginning balance of accounts payable	

Source: Reprinted by permission from *Farm Accounting and Business Analysis*, Second Edition by Sidney C. James and Everett Stoneberg, © 1979 by The Iowa State University Press, Ames, Iowa.

An income statement which has been constructed using the accrual method may in any one particular accounting period grossly overestimate or underestimate the true cash income generated by the farm. This is because increases in inventory may occur as crops are produced but not sold. As was pointed out, these increases in inventory are accounted for as receipts although no actual cash has come into the farm business from these stored crops. Likewise, expenses on the accrual

TABLE 6-3.   ACCRUAL INCOME STATEMENT

Accrual Expenses		*Accrual Receipts*	
Operating expenses		Farm production	
Hired labor	$ 8,162	Livestock sales	$111,239
Livestock	2,585	Crop sales	13,434
Crops	13,715		
Fuel and lubricants	1,467	Government payments	0
Machinery repairs	1,841	Capital asset sales gain	75
Building repairs	708	Other	570
Machine hire	3,301		
Utilities (farm)	464	Inventory increases	
Miscellaneous	494	Livestock	3,827
		Crops and supplies	4,100
Feed purchases	15,886		
Livestock purchases	22,597	Value of livestock products	
		used in home	660
Fixed expenses		Total	$133,905
Property taxes	2,460		
Insurance	1,218		
Interest accrued	5,787		
Rent	6,000	Farm accrual income summary	
		Receipts	$133,905
		Expenses	96,012
Depreciation			
Machinery	6,374	Net Farm Income	$37,893
Improvements	2,953		
Inventory decreases			
Livestock	0		
Crops	0		
Total	$96,012		

Source: Reprinted by permission from *Farm Accounting and Business Analysis*, Second Edition by Sidney C. James and Everett Stoneberg, © 1977 by the Iowa State University Press, Ames, Iowa.

income statement may be unrepresentative of the true cash flow expenses in the short run. Large outlays of cash for machinery may take place in one period but must be accounted for through depreciation over several periods on the accrual income statement. These effects, however, tend to balance out over the long run. For this reason, a calculation of net cash flow income is useful to evaluate the actual cash available for meeting production and family living expenses.

DISTRIBUTING NET FARM INCOME TO THE FACTORS OF PRODUCTION

Since net farm income measures the return to the unpaid factors of production, it is useful to distribute it to each of the factors to determine whether or not a fair return has been earned by each. A distribution of net farm income to the factors of production helps the farm manager in discovering whether the most productive use of resources has been attained.

When distributing farm income, it is necessary to account for each of the four major factors of production used in productive activity. Recall that land, labor, capital and management are the broad classifications into which each factor can be placed.

Since net farm income only includes a return to some of these factors, an adjustment should be made before the distribution process begins. This adjustment process involves adding back into net farm income any interest expense which has been subtracted. The resulting figure is called **adjusted net farm income**. This adjustment is necessary because the interest paid on liability capital represents a payment to part of the capital used in the farm production process.

There are two methods by which adjusted net farm income can be distributed to the factors of production. The first method is referred to as the **residual method**. Under the residual method a return is assigned to owned land, operator and other unpaid labor, and non-land capital. The remaining portion (if any) is assumed to have been earned by the management function.

The principle of distributing net farm income to production factors rests on the idea of opportunity costs or returns. In assigning a return to each of the factors of production, the farm manager attempts to estimate the return each of these factors could have received in their next best alternative use. The return to family and operator labor is probably the most straight-forward of the calculations. A return to unpaid family and operator labor can be estimated by multiplying the total number of hours contributed by the operator and family by an opportunity wage rate. The opportunity wage rate should be some approximation of the hourly wage which could have been earned by the operator or family members in the next best nonfarm employment. This figure represents the value of operator and family labor used in generating farm income.

The return to land can be calculated as the return which could have been received had the value of farmland been invested in its next best option. The return to land can be estimated by multiplying the total value of the land resource which is used in farming and is owned by the operator by an opportunity interest rate. However, an adjustment is required. If the land used in farming was liquidated to obtain cash for an alternative investment, the full value of the land would not be received. Sales commission costs and capital gains taxes would cause the value available for investment in alternative options to be less than the ownership value of the land used in farming. Also, only a return to the productive use of the land needs to be accounted for, since the investment return of land accrues independent of production. These adjustments lower the opportunity interest rate to something less than the current market interest rate on long-term investments. Frequently, a figure of four percent is used as the productive opportunity interest rate for land.

The return to capital used in the farm production process is calculated in a manner similar to the land return. Total book value of machinery and equipment used to produce farm income is multiplied by an opportunity interest rate. This figure represents an estimate of the alternative return which could have been received if the farm machinery were liquidated and the net proceeds invested in the next best alternative. Again, the opportunity interest rate must be adjusted for the expense associated with liquidating machinery and the discrepancy which may result between its market price and undepreciated or book value. Usually, a higher opportunity interest rate is used than the one calculated for land. The manager, because of a constantly changing economy, must decide what rate of opportunity interest is appropriate for his area and situation.

Once the return to land, labor and capital have been calculated, these are added together and subtracted from adjusted net farm income to calculate the return to the management function (See Table 6-4). This residual is considered to be an estimate of the amount of adjusted net farm income which was earned by management. Frequently, after a fair return has been assigned to the land, unpaid labor and non-land capital, the sum of these returns will be greater than adjusted net farm income. This situation gives rise to a negative return to management. It should be noted that a negative return to management does not mean that the farm is in a loss situation. It only indicates that the manager's decision to use the value of land, labor and capital in the farming process has resulted in a smaller return than if this value were placed in an alternative investment. As an extreme example, a negative return to management may mean that the operator earned a million dollar profit but could have earned five or ten million dollars if the value of farm inputs had been placed in better alternative investments. A negative return to management may indicate that the farm manager should consider alternative investments. However, the utility or satisfaction associated with farming which does not directly enter these calculations may be a reason to continue farming, even though greater money profits could be earned from another activity (Chapter 12).

The second method for distributing net farm income to the factors of production is known as the **assignment method**. This method is particularly useful when a professional farm management organization is performing the management function. In the assignment method, the return to the management function is equal to the price or cost charged by the management firm for services rendered. This figure can be as high as ten percent of gross earnings. The return to unpaid labor is calculated in the same way as under the residual method. To determine the percentage return earned by capital and land in the farm production process, the sum of the management return and unpaid labor return is subtracted from adjusted net farm income. This figure is then divided by the total

TABLE 6–4. DISTRIBUTING ADJUSTED NET FARM INCOME TO THE FACTORS OF PRODUCTION

Residual Method

Net Farm Income	$37,893	
+ Interest	5,787	
= Adjusted Net Farm Income	$43,680	

Return to Operator Labor	Return to Land	Return to Capital	Return to Management
2,500 hrs.	$475,000	$95,000	$43,680–[A+B+C]
X 3.50/hr.	X .04	X .08	$8,330
$8,750.00	$ 19,000	$ 7,600	
(A)	(B)	(C)	(D)

Assignment Method

Adjusted Net Farm Income $43,680

Return to Operator Labor	Return to Hired Management	Return to Owned Land and Capital
2,500 hrs.	(10% of gross receipts	$\dfrac{\$43,680-[A+B]}{475,000 + 95,000} \times 100 = 3.9\%$
X 3.50/hr.	crop and livestock sales)	
$8,750	= $124,673.00	
(A)	X .10	
	$ 12,467.30	
	(B)	

value of owned land and capital used in the production process. Multiplying this result by 100 gives the percentage return earned by land and capital. Table 6–4 demonstrates the distribution of adjusted net farm income to the factors of production from the accrual income statement of Table 6–3.

SUMMARY

In this chapter, the financial feasibility of a given whole farm plan was tested with the cash flow budget. Implicit in the production possibilities frontier is the means necessary to obtain the resources for producing a given combination of farm output. It is not sufficient to only test for technical feasibility; financial feasibility must also be assessed. Because the returns and expenses associated with farming are likely to occur at different times, the cash flow budget provides a way for the farmer to estimate when cash inflows and outflows are likely to take place. This budget may indicate the necessity of establishing a line of credit to accomplish farm goals.

The cash and accrual methods of accounting for receipts and expenses were discussed. The advantages and disadvantages of each were presented. The income statement was demonstrated as a means by which the farmer can establish the net earnings of a farm and the tax liability associated with it. The income statement and the resulting calculation of net farm income will be different depending upon the method of accounting used by the farm manager.

After net farm income is calculated, a distribution of this income to the unpaid factors of production can take place. When distributing adjusted net farm income, the farm manager is attempting to discover if a fair return was earned by each factor. Two methods for assigning a return to the factors of production were demonstrated. Under the residual method, the returns to land, unpaid labor, and capital were calculated and subtracted from adjusted net farm income. The remaining portion, if any, was assumed to have been earned by the management function. Under the assignment method, which can be used when professional farm management services are employed, the return to management was calculated as the cost of these services. The assignment method then calculates a percentage return to land and capital. In distributing net farm income to the factors of production, the farm manager uses the income statement to analyze whether the best possible use of farm inputs is taking place. This analysis is helpful in determining whether alternative investments (other than farming) should be considered.

TOPICS FOR DISCUSSION

1. What are some of the reasons that cash inflows and cash outflows occur at widely separated times of the year in some agricultural production?
2. What adjustments can be made on a seasonal basis to achieve a positive net cash flow?
3. What adjustments can be made on an annual basis to achieve a positive net cash flow?
4. How does a line of credit reduce total annual interest charges compared to borrowing in fixed sums on an annual basis?

5. Find the items below which do NOT belong on a cash flow budget.

   Your son's tuition payment
   Gas for the family car
   Depreciation expense for the tractor
   Feed costs
   Principal payments to the bank
   Value of farm used livestock
   Inventory increases

SAMPLE PROBLEMS

1. Classify the following items according to the category under which they would appear on the income statement (i.e. debit or credit).

Prepaid insurance premium	Value of farm used livestock
Inventory increases	Gas bill
Inventory decreases	Income taxes paid
Depreciation expense	Accounts receivable
Feed costs	Mortgage payment

   Which items would not belong on an accrual income statement (if any)?

   Which items would not belong on a cash method income statement (if any)?

2. Your farming operation has earned a net farm income of $29,000 for the past year. Total interest paid was $3,550. You have made available 2500 hours of operator labor, own $60,000 worth of machinery and own land valued at $600,000.

   a. Using appropriate assumptions regarding opportunity wage and interest rates, distribute adjusted net farm income to the unpaid factors under the residual method.

   b. Distribute again under the assignment method assuming a management fee of $12,000.

SUGGESTED READINGS

Cash Flow, Publication FM–1525, Cooperative Extension Service, Iowa State University, Ames, Iowa. Revised, 1980.

Farmer's Tax Guide, 1981. Internal Revenue Service, Department of Treasury, Washington, D.C. 1981.

Harsh, S. B., L. J. Connor and G. D. Schwab. *Managing the Farm Business*, Chapter 7. Englewood Cliffs, N.J.: Prentice-Hall, Inc., 1981.

Herbst, J. H. *Farm Management, Principles, Budgets, Plans*, fourth revised edition, Chapters 11 and 13. Champaign, Illinois: Stipes Publishing Company, 1980.

James, S. C. and E. Stoneburg. *Farm Accounting and Business Analysis*, Chapter 2. Ames, Iowa: Iowa State University Press, 1974.

Osburn, D. D., and K. C. Schneeberger. *Modern Agriculture Management*, Chapter 6. Reston, Virginia: Reston Publishing Company, 1978.

Part III

Improving the
Approximation

7

Prices

Every man has his price.

Sir Robert Walpole, 1734

Concepts

In this chapter you will come to understand:

1. Five types of price variation that contribute to risk in the farm business.
2. The difference between price movements in grain (a stock concept) and livestock (a flow concept).
3. The meaning of the cobweb cycle and other commodity cycles.

Tools

You will also gain the following skills:

1. How to measure the profitability of grain storage over differing lengths of time.
2. How to interpret the balance sheet for an agricultural commodity.
3. How to make reasonable price estimates based upon the five types of price variation.

Now that we have explored the **goals** of farm managers, the economic **principles** upon which all decisions should be based, and the **budgets** which allow the farmers to approximate those principles, it is time to consider the factors which lead to departures from expected results when the budgets are implemented. These factors include price variability, other factors which contribute to risk and uncertainty, and government programs (Figure 7–1). Because understanding price movements is so important, this chapter will be devoted entirely to them. Chapters 8 and 9 will deal with the measurement and management of risk and

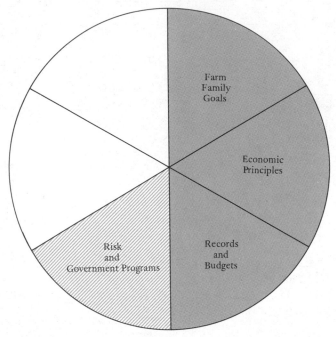

FIGURE 7-1. *The Components of Farm Business Manage-*
ment. Adding risk and government programs.

uncertainty. Chapter 10 will present different types of government
policy and how the farm operator should respond to them.

TYPES OF PRICE VARIATION

In making farm management decisions, the farmer must be aware of five
types of price variation which contribute to business risk in agriculture:

1. Random. These price movements are from unpredictable causes,
such as world petroleum crises and sudden wheat trades to Russia. Random price movements lie in the realm of uncertainty and contribute
generally to income instability in farming. No specific actions can be
taken against them.

2. Business Cycle Movements. You learned in Chapter 1 that farming,
like other industries, is affected by the rest of the economy. Business
cycle movements include the depression of 1929, the recession of late
1979, and the frequent periods of inflationary expansion in the U.S.
economy which were followed by recessionary troughs. These patterns
affect the prices of individual commodities. During an inflation, the
prices of meat and grain will rise. During a recession they will not rise
but may fall (because of the structure of the food industry, they may
be "inflexible downward").

When prices rise, consumers tend to substitute cheaper products for the more preferred expensive ones. For example, they tend to switch to pork and chicken from beef in periods of recession. This type of shift in demand, to be observed in Chapter 10, affects such decisions as whether to feed out steers or put in a new hog confinement facility.

3. Trends. This type of movement refers to a consistent increase or decrease in price over time in a particular commodity, caused by waning or waxing consumer demand (or conceivably, unusually rapid or stagnant technical progress in production). Consumer concern about cholesterol has dramatically reduced the number of eggs consumed per capita per year since the mid-1960s. Recent concern about sulfa residues and nitrites in pork may very well cause a trend away from pork consumption, especially ham and bacon. A trend toward wine consumption in this country has encouraged many new vineyards to be started on the east and west coasts.

4. Commodity Cycles. Especially in livestock production, there is a lag between the farmer's awareness of an improvement or deterioration in price and the measures they can use to take advantage of it. Similarly, there is also a lag between the increase or decrease in consumer price and the change in consumption habits which the consumer is willing to make. Therefore, for many products commodity cycles of rising or falling prices are closely related to the biology of production and the psychology of consumption. For instance, the "beef cycle" has traditionally lasted 9–12 years and the "hog cycle" four years. We shall return to these cycles in more detail toward the end of the chapter.

5. Seasonal Price Movements. This term refers to the characteristic rising and falling pattern of prices which a given commodity will evidence, not between years but between months within a single year. Seasonal movements relate to harvest and storage patterns in grains and the best period for farrowing, lambing, and calving in livestock. However, with more confinement buildings going up every year, the seasonality of meat and milk prices is becoming less apparent.

This chapter concentrates on these last two types of price movement because they are the ones over which the farmer has the most control and the ones which can be contended with most easily in the desire to achieve both favorable and stable prices. We shall discuss seasonal tendencies first, and then come back to learn about commodity cycles.

SEASONAL PATTERNS

Grains such as corn, soybeans, and wheat are produced and harvested at a particular time of the year. When harvested, they are added to the existing stock for next year; therefore, grains are usually referred to as a **stock commodity**. For stock commodities, storage costs and aggregate storage quantities have a great impact on the profitability of storage decisions.

Figure 7-2 shows the characteristic seasonal pattern for corn, based on the price history of ten recent years. Prices tend to be high just before harvest, lowest at harvest, increasing as farmers hold the grain off the market through storage, and then declining as they begin to sell it in the early part of the next year. Note also that the range of year-to-year variations around these expected values (dashed columns) is smallest in December and January and greatest in August and September. This is because of the typical pattern of three-month storage that ends between December and January and the uncertain nature of predicted harvests in August and September. As a result Figure 7-3a shows that for a crop such as corn, an individual year may be quite different from the norm. 1976 and 1979 were very typical, 1977 showed a large drop, and 1980 trended upward. Thus, the farmer can never be absolutely sure of what will happen from one month to the next.

Figure 7-3b shows that there was quite a bit more variability in price movements for soybeans from month to month, especially in the years 1976 and 1977. 1978 and 1979, on the other hand, were fairly stable.

Farm operators who hold their grain off the market through storage should know what the costs and benefits of such a practice are. Table 7-1 shows three and eight-month budgets for storage both on the farm and through such off-farm agencies as local elevators. For the three-

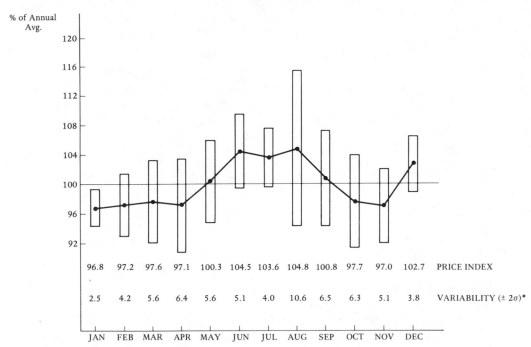

FIGURE 7-2. *Seasonal Price Index: Corn Price Received by Iowa Farmers, 1970–79. (Source: Futrell, Gene, Department of Economics, Iowa State University, Ames, Iowa, Extension Materials.*

Plus or minus two standard deviations around the mean value. Covers 95% of cases.

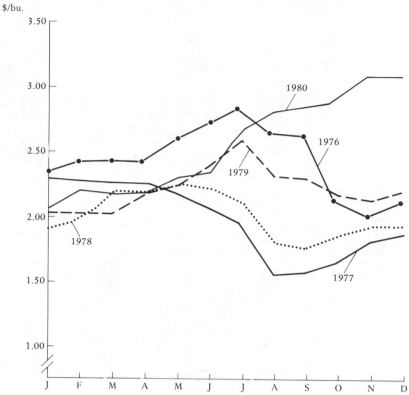

FIGURE 7-3a. *Monthly Price Movements for Corn in Specific Years.*
(Source: Futrell, Gene, Department of Economics, Iowa
State University, Ames, Iowa.)

month period, on farm storage seems to be more expensive at a constant price (marginal revenue). But the storage facilities on the farm may represent fixed costs in the short run. Therefore, on-farm storage (if the facilities are available for use) may actually be less expensive. Assuming that storage-facility costs are fixed, corn storage costs about $0.20 per bushel, so the operator needs to anticipate at least a $0.20 price rise over the three-month period after harvest to make on-farm storage worthwhile. Similarly, a $0.39 rise in price is necessary to make eight-month storage profitable. In this latter period, on-farm storage is less expensive than off-farm regardless of whether facilities are already available or have to be constructed.

It is also important to compare the profitability of these two storage strategies over a long period, say 20 years (Table 7-2). The results show that three-month storage is more profitable than eight-month. Similar patterns hold for both corn and soybeans. With three-month storage of corn, for example, the farm operator stands to make a profit in 75 percent of the years, although the size of his losses when he loses tends to be bigger than when he wins. That is why it is important to compare not just the percentage of years in which gains and losses will occur, but

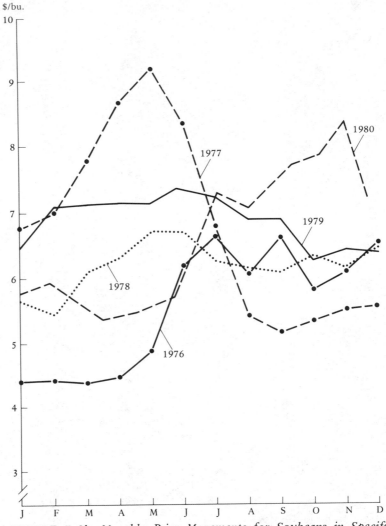

FIGURE 7-3b. *Monthly Price Movements for Soybeans in Specific Years. (Source: Futrell, Gene, Department of Economics, Iowa State University, Ames, Iowa.)*

the total expected magnitudes of each. Table 7-2 shows that three-month storage is not only more likely to lead to a profit, but that over a twenty–year period, total expected profits ($0.65) will outweight total expected losses ($-0.59). Eight-month storage is profitable in 50 percent of the cases and twelve-month storage in only 20 percent of the cases. Thus, it rarely pays to store corn or beans into the next crop year. The only exception is the case of government storage programs, such as nine-month storage through the Commodity Credit Corporation and three-year storage through the Farmer Owned Reserve program, both to be discussed in Chapter 10. The major differences in storage costs between the short run and the long run are interest, quality deterioration and shrink loss.

TABLE 7-1. CORN STORAGE COSTS ($2.80/bushel)[1]

3 Months:	Off-Farm	On-Farm
Interest	9.8	9.8
Extra Shrink	3.8	7.0
Extra Drying	2.5	1.5
Storage	12.0	(11.0) fixed
Extra Handling	0.0	1.8
Total	28.1	(31.1) 20.1

8 Months:		
Interest	26.1	26.1
Extra Shrink	3.8	7.0
Extra Drying	2.5	1.5
Storage	22.0	(11.0) fixed
Extra Handling	0.0	1.8
Quality Deterioration and Shrink Loss (1%)	0.0	2.8
Total	54.4	(50.2) 39.2

Source: Wisner, Robert, Department of Economics, Iowa State University, Ames, Iowa, 1980.

[1]Cost in cents per bushel.

TABLE 7-2. SUMMARY OF STORAGE RESULTS FOR CORN AND SOYBEANS, 1959-1978

	Years Profitable	Avg. Profit/bu. (20 yrs.)	Expected Total Profit	Years Large Loss	Avg. loss/bu.	Expected Total Loss
Corn						
3 month	15	4.3¢	$0.65	2	-29.5¢	$-0.59
8 month	10	6.3¢	$0.63	6	-37.3¢	$-2.24
12 month	4	-	—	5	—	—
Soybeans						
3 month	16	9.0¢	$1.44	2	-85.4¢	$-7.69
8 month	10	47.8¢	$4.78	6	-79.0¢	$-4.74
12 month	6	—	—	4	—	—

Source: Wisner, Robert, Department of Economics, Iowa State University, Ames, Iowa, 1980.

Table 7-3 confirms these seasonal price movements by showing the number of years out of thirty in which the operator can expect an upturn or downturn in prices between two specific months. The data suggest that April and May are particularly likely to show price rises.

In contrast to the stock commodity grains, livestock products are **flow commodities** produced all year long. They have continuous production and utilization processes and there is no storage to speak of. Thus, this major contributor to seasonal price movements in the grains is absent in livestock. Nevertheless, there are other factors which have in the past

TABLE 7-3. PRICE MOVEMENTS OVER PREVIOUS MONTH FOR CORN, IOWA, 1951-80

Month	Years Prices Increased	Average Increase (per bu.)	Years Prices Decreased	Average Decrease (per bu.)	Years Remained the Same
Jan–Feb	13	4.2¢	11	−4.5¢	6
Feb–Mar	13	3.0	9	−5.0	8
Mar–Apr	24	5.2	6	−6.7	0
Apr–May	27	5.3	2	−6.5	1
May–Jun	20	6.1	9	−2.7	1
Jun–Jul	16	7.4	12	−5.7	2
Jul–Aug	12	14.1	17	−9.1	1
Aug–Sep	11	3.5	16	−9.7	3
Sep–Oct	4	9.0	23	−9.9	2
Oct–Nov	8	7.5	18	−10.4	3
Nov–Dec	20	8.2	5	−7.6	4
Dec–Jan	15	6.8	10	−5.8	4

Source: Adapted from Ladd, G., R. Wisner, J. Choi, D. Guenther, and D. Klein, *Use of Seasonal Patterns for Corn Price Forecasting,* Iowa State University Cooperative Extension Service Bulletin M-1203. Ames, Iowa, 1981.

Note: Only 29 years of data were available for October through December. All price changes are measured mid-month to mid-month.

contributed to seasonal patterns in livestock prices (and still do in some foreign countries). For example, Table 7-4 shows data on the percentage of sow farrowings by quarter over the last thirty years. The March-May quarter used to be the major period of farrowing because of the largely portable and open-front operations. Although this period is still the most important, confinement operations have almost equalized the farrowings by quarter and cancelled out seasonality in marketing. Farrowings have always been the lowest in the December-February quarter because of the harsher winter conditions for both the hogs and the pork producer.

A further indicator of seasonal variability is monthly slaughter numbers for market hogs. Figure 7-4 shows that, except for 1979, the years 1977-1980 showed similar seasonal movements in market supply. This supply pattern traces back to the production and farrowing pattern in-

TABLE 7-4. PERCENT SOW FARROWINGS BY QUARTER

	1947-49	1957-59	1967-69	1973-75
Dec–Feb	11	20	20	22
Mar–May	51	37	32	30
Jun–Aug	17	23	24	24
Sep–Nov	21	20	24	24

Source: Futrell, Gene, Department of Economics, Iowa State University, Ames, Iowa.

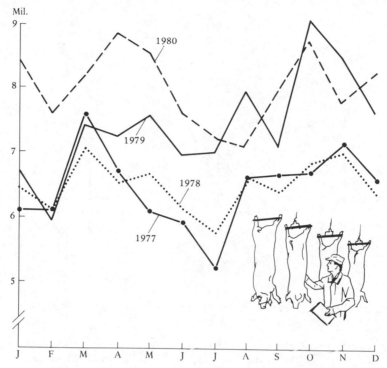

FIGURE 7-4. *Monthly   Hog   Slaughter—Commerical.   (Source:
Futrell, Gene, Department of Economics, Iowa State
University, Ames, Iowa.)*

dicated in Table 7-4, but does not exhibit nearly as much variability as
it would have, say, 25 years ago.

Figure 7-5 illustrates the seasonal pattern of the monthly pork price
index. In comparison with Figure 7-2 for corn, there are higher and
lower departures from the annual average, and significant variability (as
shown by the dashed columns) may occur in almost any month. This is
because our attempt to view one "typical" year actually involves a
statistical misrepresentation of longer term price cycles. As a result,
seasonal livestock price patterns within a given year may depart more
significantly from the norm than grain prices. Figure 7-6 shows that the
actual prices in 1977 were very similar to the normal seasonal index,
with a low point in March-April and a peak in June-July. On the other
hand, the years 1978-1980 were **not** typical, with upward or downward trends throughout the year. In fact, as we shall see, hog prices
tend to follow a four-year cycle. See whether you can trace this cycle
in Figure 7-6 by starting in January of 1977 and working through December of 1980.

As with corn, we can also compute the probability of the number of
years out of ten in which there will be an increase or decrease in hog
prices from one month to the next (Table 7-5). These data reflect the
seasonal patterns you saw earlier (Figure 7-5). Still other studies have

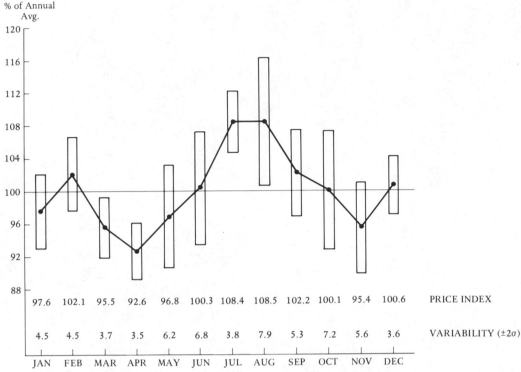

FIGURE 7-5. *Seasonal Price Index: Slaughter Hogs—Iowa-South Minnesota, 200-220 lbs. (U.S. 2-3), 1970-79. (Source: Futrell, Gene, Department of Economics, Iowa State University, Ames, Iowa.)*

investigated the daily price patterns within a given week and found distinct patterns there too. Prices tend to be highest on Wednesday, when buyers become desperate to make a final purchase, and lowest on Friday, when sellers become anxious to avoid paying for weekend housing of unsold animals. Therefore, seasonal, market supply, weekly, and other variations all contribute to the price variability faced by the pork producer.

Seasonality in livestock prices also affects the cattle market. Here, the relative availability of cow-beef, steer-beef, heifers, etc. accounts for the greater stability in seasonal supply and price than in the hog market. Figure 7-7 shows steer prices by month averaged over ten years. There is no strong seasonal movement, but prices tend to be highest in late spring and summer. As with grains and pork, some years are abnormal. Figure 7-8 shows that, among individual years, 1978 was fairly typical, but in 1979 the peak came early. Rather than trying to develop seasonal explanations for these abnormalities, it is better to remember that Figure 7-9 is only a four-year segment of a 9-12 year cattle cycle. You can verify that these four years began on the increasing part of the cattle cycle by starting in January, 1977 and tracing through time to December, 1980.

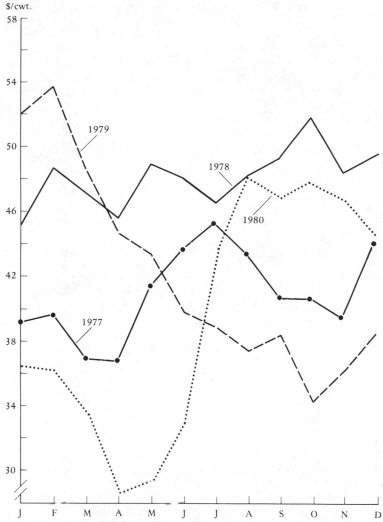

FIGURE 7-6. *Monthly Average Price of Barrows and Gilts—Interior Iowa, U.S. 1-2's, 200–400 lbs. (Source: Futrell, Gene, Department of Economics, Iowa State University, Ames, Iowa.)*

Differences exist among grades of beef as well. For example, except for likely declines in September and October, the direction of choice cattle price changes in any given month is difficult to predict (Table 7-6).

CYCLICAL PATTERNS

Cyclical patterns are much more important in livestock than in grain production. In the past, hog cycles were four years in length. The costs of feed were very stable, and there were typically two years of expan-

TABLE 7-5.   PRICE MOVEMENTS OVER PREVIOUS MONTH FOR HOGS, IOWA, 1967-76

Period	Years Prices Increased	Average Increase (per cwt.)	Years Prices Decreased	Average Decrease (per cwt.)
Jan–Feb	8	$1.25	2	–$.72
Feb–Mar	2	1.45	8	–1.87
Mar–Apr	3	.73	7	–1.49
Apr–May	8	2.23	2	–2.22
May–June	10	1.78	0	—
June–July	9	2.90	1	–2.21
July–Aug	4	3.38	6	–1.97
Aug–Sept	2	1.82	8	–2.95
Sept–Oct	2	2.06	8	–1.93
Oct–Nov.	2	.28	8	–1.79
Nov–Dec	8	1.86	2	–1.07
Dec–Jan	8	1.17	2	– .81

Source: Skadberg, Marvin, Department of Economics, Iowa State University, Ames, Iowa.

Note: All price changes are measured mid-month to mid-month.

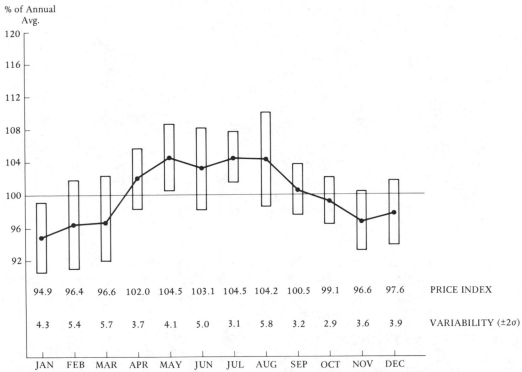

FIGURE 7-7. *Seasonal Price Index: Slaughter Steers—Omaha (Choice Grade), 1970–79.*
(*Source: Futrell, Gene, Department of Economics, Iowa State University, Ames, Iowa.*)

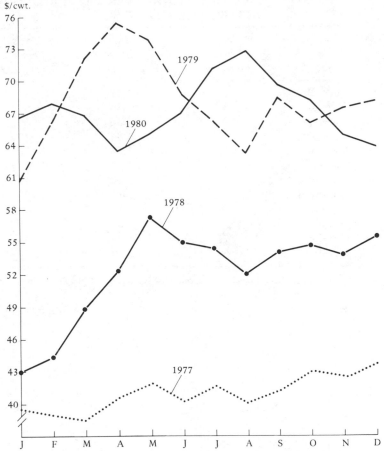

FIGURE 7-8. *Monthly Average Price of Choice Steers—Iowa and South Minnesota. (Source: Futrell, Gene, Department of Economics, Iowa State University, Ames, Iowa.)*

sion followed by two years of contraction. The reason can be shown by studying a diagram of the cobweb cycle (Figure 7-9). Farmers start producing at point **a** when the price is high; so, with a production lag due to holding back gilts, they are finally able to supply as much as they feel is justified at the price (point **b**). But, when **b** units are supplied, consumers will realize after some lag that there is more pork than necessary to support that high price and will only be willing to clear the market at a lower price (at point **c**). Then, producers will realize that the price has dropped, and after a lag for higher slaughter cut back hog numbers to point **d**. But, at the lower numbers, consumers are willing to pay a higher price, and the whole system moves back to point **a** where it began.

The cobweb cycle means that it is very difficult for livestock markets to achieve equilibrium. A further problem facing farm managers has been the breakdown of the four-year hog cycle. During several years

TABLE 7-6. PRICE MOVEMENTS OVER PREVIOUS MONTH FOR CHOICE CATTLE, IOWA, 1967-1976

Period	Years Prices Increased	Average Increase (per cwt.)	Years Prices Decreased	Average Decrease (per cwt.)
Jan–Feb	5	$1.57	5	–$1.20
Feb–Mar	5	1.36	5	–1.71
Mar–Apr	4	4.30	6	– .54
Apr–May	6	1.84	4	– .97
May–June	7	1.23	3	–1.13
June–July	7	1.33	3	–2.42
July–Aug	5	2.00	5	–1.34
Aug–Sept	1	1.13	9	–1.98
Sept–Oct	0	0	10	– .93
Oct–Nov.	3	1.00	7	–1.87
Nov–Dec	7	1.03	3	– .26
Dec–Jan	6	2.70	4	–1.30

Source: Skadberg, Marvin, Department of Economics, Iowa State University, Ames, Iowa.

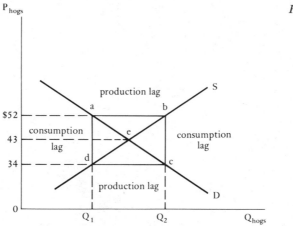

FIGURE 7-9. A Cobweb Cycle for Hogs.

after 1973, the herd-building stage lasted as little as six months and as much as four and a half years. There is some evidence that this unpredictability was induced by variability in corn price. Beginning about 1980, more stable corn prices may start to return the cycle to four years. The hog market is also complicated by the cash grain sale alternative to using one's grain for feed.

Figure 7-10 confirms two aspects of hog production cycles. First, as economic theory would suggest, there is a strong inverse relationship between the quantity supplied to the market and the price received. As a rule of thumb, farm managers feel that a one percent change in supply leads to a two percent change in price. Second, throughout the 1970s, the length of the cycles has indeed been very irregular, making price prediction difficult.

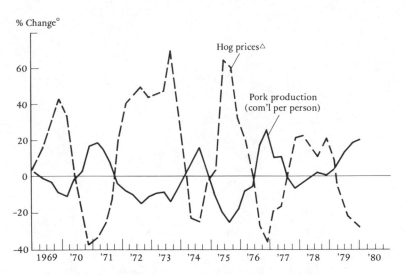

% Change°

60

40

20

0

-20

-40

Hog prices△

Pork production
(com'l per person)

1969 '70 '71 '72 '73 '74 '75 '76 '77 '78 '79 '80

°Percentage change from previous year
△Barrows and gilts, 7 markets

*FIGURE 7–10. Changes in Hog Prices and Pork Production. (Source:
USDA, Neg. ESCS 5550-79(8).*

Beef prices are often in the news, especially when cattle numbers decline and the price of beef to the consumer rises. Figure 7–11 shows
consistent patterns or cycles of 9–12 years each from the period 1928–
38 to 1967–78. This is in addition to the general upward trend in cattle
prices which resulted from rising consumer incomes and a strong preference for beef. During the most recent cycle, in January 1975 there
were 132 million head on feed, but by January 1979 this figure had declined to only 111 million head. Beef supply and prices varied widely as
a result. Still, as indicated, there has been a strong long-term trend upward over a period of years, due to inflation and the growing preference
for beef. Therefore, price analysts have not seen fluctuations in price
corresponding in magnitude to those in supply.

In general, a farm operator should consider getting into cattle raising
when herd numbers seem about to reach their lowest point and there
are good prospects for rising cattle prices during the anticipated sales
period. It is true that herd investment costs (in brood and/or finishing
animals) may also be high as herd numbers decline. Thus, the operator
should budget carefully to determine expected costs and returns. This
budgeting process is made more difficult by great uncertainty about
import quantities. In fact, cattle price is determined by a complex of
factors, as indicated in Table 7–7.

As noted, cyclical movements in grain and other crops are much less
important than seasonal movements. One cyclical factor that does enter
is the 22-year drought cycle, which brought unusually dry weather and
low grain yields to the United States in the 1950s and 1970s. Grain
farmers can shift to sorghum and other drought-tolerant crops and store
corn, wheat, and beans to anticipate these cyclical patterns. Another

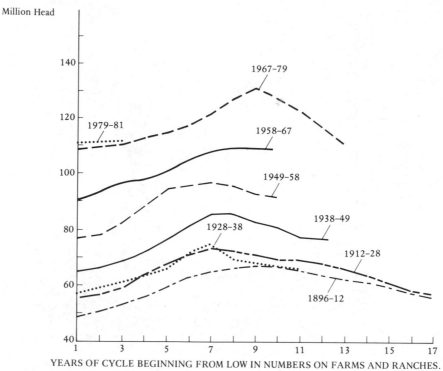

FIGURE 7–11. *Cattle on Farms by Cycles. (Source: Western Livestock Marketing Information Project, 2.100.)*

TABLE 7–7. BEEF MARKET FACTORS (INFLUENCES ON CATTLE PRICE)

Supply Factors

Domestic—fed
       —nonfed
Imports

Demand Factors

Price of competing products
Disposable income
Population growth and composition
Government programs (food stamps, school lunch, etc.)
Consumer preferences
Byproduct values, especially hides
Farm-Retail margin—farm to carcass
            —carcass to retail

---

factor that helps predict price movements for corn and other grains in a more cyclical sense is the balance sheet, which reflects the carryover stocks from one year to the next, the total size of the year's production, and changes in domestic and foreign demand. Table 7–8 compares these figures for four years.

SUMMARY

Five types of price variation contribute to risk in the farm business. These include random, business cycle, trend, commodity cycle, and seasonal price movements. Understanding how and when such movements occur and which ones can be overcome provides an important basis for marketing strategies, production decisions, and risk management. Movements involved in commodity cycles and seasonal price movements are the ones which the farm manager can most easily control.

Seasonal patterns are most obvious in the grain crops, which are a stock commodity. The major decision which affects the grain crops, then, is whether and when to store and, if one stores, for how long a period. Figures on corn and soybeans suggest that three-month storage is more profitable than eight-month storage.

The major patterns which affect livestock commodities, on the other hand, are cyclical price patterns. This is because livestock tends to be a flow rather than a stock commodity. Because it takes a longer time to develop a producing herd, careful analysis of long-term price movements and national herd size is particularly important. The goal is to enter the livestock production cycle when feeder animal numbers are low and price rises imminent, and to liquidate one's herd just before the price

TABLE 7–8. CORN BALANCE SHEET (MILLION BUSHEL)

Supplies:	1977–78	1978–79	Estimated 1979–80	Projected 1980–81
Carryover, Oct. 1	884	1,104	1,286	1,597
Production and imports	6,428	7,088	7,765	6,462
Total	7,312	8,192	9,051	8,059
Utilization:				
Feed	3,709	4,198	4,396	4,050
Food, industrial and seed	551	575	625	695
Exports	1,948	2,133	2,433	2,525
Total	6,208	6,906	7,454	7,270
Carryover, Oct 1	1,104	1,286	1,597	789
U.S. avg. farm price	$2.02	$2.25	$2.43	$3.15–$3.50

Source: Wisner, Robert, Department of Economics, Iowa State University, Ames, Iowa, 1980.

decline after the high side of the price cycle. Still, entry and exit must both be attended by careful budgeting.

TOPICS FOR DISCUSSION

1. Which types of price variation does the farm operator have the most control over? The least?
2. What are the cyclical and seasonal price patterns for the major livestock and crop commodities in your state?
3. How long do farmers in your state typically store grains? Do you think such storage is profitable? In how many years out of ten?
4. Is there a movement toward confinement livestock facilities in your state? What would the effect of such a trend be on the cobweb and other livestock cycles? Explain.

SUGGESTED READINGS

Shepherd, G. *Agricultural Price Analysis*, Fifth edition. Ames, Iowa: Iowa State University Press. 1963.

Tomek, W. and K. Robinson. *Agricultural Product Prices*, Second edition. Ithaca, N.Y.: Cornell University Press, 1972.

8

The Trade-Off Between Risk and Profit

"When in doubt, win the trick."

Hoyle, Twenty-four Rules for Learners.

Concepts

In this chapter you will come to understand:

1. The importance of the conflict between risk and profit in managing the farm business.
2. The definitions of risk, uncertainty, business risk and financial risk.
3. Interpersonal differences in attitudes toward risk.

Tools

You will also gain the following skill:

1. How to measure the trade-off between profit and risk using eight different methods.

You remember from the discussion of objectives in Chapter 1 that the farmer may have a wide range of goals including farm ownership, expansion of the farm, improving his living standard, etc. These goals are often in conflict. For example, Chapter 12 on investment analysis will show that the desire for consumption in the present must be weighed against even higher levels of consumption in the future through present investment.

But an equally important conflict in goals is that between profit maximization and the minimization of income variability. All farmers, though to varying degrees, desire to avoid the risk of poor net farm income so that they will be able to meet their fixed financial obligations in all years and, more important, retain ownership of their farms.

In this chapter, we shall begin by defining risk and uncertainty, showing how the compromise between the risk and profit that is ideal for one farmer may not be ideal for another, and introducing eight ways to assess the trade-off between the two. The collection of information, compilation, will illustrate the second of the five functions of management in any area of farm analysis. Chapter 9 will then treat the planning and implementation stages, showing individual strategies to achieve the compromise between risk and profit that best suits the farm operator's needs.

DEFINITIONS

Frank H. Knight in 1921 distinguished risk from uncertainty. He stated that **risk** occurs when the cultivator is aware of the range of possible outcomes from his decision, as well as the probability associated with each outcome. **Uncertainty**, by contrast, occurs when the probability of the outcomes or even the outcomes themselves are unknown. Typically, uncertainty involves such occasional occurrences as the flooding of a river or the death of a prize bull and can for practical purposes be ignored. But the farmer can collect data on the amount of rainfall and the incidence of limiting temperatures and assign a probability distribution to them; these phenomena fall therefore into the realm of risk.

There are two types of risk: business and financial. **Business risk** involves any factor which affects the level of net farm income. Such risks may be reduced by varying one's production decisions. Six factors contribute to business risk:

1. Yield variation
2. Price variation
3. New technology (and/or lack of knowledge of the production for current technology)
4. Government programs
5. Legal problems
6. Shifts in consumer preferences.

Every enterprise on the farm has different levels of business risk associated with it. For example, data from corn and soybean enterprises may be plotted as in Figure 8-1. Soybeans have higher expected income but also higher variability from year to year. Corn, with lower expected income, also has a lower variability.

Financial risk reflects the "safety" of the firm in a financial sense, particularly as viewed by a potential lender. It involves the proportion of debt and equity in the entire farm firm, and particularly current assets versus current liabilities. Financial risk will be treated in more detail in

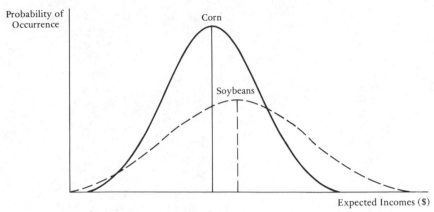

FIGURE 8-1. *Business Risk Illustrated for Corn and Soybeans.*

Chapter 13. Already, however, Chapter 4 has introduced year-to-year variability in the current ratio (current assets/current liabilities—a measure of liquidity), debt/equity ratio (total liabilities to net worth—a measure of solvency), and the net worth to total assets ratio (also a measure of solvency).

DIFFERENCES AMONG OPERATOR ATTITUDES

In assessing the trade-off between risk and profit, there is a wide range of acceptable compromises, each one of which would actually be chosen by some farmers but rejected by others. How can one tell which is best for a given operator? First, it is important to be aware that there are interpersonal differences with regard to risk aversion. The positions of the indifference curves for two farmers in Figure 8-2 differ on the curve of expected income (*E*) versus ± two standard deviations in income (± 2σ). Point **A** might indicate the profit-risk decision of a farmer in a tenant operation with a cash lease and lots of small children. He expects only a $20,000 net farm income, but is assured that in 19 years out of 20 income will not drop below $10,000 ($20,000 – $10,000). Point **B** could represent, for example, the decision a wealthy bachelor farmer with guaranteed outside income. He is indifferent to risk and can withstand years in which he earns an income of –$10,000 ($40,000 – $50,000). By enduring such years, which themselves may have some value in offsetting high nonfarm income, he can expect an average income of a full $40,000. There is also a whole range of operators in between points **A** and **B** on this curve; your own preference probably would lie in this intermediate range. For the first time in this text, one cannot dictate a single point as necessarily being correct for all farmers (although some points will be preferred by all producers). Remember to keep individual producer differences in mind.

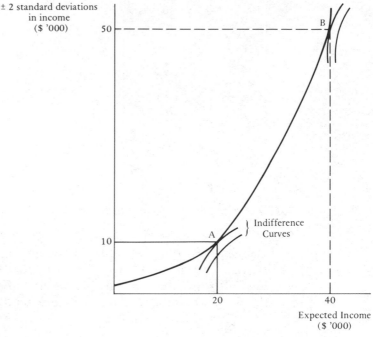

FIGURE 8-2. *Differing Attitudes of Individual Producers Toward Risk and Profit.*

EIGHT WAYS TO ASSESS RISK

There are eight common methods of assessing risk in farm management. These compilation tools are distinct from strategies which help implement the desired level of risk and are listed in the following sections.

Partial Budgeting/Minimum Returns

Let us define specific measures of profit and risk as follows:

Π = rate of return no less than x%, where x typically is two times the interest rate to repay a capital loan and compensate management

risk = average minimum returns in the worst y% of production trials, where y is typically 10 to 33 percent.

This method is often used to study experimental data or data from a group of similar farms where continuous patterns of expectations can be developed. For example, data from corn fertilizer trials conducted in Mexico are given in Table 8-1.

The first three columns are tantamount to an array of partial budgets. The best combination of fertilizers, if one considers only profit maximization, at first glance seems to be 100 kg N and 50 kg P_2O_5. But partial budgeting leaves out two very important considerations: capital scarcity and risk.

TABLE 8-1. THE EFFECT OF DIFFERENT FERTILIZATION
RATES ON NET RETURNS FROM MEXICAN CORN

Fertilization Rate[1]		Net Returns over (8 replications)[2]	Average Worst 25% of Net Returns over Variable Costs (worst 2 replications)[2]
N	P_2O_5		
0	0	20	7.2
50	0	24	9.8
100	0	26	9.2
150	0	23	6.9
0	25	19	7.4
50	25	28	17.1
100	25	28	13.8
150	25	28	10.3
0	50	16	6.0
50	50	27	17.3
100	50	29	15.7
150	50	28	14.8

Note: 1 kg = 2.2 pounds, 1 ha = 2.47 acres.
[1]Rate in kg/ha.
[2]Cost in $/ha.

Source: Adpated from Perrin, R. K., D. L. Winkelmann, E. R. Moscardi and
J. R. Anderson. 1976. *From Agronomic Data to Farm Recommendations.* Information bulletin No. 27, CIMMYT (Mexico 6).

Figure 8–3 shows the importance of capital scarcity. The net returns
over variable costs are plotted on the vertical axis against variable costs
on the horizontal. The numbers in parentheses show the various fertilizer
combinations. Again, the combination which maximizes net returns
over variable costs is the 100 kg N and 50 kg P_2O_5 combination. A
number of inferior points can be immediately eliminated because they
represent additions to variable costs (at e.g. $O\ N - 50\ P_2O_5$) which result in much lower net returns (than at e.g. $50\ N - 25\ P_2O_5$).

Now, recall that the decision rule is not only to maximize net profit;
it is to achieve a rate of return which is acceptable given a possible
operating capital shortage for each leg of investment budgeted. The rate
of return from investments in fertilizer can be calculated as:

$$r = \frac{\text{change in net returns over variable costs (\$)}}{\text{change in variable costs (\$)}},$$

where r = the rate of return. Assume one can borrow capital at 12 percent. According to the decision rule, the minimum acceptable rate of
return in going from one budgeted point to the next must be greater
than or equal to 24 percent. In the jump from $0\ N - 0\ P_2O_5$ to 50
$N - 25\ P_2O_5$, the rate of return on the $700 variable cost per hectare is
114 percent—($2800 – 2000) ÷ 700—far greater than 24 percent.

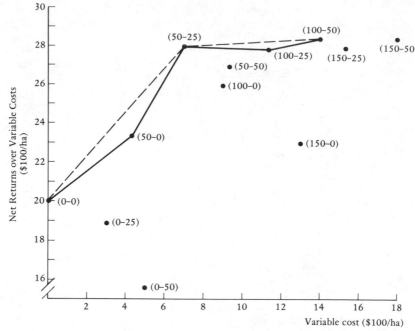

FIGURE 8-3. *Net Returns Curve for Corn Fertilizer Trials in Mexico. (Source: Perrin, R.K., D.L. Winkelmann, E.R. Moscardi, and J.R. Anderson, "From Agronomic Data to Farmer Recommendations," Inf. Bulletin No. 27, CIMMYT (Mexico 6), 1976.)*

But the situation for the next leg is less clear-cut. The rate of return to the second $700 invested is only 14 percent ($100 ÷ $700). For the small-scale producer with limited access to capital, this is probably an unwise move. By contrast, a larger-scale producer with substantially more capital of his own who has exhausted most alternative investment possibilities may have an opportunity cost of capital of only 6–7 percent. He seeks a minimum acceptable return of only 12–14 percent. Again, there is no single level of fertilization which is best for all farmers.

The second problem with partial budgeting is that, in itself, it does not take account of risk. The risk rule in this approach states that one should favor the highest average returns in the worst 10–33 percent of the cases. For the Mexico data, these values are given for the worst 25 percent of cases in the fourth column of Table 8-1. Note that $50 N - 50 P_2O_5$ is the best fertilizer combination if one looks only at the highest average of the worst years. What should a farmer choose? To summarize, there are three candidates so far:

Criterion	Best combination of N and P_2O_5
profit	100–50
capital return	50–25
risk	50–50 (with 50–25 a strong second)

The answer again depends on the farmer. The wealthy farmer might well apply 100 kg N and 50 kg P_2O_5. A small-scale farmer with capital limitations and only fairly sensitive to risk might apply 50 – 25. And a person with extremely high repayment obligations and sensitivity to risk might opt for 50 – 50. There is no single answer.

Before presenting these options to farmers, one should perform sensitivity analysis to see the effect of changes in price on these solutions.

The major disadvantage of the partial budgeting/minimum returns approach is that it generally omits year-to-year variability, largely attributed to weather and other natural factors. So, we now turn to:

Marginal/Probability Analysis

This second approach is founded not so much on budgeting as on economic principles directly. To help account for the role of nature in upsetting the predictability of yields from year to year, two decision criteria are needed:

$$\Pi = \text{use of economic principles to equate } MR \text{ and } MC$$

risk = probability distribution of the random inputs.

Before one can understand the full meaning of the risk criterion, it is necessary to consider what is meant by random versus controlled inputs. Controlled inputs are those which, like herbicide and chemical fertilizer, can be applied in controlled quantities per production unit. Random inputs, like rainfall and temperature are, by contrast, uncontrollable. Random variables interact with and affect controlled variables. Thus, rainfall may affect plant response to nitrogen or the effectiveness of insecticide spraying. The farmer may apply too little nitrogen in a wet year and lose in potential product or too much in a dry year and overspend or even burn the plant. One must therefore find a way to determine a fertilizer plan that optimizes over variable conditions. Table 8–2 shows data from a study of fertilizer on millet in Tennessee. The data embody the four steps involved in this approach:

1. Identify the random input and determine its probability distribution from historical data. Here the random input is the number of drought days per growing season. Historical records showed that the six levels of drought represented the expected range of weather conditions and all had equal likelihood of occurrence over a sixty-year period. Of course, it would have been possible to do a sixty-year-long field experiment with four replications of each level of fertilizer application each year, but this complex experiment would have involved 1,440 plots in total! The principle behind the Tennessee experiment was the same, but note its superiority to waiting 60 years to get data over two or more natural rain cycles.[1]

2. Select a range of the controlled input a farmer might consider. In this case, we are considering nitrogenous fertilizer. Most farmers in the area applied no less than 30 pounds/acre and no more than 180.

---

[1] *As noted in Chapter 7, there is strong evidence that the "drought cycle" lasts approximately 22 years and is controlled largely by sunspots. (Personal communication with Dean L. M. Thompson, Iowa State University.)*

TABLE 8-2. ESTIMATED RETURNS UNDER DIFFERENT COMBINATIONS OF DROUGHT DAYS AND NITROGEN FERTILIZATION IN MILLET AT ASHWOOD, TENNESSEE.

Amount of N Applied[1]	No. of Drought Days[2]						Expected Profit[2]
	73	56	47	38	29	19	
0	0	23	39	53	63	71	42
30	-6	26	42	56	66	75	43
60	-9	30	46	60	71	80	46
90	-7	32	49	64	75	84	50
120	-6	34	51	66	78	87	52
150	-7	35	52	67	79	89	53
180	-8	34	52	67	80	90	53

[1]Amounts in lbs/acre.
[2]Cost in $/acre.

Source: Adapted from a study by Knetsh and Parks, 1958. As quoted in Doll, G., V. J. Rhodes and J. Y. West. *Economics of Agricultural Production, Markets, and Policy,* Richard D. Irwin, Inc., Homewood, Illinois, 1968.

3. Determine for each level of the controlled input the expected profit resulting from the probability distribution of the random input. The numbers in the body of the table all represent net returns for each treatment.

4. Select the amount of the controlled input that maximizes expected profit. The profit maximizing level of N application in this case is 150 pounds/acre. It is true that if the operator hits a bad year, say one with 73 drought days, he will lose $7, whereas, if he had been more cautious and applied 30 pounds/acre, he would have lost only $6. But one should not plan for a disaster. Rather, the farm manager should develop a fertilization program that will give the best results over all types of weather and be stoic about the setbacks when they occur.

We could go on and use sensitivity analysis to be even more certain of these results. But it is important to remember that, using the marginal/probability risk approach, nothing further must be done to take account of risk. Risk, as embodied in the probability distribution of the random input, is already built into our results. Thus, the right-hand column of Table 8-2 could be renamed "Expected Profit Adjusted for Risk."

Payoff Matrices

Table 8-2 is actually a specific application of a third farm management tool commonly used in risky situations: payoff matrices. The two decision criteria for the payoff matrix approach are:

Π = the outcomes (payoffs) of a controllable decision

risk = the weights assigned to uncontrolled events of nature.

Payoff may thus be defined as the benefit the manager receives from a unique combination of a random event or state of nature and a decision alternative over which he has control. To form a payoff matrix, one usually defines the columns at the top of the table as alternative states of nature and the rows at the side of the table as the decision-maker's alternatives (Table 8–3). If all the columns or random events have an equal probability of occurrence, as under the marginal/probability approach, then one simply needs to sum the results across each row to determine the expected returns from any decision a manager might make.

More usually, however, the probabilities of individual events differ. If so, the probability of occurrence should be listed in parentheses under the heading of each column. To determine the expected returns from a decision, one simply multiplies the payoff for each column in that row by the probability weighting and adds the results. Table 8–3 shows an example for hog raising. Under the probabilities shown, the best decision would be to raise farrow to feeder hogs.

Quadratic Programming

So far we have taken examples from both economic principles and partial budgeting to show that these tools may lead to erroneous results unless modified in a way to take account of risk. Even when this is done for the single enterprises presented above, however, there is no guarantee that risk will be reduced for the farm as a whole.

Recall that whole-farm budgeting was a way to look at the optimal combination of products given various management and resource constraints and that linear programming was a convenient way to put these constraints into one format. Thus, linear programming does take into account the wide range of production alternatives on the farm, the amount of land to be devoted to each, and the most efficient allocation of each input across enterprises. Linear programming overcomes the partial nature of the tools we have looked at so far.

But linear programming still has to be adjusted for risk. Why? Because it treats—through parameterization, if at all—the variability of price and yield separately (as do the three approaches above), whereas the manager

TABLE 8–3. PAYOFF MATRIX FOR A HOG RAISING DECISION

	Possible Events Next Six Months				
Possible Decisions	*Market stable (0.45)*	*Hog Cycle Upswing (0.35)*	*Hog Cycle Downswing (0.10)*	*Nitrite Scare (0.10)*	*Expected Value (1.00)*
Farrow-to-finish	6,000	7,000	−4,000	− 6,000	4,150
Farrow-to-feeder	7,000	9,000	−2,000	− 4,000	5,700
Feeder-to-finish	5,000	12,000	−8,000	−10,000	4,650
No hogs	0	0	0	0	0

knows these interact through the market to affect net returns. Even if one builds in mimimum and maximum acreage constraints and conducts price sensitivity analyses, the linear programming solution may be very sensitive to slight changes in price.

Quadratic programming was developed to overcome these shortcomings. It is based upon a matrix of the kind used for linear programming, but it includes as a **constraint** a minimum acceptable level of income for each run of the computer and tries to **minimize** the variance of incomes from the crop and livestock combination it deems optimum. By running this quadratic program many times, economists can actually trace the path of efficient farm plans which minimize variance at each level of income (Figure 8-4).

As with the previous three approaches to the trade-off between risk and profit, there are special measures for these two parameters:

$$\Pi = \text{(parameterized) minimum acceptable net revenue}$$

$$\text{risk} = \text{minimization of solution variance}$$

One example where this technique was used is a fresh market vegetable farm in New York state, where the operators had more than 20 years of historical data on returns. Researchers at Cornell University computed the variance of each enterprise's net return over the years, as well as the covariance (the size and direction of change in net returns of one enterprise given a change in the other) among enterprises. This technique allowed the computer algorithm to select enterprises such that when one (e.g. peppers) went down in net returns, another (e.g. sweet corn) would go up; on balance, the average income would vary

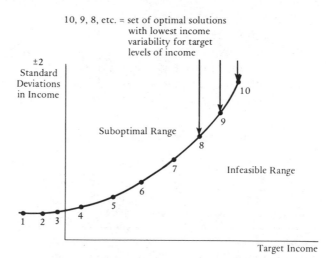

FIGURE 8–4. *Illustration of the Range of Optimal Solutions which Minimize Variance for Target Levels of Income under Quadratic Programming.*

little from year to year. The idea corresponds closely to portfolio analysis in banking or stock exchange investments.

Ten solutions were generated from the data from the New York vegetable farm (Table 8–4). Solution 10 is for the risk-lover and is exactly the same cropping pattern as would be generated by a simple linear programming model without taking into account minimum variance. It shows the maximum income ($54,000) that can be obtained from the farm; but in the worst year, the operator could lose $28,000 and in the best year (whenver that fell!) receive income so high ($137,000) that it would be difficult to shelter from heavy taxation. One of the reasons that many farmers are on the cash accounting basis for income tax purposes is that they know that equalizing the year-to-year variations in apparent taxable income is the best way to minimize tax on a total given income over a number of years. Yet, even with cash accounting and such other tax management tools as income averaging and carrying losses backward and forward (Chapter 16), after-tax earnings from solution 10 may be less than those from solution 9.

Now consider solution 9. Other early lettuces replace part of the specialty crop, early iceberg lettuces; because the two crops have high negative covariance, planting them together reduces income variability. Also, cut flower production, which has a positive correlation with iceberg lettuce, is reduced to enhance this effect. Thus, although the operator gives up $2,000 income, he assures himself of positive income in 19 years out of 20. In fact, he can be sure of being able to repay up to $9.7 thousand of annual debt and living expenses under this system. Overall taxes will be reduced.

Now, suppose the operator has minimum annual cash needs of $10,000 to pay his fixed debt obligations and meet family living expenses. Solution 9 may be cutting it too close. The farmer can retreat to solution 8, where he sacrifices another $1,000 but is assured of meeting the $10,000 with $100 to spare. Even if he does not have these specific payments to make, he may want to select solution 8 purely because of his attitudes toward risk. Once again, there is no set answer which will be best for all operators. Returning to the graphical approach, Figure 8–4 depicts those solutions from 10 at the top of the curve down to 4 before they begin to go negative.

Using a similar approach, researchers applied quadratic programming to irrigated Wyoming farms. Table 8–5 shows that as the program moves away from the profit-maximizing solution 11 (at the right), the range between the highest and lowest incomes decreases with income, as in the New York study. Moreover, the production levels of oats, corn, and alfalfa rise as those of sugar beets and dry beans decline. Quadratic programming could be used to develop a set of such income and risk trade-offs for any farming system.

Quadratic programming provides great insight into the profit-risk trade-off, but it has three major disadvantages:

1. It needs accurate and long-term historical data on costs, yields, and prices.

TABLE 8-4. CROPPING PLANS FOR EFFICIENT NET INCOME–STANDARD DEVIATION SOLUTIONS QUADRATIC PROGRAMMING RESULTS, NEW YORK FARMS

Cropping Plan	1	2	3	4	5	6	7	8	9	10
Crop Activities (acres)										
Cabbage (late)	16.9	52.7	52.7	52.1	52.3	51.6	44.3	39.7	43.3	43.4
Cabbage	–	–	–	4.2	4.3	5.9	8.4	7.0	7.8	7.7
Cauliflower (late)	2.1	14.2	14.2	14.7	14.3	13.4	18.3	24.2	19.9	19.9
Sweet Corn	–	–	–	–	–	45.5	157.5	150.5	144.0	144.0
Iceberg Lettuce (early)	1.1	6.0	8.4	8.9	10.5	15.4	12.5	14.1	15.7	58.4
Other Lettuce (early)	9.7	17.8	21.1	21.4	23.6	32.8	30.7	28.7	26.9	–
Peppers	–	12.2	13.9	15.4	16.6	24.5	43.5	50.5	57.0	57.0
Flowers (crates)	7,184	5,176	4,333	4,226	3,675	1,398	1,974	2,321	2,605	6,058
Expected Net Income (in $'000)	-48	-8	-1	2	7	32	50	51	52	54
Lowest Income ($'000) 19 years out of 20	-51	-20	-15	-13	-10	4	10.2	10.1	9.7	-28
Highest Income (in $'000) 19 years out of 20	-45	5	14	18	25	61	88	93	94	137

Source: How, R. B. and P. B. R. Hazell. *Use of Quadratic Programming in Farm Planning under Uncertainty*, Agricultural Economics Research Paper 250, Cornell University, Ithaca, New York, 1968.

212

TABLE 8-5. CROPPING PLANS FOR EFFICIENT NET INCOME–STANDARD DEVIATION SOLUTIONS, WYOMING FARMS

Cropping Plan	1	2	3	4	5	6	7	8	9	10	11
Crop Activities (acres)											
Oats	25	25	24	22	21	19	17	14	10	4	3
Sugar Beets	50	69	86	88	92	100	107	111	114	114	137
Corn for Grain	150	131	100	106	71	64	60	58	57	93	88
Corn for Silage	25	25	24	24	24	24	23	23	23	23	17
Alfalfa	150	150	148	131	130	115	99	82	64	23	16
Dry Beans	0	0	18	29	62	78	94	112	130	143	139
Steer Sales (head)											
725 lb.	192	210	245	245	248	262	274	277	280	271	180
1100 lb.	116	98	63	63	60	46	34	31	28	37	45
Expected Net Income (in $'000)	72	76	80	84	88	92	96	100	104	108	110
Lowest Income (in $'000) 19 years out of 20	35	34	31	30	27	23	19	15	12	8	-10
Highest Income (in $'000) 19 years out of 20	109	118	129	138	149	161	173	185	196	209	231

Source: Adapted from Zink and Held, 1981.

213

2. It requires the time and training of a skilled programmer and analyst.
3. It requires the expense and accessibility of a computer.

In the past, therefore, the use of this tool for plotting farmers' options has been limited to experimentation in university projects. But U.S. farms may be going in the directions of quadratic programming analysis. Computerized record-keeping associations in many states already have elaborate enterprise returns data. One could augment them with price information of the kind presented in Chapter 7 on prices and forecasting. Moreover, the importance of understanding the risk trade-off has increased over time in the United States as production patterns moved away from lengthy crop rotations and diversity for local self-sufficiency to monocropping and single-enterprise livestock production. Farmers are now much more vulnerable to business risk, and it is important to measure what this change in cropping patterns and cultivation techniques has done to the patterns of net farm income from year to year.

Game Theory

The fifth way of assessing the trade-off between profit and risk on farms is called game theory. It compares the levels and variability of benefits derived from adopting different decision-making criteria as the farmer plays games with nature. It resembles marginal/probability analysis in that it seeks to take some account of random inputs in the production process. There is a whole range of possible criteria, but we shall consider only five. These can be set out to reflect the two parameters, risk and profit:

Π = maximax (the highest single return in any year)

risk = a. maximin (highest among the worst returns from each plan)

= b. modified maximin (highest among the worst 10–33 percent of returns from each plan)

= c. Bayes or Laplace (rank all equally or according to a probability distribution, if known)

= d. Hurwicz-alpha (assign a weight to both the highest and the lowest return, depending on subjective attitude toward risk

The maximax criterion is for the reckless optimist. It is for the type of operator who likes to strut down to the local elevator or country store and brag that he cleared $47,300 this year. But what can he say when his fellow farm operators ask him about his income in the other years? The problem is that this type of approach only looks at the best and ignores the range of all possible outcomes.

The maximin criterion is almost as bad. It is designed for the excessively paranoid producer or for one who would consider it a disaster to slip below a certain floor income in any year. As it concentrates only on the worst possible outcome it fails, like the maximax, to consider the whole range of possible outcomes.

The modified maximin is an improvement for most operators. It recognizes extreme caution with regard to risk but also takes account of a few more years of outcome (two or three out of ten). As you remember, this criterion is part of the partial budgeting/minimum returns approach, so it is useful.

The Bayes or Laplace criterion involves assigning a probability distribution to each outcome. Often there is an element of uncertainty: the farm operator does not know what the distribution of outcomes is, although he knows the outcomes. For want of a better method, he ranks them equally. This has the advantage of taking all the outcomes into account. However, assigning equal weights is arbitrary. To get a better idea of the actual distribution, extension economists often recommend a modification of this technique: go visit an experienced farmer in the neighborhood, jot down a few possible yields on a piece of paper, and ask him to estimate in how many years out of twenty he would expect to see them. In his mind, or perhaps only in his subconscious, such a farmer already uses a probability distribution to make decisions.

Finally, there is an amusing origin for the Hurwicz-alpha criterion. A Mathematician named Hurwicz was appalled that anyone would base important economic decisions on the type of game theory criteria described above. He decided to discredit the lot by coming up with one that was so ludicrous that everyone would reject game theory altogether. He assigned a Greek symbol (α) to the weight of the worst return and 1 minus that symbol for the weight of the best return. The weight assigned to α reflected the relative importance the farmer in question gave to poor years versus good years. Hurwicz wrote his suggestion as a tongue-in-cheek article. But everyone who read it thought it was wonderful. The whole scheme backfired as people began using his criterion in preference to the others. Far from discrediting game theory, Hurwicz actually was partly responsible for its continued use in economic decision making.

To gain practice in applying these criteria, let us work through an example. Selected data from the Mexican corn study presented earlier can be set out in a game theory decision matrix (Table 8–6). The data points represent extreme values obtained from eight replications of each fertilizer program. (These values are not listed in Table 8–1.) The upper section of the table shows the net benefit per hectare from two programs under dry and wet years. The bottom section indicates the better fertilizer program under each game theory criterion. Make sure you understand how the values of A and B were determined for each criterion. Game theory can give a comparative view of the best production program under many criteria. It helps improve the farm manager's insights. But as a comparative method, it is perhaps the least practical for assessing the trade-off between risk and profit.

TABLE 8-6.   GAME THEORY PAYOFF MATRIX FOR MEXICAN CORN

	Dry Year	*Wet Year*
Program A (50–25)	$4,000	$1,820
Program B (100–50)	$1,500	$4,380

Game Theory Criterion	*Value A*	*Value B*	*Better Fertilizer Program*
Maximax	$4,000	$4,380	B
Maximin	$1,820	$1,500	A
Bayes/LaPlace (equal prob. wet or dry)	$2,910	$2,940	B
Hurwicz-alpha ($\alpha = 0.70$)	$2,474	$2,364	A
Hurwicz-alpha ($\alpha = 0.40$)	$3,128	$3,228	B

Source: Adapted from Perrin, R. K., D. L. Winkelmann, E. R. Moscardi, and J. R. Anderson, *From Agronomic Data to Farm Recommendations*, Information Bulletin No. 27, CIMMYT (Mexico 6), 1976.

Decision Trees

A sixth analytical tool for decision-making under risk is called decision tree analysis. The farm manager simply traces through all the possible events that might occur after each decision to determine the probability-weighted outcome of a sequence of decisions. The sequence with the highest probability-weighted outcome is selected. Even though in any given year this sequence may not yield the highest net return, over a series of years it promises to do so. Thus, as with the other approaches to risk analysis, two decision criteria are needed:

Π = the probability-weighted outcome of a sequence of decisons

risk = the probability weights assigned to natural or market events

Decision trees are particularly useful when the possible outcomes from each decision are numerous, the individual decisions in a sequence are sequentially dependent, and the probabilities of each event can be estimated with some accuracy.

Economists have identified two approaches in which decision trees may be used (Anderson et al., 1977). These are the **utility function approach** and the **certainty equivalent approach**. The utility function approach assumes that the farm operator has complete knowledge of his utility function. All final outcomes are expressed in utils (a measure of utility) rather than dollars. Utility values are even difficult for economists to determine, so it would be most unlikely that a farm operator could express relative utility with enough precision to make this method workable.

Therefore, for most practical farm management analysis, the certainty equivalent approach is used. The farm operator draws the decision process as a tree with decision points or nodes represented by squares. From each square radiates a set of rays representing the individual decisions at that node. These squares are analogous to the controlled variables of the marginal/probability and payoff matrix approaches. Random variables are denoted by change or event nodes, which are drawn as circles along the rays representing each decision. Figure 8–5 shows a sample decision tree for a cattle purchase problem. The operator can elect to buy 1000, 1200, or 1600 head at the decision square *A*. But for each choice, the random event of rainfall will determine the quality of the pasture growing season. Thus three rays radiate from the rainfall events *B*, *C*, and *D*. Note that the probabilities for each of these pasture quality levels are the same regardless of how many head the operator purchases. However, since other returns and expenses are quite different, the net payoffs from each event also differ. These are shown to the right of each probability estimate. Once these outcomes and probabilities for each event are known, then the farm operator can work backwards from the right and replace the multitude of net payoffs for each event node with a single certainty equivalent. This certainty equivalent is simply the weighted average net payoff determined by multiplying each payoff by its probability and summing at each event node. The righthand-

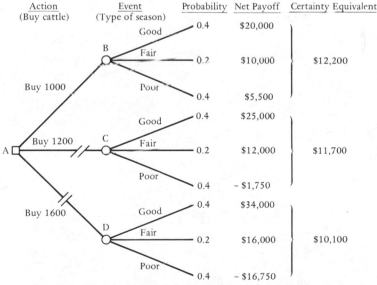

FIGURE 8–5. *Decision Tree for Certainty, Equivalent Analysis of the Cattle Purchase Decision Problem. Reprinted by permission from Agricultural Decision Analysis, by Jock R. Anderson, John L. Sillon and J. Brian Hardaker © 1977 by the Iowa State University Press.*

most column in Figure 8–5 shows that the preferred node is B because its weighted average net payoff ($12,200) is higher than for the nodes C and D. One can then put two lines (//) through rays C and D as they come out of A to simplify the tree at that point. This process is called "averaging out and folding back." Once the manager is finished with the tree, the optimal path through the decision process will be clearly visible.

The decision tree pictured in Figure 8–5 is much simpler than most. Trees can become quite complex as the manager improves his understanding of the decision process. Indeed, the very act of drawing a decision tree diagram is a great aid in understanding the details of a decision. One additional aspect that should be considered in this brief introduction, however, is the option of purchasing more information. This option E, can be added to Figure 8–5 to produce Figure 8–6. The purchased information tells which forecast (1, 2, or 3) is being reported at a given time. The probability of Forecast 1 is 0.4; Forecast 2, 0.36; and Forecast 3, 0.24. These forecasts change the original or **prior probabilities** of good, fair, and poor pasture growing conditions to other values, called **posterior probabilities** such as 0.7, 0.2, and 0.1 for Fore-

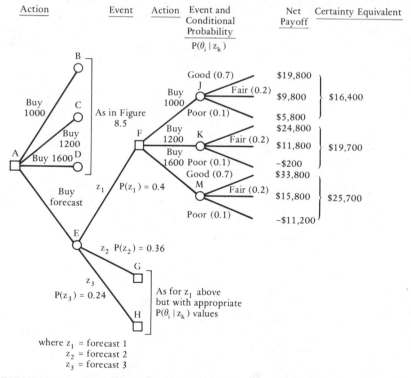

FIGURE 8–6. *Extension of Figure 8–5 to Encompass Possible Purchase of Additional Information. Reprinted by permission from Agricultural Decision Analysis, by Jock R. Anderson, John L. Sillon and J. Brian Hardaker © 1977 by the Iowa State University Press.*

cast 1. The net payoffs are also reduced by the cost of buying the information, in this case $200. If the certainty equivalent of branch E is greater than the maximum of B, C, or D then extra information should be purchased. The number of head to be raised should then be determined by the particular forecast received.

Stochastic Dominance

The seventh approach to measuring the relative risk and profits of alternative courses of action is called stochastic dominance. This is a fancy term often heard in farm management which simply refers to a method for determining the action which has the best probability distribution. The criteria for this approach may be laid out as follows:

$$\Pi = \text{expected net returns}$$

$$\text{risk} = \text{the cumulative probability distribution of returns}$$

The data collection format for this approach is straightforward. One inquires of farmers, farm management experts, or historical data the probabilities of achieving a specific outcome. Columns 2, 3, and 4, respectively in Table 8–7 show estimates of the percentage of likelihood of occurrence, cumulative probability and net return per acre for selected corn and soybean prices. To compute cumulative probabilities in column 3, we simply add the individual percentage probabilities for prices up to that point. For example, by $2.70, there is a 90 percent probability that corn price will be at that level or lower. Given the expected yield

TABLE 8–7. PRICE AND NET RETURNS PROBABILITIES FOR CORN AND SOYBEANS

Price ($/bu)	Percent Occurrence	Cumulative Probability	Net Returns per Acre ($)[1]
Corn			
2.75	10	1.00	30
2.70	40	.90	24
2.65	40	.50	18
2.50	5	.10	0
2.40	5	.05	−12
Soybeans			
7.90	20	1.00	27
7.80	30	.80	23
7.60	35	.50	16
7.40	15	.15	9
7.20	0	0	2

[1]For corn, yields are assumed to equal 120 bushels per acre and total costs $300 per acre. For soybeans, yields are assumed to be 35 bushels per acre and total costs $250 per acre.

of 120 bushels per acre and an estimated total cost per acre of $300, these cumulative probabilities can be transferred from simple prices (column 1) to net return values (column 4). Figure 8–7 shows how the net returns (horizontal axis) may be plotted against the cumulative probabilities (vertical axis). When the curves for corn and beans are compared, it becomes clear that soybeans dominate corn at lower price levels while corn dominates soybeans at higher levels. It is then up to the individual producer to determine whether he is more concerned with meeting basic cash needs or with aiming at maximum net farm income. In many cases, this approach will indicate that one alternative dominates the other throughout. Therefore, extension agents and farm managers will not have to make recommendations based upon risk aversion.

Farm management researchers in Georgia used the stochastic dominance approach to compare the risk and returns of four levels of pest control intensity. Level 1 involved $723 worth of chemicals, Level 4 only $30. Figure 8–8 shows that Level 4 (the most environmentally benign) completely dominated higher levels of control in terms of high returns and low risk and should be preferred by all producers regardless of their risk preferences. Interestingly, the Georgia researchers also compared stochastic dominance with quadratic programming analysis and determined that quadratic programming could not select between

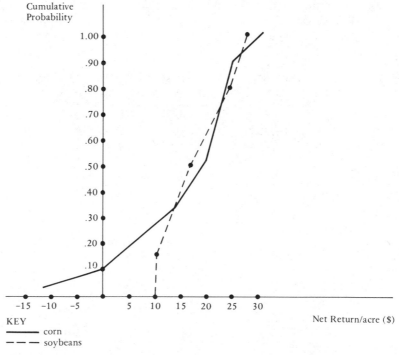

FIGURE 8–7. Stochastic Dominance Curves for Corn and Soybeans.

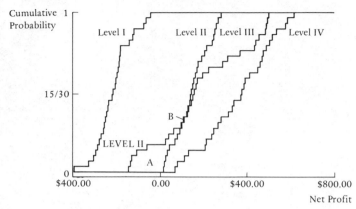

FIGURE 8-8. *Cumulative Probability Functions for Net Profits of Four Multiple-Crop Integrated Pest Management Systems, Georgia. (Source: Messer, W.N., B.V. Tew, and J.E. Epperson, "An Economic Examination of an Integrated Pest Management Production System with a Contrast between E-V and Stochastic Dominance analysis," Southern Journal of Agricultural Economics, 1981.)*

Level 2 and Level 4. Stochastic dominance was used to break the tie. These results suggest that using more than one method of risk analysis is advisable.

Composite Approach

Each of the preceding seven methods has advantages and disadvantages. An eighth and final approach that a farmer could use (with the aid of a moderately-priced calculator) involves the following criteria:

Π = expected returns (E)

risk = coefficient of variation (σ/E) in expected returns, prices and yields,
   or
   range or expected profit in 19 years out of 20 ($E \pm 2\sigma$)
   or
   worst 20 percent of cases
   or
   lowest return in any year
   or
   Hurwicz-alpha value ($\alpha = 0.65$)

Table 8-8 shows how the above criteria can be computed from historical data on corn and soybean yields and prices for a western Iowa farm. The expected value of net returns (E) is simply the average returns in constant dollars from ten years of pursuing each cropping pattern. E for

TABLE 8–8. COMPUTING MEASURES OF RISK AND RETURNS[1]

	Corn			Soybeans			Net Returns[3]			
Year	Yield bu/acre	Price $/bu[2]	Cash Production Costs $/acre[2]	Yield bu/acre	Price $/bu[2]	Cash Production Costs $/acre[2]	C	C-C-C-SB-SB	C-C-SB-SB-SB	SB
1970	50	2.60	55	20.5	5.07	39	75	70.98	68.96	64.94
1971	79	2.84	58	21.0	5.32	41	166.36	128.10	108.98	70.72
1972	100	2.17	62	36.0	6.95	43	155	175.88	186.32	207.20
1973	80	2.23	60	37.0	7.63	43	118.4	166.76	190.95	239.31
1974	66	2.26	68	22.7	5.03	45	81.16	76.37	73.97	69.18
1975	90	3.19	77	37.6	6.27	53	210.10	199.16	193.69	182.75
1976	58	2.68	76	25.8	6.05	53	79.44	88.9	93.63	103.09
1977	50	2.33	76	21.0	5.28	55	40.5	46.65	49.73	55.88
1978	130	2.20	79	38.0	6.93	56	207	207.14	207.20	207.34
1979	105	2.27	85	35.0	6.72	62	153.35	161.29	165.26	173.2
Expected value (E)	80.8	2.48		29.46	6.125		128.63	132.12	133.87	137.36
Standard deviation (σ)	26.03	.340		7.83	.922		58.62	57.85	60.62	71.23
Coefficient of variation	.322	.137		.266	.150		.456	.438	.453	.518
Upper limit on returns (E + 2σ)							245.87	247.82	255.11	279.82
Lower limit on returns (E − 2σ)							11.39	16.42	12.63	−5.1
Highest return in any year							210.10	207.14	207.20	239.31
Average returns in worst two years							57.75	58.82	59.34	60.41
Lowest return in any year							40.5	46.65	49.73	55.88
Hurwicz-alpha value (α = 0.65)							99.86	102.82	104.84	120.08
(assign a weight of .35 to highest return and a weight of .65 to lowest return)										

[1]Data from Iowa Crop and Livestock Reporting Service, Crawford County Extension Office and one farm.
[2]Prices adjusted to constant 1978 dollars.
[3]Net returns in $/acre.

each column is computed by taking the values from individual years (x_i) and dividing through by the number of observations (n), in this case 10. Thus, we may write the formula:

$$E = \frac{\Sigma x_i}{n} .$$

The standard deviation (σ) above is computed either through the following formula:

$$\sigma = \sqrt{\frac{\Sigma x_i^2 - \frac{(\Sigma x_i)^2}{n}}{n - 1}}$$

or by using a routine on a medium-priced calculator. As we shall see in the next chapter, the standard deviation is, in and of itself, worthless as a guide to measuring comparative risk unless divided by the mean (E) to yield the coefficient variation $(C.V.)$:

$$C.V. = \sigma/E$$

This by contrast, is a very effective measure of comparative variability of the yields, prices, or net returns from two or more enterprises.

The computation of the other items in the table is self-evident. Two points warrant mention, however. First, a combination of two crops will often have lower risk than either one grown individually. Second, it is important to compare the coefficients of variation of yield and price. If the former is higher, this will alert the farm manager to the possibility of improving his management through production strategies (new varieties, rotations, or cultivation techniques). If the latter is higher, he should spend his scarce management time improving his knowledge of such marketing strategies as hedging, spreading marketing dates, and so on. It is to these strategies that we will turn in the next chapter.

SUMMARY

Uncertainty refers to a lack of information while risk refers to a knowledge of the probability distributions of known outcomes but not exactly when these outcomes will occur.

Farmers differ in their willingness to accept higher risk in return for higher expected income. Therefore, it is important to measure the risk-returns trade-off curve to allow for selection of the combination consonant with the business and financial goals of the farm operation.

There are eight ways to measure the risk-returns trade-off. These are: partial budgeting/minimum returns, marginal/probability analysis, payoff matrices, quadratic programming, game theory, decision trees, stochastic dominance, and the composite approach. Quadratic programming requires the greatest amount of data and computational sophistication, while the stochastic dominance approach probably requires the least. If data are available, the composite approach gives a good set of criteria from the other seven approaches to guide the farm decision-maker.

Whichever approach is used, it is important to make an effort to measure the risk consequences of a given farm plan. Otherwise, the operator's control of his operation and even its financial viability may be severely jeopardized.

TOPICS FOR DISCUSSION

1. How does your household feel about risk and profit? Where do you lie on the curve of Figure 8–2? What choices are you aware of that have been based upon these considerations?

2. Of the six elements which contribute to business risk, which do you think were most important in 1920? Which are most important now? Which will be most important in the year 2000? Give examples.

3. Describe the relative profitability and risk of the two major crop commodities in your state. What factors account for the differences you note?

4. Which of the eight ways to assess risk and profit do you plan to use most? Explain the role of ease of application and data availability in your choice. Which aspects of the approach are most appealing?

5. Similarly, which of the eight ways to assess risk and profit do you plan to use least? Why? Which aspects are least appealing?

SAMPLE PROBLEMS

1. As a result of high death losses due to exposure in the last three winters, an experiment was done to provide northern cattlemen with information on how much feed to give their steers during the cold winter months. The number of below-zero days which had an equal probability of occurrence were determined and the cattle kept in controlled atmosphere lots to calculate their average daily gain. The results were as follows:

Units of feed fed	Number of below zero days		
	83	59	35
	Net returns ($/hd.) over feed		
100	−15	6	27
200	−26	9	38
300	−19	14	44
400	−13	18	48
500	−17	18	50

  a. How many units of feed give the greatest expected profit per head? How much profit?
  b. If each unit of feed cost $0.15 and you had an opportunity rate of return on your capital of 20%, how many units of fced would you feed?
  c. What is the name of the approach used here to measure the conflict between risk and profit?
  d. What further steps, if any, do we need in order to take account of risk?

2. To adjust yor whole farm plan for risk, you have compiled estimates for the past five years on the profitability of the top 3 feasible plans.

	NET RETURNS (in ($'000)		
	Crop-and-Livestock Plan		
Year	1	2	3
1976	7	35	8
1977	23	6	14
1978	15	21	12
1979	16	19	10
1980	12	4	17
Expected value (E):			
Standard deviation (σ):	5.86	12.59	3.49
Coefficient of variation (C.V.):			

  a. Fill in the values for E and $C.V.$
  b. Which crop-and-livestock plan has the highest expected returns?
  c. Which crop-and-livestock plan has the highest risk? Which item tells you?
  d. Define and indicate which plan is best under the following:

Criterion	Definition	Best Plan
Maximax		
Maximin		
Bayes (equal probability)		
Hurwicz-alpha ($a = 0.8$)		

e. Given all the above information, explain clearly which of the three plans you would choose if you were
1. A well-established farmer with large off-farm income.
2. A 22-year old tenant farmer with two small children.

3. In comparing fertilizer strategies, you compute the following payoff matrix:

Fertilizer strategies	Possible Events in Nature				
	Drought (0.20)	Low rain (0.35)	Medium rain (0.10)	High rain (0.35)	Expected Value (1.00)
	Net Farm Income ($)				
Low fertilizer	8000	9000	11,000	12,000	
Medium fertilizer	7000	8000	15,000	17,000	
High fertilizer	6000	7000	14,000	20,000	

a. Calculate the expected value for each strategy.
b. Which strategy should the farm operator choose?_____
c. Why?
d. Does the payoff matrix take account of capital scarcity?
_____

e. Name (another/the) approach to measuring profit vs. risk that takes account of capital scarcity? _____
How specifically does this other approach include capital scarcity?
f. How might the fertilization strategy in **3b.** change if capital scarcity were included?
g. Fill in the decision tree below with the data from the payoff matrix and demonstrate that both approaches yield the same results:

Certainty Equivalent

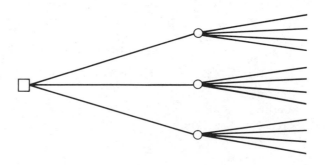

SUGGESTED READINGS

Anderson J., J. Dillon, and J. Hardaker. *Agricultural Decision Analysis.* Ames, Iowa: Iowa State University Press, 1977.

Kay, R. D. *Farm Management: Planning, Control and Implementation*, Chapter 18. New York: McGraw-Hill Book Company, 1981.

Levin R. and C. Kirkpatrick. *Quantitative Approaches to Management*, Chapter 5. New York: McGraw-Hill Book Company, 1978.

Zink R. and L. Held. *Optimum Enterprise Combinations and Risk-return Tradeoffs for Irrigated Farms: Torrington-Wheatland Area.* University of Wyoming Agricultural Experiment Station, Laramie. 1981.

9

Strategies to Reduce Risk in Production and Marketing

I knew a man who, failing as a farmer,
Burned down his farmhouse for the fire insurance.

Robert Frost, New Hampshire

Concepts

In this chapter you will come to understand:

1. The difference between the measurement of risk and strategies to reduce it.
2. The differences among production, marketing, and financial strategies to reduce risk.

Tools

You will also gain the following skills:

1. How to reduce production risk through five distinct strategies.
2. How to reduce marketing risk through five distinct strategies.

Chapter 8 presented risk from the point of view of the compilation function of management. The objective of that chapter was to help you enumerate various combinations of profit and risk in farm decision-making.

Now you are ready to go on to the planning and implementation stages of risk management. Whereas before we were discussing methods of analysis, now we will address strategies for action. To do this, assume that the farm operator has determined the desired levels of risk and profit and would still like to reduce risk to achieve a desired balance.

There are three general types of strategy which the manager can employ (Table 9-1). Each has a particular area of business or financial risk where it is most effective. Although we shall study them separately, in practice farm managers use different combinations to achieve their desired goals. Of the three types of strategy (production, marketing, and financial), we shall investigate the first two in this chapter and the last when we study capital borrowing in Chapter 13.

PRODUCTION STRATEGIES

Production strategies for risk management address four of the six aspects of business risk: variability in yield, technology, legal situation and government programs. Certainly, if the composite approach to risk measurement indicates that yield variability is more significant than price variability (and that the operator should therefore devote his limited time to improving his knowledge of yields and technology), production strategies are the kind to study. They do not treat as strongly the other aspects of business risk: variability in price and consumer preferences.

Five types of production strategies to reduce risk are: selection of stable enterprises, diversification, flexibility, insurance, and the use of other miscellaneous measures. Production strategies address the risk involved in the physical data necessary for economic decisions (Chapter 1).

TABLE 9-1.   AN OVERVIEW OF RISK-REDUCTION STRATEGIES

Strategy	*Type of Reduced Risk*
Production	Yield, technology, legal, government programs
Select stable enterprises	
Diversify	
Maintain flexibility	
Acquire insurance	
Other	
Marketing	Price, change in consumer preferences
Spread sales	
Hedge on futures market	
Forward-price inputs	
Contract sales	
Vertically integrate	
Financial	Liquidity, solvency
Maintain high proportion of self-liquidating loans	
Maintain credit reserve	
Maintain high current ratio	
Use loans of sufficient maturity	

Selection of Stable Enterprises

Stable enterprises are those that result in stable returns from one production period to the next. Table 9-2 shows average returns per $100 feed fed in four livestock enterprises: farrow-to-finish hogs in confinement, feeding yearling steers in an open lot, raising feeder calves, and managing a Grade-A dairy operation. In the period 1965-1974, dairy and hog enterprises had almost equally favorable mean returns, with the feeder calf option very close behind. One might conclude that selecting the feeder calf enterprise would be acceptable, depending upon the operator's management skills.

But just looking at average or expected returns is not sufficient. You also have to compare the variability of returns from the four enterprises if you are at all concerned with risk. Table 9-2 shows that fed cattle and feeder calves had the largest variability in 1965-1974, up to twice that of dairy, as shown in the variance figures. Now, the risk averse operator might think he prefers dairy overwhelmingly.

The mean and variance are often given in extension and research bulletins. But these are **not** sufficient to make an adequate decision as to

TABLE 9-2.   ANNUAL VALUES, MEANS, VARIANCES, AND
COEFFICIENTS OF VARIATION OF RETURNS
PER $100 FEED FED FOR IOWA LIVESTOCK,
1965-1974

| | Livestock Enterprise[1] | | | |
Year	Hogs	Fed Cattle	Feeder Calves	Dairy
1965	$189	$154	$136	$160
1966	198	123	153	168
1967	173	128	160	182
1968	180	151	171	199
1969	209	152	180	197
1970	186	119	184	200
1971	151	150	182	194
1972	218	172	203	206
1973	193	139	239	184
1974	140	63	131	145
Mean	183	135	175	184
Variance	583.67	905.44	1,025.33	399.00
C.V.	.13	.22	.18	.11

Source: Stoneberg, E. G. *Livestock Returns per $100 Feed Fed*, Unpublished data, Cooperative Extension Service, Iowa State University, Ames, Iowa.

[1]Livestock enterprises are defined as:
  hogs—farrow to finish, sow and two litters in confinement
  fed cattle—feeding yearling steers in an open lot
  feeder calves—beef cow with calf sold
  dairy—Grade A dairy operation

risk. Recall from Chapter 8 that in order to arrive at a consistent measure of variability one must take the variance (σ^2), find its square root (σ), which is called the standard deviation, and then divide through by the mean to find the coefficient of variation:

$$C.V. = \sigma/E.$$

This is the only sure way of finding the enterprise with the lowest comparative variability. Therefore, the farm operator should be careful when reading bulletins and articles in farm magazines—they rarely go that final step to compute the coefficient of variation.

In this example, a choice based upon either the total variances or coefficients of variation leads to the same conclusion: dairy has the lowest variability. But Table 9–3 shows an example that compares the expected returns and variance from corn and beans. For the period 1965–1974 corn gave two and one-half times the returns per acre that soybeans did. The huge variance figure for corn also suggests it was more variable and that the operator was forced to choose between high risk and high returns. But if one goes on to compute the coefficient of variation for the two crops, corn has a value of only 1.6 compared with almost twice that for soybeans. Corn would seem preferable to all producers, regardless of their level of risk aversion.

TABLE 9–3. ANNUAL VALUES, MEANS, VARIANCES, AND COEFFICIENTS OF VARIATION OF NET RETURNS TO IOWA CORN AND SOYBEANS, 1965–1974

	Corn	Soybeans
1965	$2.59	$ .13
1966	12.19	7.77
1967	4.03	-3.81
1968	-4.26	-4.08
1969	7.48	-8.06
1970	-4.52	-11.40
1971	15.26	-.88
1972	93.66	1.53
1973	62.66	1.53
1974	12.06	26.90
Mean	20.12	8.48
Variance	1032.96	686.33
C.V.	1.60	3.09

Source: Department of Economics extension staff, Iowa State University, Ames, Iowa.

[1]Net return is the return to management per acre after all costs have been deducted from gross income.

Diversification

Diversification to combat risk refers to combining those enterprises with negative or low positive correlations among or between their incomes. It is often possible to add two enterprises such as corn and soybeans to form mixed rotations that reduce the overall variability of crop income in comparison with raising, say, continuous corn. Alternatively, we could combine dairy with hogs, or even some more variable crop or livestock enterprise, to achieve the level of risk, profit and labor intensity that best suits the livestock manager. Table 9–4 lists the simple statistical correlations[1] in returns between pairs of the enterprises given in Tables 9–2 and 9–3. In searching for combinations whose correlations are negative or low positive, the overall winner is dairy and soybeans, although combining soybeans with fed cattle or hogs is also a good strategy. These combinations have negative correlations. Those combinations which have a low positive correlation (between 0 and 0.3) are indicated by a superscript 1 in Table 9–4. Among these, hogs and dairy are a good combination, with feeder calves and dairy, fed cattle and dairy, and dairy and corn also favorable. Thus, combining dairy or soybeans with other enterprises is a good way to achieve low variability in income.

TABLE 9–4.   CORRELATIONS IN INCOME BETWEEN IOWA LIVESTOCK AND CROP ENTERPRISES, 1965–1974

Enterprise Combination	Correlation Coefficient
Hogs and fed cattle	.658
Hogs and feeder calves	.442
Hogs and dairy	.179[1]
Hogs and corn	.445
Hogs and soybeans	-.079
Fed cattle and feeder calves	.472
Fed cattle and dairy	.254[1]
Fed cattle and corn	.352
Fed cattle and soybeans	-.237
Feeder calves and dairy	.248[1]
Feeder calves and corn	.648
Feeder calves and soybeans	.476
Dairy and corn	.266[1]
Dairy and soybeans	-.309
Corn and soybeans	.481

Source: Department of Economics extension staff, Iowa State University, Ames, Iowa.

[1]Combinations with low positive correlations.

[1] *Human capital management will be treated in greater detail in Chapter 11.*

There are other possible choices in situations where other management concerns like seasonality of labor use, conservation, and management expertise are factors. Risk is not the only factor that competes with or affects profit in the operator's decisions. As an example of the other management factors to consider there might be supplementarity on the production possibility frontier between two enterprises (Table 2–13, Chapter 2). Thus, up to a certain point, the operator may increase profit while reducing risk.

The same principles may apply to crops. Table 9–5 gives annual yield correlation coefficients for corn, soybeans, oats, sorghum, wheat and hay. All of these crops react differently to differences in weather and environmental conditions (those random inputs you learned about in Chapter 8). The lack of negative correlations shows that all crops are affected in poor years. But oats and soybeans, and sorghum and hay, have the lowest positive correlations. Meanwhile, corn and soybeans have the highest correlation. Thus, the traditional corn-oats-meadow-meadow-meadow rotation (COMMM) practiced in many states was, among other things, a way to reduce risk through yield variability. Combined with considerations of soil and energy conservation, risk reduction may constitute another argument for returning to more diversified rotations as operators endeavor to produce in an age of resource and environmental limits as U.S. agriculture approaches the year 2000. Indeed, quadratic programming might determine that a COMMM rotation, though perhaps not the most profitable production pattern, would be very acceptable for moderately risk-averse farmers on fields with slopes of five percent or more.

TABLE 9-5. ANNUAL YIELD CORRELATION COEFFICIENTS FOR IOWA CROPS, 1959-1975

	Corn Yield	Soybean Yield	Oats Yield	Sorghum Yield	Wheat Yield	Hay Yield
Corn Yield	1.0000	0.8333	0.5966	0.6971	0.7193	0.7647
Soybean Yield		1.0000	0.4963	0.6530	0.8597	0.7999
Oats Yield			1.0000	0.5459	0.6682	0.6627
Sorghum Yield				1.0000	0.6412	0.4289
Wheat Yield					1.0000	0.7669
Hay Yield						1.0000

Source: Miranowski, John A. "Annual Yield and Price Correlation Coefficients for Iowa," Sydney James, Peter Calkins and John Miranowski, eds., *Selected Readings in Farm Management*. Iowa State Bookstore Press, Ames, Iowa, 1980.

Flexibility

Flexibility involves planning the farm operation so that at any time the operator has freedom to change enterprises or production techniques. There are four types of flexibility:

1. Cost Flexibility.   The operator may seek to maintain a high proportion of variable total costs. For example, among Midwest crop enterprises, corn is more flexible than soybeans because it has only about 52 percent fixed costs versus 62 percent for beans. Among livestock enterprises, the choice depends upon the type of operation—open or confinement. Recent data suggest, however, that swine feeding on the average is more flexible, with 91 percent of total costs variable, versus about 83 percent for cattle feeding, as an example.

Another way to achieve cost flexibility is to rent or hire resources rather than buy, use custom operators for harvest or spraying, and lease rather than purchase land or machinery. Put another way, the objective is to push down the DIRTI 5 and DITIS and to raise the variable costs as a proportion of total costs (Figure 9-1). This strategy has the effect of raising the shutdown point from S to S' in the short run, which frees resources for investment in other enterprises on the farm. (The long-run breakeven point b should remain approximately the same.)

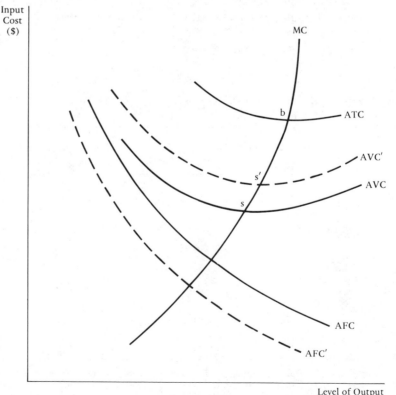

FIGURE 9-1. *The Effects of Increasing Cost Flexibility.*

2. Facility Flexibility. The operator may construct buildings and facilities that have multiple uses or can be readily converted from one use to another. For example, a machine shed may be made into a confinement livestock facility. Related to this principle is the choice by many operators of building an open or semi-confinement building in the short run before they become committed to a given livestock enterprise. Although they may achieve lower feed efficiency, such operators avoid putting in permanent facilities before they are willing to accept the risk-returns balance associated with a given enterprise.

3. Product Flexibility. This concept refers to the practice of maintaining a choice on how the product will be used or the form in which it will be sold. For example, beef-herd managers can sell offspring as feeder calves, stockers, or fed cattle. Grain-livestock producers have the choice of marketing grain or livestock. Raising storable commodities like corn also provides flexibility in the disposition of output once it is produced.

4. Time Flexibility. The operator may try to produce short-term commodities to enhance the spread between variable and fixed costs shown in Figure 9–1. For example, beef requires more time to produce than broilers. An orchard takes more time and is more inflexible than annual row crops. At the same time, you should know that maintaining flexibility has two drawbacks: 1) more choices from an increased number of alternatives may lead to more mistakes (if less costly ones) and 2) a highly flexible farm business is generally less efficient in terms of resource productivity than one that is inflexible (on the other hand, the operator can correct resource misallocations more quickly).

Insurance

The above approaches to managing production risk can be considered as three kinds of informal insurance. Formal insurance, by contrast, consists of five general types.

1. Life. Life insurance includes:
   a. Term insurance. This is good for young persons, but provides no buildup of cash value. Thus, it serves as debt insurance for the surviving spouse should the insured die before mortgages and other large purchases arc paid off.
   b. Whole or ordinary life. Under this type of insurance, premiums are payable until death but do build up value. Protection can be bought more economically than with endowment or limited payment insurance.
   c. Limited payment life. This type of insurance emphasizes savings. Although the premium is paid up after 20 to 30 years, the policy holder gets less protection.
   d. Endowment policies. These stress savings and afford very little protection per dollar spent. What is more, even though they allow

for a sum of money to be paid to survivors, no insurance program can solve discontinuity of management problems associated with intergenerational transfer of the farm.

As one progresses from term insurance (a) to endowment policies (d) the amount of savings increases as the amount of protection decreases. With a long-term rate of inflation estimated at 13 percent, the advisability of using limited payment and long-run endowment life insurance policies has decreased. They are not the most efficient mechanism for saving because one usually earns only a three to four percent return even with endowment policies. Term insurance is to be highly recommended, espeically as the potential loss of real and nonreal capital assets increases with their value over time for young operators starting out in farming.

2. Health and Disability: In case the operator or farm spouse gets ill and misses a production season it is important that the operation be compensated, not only for medical costs but also for hiring costs of replacement labor. Generous coverage is therefore recommended. It is also wise to make provisions beforehand for back-up management while the operator is indisposed.

3. Liability: If the farmer has a hired man, he will want to be covered if the man is fatally injured or hospitalized briefly through a farm accident. This is why farm operators need to participate in workmen's compensation programs and other forms of liability insurance.

4. Property: This insurance covers damage to or destruction of buildings, machinery, livestock, and stored grain. It can protect sources of wealth against natural disasters and accidents.

5. Crop: This is of two kinds—all risk and hail. No independent private insurance company could handle all-risk insurance for farmers because farming is too risky and the amount of compensation in a given year could be too large (unless the program was huge and nationwide). Thus, the farm operator has to depend upon the federal government for all-risk coverage. Even then, until recently federal insurance was not available on all enterprises or even on crops in all areas.

Hail insurance is more specialized, offering coverage for only hail and wind damage. The insurance company divides its territory up (and the bigger the better) into agronomic zones and establishes the probability of hail occurrences for each county. In other words, they transform uncertainty regarding the random input hail into risk. Then they estimate the likely severity of damage and hence the payments they will have to make in each county and add 10–15 percent for assessor's salaries and expenses and another 10–15 percent for profit to compute the rate they charge the customer. There is a consensus among some farm managers that having both forms of insurance is a good thing, particularly because hail insurance, unlike all-risks crop insurance, may be purchased on only part of the farm and up to a few weeks before harvest.

Before 1982, farmers participating in government set-aside programs were also eligible for disaster payments from the government. Now, instead, the federal government has broadened the all-risk crop insurance program to many more crops and areas of the country. As always, the operator is allowed to select the level of yield and price coverage preferred. Yet, the premiums will be more progressive. The hope is that less-specialized, small-scale producers will get by with the proportionately lower-cost yield and price combinations which could equal, say, 30 percent coverage of expected returns while large-scale wheat operators, for example, will have the desire and ability to pay for combinations that will allow for 65 percent coverage. This all-risk insurance has replaced the government's disaster payment and previous all-risk insurance programs and, in all probability, much traditional hail insurance as well. It is administered in many cases through existing hail and crop insurance companies, so that these companies suffer no adverse affects.

The federal all-risk crop insurance program is designed to cover three levels of long-term average yields in a given locale: 50, 65, and 75 percent. Thus, the program is in no way a compensation for poor management: the first twenty-five percent shortfall in yield must be borne by the operator himself. There are also three levels of price coverage per bushel among which the operator can select, the highest of which is usually about 90 percent of a favorable market price. These three levels of price and yield result in nine price-yield combinations available to the operator, each with a different insurance premium per acre (Table 9-6). To decide which level best suits his risk-returns needs the farmer must develop and use payoff matrices (Chapter 8) in six steps:

1. Determine the variable costs of production for the crop
2. Estimate the expected selling price per bushel
3. Select a range of possible yields and assign probability weights to them
4. Compute returns over variable costs with and without insurance for:
   a. three alternative price elections
   b. three alternative guaranteed yield levels

TABLE 9-6. LEVELS OF YIELD GUARANTEE, PRICE PER BUSHEL AND PER-ACRE PREMIUMS FOR CORN IN A GIVEN LOCALE

Proportion of Normal Yield Level	Bushel guarantee per acre	Available Prices per Bushel		
		$1.70	*$2.10*	*$2.70*
75%	71 bu.	$6.00	$7.00	$9.50
65%	62 bu.	$3.90	$4.60	$6.20
50%	48 bu.	$2.50	$2.90	$3.90

Note: Long-term average yield = 95 bushels/acre in this locale.

5. Construct a payoff matrix for each of the nine alternatives, as in Table 9-7
6. Compare the matrices to determine whether or not to take out federal all-risk crop insurance, and what level gives the highest expected monetary value.

The risk-neutral operator could stop after these six steps. However, operators with more concern about borrowing ability and financial obligations would also want to compute what percent of the time they could expect income to be above a certain critical level. Such "safety first" calculations might alter their preferred level of coverage.

Other Production Strategies

In addition to these four major production strategies to reduce business risk, farm operators should be aware of three other measures. First, the farm operator may invest in **yield-stabilizing technology** to permit continued operation of the farm in the event of adverse weather conditions. Such investments include the planting of pest- or drought-resistant varieties of crops, the installation of irrigation facilities and drainage pipe, the construction of confinement facilities for poultry and other livestock, and the purchase of excess machinery capacity (Chapter 14). The annual ownership and/or operating costs of such facilities may be offset by the increased stability of returns from one year to the next.

TABLE 9-7. PAYOFF MATRIX FOR NO INSURANCE AND FOR ALL-RISK FEDERAL CROP INSURANCE WITH A 22 BUSHEL GUARANTEE AT $2.50 PER BUSHEL, 500 ACRE WHEAT FARM

Events Yields	Subjective Probabilities of Yields	Actions	
		No Insurance	*FCI @ $2.50 and 22 bu.*
		Payoffs (ROVC's)[1]	
5	.01	$-16,500	$ 3,600
10	.02	-8,000	5,850
15	.03	500	8,100
20	.05	9,000	10,350
25	.10	17,500	16,350
30	.25	26,000	24,850
35	.25	34,500	33,350
40	.15	43,000	41,850
45	.10	51,500	50,350
50	.04	60,000	58,850
Expected monetary value =		$ 31,015	$30,765

Source: Casler, George L., "Should I Purchase Crop Insurance?" Working paper, Department of Agricultural Economics, Cornell University, Ithaca, New York, undated.

[1]ROVC = returns over variable costs.

Second, the farm operator may **stockpile inputs** to protect against periods of low market supply and/or excessive price rises. Such inputs include fuel, fertilizer, and other agricultural chemicals, as well as such livestock feedstuffs as hay and grain. Accompanying investments in storage facilities for these production inputs may be economically justified if they allow the farm operation to weather periods of short input supply.

Third, the farm manager should **build a knowledge base**. The more information and education the operator has at his disposal, the more quickly and accurately he will be able to cope with the price, yield, and other types of variability of a given year. Subscriptions to farm publications and newspapers, attendance of extension short courses and meetings, investments in a home computer, and even pursuit of a higher educational degree are all examples of valuable investments in the operator's human capital.[1]

MARKETING STRATEGIES

Marketing strategies for risk management address the remaining two of the six aspects of business risk: variability in prices of inputs and outputs and variability in consumer preferences. There are five types of marketing strategy: the spreading of sales, hedging, input forward pricing, contract of sales output, and vertical integration. Marketing strategies address the risks involved with the economic data necessary for decision making (Chapter 1).

Spreading of Sales

Instead of selling 100 percent of his crop on say May 11 or January 2 and risking (even with the benefit of knowledge of price forecasting and trends) that the entire crop be sold in a period of low prices, the farm operator may intentionally stagger sales and market 25 percent of the crop in each of four distinct periods.

Table 9–8 shows the results of a study conducted to measure the effects of such a marketing strategy on average returns and the level of risk. Twenty-five percent of the crop was marketed in each of the four months November, February, April, and July, and the average returns and variability of returns compared with selling 100 percent of the crop in just one month. The figures in the body of the table are returns per bushel net of storage, interest, and shrinkage costs so that we may compare like entities in each month. As you might have expected, the strategy for spreading sales does not give the highest average returns. In this particular case, holding off until July to sell all of the crop was most profitable. But the sales-spreading strategy was by no means the least successful either, as we see from the average returns in April. If the operator is just

---

[1] *Many medium-priced calculators can perform analysis between two variables to yield these estimates.*

TABLE 9–8. NET CORN PRICE RECEIVED AND VARIABILITY WHEN COMPARING SPREADING SALES AND SINGLE-MONTH MARKETING[1]

Marketing Year	Marketing Months				Spreading Sales[2]
	Nov.	Feb.	Apr.	July	
1970–71	1.24	1.313	1.228	1.131	1.228
1971–72	.94	.982	.983	.945	.963
1972–73	1.14	1.196	1.203	1.789	1.332
1973–74	2.14	2.576	2.229	2.659	2.401
1974–75	3.27	2.69	2.437	2.359	2.689
Mean	1.746	1.751	1.616	1.776	1.722
σ	.9688	.8145	.6655	.7460	.7695
C.V.	.55	.47	.41	.42	.45

concerned with profit, this approach is not the best. However, in terms of the variability of returns measured by the coefficient of variation and not the variance, selling right at harvest time and even holding off until February yield less stable expected outcomes than marketing 25 percent in each of the four months. It is not until the operator stores through April and July that returns show less than average variability, yet these options require storage facilities for a hundred percent of the crop, not just 50 and 25 percent, respectively. As it turns out, in this situation, marketing 100 percent in July is perhaps a better strategy than spreading sales. This is not always the case, and one should remember that as a general rule the farmer can trade a little bit of profit for a lot of security by spreading sales.

Hedging on the Future Market

Utilizing the futures market allows the farm manager to shift the risk of price changes to others who are willing to bear them. Other important functions of futures markets include assistance in the financing of inventories and the widespread dissemination of market prices and related information.

Hedging via the futures market allows the farm manager to accomplish a wide variety of income stabilizing options. Some of these include establishing the price of crops and livestock before they are sold, locking in margins associated with purchasing feeder cattle and fattening them, and establishing the cost of feed inputs prior to their purchase.

The process of hedging involves taking an equal and opposite position in the futures market to the expected cash market position. By being both buyer and seller, the operator can effectively hedge any price movement. When prices rise, the gain on the selling position will offset the loss on the buying side. Similarly, when prices fall the loss from the selling position will offset the gain realized from the buying activity.

Accomplishing this hedge of market prices involves trading **futures contracts**. A futures contract is a standardized agreement between two parties to buy and sell a specific amount and quality of a commodity to be delivered during a specified time to a specified location at an agreed upon price. Futures contracts also specify who pays delivery cost and any premiums or discounts for commodities delivered which do not exactly meet contract specifications. This standardization of contract allows them to be traded without the actual movement or inspection of the physical commodity until the delivery date.

Only a small volume of total futures trading is closed out by receipt or delivery of the physical commodity. Most contracts are closed out by taking an offsetting position. If you buy a futures contract, you may release your obligation to accept delivery by selling it before the delivery date. However, the threat of delivery is extremely important in maintaining a proper relationship between cash and futures prices and in making futures markets useful for hedging purposes. Without the possibility of delivery there would be no reason to expect a stable and predictable relationship between cash and futures prices.

The process of trading in the futures market begins by contacting a commodity broker. Only those persons who have a seat on an exchange can actually trade the contracts and the number of seats on each exchange is limited. The second step is to sign an agreement authorizing the broker to buy or sell futures contracts for you. The third step is to place an order with the broker giving him instructions to buy or sell contracts. This of course should not be done until you have analyzed the potential benefits from the action. Step four is to deposit a margin requirement with the broker. This provides assurance that you can cover your losses if unfavorable price changes occur. Margin requirements usually range from seven to fifteen percent of the value of the contracts and may change from time to time. Step five in futures trading is to close out the transaction at some future date. This can be done either by taking an offsetting action in the futures market or by delivering or receiving the commodity, depending upon the initial transaction. The final step is the payment of the brokerage fee. This fee varies somewhat by commodity but is approximately $40.00 per five thousand bushel contract in the grains.

Preliminary Steps to Hedging

There are several preliminary steps that should be taken before making the initial transaction in the futures market. First, the futures price should be adjusted to the cash equivalent in your local area. The difference between the futures price and the local cash equivalent is called the **basis**. Normally, the basis is closely related to the transportation costs from the local area to the futures market. The cost of storing grain to the contract maturity date is another important factor in the basis.

The second step which should be undertaken before hedging is to estimate the probable size of your anticipated cash market transaction. The volume of commitments in the futures market should be as close as possible to the volume of your cash market transaction when you actually sell your commodity. The next step in analyzing a hedge before it is placed is to estimate the net return with the hedge to determine whether this will provide a satisfactory profit. A loss can just as easily be locked–in via the futures market as a profit. Step four is to study market outlook reports to determine which direction the price of the commodity you wish to hedge is likely to move between now and the time you expect to offset your hedge. Step five is to estimate the returns without hedging. In step six you should compare returns with and without hedging to assess your ability to absorb the cash market risk if you decide not to hedge. The final step is to select the more favorable action: hedging or taking your chance with the cash market.

Futures markets can enable a farmer to assure himself within a fairly narrow range of the price that could be received for a crop at or after harvest. This is done by selling futures contracts during the growing season. At the time of harvest the farm manager sells the crop in the cash market and buys back the futures contract. This repurchase of contracts sold during the growing season is what is known as **offsetting the initial futures position**. Any decline in the cash market price which has occurred between the time the hedge is first placed and the time the cash market transaction is made is likely to be offset by an approximately equal decline in the futures market. By taking opposite positions in the two markets a loss in the cash market will be approximately offset by a gain in the futures market.

Consider the example in Table 9–9. Suppose the December corn futures contract is selling for $3.10 per bushel early in June. The producer adjusts this back to the equivalent cash market price in his local areas as follows. The normal basis for a farmer's particular area is added to the brokerage and interest costs per bushel and the total is then subtracted from the December futures price on the date the hedge is considered. Notice from Table 9–9 that the normal basis is estimated to be $.45 and brokerage and interest costs total $.03. This subtraction results in the target price at the local level of $2.62. This result means that with a perfect hedge the producer could obtain $2.62 per bushel for his corn at or shortly after harvest. Suppose that after studying the market outlook the producer decides that the corn price is likely to be considerably lower than this at harvest time. Under these circumstances, he might want to hedge a portion of his production by selling one or more futures contracts. In practice, the farm manager might want to sell a number of contracts corresponding in quantity to less than his expected produc-

TABLE 9–9. LOCALIZING THE FUTURES PRICE TO ESTAB-
LISH A TARGET PRICE.

December futures price on June 2		$3.10
minus normal basis	$ .45	
brokerage fees and interest on margin	.03	
Total		–$ .48
Target price at local level		$2.62

tion for two reasons: 1) the actual yield produced of the crop might be less than expected, and 2) the manager can sell futures contracts only in 5,000 bushel increments on most exchanges. Later on, if yield prospects become more definite, the manager might want to increase the size of his hedge by selling additional contracts.

Assume the farm manager decides that the target price is sufficient to cover all production costs and return a profit. Table 9–10 illustrates the outcome of a perfect hedge if cash market corn prices drop to $2.00 per bushel. With a perfect hedge, the December futures corn price would drop to $2.45 per bushel. Note that this difference of $.45 is the basis of the local area. The hedge would be closed out at harvest by selling the crop in the cash market and buying back the futures contracts. The net result is the target price of $2.62. The general result from hedging in periods of rising prices is also illustrated in Table 9–10. In the case of a perfect hedge, the producer would receive exactly the target price for his crop whether prices rise or fall. However, in practice the basis between cash and futures does not remain completely constant. Because of this, the actual price per bushel may vary a few cents from the target price. However, the variability in the basis tends to be much smaller than the variability in the cash market.

Producers using the futures market to establish the price of a growing crop should carefully consider the need for crop insurance if it is available. Otherwise, if a large portion of the crop is hedged or contracted at a local elevator the operator may be substituting a production risk for

TABLE 9–10. RESULTS OF A PERFECT HEDGE WHEN CASH PRICES FALL OR RISE

Situation 1—Falling Prices

Cash price received		$2.00/bushel
Futures transaction:		
Sold at	$3.10/bushel	
Bought back at	2.45/bushel	
Profit on Futures	+$ .65	+ .65/bushel
Less brokerage fees and interest		− .03/bushel
Net Price received		$2.62/bushel

Situation 2—Rising Prices

Cash price received		$3.10/bushel
Futures transaction:		
Sold at	$3.10/bushel	
Bought back at	3.55/bushel	
Loss on Futures	−$0.45	−$ .45/bushel
Less brokerage fees and interest		− .03/bushel
Net price received		$2.62/bushel

a price risk. Although a crop hedge has been illustrated in Table 9–10, the same basic principle applies to livestock hedging.

There are several common mistakes that producers make in futures trading operations. The first type of error is improper calculation of the basis or failure to subtract the correct normal basis from the appropriate futures contract price. A basis history can be developed by recording local cash prices and futures quotations once a week throughout the marketing year. The same day should be used each week to maintain a consistent record of your local basis. The second type of error which is frequently encountered is failure to relate the futures transactions to cash transactions both in size and direction of position. In hedging operations futures transactions should be such that when the hedge is closed out, transactions in cash and futures markets are in opposite directions. Also, the volume of the commitment in the futures market should be no larger than the expected volume of the cash transaction. A third type of error is failure to close out both cash and futures transactions at the same time. There are two reasons why the cash and futures transactions should be closed out together. First, a successful hedge depends upon the relationship between cash and futures prices, not on the level of either price. Second, futures prices may be very sensitive to changing market conditions and a delay in completing the futures transaction could change the futures cash price relationship. A fourth type of error frequently made is to try to trade in and out of the futures market for quick profits. There may be times when producers could wisely reverse positions in the futures market as a result of apparent changes in longer run price outlooks. However, such situations are probably infrequent and require following the market closely. In general, it is advisable to develop a careful hedging plan and follow it unless there is a very good reason to change.

Hedging Versus Contracting at Local Elevators

Most local elevators offer grain producers a chance to contract prices for delivery of their grain at future dates. When elevators purchase grain from farmers under such contracts they either hedge the resulting purchases in the futures market or resell the grain on forward contracts to grain merchants who do the hedging. But such contracts are closely linked with current futures market quotations. Contracting at the local elevator may have advantages or disadvantages when compared with hedging in the futures market. The major advantages to farmers are the lower level of technical knowledge needed for elevator contracting and the avoidance of margin deposits and margin calls. Another advantage is that most elevators are willing to contract in relatively small lots rather than the 5,000 bushel contracts traded on the Chicago Board of Trade. Thus, it is easier to spread out marketing over several intervals and to match sales with expected production through contracts than through hedging. Prices reflected in elevator contracts often tend to be slightly below those offered by direct hedging. The slightly lower prices reflect the elevator's cost of providing contracting services and the risk of missing the target hedging price by a small margin.

For some farmers hedging may offer flexibility advantages when compared with contracting at local elevators. For example, hedging permits farmers to shop around for the best local cash bid, taking into account variations in access to transportation facilities, differences in discount factors and differences in local prices. After a contract is made with the local elevator this type of flexibility is given up. Whether or not it is a significant consideration depends on your local situation. Once grain is forward contracted at the local elevator the marketing decision generally cannot be reversed. However, it is usually a simple matter to reverse a hedging decision if the market clearly has changed directions due to weather or some other unexpected development. To be successful, a hedge needs to be lifted quickly. Even then, losses could be involved. As noted earlier, reversing a hedging position offers the potential dangers of moving into a speculative position in trading in and out of the futures market for quick profits. Again, the purpose of hedging is to obtain a satisfactory, guaranteed product or input price.

Farm operators often ask whether hedging also allows them to increase profits as well as reduce risk. If one compares hedging all the time with hedging none of the time, the answer is no. In fact, hedgers should expect slightly lower average net returns because of the fees which must be paid to the commodity broker. But studies by Purcell and others show that selective hedging based on 10-day moving averages and other devices can not only reduce risk but also increase net returns. This is particularly true for livestock feeding, and especially cattle. But, in general, for the less astute hedger there is a simple trade-off between risk and profit.

You should also avoid confusing hedging with speculating. Speculating involves taking extreme positions on the futures markets in the hopes that you have read the longer-term movements of the market correctly and that it will move in your favor, giving large earnings. This strategy is just the opposite of hedging. Speculating tends to increase expected profits (if the farm manager is skillful) but also increases the magnitude of his losses and gains from any single position he takes.

Input Forward Pricing

Input forward pricing is a particularly important strategy when managing a large livestock operation. Here it is important that production costs do not exceed the calculated break-even price. Arrangements can be made to receive a certain amount of feed at a given price four or five months hence. A premium price will probably be paid for the privilege of price certainty. However, it may be worth avoiding the risk of input price variation.

Contract Sales (Forward Pricing of Products)

This strategy is often used for seed corn, soybeans, or for perishable cash crops like tomatoes or sweet corn. The farmer makes a contract to deliver a certain amount of output at a certain time. The factory or company usually provides the seeds, herbicides, and other inputs to standardize the product. The factory also supplies management assistance, and often employs either farmer representatives or special extension agents to watch the crop for the operator and put out a red flag if they see a disease or insect problem. When the operator sees the red flag, he calls the factory agent to find out what the problem is, which chemical to spray, and how much. Often the company shares the cost with the operator. Output price is often two-tiered: the operator is guaranteed a certain base price, but gets a bonus price for good quality product. Two-tiered pricing works as an incentive for the grower and also provides the company with a high-quality product to preserve their reputation and increase their market share.

Vertical Integration

Most products have a marketing channel which looks something like this:

Consumer
↓
Retailers
↓
Wholesale-retailers
↓
Wholesalers
↓
Assembler-jobbers
↓
Producers

If all of these marketing agents are involved, many people will be clamoring for their seven or ten percent cut from the gross margin, but the size of the margin may be smaller because no one can take advantage of economies of size. For this reason, there have been efforts in many industries to cut out some of these marketing intermediaries. For example, in the dairy industry, producers take over assembler-jobber and wholesaler duties in forming cooperatives to market their milk. Similarly, some large grocery store chains have been interested in acquiring produce directly from the producer, processing and wrapping it, shipping it, and delivering it through supermarkets directly to the consumer. Vertical integration has the following advantages.

1. Inexperienced growers may improve.
2. Overall efficiency may rise because of economies of size.
3. Vital pest control and other inputs and management may be provided at low cost.
4. Grower profit may be limited but more stable.
5. There may be special incentives for excellent management.
6. Marketing is usually cheaper.
7. Consumers may gain from increased efficiency and quality.
8. The firm that takes the initiative to integrate may profit.
9. Farm operators may become larger-scale and more specialized.

Producers sometimes desire quantitative estimates of the benefits from vertical integration. A study of the Maryland turfgrass industry estimated the costs and returns for different sizes of turfgrass farms as well as different levels of involvement in harvest and delivery (i.e., vertical integration). Table 9–11 indicates that return to management increased with the level of vertical integration, from the lowest amount of producer involvement (hand-directed, hand-rolled/zero transportation) to the highest (palletized/long-distance transportation). These increased returns were necessary to compensate management for the additional responsibilities of harvest and delivery and for increased financial investment.

A study of vertical integration in the Idaho cattle industry yielded similar results (Araji, 1975). The completely-integrated (cow-finished steer) system, operating at the optimal size of 480,000 pounds of live-weight production had $35,000 more net income than the optimal-sized cow-calf system and $18,000 more than the optimal-sized cow-yearling system. Vertical integration benefited producers because it allowed them to take a position farther out on the long-run average cost curve and exploit lower transportation and auction costs.

TABLE 9–11. RETURN TO MANAGEMENT FROM THE SALE AND TRANSPORTATION OF HARVESTED TURFGRASS BY FARM SIZE, METHODS OF HARVEST AND TRANSPORTATION, MARYLAND, 1976[1]

| | *Method of Harvest* | | | |
	Hand-Directed Hand Rolled	*Tractor-Powered Hand Rolled*	*Palletizer, Palletized Handling*	*Transportation Distance*
Purchase by the Acre	27.74	28.23	28.61	zero
	32.47	32.96	33.31	short
	33.94	34.43	34.78	long
Produce Less Than	28.54	29.03	29.38	zero
100 Acres	33.27	33.76	34.11	short
	34.73	35.23	35.58	long
Produce 100–150 Acres	30.40	30.89	31.24	zero
	34.13	34.62	35.97	short
	36.60	37.09	37.44	long
Produce 151–300 Acres	31.14	31.63	31.98	zero
	35.87	36.36	36.71	short
	37.34	37.83	38.18	long
Produce More Than	29.86	30.35	30.70	zero
300 Acres	34.59	35.08	35.43	short
	36.06	36.55	36.90	long

[1]In determining the return to management, gross receipts at the farmgate were based on a harvest of 4,600 square yards per acre and a harvest price of 55.3 cents per square yard. The price for delivered turfgrass was 70.8 cents per square yard.

Source: Adapted from Lessley, B. V. and I. Strand. "Effect of Farm Size and Level of Vertical Integration on Returns to Management in the Commercial Turfgrass Industry," Maryland Agricultural Experiment Station Scientific Article Number A2612, Contribution Number 5651, College Park, Maryland, undated.

SUMMARY

Once the trade-off between risk and returns has been assessed, it is important to plan and implement a combination of strategies that will help to achieve the desired level of risk. These fall into three categories: production, marketing and financial strategies, of which you studied the first two in this chapter.

Production strategies reduce variability in returns due to yield vagaries, technological change, legal contingencies, and government program changes. These strategies include the selection of stable enterprises, diversification of the enterprises included in the farm operation, maintaining flexibility (in costs, facilities, products, and the timing of operations); the use of insurance on life, health, legal liability, property, and crops; and such miscellaneous measures as investing in yield-stabilizing technology, stockpiling inputs, and building a knowledge base.

Marketing strategies reduce variability in returns caused by changes in input and output prices and consumer preferences. These strategies include the spreading of output sales, the hedging of output on the futures market, the forward pricing of inputs, contract sales of output, and taking over more of the stages in the marketing channel through vertical integration.

Through the above production and marketing strategies, the farm manager can considerably reduce the amount of business risk he confronts, though usually at the expense of some reduction in expected net farm income.

SAMPLE PROBLEMS

1. The following are data on four Iowa farm enterprises for a ten-year period.

	Fixed costs	Total costs	Expected returns over variable costs	Standard deviation in returns over variable costs	Correlation of net returns
Corn	120	210	96.5	34	1.00
Soybeans	130	190	98	36	1.00
Swine	54	635	375	49	1.00
Fed Cattle	20	121	78	6	1.00
Corn & Soybeans	—	—	—	—	0.48
Corn & Soybeans	—	—	—	—	0.45
Corn & Cattle	—	—	—	—	0.65
Soybeans & Swine	—	—	—	—	-0.08
Soybeans & Cattle	—	—	—	—	-0.24

Which enterprise would you choose if you used each of the production strategies below: (SHOW YOUR WORK AND EXPLAIN)
a. Stable enterprises

b. Diversification

c. Flexibility

In June a certain farmer begins to think about the possible price he may receive for the corn crop he plans to harvest in early November. He looks at the December futures price currently quoted for corn and finds it to be $2.60. He knows that the December futures price is normally $0.18 above the cash price at harvest, and that his brokerage fees and interest on the margin requirement would be about $0.01 per bushel if he hedged now. The current local cash price for corn is $2.00.

2. What target price would the farmer expect to receive if he hedged his corn in June?

   a. $2.00

   b. $2.60

   c. $2.81

   d. $2.79

   e. $2.41

3. If the basis that actually resulted at harvest was $0.18 and cash corn prices in his area at that time were $2.80, the above farmer would still realize only the target price for his crop.

   a. true

   b. false

4. If the basis actually turned out to be $0.18 at harvest, but cash corn prices in his area had slipped to $2.05, the above farmer would still receive the target price.

   a. true

   b. false

SUGGESTED READINGS

Araji, A. A. *Vertical Integration and Production Efficiency in Beef Cattle Operations.* University of Idaho Agricultural Experiment Station Bulletin No. 553. Moscow, Idaho, 1975.

Harsh, S., L. Connor, and G. Schwab. *Managing the Farm Business*, Chapter 14. Englewood Cliffs, New Jersey: Prentice-Hall Inc., 1981.

Nelson, A., and W. Lee and W. Murray. *Agricultural Finance*, Chapters 12 and 13. Ames, Iowa: Iowa State University Press, 1973.

Penson J., and D. Lins. *Agricultural Finance*, Chapter 7. Englewood Cliffs, New Jersey: Prentice-Hall Inc., 1980.

Purcell, W. *Agricultural Marketing: Systems, Coordination, Cash and Futures Prices.* Reston, Virginia: Reston Publishing, 1979.

Shepherd, S., G. Futrell and J. Strain. *Marketing Farm Products*, Sixth edition. Ames, Iowa: Iowa State University Press, 1976.

☐10☐

The Farm Manager's Response to Government Programs

I have heard of various kinds of government, such as oligarchies, monarchies, and democracies, but this is the first time I have ever heard of a farmocracy.

Harold L. Ickes, Speech against the United States Department of Agriculture, 1935

Concepts

In this chapter you will come to understand:

1. The factors that cause shifts in the supply and demand of agricultural commodities.
2. The meaning of parity.
3. Seven aspects of the current U.S. farm problem.
4. The past distribution of benefits from government programs.
5. The actors in the agricultural-food policymaking process.
6. The components of the 1977 and 1981 Food and Agricultural Acts and their historical antecedents.

Tools

You will also acquire the following skills:

1. How to decide whether or not to participate in a set-aside program, and at what level.
2. How to decide whether or not to join the farmer-owned reserve and when to withdraw your grain from it.

INTRODUCTION

We have investigated costs in the short and the long run for the individual farm (Chapter 3). It is time now to develop a general picture of supply for all producers of a given commodity and relate that to the demand for that commodity. Many factors underlie movements along both the supply curve and the demand curve; changes in these factors cause these curves to shift. At any time there is a balancing or "equilibrium" point at the intersection of the supply and demand curves in a competitive economy. Government policy may intentionally move producers and consumers away from that point of equilibrium. We shall compare some of the more important agricultural policies, the goals they seek to achieve, and how farm managers should determine their response.

SUPPLY, DEMAND AND EQUILIBRIUM

The Supply Curve

The segments of the marginal cost curve above the average variable cost curve in the short run (and the average total cost curve in the long run) describe the individual farm's short run and long run supply curve, respectively (Figure 10–1b). Adding together such supply curves for all

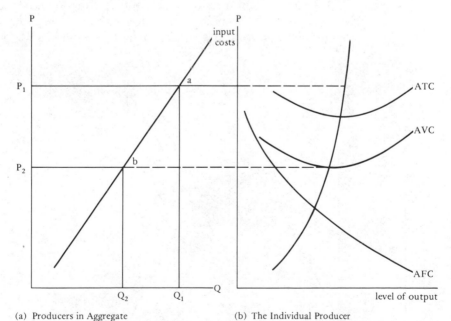

(a) Producers in Aggregate   (b) The Individual Producer

FIGURE 10–1. *The Individual and Aggregate Supply Curves for Agricultural Produce.*

producers at a series of given prices, we may form the aggregate or market supply curve for the commodity in the agricultural sector as a whole (Figure 10–1a). This latter panel shows that when price is high (P_1), producers in aggregate will be willing to supply a high amount of output (Q_1). When price falls to P_2, they will only be willing and able, given their cost structures, to supply Q_2 units. Movement between point **a** and point **b** is termed movement along the supply curve and involves a decrease in quantity supplied but not in supply itself. Movement along the supply curve occurs when price alone changes.

What, then, are the factors that underlie the supply curve? There are a total of six factors, all of which may be tied together through reference to the physical production model of inputs, technology, and outputs presented in Chapter 2 (Figure 10–2).

1. Price. ("1" in Figure 10–2). As noted, the custom in economics is to use the two-dimensional space of the graph to plot quantity supplied against price. Therefore, when price alone changes, there is a movement along the curve rather than a shift in the curve. It would be possible to plot quantity supplied against any of the factors below, but this is not the convention.

2. Yield of the commodity in question. ("2" in Figure 10–2). As the yield of a commodity increases, the quantity that may be supplied at a given price also increases. For example, say that there is an improvement in yields through the release of new B82 inbred corn crosses from your state university, which would replace the B73 inbred corn crosses. Figure 10–3 shows that for the same total and marginal costs, the individual farm can produce more corn. Alternatively, one can say that the marginal and average total costs have shifted downward and to the right,

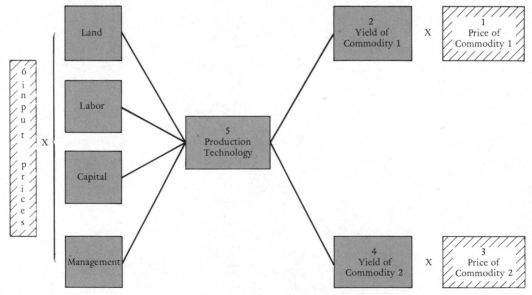

FIGURE 10-2. *The Supply Response Function as an Expansion of the Production Function.*

from MC_1 and ATC_1 to MC_2 and ATC_2 in Figure 10-3b. Since this happens for all producers who adopt the new line, there is a general increase in the ability of farmers to supply corn, and the supply curve also shifts downward and to the right, from S_1 to S_2 in Figure 10-3a.

3. The Price of Competing and Complementary Goods that the Producer Could Grow. ("3" in Figure 10-2). This factor relates to the shape and position of the production possibility curve for the farm. If in terms of Figure 2-12, Chapter 2, the price of alfalfa increases, then it will pay to produce more by moving toward the lower end of the competitive range. If the price of some competing commodity, such as sorghum, increases, it will pay to divert land from corn to sorghum. In either case, there will be a shift backwards in the supply curve for the commodity.

4. The Yield of Competing and Complementary Crops. ("4" in Figure 10-2). Clearly, if the yield of other crops that may be grown in place of a given crop increases, then there will be a reduction in the amount of that given crop that the producer will be willing to supply. In other words, there will be a shift backwards in the supply curve, say from S_1 to S_3 in Figure 10-3a.

5. The Technology Available for Producing the Crop or Livestock Commodity. ("5" in Figure 10-2). If, for example, field tests show that minimum tillage methods will provide comparable yields with much less machinery and field time, then the supply curve for a crop will shift outward and to the right. Alternatively, the development of

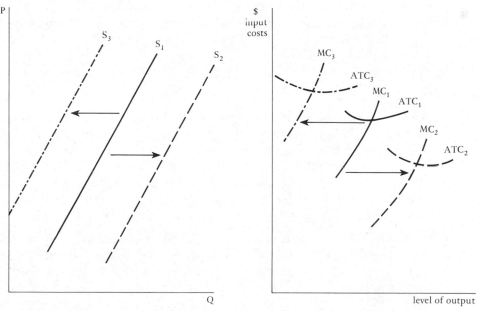

(a) Producers in Aggregate   (b) The Individual Producer

FIGURE 10-3. Shifts in the Supply Curve for Individual and Aggregate Producers.

hormone injections for cattle may represent a technological advance that will help to shift outward the supply curve for beef.

6. The Prices of the Production Inputs (Land, Labor, Capital and Management) Needed to Produce the Crop. ("6" in Figure 10-2). As these costs go up, there will be a contraction in the supply that farmers can produce. For example, assume that there is a large increase in the cost of petroleum-based fertilizer, pesticides, and fuel inputs needed to produce the commodity in question. To produce any given level of output the marginal and average total costs will increase, say from MC_1 and ATC_1 in Figure 10-3b to MC_3 and ATC_3. As a result, there will be a shift backwards and upward in the supply curve, say from S_1 to S_3 in Figure 10-3a.

When considering movement along the supply curve, we assume that factors 2 through 6 above are being held constant. When any one of them changes, a shift in supply occurs because the supply curve actually moves. Each example given above is for a change in only one direction. Can you think of examples where movement in the supply curve would be in the opposite direction from that mentioned for each factor?

Economists often perform supply response studies for producers and government analysts to estimate the relative importance of the various factors underlying the supply curve. A study of Delaware dairymen, for example, found that the most important determinants of dairy herd size were farm wages, milk prices for as many as eleven previous quarters, the price of concentrates, and the purchase price of milk cows (Elterich and Masud, 1980). By contrast, the most important determinants of milk production per cow were the price of concentrates, the price of alfalfa hay, technological improvements, season, and the price of milk for six previous quarters. Such studies are important in not only explaining producer behavior, but also predicting future cow numbers and levels of milk production.

The Demand Curve

Again, by convention, the two-dimensional space shows the relationship between price and quantity. For example, when price is P_1 in Figure 10-4, consumers will only demand Q_1 units of the commodity. However, when price falls to P_2, consumers will be willing and able to buy more, say Q_2 units. This change is called a movement along the demand curve and involves a change in quantity demanded rather than a change in demand itself. A total of five factors underlie the demand curve:

1. Price. This factor is what is actually plotted with quantity to determine the demand curve. Whenever price alone changes in either direction, there is movement along the demand curve rather than a shift in the demand itself.

2. Income. As consumers' incomes rise, the demand for some commodities (such as steak) rises while the demand for others (such as pinto

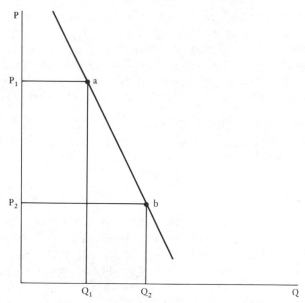

FIGURE 10–4. *The Demand Curve for Agricultural Produce.*

beans) decreases. These two situations involve a shift outward or backward in the demand curve, respectively. Over the past decade income
increases in the less-developed countries have been a major contributor
to shifts outward in the demand curve for U.S.-produced grain crops.
At their level of development, consumers in such countries will spend a
high percentage of each increased dollar of income on the purchase of
food.

3. Price of Complementary and Competing Goods.   In terms of the consumer, the ingredients in steak sauce are a complementary good to steak
while pork chops are a competing good. If the price of steak increases,
the demand for steak sauce will go down (there will be a shift upward
and to the left in the demand curve). If the price of pork goes up, there
will be, by contrast, an increase in demand for steak.

4. Population Size.   In the early days of our country, population increased at a high rate, and contributed greatly to a continuous expansion
in the demand for food products. In the last half of the twentieth century, demographic and cultural factors, aided by ZPG (zero-population-
growth) campaign, have meant that the population of the United States
grows only by small amounts each year. Again, one must look to other
countries, such as the less-developed nations with higher rates of population growth, as potential sources of increased demand for U.S. agricultural production. In addition, the recent expansion of trade with the
People's Republic of China has increased the demand for feedgrains to
help expand the Chinese livestock industry.

5. Consumers' Tastes and Preferences. Over the past 15 years, the American diet has changed to include more natural food and wine, fewer eggs and less nitrite-containing meats. The demand curves for natural food and wine have thus shifted outward. The demand curves for bacon and eggs have shifted backward, both in their own right and because they are complementary to each other (factor 3 above).

Remember that Figure 10-4 assumes that factors 2 through 5 above are held constant. Only if one or more of them changes will there be a shift or change in demand itself.

Market Equilibrium

Figure 10-5 shows the effect of combining the supply and demand curves of Figure 10-3a and 10-4. You will note that at a high price (P_1), producers are willing to produce Q_1 units of output, but consumers can only purchase Q_2. Therefore, a surplus develops. By contrast, if price falls to P_2, consumers will be willing to purchase Q_1 units of output but producers can only supply Q_2. A shortage develops. In a competitive economy, these two extremes will tend to work toward the center to achieve an equilibrium at price P_e and Q_e. This equilibrium point is rather magical, because it is at this point that natural market forces meet. Marginal cost of production is just equal to price, which is in turn just equal to the marginal satisfaction obtained by consumers.

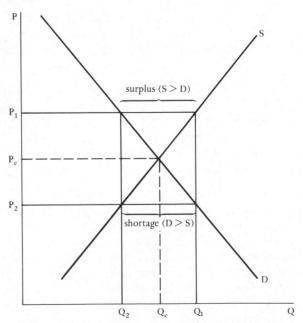

FIGURE 10-5. *Supply and Demand Equilibrium, Surplus, and Shortage for an Agricultural Commodity.*

Inputs and outputs of a society are allocated most efficiently. If all markets reach equilibrium in this manner, then all three economic questions (the factor-product, factor-factor, and product-product) are efficiently satisfied for the society. Society is then operating at the optimal point on its production possibility curve.

THE FARM PROBLEM

Parity

Who would ever wish to depart from this efficient world? Perhaps the most vocal advocates of ignoring equilibrium prices are the members of the American Agriculture Movement. They drove their tractors to Washington in 1977 to insist that farm incomes were too low. They claimed that the most straightforward way to improve those incomes was to guarantee that the prices of wheat and feedgrains be maintained at a level at least 90% of parity.

The concept of parity was first used as the basis for commodity loans to farmers in the Agriculture Adjustment Act of 1933. It did not originate with the American Agriculture Movement. It is still used to determine the support price for dairy products, although this may change in the future. Parity prices are computed to reflect equality over time in the purchasing power of farmers for the nonagricultural production inputs and consumer items they must buy with their farm earnings. The parity price for a given commodity is defined as follows:

$$\text{Parity} = \frac{\text{average price of a commodity last 10 years}}{\text{average index of all prices received last 10 years}}$$
$$\times \text{ current index of prices paid.}$$

In a static world, this formula would be one way to assure that the income of farmers kept up with the income of nonfarmers. However there are two forces which make the use of parity an unreliable guide to income maintenance:

1. Technological Change. As you have seen, this is one of the factors that can shift outward the supply curve on the supply side of market equilibrium. Specifically, technological change means that at the same level of prices and input costs, farmers can increase their incomes. If technological change continuously increases the yields per unit of production or reduces input costs, a falling parity price may actually accompany rising comparative incomes for farmers.

2. Changes in the Tastes and Preferences of Consumers. You have seen that this factor on the demand side can affect the position of the demand curve in market equilibrium. The relative amounts purchased by consumers in 1990 may be very different from the quantities purchased in 1980, particularly for such items as eggs and wine. However, the parity formula assumes constant weights for the index of prices received for food and fiber commodities. By undervaluing the prices of the commodities farmers sell more of over time, and overvaluing the prices of commodities farmers sell less of, the parity formula is not a true reflection of what the adjusted parity price should be.

If parity prices were used as the basis for income support programs for farmers, resource allocation would be distorted, and the distribution of income would deteriorate. Inefficient farms would be perpetuated rather than encouraged to expand, the location of production would be frozen among regions, and the farmers' share of U.S. and foreign markets would diminish.

To illustrate why, consider the demands of the American Agriculture Movement in 1977. The price of corn at the time was about $2.00 per bushel, but the price at 90% of parity would have been approximately $3.25. If the grain farmers were paid this price, one U.S.D.A. study has estimated the following effects would occur:

1. The supply curve for livestock commodities would shift backwards dramatically, resulting in higher price and limited quantities to the consumer. This is because feedgrains are a major production input in the livestock industry. The smaller-scale producers of livestock commodities would be driven out of operation entirely.

2. The higher prices would soon be built into the cost of land to crop farmers. In other words, the gains would be capitalized into higher costs of land and would cease to be reflected as an increase in net farm income over variable and fixed costs. Because of the higher cost of land, the small-scale farmers, who already had higher production costs and hence faced a greater cost-price squeeze, would be unable to buy land for expansion or even continue to rent the land they were leasing. The study estimated that about 25 percent of all U.S. farms would go out of operation.

3. The quantity and value of U.S. exports would be drastically reduced. With the increase in grain prices, other nations, on whom expansion in U.S. grain crop demand depends (through their higher rates of population growth and spending on food per dollar of income), would seek their grain imports from Argentina, Canada and Australia. Currently, agriculture is the sector with primary responsibility for lessening the balance of trade deficit to allow the United States to improve the living standards of its citizens through continued imports. Without the earnings from feedgrain and wheat exports and the increased imports of livestock commodities, the United States would become less able to purchase consumer goods in which other nations enjoy a comparative productive advantage.

The U.S. Farm Problem

Clearly, parity pricing is an oversimplified way to solve the problems of low farm incomes in agriculture. In fact, there is not just one U.S. farm problem, but seven separate problems which combine to cause decision-

TABLE 10–1. THE PRESENT FARM PROBLEM

Issue	Value	Alternatives
1. Excess capacity and low prices	Efficiency	Parity, marketing quotas, acreage reduction
2. Price instability	Security	CCC stocks, PL 480, world grain reserve
3. Low farm income	Commutative justice	Support prices transfer payments
4. Structural problems	Charity, equity	Payment ceiling, revise laws
5. Resource use, productivity, and returns	Enterprise, work ethics	Expand demand, limit research
6. Unfavorable input markets	Distributive justice	Farm Credit System, Minnesota Young Farmers Plan
7. Unfavorable output markets	Commutative justice	Capper-Volstead, AMA 1937, holding actions

making and earnings problems for farm operators. These, along with the American values they disturb and some possible solutions, are listed in Table 10–1.

The first issue which contributes to the present U.S. farm problem is that of excess capacity and low prices. It has been estimated that a full two-thirds of all farms could go out of operation in the United States and that the remaining, generally large-scale, farms could meet both domestic and foreign demand for U.S. farm products. This situation flies in the face of the American value of efficiency in resource allocation: if the land, labor capital and management used on these farms are unnecessary, why not use them to some other purpose?

But it is that very value of efficiency that has contributed to creating the problem. Landgrant university and private research efforts in the United States have caused supply curve to shift outward through technological change at the rate of 2.6 percent per year, even with set-aside programs and other efforts to limit supply (Figure 10–6). At the same time, however, the demand curve has been shifting outward at the rate of only 1.7 percent per year, largely as noted through steady increases in demand from foreign nations. Therefore, price has been trending downward at the difference between these two rates: 0.9 percent per year[1]. Fewer and fewer farms are required to meet society's demands. Because the equilibrium price is trending downward, only those farms that are best able to move out along the long-run average cost curve to keep production costs below prices received will be able to survive. This fact helps to explain the trends toward both fewer farms and a greater percentage of part-time farms in the United States.

One alternative that has been suggested for solving this aspect of the

[1] *Some economists feel that the U.S. agricultural economy in the 1980s and 1990s is going through a period of "scarcity syndrome," in which domestic technological advances will decline, greater conservation practices will be enforced, and the effective demand for food in developing countries will increase. Although such a situation would ease the downward pressure on prices received by U.S. farm producers, there is no firm evidence that the scarcity syndrome is materializing.*

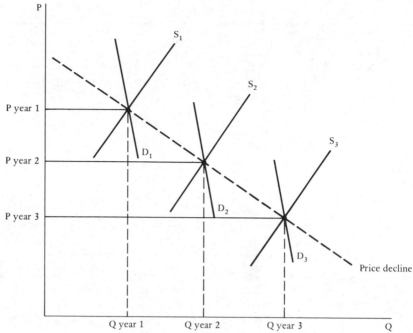

FIGURE 10-6. *The Problem of Excess Capacity and Declining Price in Agriculture.*

farm problem is to use parity prices. However, we have noted that fallacies attend the parity approach, especially in periods of rapid technological change. The other approaches are the use of marketing quotas and acreage reductions, which shift backward the supply curve in a given year to help counteract the outward shift caused by technological change and thus maintain constant prices.

The second aspect of the present farm problem is price instability. This, as you learned in Chapter 1, is largely because of the biological nature of farming and the inability to predict the exact amount of harvest in a given year. Figure 10-7 shows the price stabilization approach which has been used in the United States since the 1930s and constituted the primary instrument of farm policy until 1973. The government determined a support price through reference to parity concepts. In a good year, when yields and production were so high that price would fall below the support price, the government would buy up the amount of grain necessary to reduce the quantity on the market to Q_2. This would guarantee the producers the support price. The Commodity Credit Corporation (CCC) would then hold the stocks for the following purposes:

1. To add to market supply in a very poor year to keep the price from exceeding the support price.
2. To distribute through domestic food programs such as foodstamps, the school-lunch program, and the Women and Infant Care program.
3. To sell to earn income for the Food for Peace Act, also known as the P.L. 480 program.

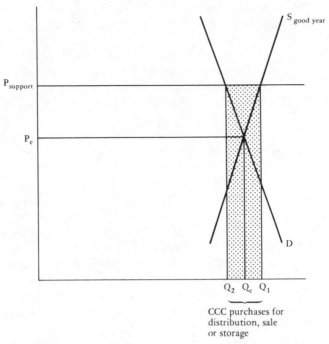

FIGURE 10-7. *The Commodity Corporation Price Support and Stabilization Program, 1933-72.*

The net cost of the above program was the cost to the CCC of acquiring and distributing the stocks through aid programs less any earnings from overseas sales. This cost had to be paid by the taxpayers. However, the burden of the program was also felt, often severely, by low income consumers, for whom the cost of food was a major item of household expenditures. Since the program restricted the supply of food and caused a higher price in the market, it tended to discriminate against such low income consumers.

Another program which could reduce the instability in domestic and world grain prices would be the formation of a world grain reserve. The United States is a strong supporter of this proposal because very few other countries have programs which help to stabilize grain prices. To date, suggestions for distributing the burden of storage problems among other countries have not been met with an enthusiastic response from the other grain importing or grain exporting nations.

In the absence of a world grain reserve, another measure to solve the price stabilization aspect of the farm problem is the domestic Farmer-Owned Reserve (FOR) program. First mandated in the Food and Agriculture Act of 1977, it included total target amounts for storage in both government and farmer-owned bins of 555 million bushels of wheat (of which a full 400 million bushels were to be held by farmers), 500 to 575 million bushels of corn, and 95-170 million bushels of other grains. The wheat stocks were designed to meet the needs of foreign aid and exports, while the corn and other grain reserves were directed at the needs of livestock producers at home and abroad and for human consumption in some less developed nations.

1. It ensures that government and farm reserves are held in adequate quantity to meet the needs of consumers, export to foreign nations, and foreign aid.
2. It permits the recall of loans and the resale of government stock during high prices and low reserves.
3. It reduces the high and low extremes of farm prices to benefit farmers in their production and tax management.

Figure 10–8 shows how the farmer-owned reserve helps improve price stability and rational marketing of grain commodities as compared with the CCC program alone or the CCC program set-aside. Figure 10–8a shows the demand and supply curves for the supported commodity with just the CCC program. There is a support price of $2.35, below which the government will not let the price fall. However, without acreage reductions, the supply curve lies far to the right and an excessive amount of production occurs. The government is forced to spend a substantial amount of money on maintaining the CCC reserves it buys from the farmers. Only if the price reaches a very high level will the government dump the extra amount in the reserves on the market. This either-or decision may cause the price to drop quickly. Thus, the use of the CCC program alone is clumsy and ineffectual in raising prices and does not allow for the gradual release of stocks onto the market to stabilize price.

Figure 10–8b shows the case for the set aside plus CCC program. Here the situation is improved because the supply curve is shifted to the left. Therefore, the price is supported at $2.70 rather than $2.35 because of a higher intersection of the demand and supply curve. Note that the demand and supply curves in both panels 10–8a and 10–8b are not straight lines. This is because government intervention into markets has changed their shape.

Figure 10–8c shows the case for the addition to the above programs

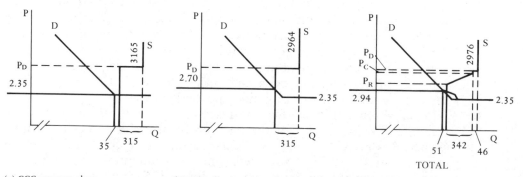

(a) CCC program alone   (b) CCC plus set-aside programs   (c) CCC plus set-aside and FOR

FIGURE 10–8. *Supply and Demand Configuarations under Three Policy Alternatives. (Source: Meyers, Willi, Department of Economics, Iowa State University, Ames Iowa, Unpublished Class Exercise.)*

of the Farmer-Owned Reserve. Because farmers are also encouraged to withhold production through storage payments on their own farm, the intersection of the supply and demand curves is at its highest point ($2.94). Note also that the shape of both the demand and the supply curves has changed. A much smaller amount of the supply curve is represented by CCC stocks, and a substantial portion with a gradual slope has been added. This latter section is attributable to the FOR program. The upward bulge in the demand curve is also attributable to the FOR program, because the farmers themselves are now responsible for an added component to the demand for the commodity: the demand for stocks to fill their bins in order to take advantage of the government programs. Along the gradual slope of the supply and demand curve, individual farmers make decisions on whether to enter or withdraw from the reserve based upon their perceptions of how price will move in the future, their willingness to bear risk, and their needs for immediate cash.

The third aspect of the present farm problem is chronically low farm income. The existence of unusually low incomes to producers in the agricultural sector goes against the American ideal of commutative justice, which states that all workers should get a fair return to their labors. One reason agricultural producers tend to receive low incomes in any economy is that they produce a commodity for which the demand is fairly constant regardless of the price that consumers must pay. Economists say that the demand for agricultural commodities is therefore "price inelastic."

Figure 10-9 shows that because of the very steep demand curve which accompanies most agricultural commodities, the less that farmers as a group produce, the more total revenue they will earn. You can prove this to yourself by comparing the areas **obcf** and **oade** in Figure 10-9a. The difference in net revenue is even greater because by producing and

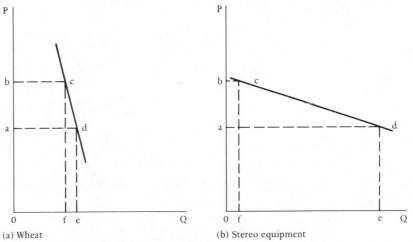

(a) Wheat (b) Stereo equipment

FIGURE 10-9. Elasticity and Its Effect on Total Revenue for Agricultural and Nonagricultural Commodities.

marketing **of** units of output farmers are saving costs compared with producing and marketing **oe** units. Figure 10–9b shows the situation for the producers of such nonagricultural goods as stereo equipment. Because of the different slope of the demand curve, the area **oade** is larger than **obcf**. This, it pays the producers of stereo equipment to try to produce and market as much as they can to maximize total revenue.

A second reason for low farm incomes is that it is hard for widely scattered and independent-minded agricultural producers to organize to restrict the amount marketed. It is often each producer for himself. Thus, there is no market mechanism to restrict the quantity of food produced and marketed in order to earn higher incomes. Such American farm groups as the National Farmers' Organization have tried to reduce marketing by 30 percent, but they have not been able to get the majority of the producers of a good to agree to such a plan.

The problem of low farm incomes may be solved through the Commodity Credit Corporation programs designed to ease price instability. However, as noted, the effects on the poorer consumers may be unacceptable to society as a whole. Therefore, in 1973, a program of supporting farm incomes through transfer or deficiency payments to producers was adopted as a substitute for increasing incomes through higher prices. Figure 10–10 shows the basic principles of the deficiency payment program, first suggested by then Secretary of Agriculture Brannan in 1949 but not adopted until the 1970s.

As under the CCC program, the government wishes to support prices at the price P_s by taking some land out of production. However, because not all farmers will join the program, it sets a target price P_t so that the net support price will work out to P_s. The target price was set by reference to the parity concept in the 1973 Agriculture and Consumer Pro-

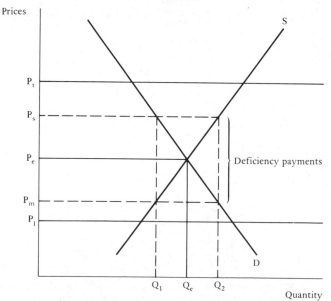

FIGURE 10–10. The Operation of the Target Price and Deficiency Payment Program.

tection Act, but in 1977 the target price was set by referring to actual production costs over the previous three years.

The program works as follows. The producers are willing to, and do, produce as much as is consonant with the support price and the supply curve for the commodity in question, Q_2. This means that there is greater production than would be indicated by the original equilibrium price. However, instead of buying up this extra production, the government allows it to be marketed. Market price falls from P_e to P_m, with consequent savings to the lowest income consumers, for whom food, a major item of their budgets, is now both plentiful and cheap.

Agricultural producers who participate in the program receive their income through two means. First, they receive the market price P_m times the amount they sell. Second, they receive a check from the government, called a "deficiency payment," based on the amount they produce times the difference between the target price and either the market price or the loan rate (P_1, a price floor), whichever difference is less. The formula to determine the amount of deficiency payments to an individual producer is:

$$\text{Deficiency payment} = \min(P_t - P_m, P_t - P_1)^1 \times \text{normal acreage} \times$$
$$\text{normal yield} \times \text{national allocation factor},$$

where the national allocation factor reflects the percentage of total target land taken out of production by program participants in a given year.

The deficiency payment program is preferable to the CCC program because:

1. Producer incomes are still supported at the support prices.
2. There is a strong inducement for farmers to participate by reducing acreage planted, because they are ineligible for government checks to augment their income if they do not.
3. Low-income consumers receive plentiful food at low costs.
4. The major cost of the program is borne by the government, and ultimately the taxpayers who must pay for the checks to producers.

Since the tax structure in the United States is, despite its loopholes, still primarily progressive, it is the high income taxpayers in society that are subsidizing the low income consumers and the risk-bearing agricultural producers. Because of this new component to the agricultural acts of 1973 and 1977, the CCC program has been reduced considerably. Another reason for the reduction in size of the CCC program has been the farmer-owned reserve already described.

The fourth aspect of the present farm problem is that of the distribution of incomes and government program benefits between small and

---

[1] *The expression, min $(P_t - P_m, P_t - P_1)$, is read: "the difference between the target price and the market price or the target price and the loan rate, whichever is less."*

large farms within the agricultural sector. It is not enough to assure that farmers as a group get a fair and stable income; Americans also place a value on equity and charity. Many would like to see that small and/or beginning farmers receive higher proportional returns to help them continue farming. Table 10–2 shows the situation for the distribution of farm income and program benefits for 1978. The smallest 50 percent of producers received only 10 percent of the program benefits from commodity support programs. Similar patterns held for other supported commodities in the 1960s and for farm programs in general through the 1970s. In fact, then Secretary of Agriculture Robert Bergland candidly admitted in a speech in 1979 that government programs to help farmers— whether in terms of market prices, deficiency payments, or credit— systematically favored the haves over the have-nots within the agricultural sector. Even though the sophistication and effectiveness of programs to help farmers as a whole have increased over time, the goal of equity within the farm sector is not being met.

Attempts have been made to channel the benefits of government programs to smaller-scale producers. However, as long as government program benefits are calculated on the basis of acreage or yield, there will be a natural tendency for the larger-scale producers to receive a greater share of the benefits. Moreover, the limit on government commodity payments to any individual producer was $50,000 per year through 1985, a sizeable amount of **extra** income in addition to normal net farm income. Thus, unless the laws are revised in future Agriculture and Food Acts, the question of equity in the agricultural sector may continue to be a problem.

The fifth aspect of the present farm problem relates to the efficiency of resource allocation to maintain high rates of output and fair returns to the owners of the factors of production. American society values hard work and no interference with the efficient allocation of resources. On the other hand, the increasing concern for the environment has meant that society is now seeking to restrict the use of agricultural chemicals and control the rate of soil erosion so that resources can be

TABLE 10–2.   DISTRIBUTION OF PROGRAM DIRECT PAYMENTS BY COMMODITY, 1978

	Percent of Total Payments Received by			
Commodity	*Smallest 50% of Farmers*	*Largest 50% of Farmers*	*Largest 10% of Farmers*	*Numbers of Farmers*
Wheat	10.9	89.1	50.5	38,734
Cotton	6.2	93.8	53.3	5,045
Rice	7.0	93.0	39.8	1,658
Feed grain	13.3	86.7	39.5	62,037
Total	9.7	90.3	46.0	73,635

Source: Lin, W. and L. Calvin. *Farm Commodity Programs: Who Participates and Who Benefits.* USDA Agricultural Economic Report No. 474, Washington, D.C., 1981.

husbanded for future generations as well as allocated to maximize returns in the present. Rather than see land set aside, our values prefer to see it used to produce more. Ways to ameliorate this aspect of the farm problem include:

1. Expanding foreign and domestic demand so that increases in productivity and efficiency in resource allocation can supply the demand at a still-acceptable price, and
2. Limiting the research of land grant and private scientists and entrepeneurs so that the supply curve will cease to shift out more quickly than the demand curve.

This latter solution is, however, untenable given both our cultural values and the rapid increase in the size of the world's population that must be fed.

The last two aspects of the farm problem relate to marketing rather than production. Farmers often find it difficult to obtain credit and manufactured inputs at fair prices because of the less-than-competitive structure of input supply markets into agriculture. As Bain has asserted, there is an intimate relationship among the structure, conduct and performance of marketing systems. Because the machinery supply market, for example, has oligopolistic tendencies, one has to question whether the prices that the farmers pay are fair.

Not only do farmers have an unfavorable bargaining position for inputs as a group, but small-scale and beginning farmers have particular trouble gaining access to the factors of production, notably land and credit, as you will study in Chapters 12 through 14. Therefore, the Farmers' Home Administration has been established to help farmers receive credit if they are unable to obtain it elsewhere. Certain states have also set up low-interest credit programs, especially for the purchase of land and machinery, to aid young farmers as they begin their farming careers.

In the same way that farmers face imperfect markets as they try to buy their production inputs, they also face imperfections in the output markets for their produce. They have found it difficult to assert their market power as they sell to grain companies and even local elevators because farmers have typically not been organized into marketing associations. Thus, at the same time the federal government was working towards controlling the concentration of power in the nonagricultural sector through the Sherman Anti-Trust Act of 1890 and the Clayton Act of 1914, it actually **encouraged** farmers to collude in the Capper-Volstead Act of 1922 and the Agricultural Marketing Act of 1937. In some cases, such as that of Ocean Spray cranberry producers and the Sunkist citrus producers, such cooperative associations of farmers have themselves come to control a large share of the market. In general, however, such facilitative legislation has failed to give farmers an equal bargaining position in their efforts to achieve a fair price for their products.

THE NEW AGENDA FOR AGRICULTURAL POLICY

The seven aspects of the farm problem listed in Table 10-1 have always posed hardships for U.S. farmers. It is now more difficult for farmers to get a favorable hearing of them because of the shrinking importance of farmers as a percentage of the population and because of additions to the policy agenda for food and agriculture over the decade of the 1970s. It is true that the clout of farm groups is disproportionate to their numbers, now less than 2.7 percent of the population. But farmers no longer have sufficient political power to obtain the legislation that they desire without compromise. As an example, farmers had to form a coalition with labor groups during passage of the 1977 Food and Agriculture Act. In return for labor's support of a high target price for peanuts, the farm groups had to drop their support of a work requirement as part of the eligibility standards for receiving foodstamps.

Figure 10-11 shows that the traditional inner triangle of Congress, farm organizations, and the executive branch of the government that used to set farm policy has now been joined by at least three other major actors in the policy area:

1. The Hunger Lobby and Consumer Protection Lobby. Their concern for safe, inexpensive food for all grew out of the efforts of Michael Harrington (who wrote *The Other America*, 1962) and Ralph Nader in the 1960s to rally support for the low-income consumer.

2. The Conservationist and Environmentalist Lobby. The key book in this area was Rachel Carson's *Silent Spring*, also published in 1962,

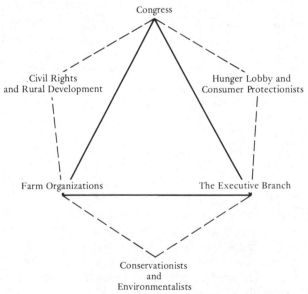

FIGURE 10-11. *The Expanded Cost of Contenders over the Food and Agricultural Policy Agenda.*

which described the effects of agricultural and other chemicals upon the natural ecology.

3. The Civil Rights and Rural Development Lobby. These lobbyists advocate fair treatment of all, regardless of race or income group, and efforts to retain and strengthen the quality of rural communities.

As a result of these new actors with a strong and increasingly powerful voice in programs that affect farm policy, the need for compromise by farm groups has increased. The very organization of the United States Department of Agriculture now reflects the changed agenda. Figure 10–12 shows that, in addition to their traditional responsibilities for marketing and international and commodity programs, the under-

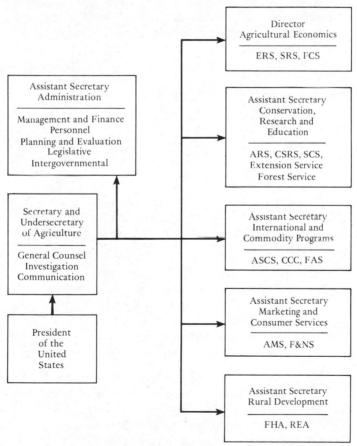

FIGURE 10–12. *Organization of Main Functions and Services of the U.S. Department of Agriculture. (Source: O'Rourke, A.D., The Changing Dimensions of U.S. Agricultural Policy, © 1978, p. 19. Reprinted by Permission of Prentice-Hall, Inc., Englewood Cliffs, N.J.*

secretaries of agriculture now have responsibilities for conservation, rural development, and consumer services, areas which reflect the three lobbies described above. Out of 9.7 billion dollars, the total 1979 USDA program budget, about two-thirds went for foodstamps and other food distribution programs (which increase farm incomes indirectly) and only about one-third to programs which directly helped support farmers.

To illustrate the conflict of interest between farmers and such other groups as the government, agribusiness firms, and consumers, Table 10–3 shows the positions that such groups might be expected to take with regard to various types of farm programs. Except for programs to expand demand, farmers are at odds with some group in regard to every type of government program. For example, while producers favor land retirement as a means of receiving income for not producing, all other groups (notably agribusiness, whose level of income depends upon input sales to farmers) are opposed to the program. On the other hand, producers and agribusiness firms find it in their self-interest to oppose measures to improve the environment favored by the consumers and the government.

THE FARM MANAGER'S RESPONSE

Given the provisions of the 1977 and 1981 Food and Agriculture Acts described previously, there are two decisions which the farm operator must face as he goes about maximizing and stabilizing his net farm income:

1. Whether or Not to Participate in the Set-aside Programs for the Crops He May Raise. A corollary decision regards the level, usually 10 or 20 percent, at which he will elect to set aside land from the production of these commodities.

2. Whether or Not to Place Crops in the Farmer-Owned Reserve. A corollary decision relates to when he should withdraw commodities from the program once he has placed them in reserve.

We have seen that the above programs help the government to control and stabilize the amount of grain supplied to the market place, to lower and stabilize food costs, and to offer farmers a chance to improve their income.

From the farmers' viewpoint, both questions involve a trade-off between taking the risks of private storage and uncontrolled production vs. the likelihood of higher, more stable prices as the operator endeavors to maximize total revenue and net farm income. Stated in its simplest terms, the set-aside question asks the farmer to calculate whether taking a certain amount of (often marginal) land out of production will justify, to him as an individual, the increased price from selling an inelastic commodity. The Farmer-Owned Reserve decision asks the farmer to calculate whether shifting the costs and risks of storage to the government is worth the loss of some of the farmer's cash flow flexibility.

TABLE 10-3. A SUBJECTIVE EVALUATION OF THE POSITION AND RELATIVE
INFLUENCE OF VARIOUS INTEREST GROUPS IN FOOD POLICY ON
CONTEMPORARY POLICY ISSUES

Issues	*Producers*	*Consumers*	*Government*	*Agribusiness*
Supply programs:				
Land retirement	+++	–	–	– –
Reserves	– –	++	+	++
Marketing orders	+++	– –	–	– –
Demand programs:				
Market development	++	n	++	+++
School lunch	++	++	+	+++
Food stamp	+	++	+	+++
Generic advertising	++	n	n	+
Price programs:				
Price supports	+++	–	–	++
Bargaining	+	–	–	– – –
Electronic pricing	n	n	n	– – –
Structural programs:				
Deconcentration	n	++	++	– – –
Countervailing	+	– –	–	– – –
Consumer programs:				
Specific issues[1]	n	+++	n	– – –
Consumer agency	n	+++	–	– – –
Input programs:				
Finance	++	n	–	–
Research	++	n	+	++
Conservation	++	n	(+–)	++
Water	+	+	n	++
Labor	– –	+	+	(+–)
General economic programs:				
Price controls	– –	++	– –	– – –
Energy	–	+	+++	–
Environment	– –	++	++	– –

[+]favor;–oppose

[n]is unknown or not applicable

[1]Refers to issues such as unit pricing, grade labeling, and false advertising.

Source: *Agricultural Food Policy Review No. 1.* U.S.D.A. Washington, D.C., 1977.

The Set-aside Decision

To answer the first question, the farmer must calculate a series of block
budgets, as illustrated in Table 10-4. Participation in the set-aside program may reduce potential income because of the fewer acres planted.
Therefore, every individual farmer must calculate whether the expected
price and yield for his farm will result in enough extra income to make
the set aside worthwhile. Note that, in the case of this farm, they do

TABLE 10-4. BUDGETING THE EFFECTS OF PARTICIPATION VS. NONPARTICIPATION IN SET-ASIDE PROGRAMS FOR A TYPICAL INDIANA FARM, 1978

	Corn	Soybeans	Wheat	Wheat-Beans Dbl. crop	Corn percent set-aside		Wheat	Wheat-Beans Dbl. crop
					10	20		
1. Harvested acres	600	600	600	600	545	500	500	500-500
2. Set-aside acres	–	–	–	–	55	100	100	100
3. Yield	110	35	50	50-21	111	111	50	50-22
4. Assumed price	$1.90	$4.75	$2.25	$2.25-4.75	$2.00	$2.00	$2.25	$2.25-4.75
5. Gross sales	$125,400	$99,750	$67,500	$127,350	$120,990	$111,000	$56,250	$108,500
6. Estimated deficiency payments	–	–	–	$5,450	$16,000	$16,000	$15,000	$15,000
7. Gross receipts	$125,400	$99,750	$67,500	$127,350	$126,440	$127,000	$71,250	$123,500
8. Direct costs (harvested acres)	$47,190	$25,350	$25,620	$60,000	$42,864	$39,325	$21,350	$50,000
9. Direct costs (set-aside acres)	–	–	–	$412	$750	$750	$750	$750
10. Income over direct costs	$78,210	$74,400	$41,880	$67,350	$83,164	$86,925	$49,150	$72,750
11. Income over direct cost/acre	$130	$124	$70	$112	$139	$145	$82	$121

Source: Robbins, Paul R., "Participation vs. Nonparticipation in Set-aside Program," The Food and Agriculture Act of 1977, Purdue University Cooperative Extension Service Bulletin EC-469, West Lafayette, Indiana. p. 28.

not without deficiency payments. However, by participating in the set-aside program, the farm qualifies for the deficiency payments noted earlier, subject to a limit across all supported commodities of $50,000. On this farm, such deficiency payments result, even in the ten percent set-aside case for corn, in enough added income to make participation beneficial. Thus, if one only considers the deficiency payments, it is worthwhile on the farm we have chosen, to participate in the set-aside program. On other farms it may well not be, depending upon individual conditions.

But there are two further benefits from participation in the set-aside program. First, the farmer has been eligible in the past for disaster payments on any supported commodity he is unable to plant or which is damaged because of poor weather conditions. Payments were calculated at one-third of the target price multiplied by 75 percent of normal production. However, if yields were less than 60 percent of normal production, the farmer received 50 percent of the target price for any shortfall on planted acres for which the production was less than 60 percent of normal.

After 1982, the disaster payment program, along with the disaster loan programs administered under the Small Business Association and the Farmers Home Administration, was replaced by an expanded all-risk Federal Crop Insurance Corporation program to sell insurance to farmers (Chapter 9). It is believed that the larger more specialized, higher risk farmers will choose to purchase the insurance at higher levels of coverage with larger premiums while the smaller-scale, less specialized, lower-risk farmers will purchase it at lower levels of coverage and premiums. The federal government hopes that this program will, unlike many other federal programs, have a positive effect on income distribution. At the very least, it is hoped that income will be transferred from wealthier to less wealthy people, rather than the reverse.

The second further benefit from participation in the set-aside program is that the farmer qualifies for entry into the program of nonrecourse loan benefits under the CCC as well as the farmer-owned reserve. Thus, the second question only becomes relevant once the first question has been answered in the affirmative.

The Government Storage Decision

If a farmer wishes to place his crop under CCC loan, he must first go to the local Agricultural Stabilization and Conservation Service (ASCS) office, which inspects his facilities for adequate quality. The amount of loan he receives depends upon the quantity of grain the farmer puts up as collateral.

Interest is substantially below market rates from other sources of loans, and has been as low as seven percent. The farmer is required to hold the grain for at least nine months, after which time he has three choices:

1. Turn the grain over to the CCC in lieu of total principal and interest payments for the loan. The CCC has no recourse but to accept this payment in kind, hence the name "nonrecourse" loans.
2. Sell the grain at a (higher) price in the market and pay off the loan plus interest.
3. Enter the Farmer-Owned Reserve program for an indefinite period. The farmer is then required to pay interest at the subsidized rate for only the first nine months plus one additional year, after which there are no additional interest payments. As with other types of grain storage, the farmer is investing in a way if he continues to store. He obviously is forgoing marketing in the current period in expectation of higher future prices. The farmer will decide to store if:
   a. He believes the move will help him reduce risk.
   b. He can continue to operate his farm without cash from the sale of the commodity. In other words, if the market value is significantly higher than the value of the original CCC loan principal, there may be a cash-flow aspect to this decision.
   c. The anticipated increase in market price will exceed the costs of storage. In short, the farmer has to calculate whether the present value of the loan rate, the net storage payment, and the net final value of sales minus principal and interest will be greater than the current sale value of the commodity. This is basically a question of whether marginal revenue is greater than marginal costs, except that is involves discounting future returns into the present. Chapter 12 will demonstrate how this is done.

Once the farmer joins the Farmer-Owned Reserve, the government has a great deal of control over when he can withdraw the grain from reserve. The farmer is not allowed to withdraw the grain from farmer-owned reserve until the market price is at least equal to the release price (P_r in Figure 10–8c). This is defined as 125 percent of the loan rate for corn and 140 percent of the loan rate for wheat. When market price reaches this level, there is obviously a relative market shortage for the crop in question. The government "releases" the farmer from the FOR contract and allows him to sell his grain at this level without paying a penalty for early sale.

The farmer may continue to store grain after market price reaches the release level if he feels that future increases in price will exceed the storage costs. Again, however, he must base the decision to continue storage on his own cash-flow needs and his perception of and preferences for risk. Because all farmers differ with regard to these considerations, there is a gradual release of grain as price rises above the release level, as depicted by the segment of the supply curve between P_r and P_c in Figure 10–8c.

The endpoint of the segment is termed the call price, P_c, so named because if the market price rises to this level, the government "calls" the grain out of storage. The 1977 act set the level at 140 percent of the loan rate for corn and 197 percent of the loan rate for wheat. Clearly, when market prices reach this level, the shortage of the commodity in question has become marked. The producer has two choices at this point. He may:

1. Forfeit the grain in repayment of the loan, so that the government can put it on the market to reduce the market price.
2. Pay off the loan plus interest and keep the grain in expectation of even higher prices.

The second option involves a careful perception of what price trends will be. If the price declines, the farmer will have lost. If the price increases, the farmer will gain, but only if the market price increases by less than ten more percentage points of the loan rate (i.e., to P_d, 150 percent of the loan rate for corn, for example). This level is called the "dumping" price for the commodity, at which the government enters the market and sells off its CCC stocks. If such an event occurs, the market price will fall and the farmer may fail to maximize returns.

The Farmer-Owned Reserve program provides for the more gradual release of stocks onto the market. It is more attractive than ordinary storage to farmers because:

1. The cash payments by the government reduce the cash-flow problems which attend any storage investment decision by farmers.
2. Storage costs are less than under normal storage because of the storage payment and the waiver of interest on the loan after the first 21 months.
3. Because the government has no recourse but to accept the grain lieu of payment, downside risk from price movements is limited.

Thus, the Farmer-Owned Reserve program benefits both the government and farmers. However, early studies have suggested that since, like most other government programs to farmers, it depends on volume, it tends to be the large-scale cash grain farmers who are the major program participants and beneficiaries. Nevertheless, because of the complex nature of the farm problem, the Farmer-Owned Reserve, in combination with the set-aside, CCC and deficiency payment provisions of the current agricultural legislation, provides a package superior to any single and simplistic answer to the farm problem, such as parity pricing.

SUMMARY

Six factors underlie the supply curve: price, yield of the commodity in question, price of competing and complementary goods, yield of competing and complementary crops, technology, and prices of the production inputs. Five factors underlie the demand curve: price, income, price of complementary and competing goods, population size, and consumers' tastes and preferences. For both types of curves a change in price involves a movement along the curve, whereas a change in any other factor involves a shift of the curve itself.

Market equilibrium occurs when the quantity supplied and the quantity demanded are equal. When this equilibrium price does not result in high enough income for farmers, a farm problem results. The current United States farm problem not only involves low prices and excess capacity, it is also related to six other issues. These are: price instability, chronically low farm income, income distribution within the agricultural sector, inefficient resource allocation, and the unequal bargaining position of farmers in both the input and output markets. The seven aspects of the current farm problem violate values in American society which may themselves be in conflict. Therefore there are no easy answers to achieving greater equity and efficiency of agricultural production in this country.

The consumer protection lobby, conservationists, and the rural development lobby have joined the traditional actors in formulating food and agricultural policy. This means that farm groups must rely increasingly on compromise to achieve their ends. The set-aside program and the Farmer-Owned Reserve are two areas of agricultural policy which have resulted from such political compromises. To decide whether or not to join the set-aside program, the farmer must calculate a series of block budgets to assess the benefits and drawbacks of participating. In order to determine whether or not the store crops under the Farmer-Owned Reserve program, the farmer must decide whether or not his risk will be lessened, if he can continue to operate his farm without the cash from the sale of the commodity at favorable current prices, and whether or not he anticipates a rise in the price of the commodity. Because of the complex nature of the farm problem, such combinations as the Farmer-Owned Reserve and the set-aside programs provide a package of balancing measures superior to parity prices and other single and simplistic resolutions to the United States farm problem.

TOPICS FOR DISCUSSION

1. What would be the effect of a sudden large sale of corn to the People's Republic of China on the corn and fed cattle markets in the United States? Support your answer by reference to the factors which underly the relevant supply and demand curves for the two commodities.

2. How has the price of the major farm commodities from your state moved in comparison with the general price level in recent years? What factors underlying the demand and supply curves for these commodities have been responsible?

3. Which aspect of the seven that make up the current farm problem is most severe in your state? Which commodities are most affected? What programs do you think would be most effective in alleviating the problem?

4. What is the participation rate of farm operators in your state in the set-aside and farmer-owned reserve program? Do farmers participate in government programs for milk, tobacco, and other commodities? Are farmers satisfied with the options these programs provide? How have transportation rates trended over recent years for individual commodities?

5. What are the two major farm organizations in your state? What are their stated goals? Would these goals, if implemented, have the effect intended by the members of the organization? What adverse side effects might result, and who would be most affected by them?

6. What nonproducer actors in the policy process (environmentalists, consumer-advocates, etc.) have entered the policy debate in your state in recent years? What specific programs do they advocate? Discuss these programs in terms of economic efficiency and social equity.

SUGGESTED READINGS

Agricultural Food Policy Review No. 1. U.S.D.A. Washington, 1977.

Bain, Joe S. *Industrial Organization.* Wiley, New York, 1968.

Carson, Rachel. *Silent Spring*, Houghton Mifflin, Boston, 1962.

Cochrane, Willard. *The Development of American Agriculture: A Historical Analysis.* Minneapolis: University of Minnesota Press, 1979.

Elterich, G. J. and S. Masud. "Milk Supply Response in Delaware," *Journal of the Northeastern Agr. Econ. Council*, Vol. 9, No. 1., 1980.

"Estimated Impacts *with* Exporter Cartels." Unpublished mimeographed study on the effects of the 90 percent parity proposal. USDA. Washington, undated.

Harrington, Michael. *The Other America: Poverty in the United States.* MacMillan, New York, 1962.

O'Rourke, A. Desmond. *The Changing Dimensions of U.S. Agricultural Food Policy.* Englewood Cliffs, New Jersey: Prentice-Hall Inc., 1978.

Paarlberg, Don. *Farm and Food Policy: Issues of the 1980s.* Lincoln, Nebraska: Univeristy of Nebraska Press, 1980.

Tweeten, Luther. *Foundations of Farm Policy.* Second edition. Lincoln, Nebraska: University of Nebraska Press, 1979.

Part IV

The Real World

11

Managing Labor and Human Capital

Then He said to his disciples, "The harvest is abundant
but laborers are few."

Matthew 9:38

Concepts

In this chapter, you will come to understand:

1. Two major sources of management expertise for operating a farm
   business.
2. Two major sources of labor for the farm business.
3. The relationships between the value marginal product, wages, and
   the most economic level of labor hiring.
4. The tangible and intangible factors sought by employers and
   employees in satisfactory labor agreements.

Tools

You will also gain the following skills:

1. How to increase labor efficiency on the farm.
2. How to plan a labor calendar.
3. How to make effective use of hired labor.
4. How to analyze and improve work methods.
5. How to reduce seasonal variations in labor use.
6. How to become a successful personnel manager.

We have already covered farm **objectives**, economic **principles**, **budgets**, and **adjustments** for risk and government programs. Now we are ready to look at the fifth piece of the farm management pie, acquiring control of and managing the **factors** of production: land, labor, capital and management (Figure 11–1). Note that acquiring control of the factors of production does not necessarily mean owning them. The idea of ownership is secondary. While ownership allows production in the short-run periods of low product prices and constitutes a form of investment for capital gain, it may also limit the flexibility of the farm operation, as you have seen.

We shall discuss each factor of production in order of decreasing ease of initial acquisition: management, labor, capital, and land. For each, we shall first study the possible sources for obtaining control of the production factor and note advantages and disadvantages associated with each source. Then we will address the principles for wise use of each resource.

MANAGEMENT

There are two sources of management: that of the farm operator and his/her family, and professional management hired from outside. Operator management skills can be obtained by working on a farm from childhood, by serving as a farm laborer through experience in a lease or other farm business arrangement, or through owner-operation. Partnership with other individuals further enhances the pool of management

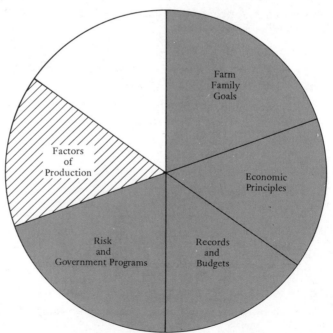

FIGURE 11–1. *The Components of Farm Business Management. Adding the Factors of Production.*

skills. Management assistance is also available from publicly supported sources such as state and local Agricultural Extension Services, the Soil Conservation Service, the Forestry Service, and so on.

Everyone has management skills. This text cannot make you a farm manager, because you already are that to a certain degree. However, it can make you a better farm manager by alerting you to all of the important aspects of farm management that must be taken into account and the tools for successfully handling each. The quality of an individual's management should improve over time.

Professional management, by contrast, involves payment by often absentee or affluent owners to an individual manager or management firm to meet the management objectives laid down by the owners. Professional firms are quite willing to manage your farm for you. But they pose two disadvantages. First, each manager has twenty to forty farms to oversee (if they are primarily livestock operations, it will be closer to twenty, if they are cash grain operatons, it will be closer to forty), and he cannot feel the personal commitment to any one farm that the owner-operator can feel toward his own. Nor can he possibly know the spots of poor drainage and other problems as well as the owner-operator.

Secondly, such managers treat returns to management differently from the average farmer. For the owner-operator, returns to management = NFI—return to equity capital—returns to unpaid labor. As you saw in Chapter 6, this figure is often negative. If the operator manages his own farm, he can simply shrug his shoulders and hope for better success next time.[1] Better still, he can exercise the evaluation function and learn from experience.

But the professional farm manager takes out the return to management (often eight or ten percent of the gross value of production!) first, leaving the other factors of production to fight over the remainder. By hiring a farm manager, the owner may often accept lower rates of return to the other factors of production that he contributes. Only if hired management is of sufficiently higher quality to generate a much greater return than the operator's management can it pay for itself. Therefore, the farm owner should make sure the hired manager is worth his charge before hiring (or continuing to hire) his services. The major unequivocal benefit of a hired farm manager is his nearby location to handle on-the-spot arrangements for the absentee farm owner.

LABOR

There are two sources of labor: **fixed** and **variable**. The first source includes operator, family, permanent hired, and partnership labor. These types of labor represent a fixed cost in operating the farm. The second source is short-term hired and cooperative labor. By contrast, these

---

[1] *Of course, a truly disastrous year may have more serious consequences: reduced level of living, delayed machinery replacement, no vacation, inability to service debts, and possibly even complete liquidation of the farm assets.*

types of labor represent a variable cost. In addition, these different types of labor have different capabilities, seasonal availabilities, and attitudes. They must be managed accordingly.

Why should the farm operator be concerned with managing labor in the first place? If any fixed or variable resource is used inefficiently, it can pull down the efficiency of the whole farm operation. There are three important reasons for maintaining high efficiency in the use of labor:

1. Labor productivity varies among individuals and farms. In a study of labor productivity on otherwise similar Illinois farms where hogs were produced in confinement, labor efficiency ranged from below 65 percent to over 140 percent of the average. Only 30 percent of the farms were at the average. If the operator compares output per man and per hour on his farm with those on other farms and discovers less than average productivity, he should ask himself, "Do I have an inefficient feeding system?", "Could I run more hogs with the same amount of labor?", "Do my workers work?" "Are they disorganized in their work routines?" and other questions. Some of the possible reasons for low productivity have to do with inefficient operating techniques and some with poor personnel management (to be discussed later).

2. Labor is a major farm cost. With the migration of more and more labor to the cities (between 1929 and 1965 there was a net migration of 47 million workers!) the agricultural wage has been bid up. Now, in many parts of the Midwest, one cannot hire teenagers to weed beans for less than \$5/hour. It is true that the costs of other variable inputs are also going up, but there has been greater technological advance in those inputs. Study Figure 11–2 for a moment. If the wage increases from MIC_1 to MIC_2, the farm operator will have to cut back on labor use from L_1 to L_2 unless:

   a. He can think of ways to make labor more efficient. Higher labor efficiency increases production and earnings. This is because increasing the MP of labor (which multiplied by the output price equals VMP) gives him a greater value of production for any given labor input by pushing out the VMP curve from VMP_1 to VMP_2.

   b. There is a dramatic increase in output price.

3. There are fewer **qualified** farm workers available. Not only has there been a reduction in the total number of farm workers needed per acre, there have also been great technological changes which have made the skill levels required of the labor we use much higher. Would you be willing to go to the Bahamas for a month to take a well-earned vacation, give someone else the keys to your brand-new, air-conditioned combine and have him take over your brand-new hog confinement facilities? Probably not. One hundred years ago, agricultural technology was very simple: farmers plowed by horse and picked corn by hand. Now, a great deal more trust is required by management, and there is more chance of permanent damage to

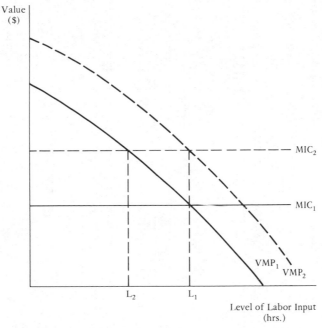

FIGURE 11-2. *The Labor-Hiring Decision as Costs Change.*

valuable equipment and enterprises by workers. The relative short-age of skilled labor makes labor management in agriculture even more difficult.

For these three reasons, labor efficiency is important. But, how does the manager go about increasing efficiency? The first step is to try to balance the supply and demand of labor on the farm to make sure there is enough labor (to use the other resources efficiently) but not too much (to involve excess wage or opportunity cost). The operator must inventory supply, i.e., how much of each of the six types of labor listed earlier he has available (Table 11-1). It is very important to list the labor not just as an annual total, but on a much more frequent basis: by month, or better still, bi-weekly periods. Otherwise, the operator may find he has enough labor overall, but faces real shortages at the time of harvest or farrowing.

Against this supply question on the individual farm, it is interesting to note how labor availability in the country is changing. The USDA defines four classes of farm labor:

year-round ≥ 250 days
regular   = 150–249 days
seasonal   = 25–149 days
casual   =   1–25 days

Of the classes listed the fastest declining are year-round labor and regular labor, exemplified by the old concept of the hired hand who was needed for the entire growing season but often not the entire year. The largest

TABLE 11-1. LABOR AVAILABILITY BY SEASON IN HOURS

| Season/period | Fixed | | | Variable | |
	Operator	Family	Permanent Hired	Partnership	Short-term Hired	Cooperative
WINTER						
Dec 6–Mar 28						
SPRING						
Mar 29–Apr 11						
Apr 12–25						
May 10–23						
May 24–Jun 6						
SUMMER						
Jun 7–Jul 4						
Jul 5–Aug 1						
Aug 2–Sep 5						
FALL						
Sep 6–19						
Sep 20–Oct 3						
Oct 4–17						
Oct 18–31						
Nov 1–14						
Nov 15–Dec 5						

percentage of total farm workers is seasonal and casual (71 percent in 1979). The large numbers of custom-hired help, summer help from youths, and migrant cash-crop labor mean that the farm operator must often deal with more people on a shorter-term basis. Special training and instructions have to be repeated more often and are understood less well. This again increases the need for personnel management skills.

Once the operator has inventoried his labor supply, he must also estimate total farm labor needs (or demand). There are three ways to do this:

1. Consult Standards of Different Farm Sizes and Types. This is an acceptable approach if one is just starting out in farming and wants to estimate how much labor may be needed for a 240-acre hog-and-cash-grain farm or whatever size and type of farm is being considered. The problem is that the prospective farm operator will only get the data on an annual basis, and will have no idea of the seasonal bottlenecks he may run into. Therefore, the second method is preferable:

2. Keep Detailed Labor Records, Adding Overhead Labor to the Labor Needed for Each Enterprise. This should be done not only on a per year basis, but also per month or half-month. In other words, the time period subdivision used to measure supply should also be used to measure demand. All too many farmers keep accurate records for income tax purposes but totally neglect their labor data. Important types of analyses that can be done with labor data will be presented below so you should realize the importance of accurate estimates of labor needs.

3. Budget. If records are not yet available, one can estimate enterprise budgets based on the specific production practices to be used. Then one should multiply the per unit labor requirements by the number of units of each enterprise in the whole farm plan and sum the enterprises for each time period. Finally, overhead labor needs (both quantities and timing) must be added.

Suppose, that having measured his supply and demand of labor, the manager finds they are unequal, as they almost always will be. In the case where supply is greater than demand, he may pursue any or all of four strategies:

1. Increase the Volume of Business. By adding more land (perhaps through renting) and/or capital (e.g., machinery), he can complement his surplus labor and increase the productivity of the whole farm by shifting out the production possibility frontier. Alternatively, he may wish to move to a higher isoquant with the same amounts of land and capital by adopting more labor intensive technologies such as intensive hog farrowing.

2. Produce Higher Quality Products. The manager can push out the price of the products he produces by improving their quality, in other words, increasing P_1 will raise the *VMP* curve from VMP_1 to VMP_2 (Fig. 11-3). If this is possible, increasing labor use from L_1 to L_2 will increase his profit. For example, many farmers sell hogs on a grade-and-

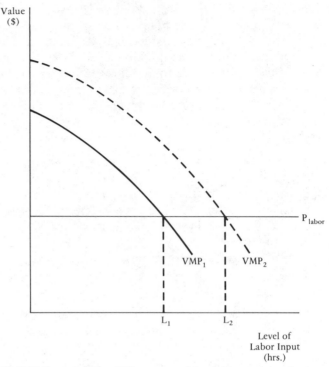

FIGURE 11–3. *The Effect on Labor Hiring of Producing Higher-quality Products.*

yield basis. They know that it takes more time and care to produce grade 1 hogs, but they can use their excess labor to do so and thereby push out the *VMP* curve. Similarly, farmers on contract with horticultural processing firms and seed companies can invest their labor to produce higher quality output, for which they are paid a premium price.

3. Perform Custom Work.   One can buy a machine and plow, harvest, or spray for neighbors who may have a labor shortage.

4. Perform Non-farm Work.   Especially if the farm operator has a large surplus for a continuous period (say, two or three months during the winter, or even one or two days per week during the year)[1] then it will be profitable to take a full or part-time job in town.

In the case where supply is less than demand, the farm operator has five options open to him:

1. Work longer. This may be the easiest solution in the short-term: most farmers are willing to and can work 16 to 18 hours a day during the planting and harvesting season and run their tractors all night. But, if they continue doing so for an extended period, they may be risking their health or even lives. Therefore, we must also consider other options:

[1] *You will learn in this chapter how to create this situation if you so desire.*

2. Hire additional labor, provided its *VMP* is greater than or equal to the wage the manager has to pay. Figure 11–4 shows the labor situation for a typical family-operated farm. "Fixed" represents all sources of fixed labor supply on the farm while "hired" represents the variable labor supply. If the operator finds himself at L_f, i.e., using only fixed labor, and wants to produce up to the point where he is equating the value produced with the wage, and profits are maximized, it will pay him to go out to L_t by hiring $t - f$ hours of outside help.

3. Exchange labor. In many farming contexts, a farmer and one or more neighbors will share a combine and hauling equipment at the time of harvest, in addition to their own labor. This practice reduces total machinery investment and increases the timeliness of these critical operations. With a little forward planning, they can reach an agreement on the order of harvesting among the cooperating farmers and rotate the order in following years. They not only reduce each person's fixed costs, they also reduce the labor shortage. Finally, they can actually save on record-keeping for purposes of tax reporting. Another example involves exchange labor between seasons. Suppose Farmer One, who raises apples, has excess labor in the spring while Farmer Two, who raises sheep, has excess labor in the fall. If One helps Two lamb in the spring and two helps One harvest in the fall, both can smooth out their respective seasonal differences in supply and demand.

4. Hire custom work. Of course, this is the converse to the third approach

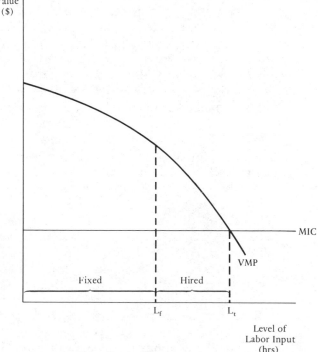

FIGURE 11–4. *The Labor-Hiring Option.*

of reducing excess labor supply. If, by using the other methods, the farmer still does not have enough time to plant or harvest, then he may hire someone else to come and do it. There may be timeliness losses, however. For example, if the job should be done on Tuesday but the custom operator does not get around to coming until Saturday, then field losses may be higher and the portion harvested may be of lower quality. There are trade-offs involved in almost every farm decision.

5. Finally, the operator can improve the efficiency of the labor hours he does use. This is easier said than done, but there are four basic methods of improving labor efficiency which he may consider:

   a. Plan a labor–use calendar by dividing all jobs into inflexible, semi-flexible and flexible. Setting up a table at the beginning of the year (or more frequently) is increasingly important because of the growing demands on the time of the farm operator. The consequences of forgetting something may be disastrous. The table usually resembles that shown in Table 11–2.

      In February, for example, the operator absolutely must prepare for calving, because he knows the cows are going to calf in March. He should also use records and price expectations to formulate budgets for the coming year. It is less important to finish his tax forms; less important still to paint buildings. In each month, he should start with the chores at the top of the list. Whatever he cannot finish in one month he should carry over to the next and move up in priority. This type of approach helps the farmer avoid waking up in a panic because the cows are calving that afternoon and he has not done anything to prepare for it.

   b. Make effective use of hired labor. The manager can implement this approach by paying good wages, maintaining good personal relationships, providing housing and good working conditions and providing incentive plans. Details of these and other aspects of personnel management will be presented at the end of this chapter.

   c. Improve operating techniques. There is a whole discipline entitled "motion studies and work simplification." Packing plants can completely process and wrap a hog every six seconds partly because an efficiency expert planned very carefully what was done, why, where, and how, and tried to make it as simple as possible. Of course, the farmer doesn't have time to become a motion-and-work expert. But he does have time every January to sit back and think through all the routine jobs he does and ask himself whether he always has to walk from the house to the back of the barn to get something he needs to use in the front of the barn. Or, whether there is some routine operation in the farrowing house that requires constant backtracking. If he can identify such problem areas, he should reorganize his equipment to increase the speed and simplicity of his valuable labor input. It is all too easy to fall into set habits, but every simplification will push out the *VMP* curve.

TABLE 11-2. A LABOR CALENDAR FOR A MIDWESTERN FARM

Urgency Level	January	February	March	April	May
Inflexible	Complete records Compute efficiency measures	Budget for coming year Prepare for calving	File tax forms Calving Apply for loans Buy machinery	Plow for row crops	Plant row crops
Semi-flexible	Budget for coming year Prepare for calving	Finish tax forms Apply for loans Buy machinery	Plow for row crops Paint buildings	Plant row crops	Renovate pasture
Flexible	Finish tax forms Buy machinery	Paint buildings		Renovate pasture	Repair fences

d. Reduce seasonal variations in labor use. Because labor is so scarce and valuable, the manager should avoid having either too little when he really needs it or long periods of "seasonal underemployment." Often if a farm operator can smooth out the peaks and the troughs in month-to-month labor use, he will find that he can free one family member to take a part-time or full-time job in town. Even if this is not feasible, he will reduce the strain of the peak periods.

There are two ways to study seasonal patterns of labor use with a view to reducing variability. The first is to graph actual labor use for the farm as a whole and for individual enterprises as shown in Figure 11–5. The data plotted are from an actual 320-acre farm in Illinois which raises crops and livestock and has maintenance and other overhead labor as well. The figure shows that crop labor use is what contributes to the seasonality. If crop production operations were not so variable, the farmer could probably get along with one and a half workers instead of two. This type of approach is important to problem identification but another step is helpful in showing how to improve on the situation. Therefore, using the second method is also advised.

Table 11–3 shows labor use on the Illinois farm using the same mean-and-coefficient-of-variation format used in the risk analysis of Chapter 8. Along the top the manager lists corn, soybeans, wheat, hogs, overhead, and total labor for the farm. Along the side, he lists not years

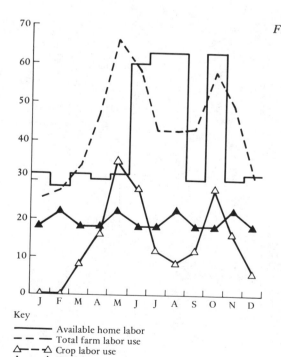

FIGURE 11–5. *Seasonal Patterns of Labor Use on a 320-Acre Illinois Farm. (Source: Adapted from Herbst, J.H., Farm Management, Principles, Budgets, Plans, Champaign, Illinois, 1976.*

Key

——— Available home labor
— — — Total farm labor use
△—-△ Crop labor use
▲—-▲ Hog labor use

(as in the risk analysis) but months. The goal is to minimize the variability of labor use, i.e., its coefficient of variation. On this farm, the variability in labor use is high for wheat (116%), lower for soybeans and still lower for corn. But the hog enterprise is the most stable: labor requirements vary only by five percent from month to month. Thus, the total variability of labor use on the farm is only thirty percent. If the manager wanted to get this down to ten or fifteen percent to free someone to go to work in town, all he would have to do is decrease wheat acreage, increase hog numbers, and perhaps achieve a better balance between corn and soybeans. Of course, this decision would only be profitable if the gains from outside employment outweighed the cost of shifting the farm plan away from the income-maximizing enterprise combination. This variability-of-labor-use management (to maximize the returns of both farm and nonfarm labor) is another important factor in choosing the combination of enterprises on the farm. This factor was included in a general way in the bi-monthly labor breakdown in the crops-livestock matrix of the whole-farm budget (Chapter 5). Now, however, you know a method which is much more precise and improves upon such yes-no decisions.

Finally, one should not neglect the inclusion of other enterprises which require labor mainly during the slack months of the base enterprises currently produced. Addition of these enterprises could also even out labor use. But their main benefit may be in employing the hired labor in slack periods to make sure it is available when needed during

TABLE 11–3.   COMPARATIVE VARIABILITY IN LABOR USE AMONG FARM ENTERPRISES[1]

	Corn	Soybeans	Wheat	Hogs	Overhead	Whole Farm
January	0	0	0	154	48	202
February	0	0	0	173	48	221
March	43	20	1	154	47	265
April	87	42	1	154	95	379
May	175	84	0	173	95	527
June	131	84	6	154	95	470
July	44	42	5	154	95	340
August	44	21	3	173	95	336
September	44	42	6	154	95	341
October	131	84	6	154	95	470
November	131	0	0	173	95	399
December	43	0	0	154	47	244
Full Year	873	419	28	1920	950	4194
$\overline{X}$	73	35	2	160	79	350
σ	57	34	3	8	23	105
C.V. (%)	78	97	116	5	29	30

[1]Calculated in terms of hours of labor use.

Source: Adapted from Herbst, J. H., *Farm Management, Principles, Budgets, Plans,* Champaign, Illinois, 1976.

peak periods of more profitable enterprises. This principle is vital, for example, to successful farming of tobacco, a high-value crop, in the southeastern United States.

PERSONNEL MANAGEMENT

Once the farm manager has decided how much labor he must hire for what task and which periods of the year, he must transform himself from a general economic analyst to a personnel manager. He must become a skilled psychologist, actor, teacher and at times even staff sergeant, because labor is a psychological as well as physical input. This dual nature of the labor resource makes it one of the most difficult but also one of the most rewarding to manage. A further complexity is that labor is a lumpy input: it cannot be conveniently divided into fractional units or employed only when it is strictly needed. Personnel management is a skill often overlooked in courses in agricultural colleges. But without these skills the productivity of the farm and the happiness of the farm family may be greatly reduced.

The farm operator must go through six labor management functions as he goes about dealing with hired help. These are acquisition, training, motivation, compensation, discipline and compliance. The prospective personnel manager must not only understand the principles of each of these functions, he must also be a good communicator. Communication is the lubricant which makes all of the above functions work smoothly. In the following sections, these six functions of personnel management will be described.

Acquiring Labor

In hiring labor it is extremely important that you take the time and effort to interest and attract the best possible candidates for the job. Although a formal application process may seem to take away valuable time from the rest of your operation, it is well worth the effort to hire workers as competent and productive as possible. Four principles are involved in successful acquisition of hired labor. First, you should try to sell the job as an opportunity for the employee to gain in experience and income. There clearly are advantages and disadvantages to working on the farm, but the prospective employee will not have applied unless he has some affinity for agricultural work. Therefore, in describing the job you should list the advantages in as favorable light as possible and portray the disadvantages as the inevitable reverse side of these positive aspects. For example, even though agriculture is one of the three most dangerous occupations in the United States, it allows the worker to enjoy outside and inside work. Moreover, even though it is hard to advance to a higher level position on the farm, the experience of having worked on one farm lends horizontal mobility for finding another farm job in the future. Also, even though the hours are long and sometimes unpredictable, the variety of tasks that can be done on an individual farm leads to both interest in the job and a sense of accomplishment.

Second, it is important to request formal applications and to interview the most likely candidates in person. Table 11–4 shows a typical application form for an Indiana farm. When the applicant comes for

TABLE 11–4. APPLICATION FOR EMPLOYMENT

Full Name _____

Address (Present) _____

_____ Zip Code _____

Social Security No. _____ Phone No. _____

Date of Birth _____ Place of Birth _____

Height _____ Weight _____

Education: Grade School _____ Yrs in High School _____ College _____

Married _____ Unmarried _____

Number of Children at Home _____

Number of Dependents Other Than Spouse & Children _____

_____

Most Recent Employer _____

Address _____

Type of Work _____

Reason for Leaving _____

Number of Years Farming Experience _____

Names and Addresses of Persons for Whom You have Worked or Who have Known You for Several Years:

Name and Address _____

_____

Name and Address _____

_____

Source: Adapted from Robbins, 1977.

the oral interview you should take the time to give him or her a tour of the farmstead, and to explain in as much detail the conditions of employment and the advantages and disadvantages of the job in question. You should be tolerant of and even respect penetrating questions by prospective employees.

Training Hired Labor

The training of hired labor is in fact a process of building human capital. **Human capital** was defined by Nobel laureate T. W. Schultz as "the capacity of a population to do mental and physical work to produce goods and services and manage society." It is a function of, among other things, education, leadership ability, and health. You should remember that, like other types of capital, human capital can depreciate, become obsolete, and break down. Therefore, it is necessary to have a continuous training process for the labor on your farm. A study by Huffman has found that training and other types of education can have two positive effects on the efficiency of a farm:

1. A worker effect which increases the marginal productivity of labor, and
2. An allocative effect which helps the farm worker to make wiser decisions as he goes about his day–to–day chores. For example, Huffman found that the rate of adjustment of the proper rate of nitrogen to corn is a function of education and extension on Cornbelt farms.

Given the importance of education of your hired labor, there are three types of training which you can consider. The first is **orientation** to the farm operation as a whole. Orientation is best handled during the trial period. Many farm workers have eventually quit because of inadequate information at the beginning of their employ. The second type of training relates to Huffman's worker efficiency. This is training in **task-oriented skills** and involves such abilities as the farrowing of sows, the fine-tuning of a tractor engine, and the setting of the seeding rate on a tomato planter. This stage is intermediate in the career of a farm worker. The third type of training relates to Huffman's allocative effect. This involves **decision-oriented skills**. To the extent that the worker will be able to make efficient day-to-day decisions on your behalf, you will be free to worry about even larger long-run planning on the farm. As you will see, these decision-oriented skills are the ones that give the greatest feeling of job satisfaction to most employees.

Table 11–5 shows that there are four levels of task complexity that the worker can grow into through these types of training. Level I includes jobs that the worker can do after the orientation stage. Levels II and III are primarily directed at task-oriented skills while Level IV allows the worker to use the decision-oriented training.

In all types of training, it is very important to have patience. Different workers learn at different rates and all go through periods of discourage-

TABLE 11-5. EMPLOYEE SKILL LEVEL BY ENTERPRISE AND JOB PER-
FORMED, INDIANA HIRED FARM LABOR SURVEY, 1975

Skill Level	*Percent of 1975 Employees*	*Enterprise*	*Example of Jobs Performed*
I	5	Crops	Haul grain from fields
		Swine	Scrape and clean floors
		Dairy	Clean barns and milkhouse; assist operator with milking
		Beef	Unskilled manual assistance with feeding and cleaning up of facilities
		Other	Provide unskilled manual assistance
II	14	Crops	Plow and disk with operator's largest tractor
		Swine	Deliver feed to feeder with auger wagon
		Dairy	Milk & feed on occasion unsupervised
		Beef	Operate tractor & loader or mechanical feeding equipment, etc.
		Other	Perform semi-skilled jobs
III	45	Crops	Safely & correctly operate all major equipment without close supervision
		Swine	Be in charge of care, feeding & farrowing for week or so
		Dairy	Milk & feed for a week unsupervised
		Beef	Look after cattle feeding operation for a week or so unsupervised
		Other	Be in unsupervised charge for a week or so
IV	36	Crops	Be in almost complete continuous charge of the crop enterprise (including chemical usage, planting, and harvesting)
		Swine	Be in almost complete charge of the swine enterprise (i.e. herdsman)
		Dairy	Be in almost complete charge of the dairy enterprise (i.e. herdsman)
		Beef	Be in almost complete charge except for buying and selling
		Other	Be in almost complete, continuous charge

Source: Robbins, 1977.

ment, frustration or boredom. It is important at those stages that you
exercise your skill as a psychologist and teacher.

Motivation

The hiring and training of workers is itself a way to motivate people to
help you run the farm efficiently. However, motivation is a very complex human phenomenon and one of the most difficult aspects of per-

sonnel management. Because each person is unique, there are no easy answers and no set approaches which you can use in all cases.

Table 11-6 shows that laborers, as they consider whether or not to supply their labor to you, have both intangible and tangible needs. A number of psychologists and farm economists, including Shapley, Herzberg, and Maslow, have listed various factors they consider to fall into these intangible and tangible categories. In addition, McGregor has asserted that there are two polar views of why people work: Theory X, which relies on threats, and Theory Y, which relies on stimulation to greater creativity. But the main conclusion from these psychologists is that both physical (tangible) and psychological (intangible) factors drive people to seek employment. The list of factors presented in Table 11-6 is still probably incomplete. What you must remember is that potential workers must feel they are getting access to most or all of these factors. One helpful rule of thumb is that money is a compensator not a motivator. You do not necessarily satisfy your employees by giving them everything money can buy.

At the same time, Table 11-6 shows that you, the farm manager, also have demands for certain intangible and tangible aspects of the labor that you hire. The tangible factors of physical strength, the ability to tinker with tractors and perform other technical operations, and the diligence to put in a forty or a sixty hour workweek are not sufficient as you seek to hire laborers that will meet all of your needs. In addition, you must look at the initiative, creativity, intelligence, and the potential management skills of the employees among whom you are choosing. This is another reason why an oral interview is an extremely important way for you to select the best employee.

One of the best ways to motivate workers is to use an incentive program. Often such programs link tangible output in the form of physical production with management programs that allow the employee to share net income. Thus, both parts of the worker's criteria in Table 11-6 are satisfied. As Table 11-7 shows, incentive plans may be based on a wide range of factors ranging from physical production to equity building. Each of these plans has advantages and disadvantages. For example, the physical production plan is easy to understand and may be adjusted to the time of performance, i.e. when calves are sold or oranges harvested. However, costs are often disregarded, adverse weather and other conditions may lead to low yield despite the employee's best efforts, and the employee may short-change other enterprises on the farm for which there are no incentive programs.

Incentive programs help to increase the overall profitability of the operation by prolonging the tenure of good workers, increasing their efficiency and feelings of common destiny with the farm, and improving worker morale in general. However, the effectiveness of an incentive plan depends upon a number of factors. These include an agreement in written form, compatible objectives of the employer and employee, sufficient reward to significantly improve performance, a straightforward and clearly expressed system of compensation, and, above all, the appli-

TABLE 11-6. TANGIBLE AND INTANGIBLE FACTORS IN MOTIVATING EMPLOYEES AND SATIS-
FYING EMPLOYERS

Motivate Employees	Shapley	Herzberg	Maslow	McGregor	Satisfy Employer
Intangible Factors					*Intangible Factors*
Achievement & self-fullfilment	√		√		Intelligence
Recognition & esteem	√	√	√	Theory	Initiative
Responsibility		√		Y	Creativity
Promotion & growth (incl. training)	√	√			Management skill
Tangible Factors					*Tangible Factors*
Wages & other compensation	√	√			Physical prowess
Work conditions	√	√			Technical skills
Social needs (including affection)			√	Theory X	
Physical needs	√		√		Diligence
Relations with supervisor and co-workers		√			
Vacation		√			
Security	√		√		

Sources: Shapley, 1970; Herzberg, et, al, 1959; Maslow, 1970; McGregor, 1967.

TABLE 11-7.   TYPES OF INCENTIVE PLANS FOUND
ON INDIANA FARMS IN 1975

Item	*Percent*
Farms on an incentive plan	34
Full-time employees on an incentive plan	23
Plans based on:	
(a) Physical production	36
(b) Gross income	9
(c) Net income	11
(d) Tenure	4
(e) Equity building	6
(f) Other	2
(g) Two or more of above plans[1]	32

[1]When two or more plans were used, the second plan was often
the equity building plan (employee permitted to keep a few
livestock, etc.).

Source: Robbins, 1977.

cation of the incentive agreement to tasks over which the employee has
control.

Compensation

The tangible elements in Table 11-6 all represent possible forms of
compensation and are distinct from those intangible factors which relate primarily to motivation. Compensation can thus take the form of
cash wages, acceptable working conditions, favorable employee relations,
and periodic upgrading of the employee's title. Of these, the most critical
to establish is the cash equivalent value of wages and fringe benefits.
Table 11-8 illustrates a useful format for summing different types of
benefits. If these benefits are established by reference to the supply
factors of Table 11-6, then you may consider the rate that is required
to keep an employee under your employ, the salaries that previously
hired employees are already paid, the established wage rate in the farm
community as a whole, or an incentive plan. If the wage is set from the
point of view of the demand factors in Table 11-6, in other words from
the point of view of the employer, then the value of that added worker
to the farm can be assessed through analysis of the value marginal product curve. You can then offer a wage which is less than or equal to
the value of the last day of work that you anticipate to be contributed
by that employee.

A study of the total wage and benefit packages on typical Indiana
farms was conducted in 1975. Although by the single largest component
of overall compensation was a cash wage, incentive payments, the value
of housing, rent, room and board were also significant factors. Incentive
payments represented about three percent, housing about seven percent
and bonuses about five percent of the total wage and benefit package.

TABLE 11–8.   EMPLOYEE WAGE AND BENEFIT STATEMENT

Employee _____ Social Security No. _____

Address _____ Base Wage _____

Items	This Pay		Brought Forward		Total to Date	
	Quantity	Dollars	Quantity	Dollars	Quantity	Dollars
Cash Wages						
1. Basic rate						
2. Overtime pay						
3. Incentive or bonus pay						
4. Total cash benefits						
Wages Withheld						
5. Social security	XXXX		XXXX		XXXX	
6. Income tax	XXXX		XXXX		XXXX	
7. TOTAL (5 + 6)	XXXX		XXXX		XXXX	
8. Net Pay (4 – 7)	XXXX		XXXX		XXXX	
9. Less advanced pay	XXXX		XXXX		XXXX	
10. Net check (8 – 9)	XXXX		XXXX	XXXX	XXXX	XXXX
Non-cash Benefits						
11. Housing						
12. Food items						
13. Utilities						
14.						
15.						
16.						
17. TOTAL (11 – 16)						
18. TOTAL BENEFITS (4 + 17)						

Source: Robbins (1977) as adapted from: "Rural Manpower Center Special Paper #1," L. H. Brown, Michigan State University.

Discipline

Discipline is one of the least pleasant functions of personnel management for most farm operators. It is here that one must be either an actor or a staff sergeant or both. One must be firm but also reasonable and consistent in meting out disciplinary actions consistent with the nature and magnitude of the transgression. Again, it is best to have the consequences of failing to behave according to the contract spelled out in writing at the time the labor agreement is made. The necessity of discipline falls into the theory of threats and punishment of McGregor's Theory X (Table 11–6).

A helpful rule of thumb in disciplinary action is as follows: when pressed, employees will respond in ways atypical of their usual personalities. The person who is usually meek and conscientious will usually turn defensive and aggressive if confronted. Therefore, meek individuals should not be treated harshly. On the other hand, people who tend to arrogance and cockiness may be cowed into submission by an employer taking a strong stance. Thus, a given employer must develop the ability to act out often unpleasant roles to elicit improved behavior from diverse employees.

Compliance

There are a wide range of laws and regulations passed by federal and state governments of which the farm operator must be aware. These fall into nine categories:

1. Minimum Wage Law.   All agricultural employers who use more than 500 person days of labor in any three-month period of the preceding year are required to pay a federal minimum wage. In 1981 this was $3.35 per hour but it will increase over time with inflation. Paradoxically, although the minimum wage rate increases the incomes of those employees that are hired, it also tends to reduce the number of agricultural workers who are offered employment. Therefore, it may actually have an adverse affect on the distribution of rural incomes as a whole.

2. Unemployment Insurance.   The farm operator must pay unemployment insurance if he pays $20,000 in total wages and salaries in any three-month period or hires at least ten workers for at least 20 weeks.

3. Workers' Compensation Insurance.   The farm operator is required to purchase this insurance in certain states. The employer pays a premium based upon the total amount of salaries and wages that he pays in a given year. If there is a farm accident of any type, participation in workers' compensation insurance programs frees the individual employer from liability for damages and injuries and the possibility of being sued. Therefore, even though the rates tend to be high, many farm employers are happy to pay for this type of insurance.

4. Social Security.   If the employee receives $150 or more or works for 20 days or more for cash, the farm operator must pay an amount equal to the social security deduction from the employee's pay. The exceptions to this rule are the farm operator's own family members under the age of 21 and the farm spouse.

5. Federal Income Tax Withholding.   This is an optional program, but the farm operator must be careful to handle all of the forms required.

6. Health and Housing.   If the operator hires migratory farm workers, he must house them and provide health and other sanitary facilities in compliance with statutes imposed by the Departments of Labor and Health and the Occupational Safety and Health Administration (OSHA). OSHA also requires that the farm operator provide safety training, a safe place in which to work, and warning signs for all areas of the farm operation.

7. Child Labor Laws.   The farm operator cannot hire workers under the age of 16 in hazardous tasks or during school hours. Children ages 12 and 13 can be employed within these rules only with parental consent.

8. Discriminatory Hiring.   The farm operator cannot discriminate on the basis of race or ethnic background if he hires 15 or more employees.

9. Employee Retirement Plans.   These may be required in certain states. The farm operator must contribute to the buildup of a farm retirement fund for each employee. Another responsibility is to maintain records on these retirement plans.

LABOR ISSUES FOR THE 1980s AND 1990s

Hired workers were only 23 percent of the agricultural workforce in 1950 but by 1980 had increased to 35 percent. As the total size of the agricultural work force declined, the percentage of family farm workers declined even faster. This is because mechanization has progressed most rapidly on the family farm. Hired labor is most important in the coastal areas. Figure 11–6 shows that a full 73 percent of the agricultural work-force in California and Nevada was hired, followed by 47 percent in the northwestern states and 45 percent in the northeastern states. By contrast, only 18 percent of the agricultural workforce was hired in the six states centered on Kansas City. Contrary to popular belief, the hired farm labor force is not dominated by migrants, who composed only eight percent of the hired farm population in 1980. However, migrants included up to 0.36 billion undocumented farm workers in the southwest and Pacific states.

Most analysts agree that these patterns of the past 20–30 years will continue. It is expected that most of the hired agricultural labor will continue to be on the coasts, that the percentage of hired labor in the overall farm population will increase, but that enough people will seek agricultural employment to meet the overall demand. Therefore, successful personnel management will become even more important as U.S. agriculture faces the year 2000.

The validity of this projection is, however, contingent upon at least five factors:

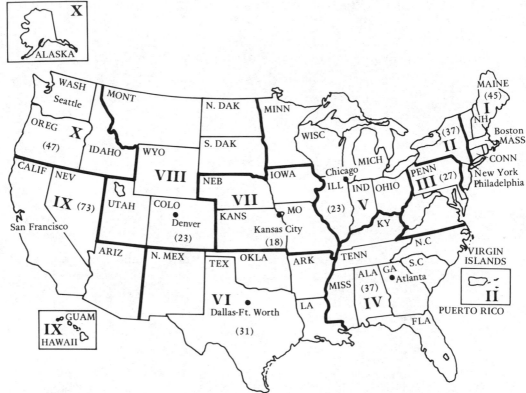

FIGURE 11–6. *Hired Labor Percentages in Standard Federal Regions. (Source: U.S. Department of Agriculture, ESCS, Crop Reporting Board, Farm Labor, Washington, D.C., 1978.)*

Note: Figures in parenthesis represent the percentage of the total agricultural labor force that was hired.

1. Technological Change. If there are dramatic increases in such labor saving technology as large-scale farm machinery and animal handling systems, overall agricultural demands and the overall level of labor hiring may decline.

2. The Structure of Agriculture. These predictions are dependent upon ever increasing acreages under the ownership of farm families.

3. Labor Programs. The Bracero Program of 1942 to 1964 encouraged Mexicans to immigrate to the United States to meet the labor needs of World War II and the Korean War. Since 1974 the Immigrant and Nationality Act administers the foreign labor certification program (H–2). However, this program now handles only one percent of the hired workers versus thirteen percent during the Bracero period. In 1972 the Comprehensive Employment and Training Act was passed in response to criticism that other related legislation had only been designed to take hired workers out of agriculture.

4. The Relative Prices of Energy and Other Inputs. One Iowa study has shown that under all five scenarios posited for future petroleum fuel price rises, the use of total labor per farm and the hired labor expense per farm will increase.

5. Legislation with Respect to Collective Bargaining.   If such programs are implemented, the benefits of those workers employed will probably increase. But there may be some question as to the total number of beneficiaries of such collective bargaining.

SUMMARY

Management and labor are often easier to acquire than capital and land as production factors in agriculture. Management may be obtained either through the experience of the farm operator and his family or through a hired professional consultant. Labor may be obtained through the fixed contributions of the family members and permanent hired and partnership personnel, or through short-term hiring and cooperative exchange.

It is essential to use labor efficiently because labor productivity varies among individuals, labor is a major farm cost, and the availability of hired workers adequately qualified to operate sophisticated machinery and understand the delicate biology of livestock is declining.

To use labor efficiently, the manager must balance the supply and demand of labor on the farm on a seasonal basis. If supply is greater than demand, he may increase the volume of business, produce higher quality products, and/or perform custom and nonfarm work. If demand is greater than supply, he may work longer, hire outside labor, use cooperative exchange labor, hire custom work done, and/or improve the efficiency of the labor he does use.

Labor calendars, good treatment of hired labor, improved operating techniques, and steps to achieve greater month-to-month consistency in labor use levels are all ways to improve on-farm labor efficiency.

Personnel management is difficult and involves the functions of acquisition, training, motivation, compensation, discipline and compliance. Adequate time should be spent in screening and hiring personnel and in training farm workers not only for performance of tasks but also for decision making. It is important to motivate farm workers through both tangible and intangible rewards. Discipline is often a problem, but successful communication and consistent implementation of policies can go a long way to solving disciplinary problems. Hired labor will increase as a percentage of the farm labor force. Therefore, successful personnel management will become even more important as American agriculture faces the year 2000.

TOPICS FOR DISCUSSION

1. Suppose that the government has just increased the parity percentage for dairy product prices and the eldest son must leave the farm for four years of university education. Demonstrate through figures

and clear reasoning the effect on the fixed and variable labor input on the farm. What do you expect will happen to farm income, to fixed versus variable costs, to the variability of seasonal labor use?

2. Of the four ways to adjust for on-farm labor supply being greater than demand, which do you think has most promise for typical farms in your state?

3. Of the four ways to adjust for on-farm labor supply being less than demand, which do you think is best for typical farm enterprises in your state? What opportunities do you see for the exchange of labor among farms with different enterprise orientations?

4. What factors should you take into account in determining whether or not it is wise to reduce the seasonal variability of on-farm labor use in order to send one family member to take a job in town? Be sure to include both hidden and obvious costs.

5. What wage and non-wage components are typical of agricultural labor agreements in your area? What areas of personnel management do you personally feel most capable of handling, least capable? Why?

SUGGESTED READINGS

Forster, D. L. and B. L. Erven. *Foundations for Managing the Farm Business*. Chapter 9. Columbus, Ohio: Grid Publishing, Inc.

Harsh, L. S., Connor and G. Schwab. *Managing the Farm Business*. Chapter 12. Englewood Cliffs, New Jersey: Prentice-Hall Inc., 1981.

Herbst, J. H. *Farm Management: Principles, Budgets, Plans*. Fourth revised edition. Chapter 8. Champaign, Illinois: Stipes Publishing Company, 1976.

Herzberg, F., B. Mausner, and B. Snyderman. *The Motivation to Work*. 2nd Edition, New York: Wiley, 1959.

Huffman, W. "Decision-Making: The Role of Education." *American Journal of Agricultural Economics*. Vol. 56, No. 1., pp. 85–97, 1974.

Kay, R. D. *Farm Management: Planning, Control, and Implementation*. Chapter 15. New York: McGraw-Hill Book Company, 1981.

Maslow, A. H. *Motivation and Personality*. 2nd Edition. New York: Harper and Row, 1970.

McGregor, D. *The Professional Manager*. C. McGregor and W. G. Bennis, ed. New York. McGraw-Hill Book Company, 1967.

Robbins, P. R. *Getting and Keeping Good Hired Farm Labor*. Purdue University Cooperative Extension Service bulletin EC–459. West Lafayette, Indiana, 1977.

Shapley, A. E. *Personnel Management in Agriculture—Instructor's Manual*. Rural Manpower Center Special Paper No. 12, Michigan State University, East Lansing, 1970.

12

Capital Investment

The future is the most expensive luxury in the world.

Thornton Wilder, The Skin of our Teeth

Concepts

In this chapter you will come to understand:

1. The various types and classifications of capital.
2. The importance of, and reasons for, the time value of money.
3. The pitfalls in using the necessary-and-urgent, payback period, and return-on-investment approaches to capital investments.
4. The effect of inflation on cash flow and cost-price squeeze problems.

Tools

You will also gain the following skills:

1. How to compute the present value and net present value of future investments using four alternative formulas based on magnitudes and frequency of returns.
2. How to compute the present value of costs devoted to past investments as a guide to pricing improved farm assets you wish to sell.
3. How to use seven investment strategies to reduce the adverse effects of inflation.

The previous chapter treated the acquisition and effective use of management and labor. We now proceed to study capital as one of the factors of production that must be effectively controlled. The issues relating to capital management are much more complex than those regarding labor use. Therefore, we shall start by looking at capital investment in this chapter and then proceed to address the effective use of credit for acquiring that capital in Chapter 13.

TYPES OF CAPITAL

The first major distinction with regard to types of capital is that between real capital (land and permanent improvements) and nonreal capital. In farm management, land or **real capital** is so important that economists distinguish it from the other types of capital for analytical purposes.[1] Therefore, discussion of land will be put off until Chapter 15.

The other types of capital are collectively called **nonreal capital** to distinguish them from land and permanent improvements. The term nonreal does not mean "imaginary," but simply "nonland." This nonreal capital is further subdivided to include short-run operating capital and medium- to long-run investment capital. Operating capital refers to the cash and physical inputs (seed, fertilizer, chemicals, etc.) needed to **operate** the business in a given year.

By contrast, investment capital refers to machinery, equipment, buildings, and brood animals which form the basic plant for operating the business over a period of years. These items are what the farm operator must **invest** in to provide a larger capital base and scale to his operation. Thus, operating capital can be thought of as the money used to cover variable costs while investment capital is the money used to cover fixed costs.

Finally, in addition to these dimensions of time and form, capital is also distinguished on the basis of ownership. There is a continuum of sources of funds to obtain capital assets. At one end, there is **owner equity**, which is the total value of the farm operator's share in all assets he owns outright or in part to run the farm. It is added to each year by savings from net farm, off-farm and nonagricultural income.

At the other end of the continuum is **debt capital**, which is that portion of operating, investment, and real capital which must eventually be paid back to someone else, along with accumulated interest. The maximum amount of debt capital that a farm operator can obtain is determined by his/her owner equity, willingness to assume the risk of high debt, and realiability as a credit risk in the eyes of potential lenders.

Between equity and debt capital, there are other options for acquiring control of capital. These include leasing, renting, partnerships, and capital pooling, all of which are important sources of investment capital in U.S. agriculture. More about these sources will be presented in Chapters 13–17.

---

[1] *Historically, this distinction can be traced to legal terminology of ownership and transfer that differentiated real estate from personal property.*

THE TIME VALUE OF MONEY

If we said that we would give you $1,000 (remember, this is a hypothetical example!) either today or one year from today, which time would you choose? Probably, you would decide to take the money now. Now, ask yourself why you chose as you did. You should be able to convince yourself that the following three reasons figured in your choice:

1. Uncertainty.   There is no guarantee that we will be alive next year or able and willing to make good on our promise. Nor, for that matter, is there any guarantee that you will be alive to enjoy the money. Because of these and other aspects of uncertainty, it is better for you to enjoy the money now, while you can.

2. Alternative Uses.   You could take the $1,000, put it under your mattress, and take it out only after one year. In this case, the two time period options would be equivalent.

But there are alternative uses for the money which could make it work for you during the year. You could, for example, deposit it in a savings account to earn interest, invest it in stocks or bonds, use it to increase the operating capital of your farm operation to gain more net farm income, or put in an apple orchard one year earlier to hasten the day when you can harvest its fruits. These alternative uses all make having the capital now more attractive than waiting.

3. Inflation.   Because of inflation in the prices of production inputs or the consumer items you could purchase with the $1,000, the money will allow you to buy 10–18 percent greater real value now than in one year. Thus, inflation makes current receipt of the $1,000 preferable to waiting a year.

All three of the above reasons contribute to the principle of the time value of money. This principle states:

> Money is worth more to the holder today than at any future time because of uncertainty, alternative uses, and inflation.

If you have taken a principles course in macro-economics, you will remember that John Maynard Keynes, in his famous *General Theory*, published in 1936, discussed three motives for people's desires to have cash on hand, which he called their "liquidity preference." Table 12–1 shows that these three reasons are the same three reasons we have discussed for the time value of money:

1. The **precautionary motive** says that because of uncertainty, people prefer to have cash on hand now.
2. The **transaction motive** says that because people realize there is an opportunity cost to waiting one year to receive their money, they prefer to invest and put their money to work.

TABLE 12–1.   A COMPARISON OF THE TIME VALUE
OF MONEY AND MOTIVES UNDERLYING
LIQUIDITY PREFERENCE

Time Value of Money	Keynes' Liquidity Preference
Uncertainty	Precautionary Motive
Alternative Uses	Transactions Motive
Inflation	Speculative Motive

3. The **speculative motive** recognizes inflation and seeks to hedge against it through investments in land, long-term bonds, or the stock market.

In short, each of the three factors underlying the time value of money implies a strategy or motive for exploiting it through a preference for liquidity. Thus, the reason that the farm operator must pay interest to the lender of money is to offset the costs to the lender of uncertainty, alternative uses and inflation.

HOW TO MAKE INVESTMENT DECISIONS

There are five approaches to analyzing investment decisions: the necessary-and-urgent, payback period, return on investment, present value, and cost compounding methods. They will be presented in order, from the least to the most acceptable. Only the last two methods are recommended because only they take into account the time value of money.

1. The **necessary-and-urgent approach**. This is simply a fancy name for hunches, guesses, intuition, and unbridled desire; there is little or no formal analysis made.

   For example, a farm operator may wake up some fine Saturday morning and know he absolutely must have a new green tractor with air-conditioned cab and stereo. Nothing else will do. He likes the green color, does not like the white of some tractors because it gets dirty too quickly, does not like the red of others because it looks like a fire engine. So, he rushes down to the nearest dealership, strides in, and says, "I'll take it! How much does it cost?" If he waited another week to pencil out some alternatives, the thrill of excitement would wane. Perhaps in this case, he is valuing prestige as one of those conflicting goals in running a farm.

   But this approach is clearly inadequate and unscientific. It does not take into account the time value of money or the size and timing of returns. So, one should look for some criteria such as:

2. The **payback period approach**. This approach is actually used by many dealers. If, instead of saying, "I'll take it" as soon as he walks

in the door, the farmer shows some hesitation, the machinery dealer may produce a formula to impress him. To do so, he will specify some variables:

P = the payback period (in years)

C = capital required

E = average annual after-tax earnings before depreciation.

And, the formula he will show the farmer is:

$$P = C/E.$$

The dealer may say, "With this machine you can earn $10,000 per year in added efficiency and its purchase price is only $40,000." He can then compute:

$$P = \$40,000/\$10,000 = 4 \text{ years},$$

and insist that the machine will pay for itself in four years while a red tractor will take five years to pay for itself. All of that is true, as far as it goes. And this is a better approach than urgency because it requires conscientious appraisal of costs and expenses.

But the payback period is not a measure of profitability. It fails to consider the entire economic life. The green tractor may pay for itself in four years and fall apart the next day, while the red tractor may take five years to pay for itself but run another twelve years. Another failing is that the cash flow aspects and time value of the returns on the investment are entirely ignored. One must, therefore, go on to the third approach, which is a slight improvement:

3. The **return on investment (*ROI*) approach**. This approach takes account of depreciation, already an advantage over the payback period approach. Two more variables are needed:

R = average percentage rate of return on investment

D = annual depreciation.

The formula for this approach becomes:

$$R = \frac{E - D}{C}.$$

If we assume that the green tractor will last ten years and use the ACRS straight-line method to compute depreciation, then:

$$D = \frac{40,000}{12} = \$3,333$$

and

$$R = \frac{10,000 - 3,333}{40,000} = 16.7\%.$$

This rate of return is not bad. But the *ROI* approach has two major weaknesses:

a. Through no fault of its own, it is inconsistently applied. Specifically, some people say C is the capital cost over the entire project, as above; but others compute it as an annual average capital cost (total capital required divided by the number of years of the investment). Under the former, R = 16.7%, and under the latter, a full 167%. This would not be a problem if all dealers and consumer reports used it in the same way. However, the operator may be persuaded to buy an inferior machine simply because a promoter calculated a higher R using the average annual cost estimate for C. Therefore, one must apply a great deal of caution in using this approach.

b. The operator knows nothing about the timing of costs, returns, and depreciation. This second weakness is more serious. Even though the operator has now taken depreciation into account, he has no way to include the time value of money. Therefore, one must go on to the fourth approach:

4. The **present value approach**. This has four forms but they are all really variations developed from the first form:

a.
$$PV = \frac{E}{(1 + r)^t}.$$

Three more variables must be added to our arsenal:

PV = the present value of future income, i.e., the value today of some investment subject to uncertainty, alternative uses, inflation

r = the opportunity rate of return. Simplistically, one can think of this as the interest earned by putting the money in the bank. Later in this chapter, you will learn how it can be adjusted for risk, inflation, and appreciation.

t = the number of time periods over which the investment gives us returns

Now, compute the present value of a cow which the farm operator can sell for $600 in one year or sell now and invest the money elsewhere at 10 percent. To make this calculation, one need only fill in the formula:

$$PV = \$600/(1.10)^1 = \$545.$$

Therefore, if someone came up to the farmer and offered $550 for the cow right now, he should take the money. Alternatively, if someone comes by and offers $600 after six months instead of one year, the farmer should also take his offer. Now, think about this: is there a hidden cost to the tactic, put forth in Chapter 6, of delaying cash sales to even out reported income tax earnings to the IRS on the cash method of accounting?

The above example was simple, though real. In fact, the first formula for present value is based on two assumptions:

(1) variable returns
(2) finite period.

Consider another example given the same formula but using a multiple rather than a single time period. A beef heifer will give a calf with a net value of $55 in each of the following four years and will be sold in the fourth year for a net return (after feed and other costs) of $140. Suppose now the opportunity rate of return is nine percent. What is the present value of investing in the heifer? In this case of multiple time periods, we use an expanded formula as follows:

$$PV = \frac{E_1}{(1 + r)^1} + \frac{E_2}{(1 + r)^2} + \frac{E_3}{(1 + r)^3} + \frac{E_4}{(1 + r)^4}$$

$$= 55/(1.09)^1 + 55/(1.09)^2 + 55/(1.09)^3 + 195/(1.09)^4$$

$$= 50.46 + 46.29 + 42.47 + 138.14$$

$$= \$277.36.$$

So, the present value is about $277. If the cow is selling for less than that, the farm operator should buy it; if it is selling for more he should not. Related to the concept of present value is that of net present value. This is simply the present value minus the cash outlay at the present time:

$$NPV = PV - C.$$

In the previous case, if the heifer was selling for $250, what would be the net present value of investing in her?

$$NPV = \$277.36 - \$250$$

$$= \$27.36$$

b. The second form of the present value formula is:

$$PV = E/r - \frac{E/r}{(1 + r)^t}$$

This is a short-cut approach to the expanded version of formula (a) when:

(1) returns are constant, i.e., you are considering an annuity, and
(2) there is a finite (but typically long) time period.

Suppose one is trying to compute the present value of something which will give constant returns over 25 years. One could always use the first form of the formula and make 25 separate computations, but the easiest way is to use this second form.

For example, suppose you are considering leaving the farm and taking a nonfarm job in town for 25 years. You expect after tax earnings to average $25,000 per year (for simplicity, assume that any wage increases you get just match the inflation rate). Say your opportunity rate of return is 10 percent. Thus, $r = 0.10$, $E = $25,000$, and $t = 25$. You can enter these values into the formula as follows:

$$PV = \frac{25,000}{.10} - \frac{25,000/.10}{(1.10)^{25}}$$

$$= \$226,926.$$

This is the value to you today of taking that job for 25 years. Bear this figure in mind because in just a moment you will compare this present value to that from working on the farm for a similar time period.

c. The third form of the present value formula is derived from the second except for a change in assumptions:

(1) returns are constant, but
(2) they continue indefinitely

One example of a farm investment asset that has these characteristics is land. So, the formula for investing in land and other real capital is the simplest form yet of the present value formula:

$$PV = E/r.$$

Notice that this formula is simply the lefthand side of formula (b). What happened to the righthand side? Remember, these returns will continue indefinitely. Thus, in the denominator of formula (b), t tends toward infinity. As the denominator gets larger and larger, the value of the righthand side gets smaller and smaller. Thus, if one is considering an indefinite time period, the righthand side goes to zero, and our formula reduces to $PV = E/r$.

In the context of land values, E simply stands for the return to land and improvements. This return is computed by subtracting charges for operator management and unpaid labor from net farm income. The annual net rental income may also be used to estimate E. Suppose that a young prospective farmer is considering the purchase of a 100-acre farm that yields $25,000 total revenue per year with $5,000 in variable costs, $3,000 in fixed costs, and $7,000 in management and unpaid labor costs. On a per acre basis, total revenue is $250, variable costs are $150, fixed costs are $30 and management and unpaid labor costs are $70. Suppose also that he uses the value of r commonly used by farm management firms through the end of the 1960s of .05. He can figure the expected market price for an acre of that land as follows:

$$PV = \frac{E}{r}$$

$$= \frac{\$250 - \$50 - \$30 - \$70}{.05}$$

$$= \$2,000/\text{acre}.$$

He feels proud of himself for successfully making the calculation and perfectly capable of buying that land in the next auction until he goes and finds out it is selling for $3,330! What happened? Is the formula wrong? No. Is his estimate of farm income and costs wrong? No, he has checked and rechecked those figures. Is the selling price in the marketplace wrong? No, it cannot be: he has seen with his own eyes people paying hard money for that land.

What is left? The opportunity rate of return r. This value r has been shaken by great economic forces over the past ten or eleven years. It is no longer enough to heedlessly use an opportunity interest rate of, say, five percent. Prospective farmers must also realize that risk, inflation, and appreciation are at work. Specifically:

r = opportunity rate of return,	.05
which has to be adjusted by:	
rate of inflation	+.13
risk, e.g., variation in price and yield	+.01
(differs by operator)	
appreciation in land asset since 1974 which = 16%,	−.16
to yield the value of r:	.03.

When one enters the adjusted value of r into the formula, one obtains:

$$PV = \frac{\$100}{.03} = \$3,300.$$

This recalculation reconciles farm returns with the observed selling price in the market.

This technique seems to be going through the back door to determine r, but is in fact one method land appraisers and other economists have been forced to adopt in recent years. They observe the actual sale price of similar land in 50 or 60 auctions, compute farm income and costs, and then deduce what the opportunity rate of return must be. Far from falsifying the numbers, this approach gives them valuable insight into farmers' perceptions of risk, opportunity interest rates, etc., because they already know the rate of inflation and percentage increase in the value of land. No matter which variable is used to solve it, this formula will provide a great deal of information.

d. The fourth form of the present value formula has still different assumptions from those of the preceeding three:

1. constant returns
2. one has to wait until the last period to receive them. This assumption applies, for example, to the build-up of equity or capital gains on a farm.

The formula is as follows:

$$PV = \frac{E(t)}{(1 + r)^t} \, .$$

If the farm operator expects capital gains of $5,000 per year over a ten-year period with an opportunity interest rate of ten percent, then,

$$PV = \frac{5000(10)}{(1.1)^{10}} = \$19,277.$$

To tie all these concepts together, let us compare the cash-flow, equity, and capital gains components of the present value of working on the farm with the present value of working off the farm computed earlier. Suppose you are thinking of purchasing a 300-acre farm for $2,250 per acre. The farm will return $45,000 after taxes and interest payments each year, plus capital gain of $4,000 per year which will be taxed at 20 percent[1] when converted to cash at the end of the 25 years if you sell the farm. Principal payments on the farm are $27,000 per year and are recoverable through sale at the end of the 25-year period. Assume a 10 percent discount rate.

$$PV_{\text{cash flow income}} = \frac{\overset{\$18,000}{\overbrace{\$45,000 - \$27,000}}}{.10} - \frac{\$18,000/.10}{(1.10)^{25}} = \$163,387$$

$$+ \, PV_{\text{equity}} = \frac{\$27,000(25)}{(1.10)^{25}} \qquad\qquad = \$ \ 62,300$$

[1] *Under the Economic Recovery Act of 1981, 40 percent of capital gains are taxable and at a maximum rate of 50 percent.*

$$+ PV_{\text{capital gains}} = \frac{\$4,000(25)(0.8)^*}{(1.10)^{25}} \qquad = \$\ \underline{7,384}$$

$$= PV_{\text{TOTAL}} \qquad\qquad\qquad = \$233,071$$

Remember, the present value for off-farm work was $226,926. Of course, the choice of a nonfarm occupation also allows the worker to make investments with his savings. Let us assume that you choose to invest in owning a house in town worth $60,000 over and above a downpayment, and to pay for it over the twenty-five year period. You will be building up both equity and capital gains. The present value of these can be computed in a similar manner as for the farm option:

$$PV_{\text{equity}} = \frac{\$2400(25)}{(1.1)^{25}} \qquad = \$5,538$$

$$PV_{\text{capital gains}} = \frac{\$1000(25)(0.92)^{**}}{(1.1)^{25}} = \$2,123$$

Further, as a result of investing in the house, you must adjust the estimated present value of your cash flow income downward by subtracting out the value of annual principal and interest payments. Assuming a loan at twelve percent, the annual principal plus interest payments for the 25-year period on a $60,000 mortgage are $7650 ($127.50 annual payments per $1000 of loan multiplied by 60.)† After-mortgage cash flow income becomes $19,584 when changes in the marginal tax rate are also taken into account.

The new estimate of the present value of nonfarm after-tax cash flow earnings thus becomes

$$PV_{\text{cash flow income}} = \frac{\$19,584}{0.1} - \frac{\dfrac{\$19,584}{0.1}}{(1.1)^{25}} = \$177,765$$

When this figure for cash flow income is added to the present value of equity and capital gains incomes ($5,538 and $2,213, respectively) the total present value of the nonfarm option with house purchase is $185,426.

Given these calculations would you choose to work on the farm or in town? The cold economics of investment says that every individual faced

---

*0.8 equals 1 minus the 20 percent capital gains tax rate.

**Assuming that 40 percent of your capital gains will be taxed at the 20 percent rate, 1 − t = 1 − (0.4 × 0.2) = 0.92. If you wait until after age 55 to sell the residence, there is a once-in-a-lifetime waiver of capital gains tax on up to $125,000 of gain.

†See Table 13.8. Further examples of this procedure will be presented in Chapter 13.

with this choice should go into farming. But, in addition to present value considerations, other economic and noneconomic factors also enter the picture.

Economic

The family only has about two-thirds as much take home pay ($18,000 vs. $25,000[1]) in farming to pay for clothing, food, amusements, and other expenditures.

Income is much more variable in farming, which leads to:

1. risk of defaulting on loan repayment obligations
2. unexpected disappointments in terms of the family's nonagricultural expenditures

There is an opportunity cost of labor for whichever option (farming or working in town) uses more. This labor could otherwise be used to find additional work to supplememt income from the first job.

Living expenses are often greater in town, while transportation costs for shopping and commuting to off-farm jobs are often higher in the country.

Noneconomic

Health and Safety.   Agriculture is the nation's third most dangerous occupation after mining and construction. Recent studies also indicate that a growing number of farm women are being killed in machinery accidents. Accidental poisoning from agricultural pesticides and herbicides has long been common.

Quality of Life.   Many people love farm work, getting up with the birds and smelling the fresh country air. It is difficult to place a value on such external benefits from living in the country.

The Environment for Raising Children.   Some argue that a farm childhood is more wholesome than an urban one. Others point to the lack of playmates. These factors vary from location to location, but should always be considered.

Continuing our outline:

5. **Compounding costs.** The last method of investment analysis is really just a variation on present value. The only difference is that it looks at the past rather than at the future.

   a. The formula for compounding costs is as follows:

$$C = E(1 + r)^t,$$

where

C = the compounded costs at the time of sale.

E = the actual expenditures by years.

[1] *Or $19,584 if they purchase a house in town.*

TABLE 12-2. COMPOUNDING COSTS OF ESTABLISHING AND DEVELOPING A FOUR-YEAR-OLD ORCHARD

Year	Actual Dollar Outlay/Acre	Compounding Factor at 12 Percent	Compounded Cost of Outlay in Present
1	$2006	1.573	$3155
2	769	1.405	1080
3	930	1.254	1160
4	1089	1.120	1220
Total	$4794		$6621

Source: M. Ferree, and O. C. Smith, *Apples Enterprise Cost Analysis,* University of Georgia Cooperative Extension Service Miscellaneous Publication No. 82, Athens, Georgia, 1981.

b. If more than one year is involved, the expanded version of the above formula becomes:

$$C = E_1(1 + r)^t + E_2(1 + r)^{t-1} + \ldots E_n(1 + r)^1$$

Note that, in contrast to the present value formula:
(1) The exponent declines as one moves left to right in the formula. However, exponent values in both formulae are smallest closest to the present:

Compounding Range	Present Value Range
$t - 1 \; t - 2 \; t - 3 \; t - 4$ The Present	$t + 1 \; t + 2 \; t + 3 \; t + 4$

(2) The E's of the formula are multiplied by the $(1 + r)^t$ components rather than being divided by them.

c. To demonstrate these concepts, consider the example of land that a grower has invested in improving for the past four years by starting an apple orchard. The left side of Table 12-2 shows the actual dollar costs invested, without taking into account the other uses to which the grower could have put that money and other aspects of the time value of money. The right side of the table adjusts the investments for the time value of money using the formula for compounding costs. Note that the grower should sell the orchard for nothing less than $6621 per acre plus the market value of unimproved land. If he took only the $4794 he invested, he would be selling himself short. Remember, the buyer would otherwise have to start from scratch in the biological process of establishing an orchard, which cannot be hurried. Therefore, he should be willing to pay extra for an orchard four years closer to peak production.

d. A variation on the cost compounding formula is the future value formula. This equation allows the farm manager to estimate the value of an investment asset a few years hence to determine, for example, what he could sell it for then. It is written:

$$FV = E(1 + r)^t,$$

where FV stands for future value and all other variables are the same as defined for the compounding costs. If, for example, the farm operator will be investing $1000, $2500, and $1500 respectively in each of the next three years, and the discount rate is 11 percent, the future value of these investments after three years will be:

$$FV = E_1(1+r)^3 + E_2(1+r)^2 + E_3(1+r)^1$$

$$\$1000(1.11)^3 + \$2500(1.11)^2 + \$1500(1.11)^1$$

$$= \$1368 + \$3080 + \$1665$$

$$= \$6113.$$

PROBABILITY-WEIGHTED AFTER-TAX INVESTMENTS

Now that you understand the basic concept of present value analysis, it is important to learn to apply it to even more complex real-world situations. Such situations include the purchase of improved poultry houses and other livestock facilities, investments in improved machinery with variable depreciation deductions and operating and repair costs,[1] and investments in brood animals such as sows, heifers, ewes, and hens.

Table 12–3 shows an example of investing in a replacement heifer for a dairy operation typical of those across the nation. The purchase price for the heifer is $1400. The dairyman predicts that the heifer will produce an average of 13,500 pounds of milk per year over a six-year investment period, ranging from 11,500 pounds in year 1 to 14,750 pounds in year 6. He expects to sell the animal at the end of the sixth year. The probability of success in milk production, as well as the probability that the cow will be culled and sold must be used to weight the returns in each year. The marginal tax rate for this farm operation is 30 percent. Therefore, net return in each period must be multiplied by 0.70 (1 minus the tax rate) to determine the after-tax returns.

The table shows that the present after-tax value of the replacement heifer, weighted for the probabilities of successful milk production and possible culling, is $1628. This figure implies a positive net present value of $228 ($1682 – $1400). Provided he can manage the cash-flow aspects of the investment and has no more profitable investment alternatives than those implicit in his 10 percent discount factor, the farmer would be advised to purchase the heifer.

Annuity tables or simple experimentation can be used to find the **internal rate of return** that would equate the present value of the after-tax income stream to the $1400 purchase price for the heifer. In this case it is roughly 14.5 percent. In other words, if the farmer can find no alternative that yields a rate of return as high as 14.5 percent, he should invest in the replacement heifer.

[1] *An example of investment in a tractor will be given in Chapter 14.*

TABLE 12-3. EXPECTED NET INCOME FROM MILK PRODUCTION AND CULL COW SALE FOR DAIRY HEIFER BY LACTATION PERIOD

	(1)	(2)	(3)	(4)	(5)	(6)	(7)	(8)	(9)
Lactation number	Probability of success in milk production	Net income from milk production	Expected[1] net income from milk production	Probability that cow will be culled and sold	Net value of cull cow if sold	Expected net income of cull cow if sold[2]	Expected net income	Expected net income adjusted for taxes[4]	Discounted expected after tax income[6]
1	.9326	322	300	.0607	365	22	322	226	205
2	.9165	447	410	.0752	397	30	440	308	255
3	.8778	578	507	.1100	454	50	557	390	293
4	.8562	656	562	.1294	466	60	622	435	298
5	.8322	650	541	.1510	480	72	613	429	266
6	.8249	716	591	.1576	490	77	668	468	264
Cow culled	.0000	–	–	.2402[5]	490	118	118	83	47
Totals	–	3,369	2,911	–	–	429	3,340	2,339	1,628

[1]Derived by multiplying probability of success in milk production (column 1) times net income from production (column 2).
[2]Derived by multiplying probability that the cow will be culled and sold (column 4) times net value of cull cow if sold (column 5).
[3]Expected income from milk production (column 3) plus expected net income of cull cow if sold (column 6).
[4]A tax rate of 30 percent is assumed.
[5]Equals the probability that the cow hasn't either died or been culled prior to the end of the sixth lactation period.
[6]The discount rate assumed is 10 percent.

Source: Adapted from Willett, Gayle S., *How to Place a Value on a Dairy Heifer: An Application of the Rate of Return Method for Evaluating Investment Opportunities,* University of Wisconsin Cooperative Extension Bulletin, Vol. 3, No. 12, 1971.

INVESTMENT MANAGEMENT IN AN INFLATIONARY PERIOD

The period of the late 1970s and early 1980s has been one of unprecedentedly high levels of inflation. The prime interest rate has reached, and exceeded, 20 percent. Even if input and output prices faced by farm operators moved exactly in tandem with each other, such inflationary pressures would make careful estimate of the present value of future returns all the more important. Gone are the days when simple partial budgets can be computed without supplemental estimates of the magnitudes and timing of returns over the investment period.

An added burden to the farm decision-maker has been the fact that capital-intensive U.S. farms are facing unprecedented cost-price squeeze and cash flow problems. A **cost-price squeeze** occurs when input prices rise relative to output price without compensating improvements in yields or productive efficiency. Cost-price squeezes are not new to U.S. agriculture, nor are they unique to inflationary periods. For example, in the last thirty years of the nineteenth century, a period of **deflation**, farm output prices fell. But interest payments on mortgages, legally-binding contracts, remained constant. Therefore, the **relative** price of the land input rose, causing many farm foreclosures. As a result, farmers supported the Greenback Party, which promised to create inflation!

Clearly, times have changed. Farmers now oppose fiscal policies that fuel inflation. But the underlying cost-price problem is the same. The prices of inputs, especially petroleum-based fertilizers and fuels, have increased faster than output prices in the past decade. As if this were not enough, fuel price increases have also been a major contributor to increases in the price of borrowed capital. The view of land as an investment asset has increased its price (Chapter 15), while continuing agricultural labor-force reductions, hastened by the cost-price squeeze, have increased farm wages (Chapter 11). Nearly all the inputs that the farm operator must purchase have increased in price faster than the farmer's output. The cost-price squeeze is in evidence again.

A **cash-flow problem** occurs when the timing of cash returns does not match the timing of cash outlays. This problem can happen within a production season. If it does, it can often be solved by taking out short-term operating loans. However, serious cash-flow problems have appeared in the last decade with respect to investments in and returns from land. Much of the return from land investments is in the form of long-term capital gains, which are realizable only when the asset is sold. In the shortrun, the purchase price of land is far out of proportion to its earning power. Therefore, especially in periods of inflationary cost-price squeezes, farmers also face a severe cash-flow problem. These twin problems have put enormous financial pressure on U.S. farm operators, particularly those of small-scale farms.

What can be done to survive such periods of inflationary cost-price squeeze and cash flow problems? With this understanding of the reasons behind these problems, seven investment management strategies can be outlined:

1. *Use Production Strategies to Diversify Output Mix.* A diversified farm is less vulnerable to problems of low output price in any single commodity. It also will not be locked into the continued production of energy-intensive enterprises during sharp upward jags in energy prices.

2. *Put Off the Purchase of Land.* It may be far better in the near future to rent land, and perhaps to operate a smaller area than otherwise, to avoid high principal and interest payments and/or high cash rents. Crop-share leases are an excellent means of reducing the burden of declining relative output prices.

3. *Try to Assume a Mortgage if You Must Buy Land.* Often, mortgages are available at far below the going interest rate if the bank agrees to continue the mortgage under a new land-owner. The major disadvantage is that you must be able to put down the entire amount of equity that the pervious owner had built up. In some cases, this is a substantial amount. To exploit this strategy eventually, one can begin to rent and/or perform nonfarm work to build up enough equity to make such payments.

4. *Invest Any Extra Capital Not Essential to the Operation of the Farm in Assets Whose Values Are Tied to and Fluctuate with the Inflation Rate.* To the extent possible, these should have a short redemption period to maintain adequate liquidity. Six-month money-market certificates are an excellent form in which to implement this type of strategy.

5. *Contract with Seed, Horticultural, and Other Vertically Integrated Industries.* Vertical integration allows such companies to contain much of the increase in farm inputs necessary to the production of the given commodity, and to offer a stable and reasonably high price for a specialized output. Therefore, such contracts can minimize the plight of many farmers as farm-gate price takers with no control over input and output prices.

6. *Have One or More Family Members Take a Part- or Full-time Off-farm Job.* The wages from many jobs increase with the inflation rate, particularly unionized occupations, whose compensation is often tied to an index of inflation.

7. *Use Accelerated Depreciation or Cost Recovery.* This practice helps ease the cash flow problem by creating larger net cash flows in the early part of an investment period. For example, in a study of alternative haying systems in irrigated wheat operations of southeastern Wyoming, researchers found that accumulated net cash flows at the end of a 5-year-planning period were $2809 higher for accelerated depreciation than for straight line.

SUMMARY

There are many classifications and subdivisions within the broad term capital. In this chapter you have learned to distinguish real from nonreal, operating from investment, and equity from debt concepts as they relate to the types of capital available to the farm operator.

Because of the time value of money and the possibilities for uneven patterns of expenses and returns over time, the necessary and urgent approach, the payback period approach, and the return on investment approach to capital investments are inadequate guides for the farm manager. Rather, if the farm manager is planning to invest in the future, he should use any of four different formulas which express the present value or, alternatively, the net present value, of each investment. If on the other hand, he is trying to value an asset in which he has invested over a period of past time, then he should use the compounding cost method, closely related to the present value approach, to determine the minimum amount that he should be paid in order to recoup his investment.

Three factors underlie the time value of money: uncertainty (which relates to Keynes' percautionary motive), alternative uses (which relates to the transaction motive), and inflation (which relates to the speculative motive).

Investment analysis can be particularly helpful in making the decision between a farm and a nonfarm career. Nevertheless, such noneconomic factors as health and safety, the quality of life, and the environment for raising children should also have an impact on the decision. A comprehensive evaluation of a farm versus a nonfarm career must include the present value not only of the cash flow income but also of the equity and capital gains built up from each alternative. Employing the present value formula to determine the price which should be bid at an auction for land is particularly complex because of the changes which have occurred in the opportunity rate of return, r. The opportunity interest rate must be adjusted for risk, inflation, and appreciation in order to derive an adjusted value of r.

Wise investment analysis must increasingly take account of inflation as farm managers face the year 2000. Inflationary pressures have worsened farmers' cost-price squeeze and cash flow problems. Measures to help survive inflationary periods include output diversification, deferred land purchase, assumption of existing mortgages, investment in money-market certificates, contracting with vertically-integrated firms, nonagricultural employment, and the use of accelerated cost recovery.

TOPICS FOR DISCUSSION

1. What is the method that automobile and machinery dealers in your area use to persuade customers of the wisdom of making a given investment? What reasons can you name for their using these methods?
2. Compare net present value and the market value of land in your area.

Try to disaggregate the components of the discount rate and measure their magnitudes. Given the results, what can you say about land as a productive versus investment asset?

3. Calculate whether it would be better for you to enter farming or take a nonagricultural job you are reasonably sure you could get. What economic and noneconomic factors are most important to you in making the decision? Do they reinforce or work against the results of the pure investment analysis?

SAMPLE PROBLEMS

1. A capital investment requires $20,000 worth of outlay at the beginning. It has average annual after-tax earnings before depreciation of $8,000 ($12,000 the first year, $8,000 the second year, and $4,000 the third year) and an annual rate of depreciation of 10% of the purchase price. You have an opportunity rate of return of 11% in another investment which has about the same amount of risk as this one.
   a. Compute the payback period for the investment, the return on investment (ROI), and the present value of the investment.
   b. Which of the three methods is best for analyzing investment decisions? What are the disadvantages of the other two?

2. A farm operator has invested in a hog farrowing operation over the past three years putting in $35,000 the first year, $12,000 the second year, and $9,000 the third year. If he wants to sell it to another farmer, what price should he ask? (Assume a discount rate of 13%.)

SUGGESTED READINGS

Agee, D. *Analyzing Alternative Haying Systems, Big Baler Versus Custom Baling and Stacking*. Agriculture Extension Service Division of Agricultural Economics report AE 80–20. Laramie, Wyoming: University of Wyoming, 1980.

Harsh, S., L. Connor, and G. Schwab. *Managing the Farm Business*. Chapter 11. Englewood Cliffs, New Jersey: Prentice-Hall Inc., 1981.

Kay, R. D. *Farm Management: Planning, Control, and Implementation*. Chapter 13. New York: McGraw-Hill Book Company, 1981.

Nelson, A., W. Lee and W. Murray. *Agricultural Finance*. Chapter 3. Ames, Iowa: Iowa State University Press, 1973.

Osburn, D. and K. Schneeberger. *Modern Agriculture Management*. Chapter 18. Reston, Virginia: Reston Publishing, 1978.

Penson, J. and D. Lins. *Agricultural Finance: An Introduction to Micro and Macro Concepts*. Englewood Cliffs, New Jersey, Prentice-Hall Inc., 1980.

13

Credit and Financial Risk

Everybody likes a kidder,
but nobody lends him money.

Arthur Miller, Death of a Salesman

Concepts

In this chapter, you will come to understand:

1. The growing importance of borrowed capital in U.S. agriculture.
2. The role of borrowed capital in pushing U.S. agriculture toward a polar structure of small and large farms.
3. The meaning of financial risk, leverage, and the increasing risk principle.
4. The continuum of sources of borrowed capital.
5. The three R's of credit: risk, returns and repayment.
6. The valid uses for credit and how they relate to economic principles.
7. Different credit sources by length of loan and sector (private, public, or government).

Tools

You will also gain the following skills:

1. How to determine the amount of your credit capacity you should use, given your age, farm size, and attitude toward risk.
2. How to use farm records to demonstrate to your banker that you are qualified to receive a loan.
3. How to compute the repayment feasibility of making a capital investment.
4. How to compute the annual effective interest rate.

TRENDS IN CAPITAL ACQUISITION

You now have studied different ways to measure the value of a given investment alternative for capital. What remains to be considered is the problem of acquiring the capital to do so. The previous chapter assumed that the farm operator had the necessary capital and was just looking for the best way to invest it. In fact, especially in heavily- and increasingly-capitalized agriculture, the acquisition of nonreal capital is second in difficulty only to acquiring land itself.

A study of the increasing importance of borrowed capital in U.S. agriculture will set the stage for our inquiry. It is possible to develop a balance sheet for agriculture similar to that presented in Chapter 4 for an individual farm. Table 13-1 shows the percentage of capital in U.S. agriculture that was borrowed in selected years. The figures indicate that the proportion of borrowed capital in U.S. agriculture has doubled in the last 30 years and has increased eleven times in absolute dollar terms. Because of the sharp decline in the number of farms, the dollars of borrowed capital per farm have increased over 22 times over the period, showing a substitution of capital for labor along the farm production isoquant.

Will these trends continue? Table 13-2 indicates that under government efforts to reduce inflation, the debt:asset ratio for U.S. farms will likely reach a peak in 1984 or 1985. However, high inflation scenarios (II and IV) suggest that the proportion of debt in total assets may increase steadily to the year 1990 when it may become as high as 0.27.

But these are aggregate figures and neglect the role of borrowed capital in determining structural issues in U.S. agriculture. Table 13-3 shows a dramatic difference in borrowing patterns between small and large farms. On the largest farms, assets were four times, liabilities sixteen times, equity three times, and the debt:asset ratio four times that on the smallest farms. The greater borrowing by larger farms has its roots in many factors. Operators of smaller farms are closer to subsistence (with a greater risk of not being able to pay for food, shelter, clothing, and education in a given year), are more timid in borrowing, are viewed as less creditworthy by financial institutions, and thus have a lower pro-

TABLE 13-1.   A BALANCE SHEET FOR U.S. AGRICULTURE

	Year		
	1950	*1977*	*1980*
Assets ($ billion)	135	566	821
Liabilities ($ billion)	13	95	146
Owners' equity (net worth, $ billion)	122	471	675
Debt: asset ratio (%)	9	17	18

Source: *Economic Indicators of the Farm Sector: Income and Balance Sheet Statistics, 1979,* USDA, Washington, D.C., 1980.

TABLE 13-2. SIMPLIFIED U.S. AGRICULTURAL BALANCE SHEET UNDER FOUR INFLATION AND GOVERNMENT INVOLVEMENT SCENARIOS, 1980–90

	1980	1981	1982	1983	1984	1985	1986	1987	1988	1989	1990
Scenario I											
Low Inflation, constant government											
Assets ($billion)	1002	1090	1233	1410	1571	1771	2008	2280	2603	2998	3493
Owners' equity ($billion)	817	881	997	1140	1267	1430	1627	1859	2145	2504	2970
Debt: asset ratio (%)	18.5	19.2	19.1	19.2	19.3	19.3	19.0	18.5	17.6	16.4	15.0
Scenario II											
High inflation, high government											
Assets ($billion)	1002	1090	1227	1395	1538	1735	1970	2253	2587	2977	3451
Owners' equity ($billion)	817	881	988	1116	1217	1359	1525	1725	1958	2224	2546
Debt: asset ratio (%)	18.5	19.2	19.5	20.0	20.9	21.7	22.6	23.4	24.3	25.3	26.2
Scenario III											
Low inflation, low government											
Assets ($billion)	1002	1089	1230	1403	1562	1758	1987	2253	2568	2955	3442
Owners' equity ($billion)	817	881	994	1133	1259	1416	1605	1830	2107	2457	2911
Debt: asset ratio (%)	18.5	19.2	19.2	19.2	19.4	19.4	19.2	18.7	18.0	16.9	15.4
Scenario IV											
High inflation, low government											
Assets ($billion)	1002	1089	1224	1387	1539	1734	1966	2248	2581	2972	3362
Owners' equity ($billion)	817	881	985	1109	1218	1357	1521	1719	1949	2211	2443
Debt: asset ratio (%)	18.5	19.2	19.5	20.0	20.9	21.8	22.6	23.5	24.5	25.6	27.3

Source: Hughes, Dean W., "An Overview of Farm Sector Capital and Credit Needs" USDA/Economics and Statistics Service, Agricultural Finance Review, Vol. 41, July 1981, Washington, D.C.

TABLE 13-3. BALANCE SHEET FOR U.S. FARMS ON JANUARY 1, 1980 BY GROSS SALES SIZE CATEGORY

	Annual Sales ($'000)					
	5-10	*10-20*	*20-40*	*40-100*	*100-200*	*>200*
Assets ($ billion)	38	58	103	243	137	156
Liabilities ($ billion)	3	6	13	44	28	47
Owner's equity (net worth $ billion)	35	52	90	199	109	109
Debt: asset ratio (%)	7	10	13	18	20	30

Source: Adapted from *Economic Indicators of the Farm Sector: Income and Balance Sheet Statistics, 1979,* USDA, Washington, D.C., 1980.

portion of debt. Operators of the larger farms are often less risk-averse, can exploit economies with good return, and therefore borrow to take advantage of these economies of size. By starting bigger, the larger farms get bigger. The rich get richer, the poor poorer (and fewer as operators leave for full- and part-time off-farm, jobs), and U.S. agriculture is increasingly polarized into two camps.

Figure 13-1 shows the projected distribution of U.S. farms for the year 2000. In comparison with 1974, there will likely be a huge decline in the numbers of farms under 500 acres, particularly those operations of less than 100 acres. At the same time, and partly as a result, there will be a proportional increase in the number of farms greater than 500 acres even though their numbers remain constant. Particularly because of the rising ratio of farm production expenses to gross farm income, there is a cost-price squeeze between average total costs and marginal revenue which hits smallest farms hardest because of their higher position on the long-run average cost curve.

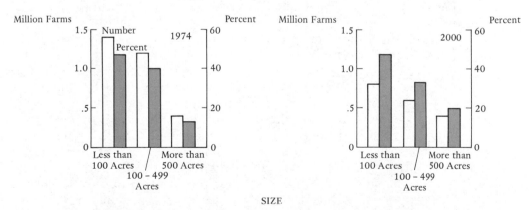

FIGURE 13-1. *Distribution of U.S. Farms by Acreage, 1974 and 2000. (Source: McDonald, T., and G. Coffman, "Fewer Larger U.S. Farms by Year 2000—and Some Consequences," USDA Economics and Statistics Service Agricultural Information Bulletin No. 439, Washington, D.C. 1980.)*

FINANCIAL RISK: AN EXAMPLE

This conclusion leads to the introduction of three concepts which will help to show the different positions of small and large farms and highlight a new trade-off in farm management: that of financial risk versus rate of growth in owner equity.

Financial risk can be defined as "any financial situation which jeopardizes the variability (solvency or liquidity) of the farm firm." Chapter 4 explained that solvency refers to the ability of total assets to cover total liabilities in case the farm had to be sold. Liquidity refers to the ability of assets to cover liabilities for the current period. Another measure of financial risk is the debt:asset ratio, defined as debts divided by the total value of assets controlled. This ratio should be maintained well below 0.7. In other words, the farmer should incur no more than 70 cents worth of debt for every dollar of total assets he controls. Because bankers prefer debt:asset ratios of 0.5 or below, this value of 0.7 may be considered a danger point: it is the maximum permissible debt:asset ratio even for farmers with a good credit rating. Similarly, while the preferred level for the debt:equity ratio is 1:1 or less, bankers have set a danger point of 2.3:1 for the maximum permissible value of borrowed to owned assets. Preferred levels of the current ratio (current assets to current liabilities) lie in the range 1.5:1 to 2:1 or above; the danger point is 1:1. This view of financial risk leads to the second concept.

Leverage may be defined as "the percentage of debt in total asset value". You learned in Chapter 4 that another measure of leverage is the debt:equity ratio. These two measures are variants; once you know one, you can compute the other. As the operator increases his leverage, he allows the firm to grow faster, but he also increases his financial risk. And this leads in turn to the third concept.

The **increasing risk principle** states that the greater the percent of borrowed assets in total farm assets (i.e., leverage), the greater the risk of becoming insolvent or illiquid; in other words, the greater the financial risk.

Let us apply these three concepts to two farms to see how they work. Suppose that two beginning farmers, Y and Z, are identical twins who have inherited, from their parents, identical small-scale farms of a total value each of $50,000 in equity capital. Each can borrow money at fifteen percent interest (i) and each expects a rate of return (r) of twenty percent. All they differ in is their attitude toward financial risk. Z is willing to borrow three times as much as Y. Table 13-4 shows the situations of the two farmers. Farmer Z is willing to take more risk, although the 0.60 level of debt to total assets is still perfectly acceptable to most bankers, and is by no means reckless. Because of his greater willingness to take financial risk, Farmer Z can expect his farm to grow faster than that of Farmer Y.

Why would anyone be so foolish as not to borrow as much as he could? The answer lies in expected returns, **r**. In fact, although for analytical purposes economists distinguish between business and finan-

TABLE 13–4. THE EFFECT OF LEVERAGE ON RETURNS
ON EQUITY CAPITAL IN A TYPICAL YEAR
VS. A POOR YEAR

	Farmer Y	Farmer Z
Equity ($)	50,000	50,000
Debt ($)	25,000	75,000
Total assets controlled ($)	75,000	125,000
Typical year (r = 20%)		
Ratio of debt on total assets ($)	33%	60%
Returns on total assets ($)	15,000	25,000
Interest on debt capital ($)	–3,750	–11,250
Net return ($)	11.250	13,750
Percentage return on equity capital	22.5%	27.5%
Poor year (r = 10%)		
Returns on total assets	7,500	12,500
Interest on debt capital ($)	–3,750	–11,250
Net return ($)	3,750	1,250
Percentage return on equity capital	7.5%	2.5%

cial risk, business risk (the variability in prices, yields, etc.) is one of the major contributors to financial risk. The lower the returns, the lower the net farm income, the current assets, the ratio of current assets to current liabilities, and the ratio of total assets to total liabilities. Whenever r dips below the level of i, the farmer gets into trouble.

So assume now that, instead of 20 percent, r equals 10 percent. (Of course, in some years, it could probably range as high as 30 percent; the farmer really does not know until he harvests the crops, finds out the level of death loss, and so on.) The lower half of Table 13-3 shows the results of increasing leverage in a bad year. Farmer Y receives $7,500 return on total assets, a $3,750 net return, and still a 7.5 percent return on equity. These results are not wonderful, but not disastrous either. However, Farmer Z gets $12,500 return on total assets but only $1,250 net return, for a return to equity of only 2.5 percent. Although Farmer Z will average 27.5 percent return in the long run, his short-run percentage return may be only 2.5 percent and his money available for family living only $1,250. Instead of growing at a faster rate, he may lose the farm altogether.

The twin farmers exemplify the principle of increasing risk: the more leverage, the faster the growth, but the greater chance of losing the farm. The increasing risk principle has three corollaries:

1. As Leverage Increases, the Spread between Possible Gains and Losses Increases. In this example, for r values of 10 versus 20 percent, the spread in Farmer Y's returns is $7,500, compared to $12,500 for Farmer Z. For r values of 10 versus 30 percent, the spread is even greater: $15,000 for Farmer Y compared to a full $25,000 for Farmer Z.

2. With Equal Percentage Gain and Loss on Total Assets, the Dollar Loss on Owner Equity is Greater than the Dollar Gain. In other words, if the rate of return had been –20 percent instead of +20 percent, then Farmer Z would have lost $36,250 rather than gaining $13,750.

3. The After-tax Gains Do Not Encourage Increased Borrowing. Although interest payments are a deductible business expense and operating losses may be carried back and forward (Chapter 16), there is no negative tax. Even with income averaging, the progressive nature of the U.S. tax structure means that the farmer with higher leverage will lose more on the downside than he can gain on the upside of variations in the rate of return (**r**).

Despite these corollaries to the principle of increasing risk, the interaction among the interest rate, the rate of returns, and the debt to asset ratio allows larger farms to grow more quickly and absorb higher levels of financial risk. Let us state simply that the rate of growth of the farm firm is a positive function of the rate of returns and a negative function of the interest rate, i.e.,

$$g = f(\overset{+}{r}, \overset{-}{i})$$

where

g = rate of growth of the farm firm

r = the rate of return

i = the interest rate.

We may then imagine the growth rays of a large and small farm as shown in Figure 13-2. The upper ray shows the situation for a typical

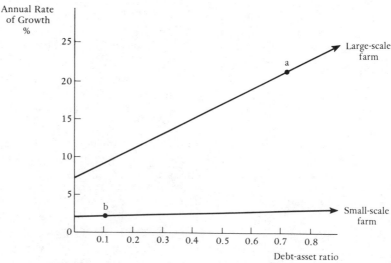

FIGURE 13-2. *Growth Rays for Large and Small Farms.*

large farm. Because of economies of size, larger farms enjoy a higher level of **r** because they lie farther out on the long-run average cost curve. They also may enjoy (though not always) a lower interest rate because of their greater creditworthiness, greater ability to meet family living expenses, greater access to information on financial options, and so on. In both respects, they may be aided by the county extension agents, who have an understandable urge to try to affect the largest possible number of acres with improved technology. The lower ray shows a much tighter margin between **r** and **i** for smaller farms because they do not enjoy these advantages. Already, smaller farms are doomed to grow much more slowly.

But there is also another factor at work: the position on the ray. Larger-scale farms are more tolerant of financial risk than smaller-scale farms and may lie out at point **a**, with a debt:asset ratio of 0.7 versus 0.1 for many small-scale operations (point **b**). This further difference polarizes U.S. agriculture into the fast-growing large farms and the slow-growing small farms. Differing attitudes toward financial risk also provide the very means by which large farms can grow: acquiring the land of the small farms whose operators decide to leave agriculture and take urban jobs.

Is the smaller-scale farmer wrong for not trying to move out farther along the ray? Probably not, for there are both economic and psychological reasons why he should use less of his credit capacity. To understand why, study Figure 13–3, oftentimes effectively used in agricultural

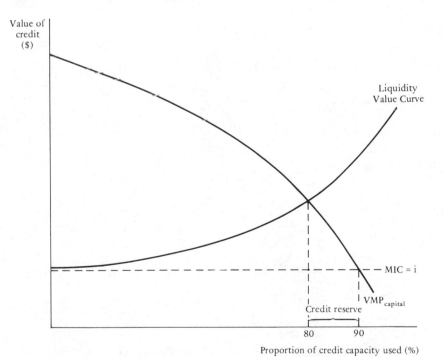

FIGURE 13–3. *Determinants of Credit by Capacity Used.*

extension to reassure farmers that they are right not to give in to the peer pressure of their friends down at the elevator who say they should purchase that extra 160–acre tract of land. The vertical axis of Figure 13–3 represents the value of credit, the horizontal the percentage credit capacity used in borrowing. This is essentially the approach to viewing the most efficient use of an input (in this case, borrowed capital) that we saw in our study of economic principles. One would normally expect that the optimum percentage of credit capacity to be used would be where the *VMP* of borrowed capital equals the marginal input cost of capital. But another factor enters the picture: most farmers assign a positive value to liquidity (cash on hand) because they want to have money in case of an emergency, such as a sickness in the family or the necessity of replanting a poor crop stand. Obviously, as the percentage of credit capacity used increases, the importance of keeping some resources liquid also increases. Hence, the liquidity value curve has an upward slope. The farmer should now borrow where the liquidity value curve intersects the *VMP* curve, at say, 80 percent. The percent of credit unused is called the **credit reserve**. As you will learn, maintaining a credit reserve is one of the four major financial strategies to reducing risk in farming.

Not all farmers have the same optimum percentage of credit reserve. In the first place, the size of operation determines the optimum percentage of credit used. If the solid line in Figure 13–4 is that of a large-scale farmer, the *VMP* curve for a small-scale farmer could be represented by the dashed line. We use percentages here because we are comparing

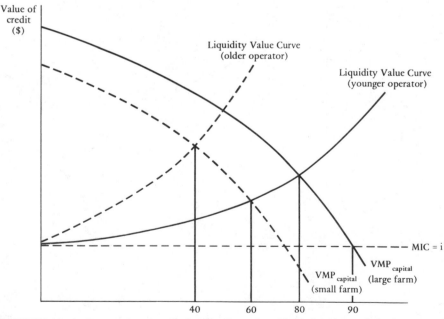

FIGURE 13–4. *Determinants of Credit Capacity Used by Age of Operator and Farm Size.*

across farms and it would be inconvenient to use dollar amounts. Therefore, at the same marginal input cost of credit (i.e., interest rate), the small-scale farmer is economically justified in borrowing only, say, 60 percent of his credit capacity. If he is faced with a higher interest rate, as he often is, then he should borrow even less.

Farmers may also differ in terms of their stage in the farm life cycle. Imagine two farmers: one young and old. The young farmer is just starting out in agriculture and is trying to build up the size of his equity as fast as possible. The older farmer is interested mostly in stability and does not want to rock the boat as he coasts into his final years. He wants to have plenty of money on hand in case of medical emergency or a trip to the Bahamas. Therefore, the liquidity value curve would be higher for the older farmer. Figure 13–4 shows liquidity value curves for both a young and old farmer.

Now take the example of an old, small-scale farmer. This is quite a common type in U.S. agriculture; over half of the small-scale farmers in the Midwest, for example, are 55 years or older. It is clear that this type of farmer would be economically and psychologically justified in borrowing only 40 percent, while a younger, large-scale farmer should borrow 80 percent. This diagram also helps to explain some of the father-son conflicts to be presented in Chapter 17. Therefore, when a small-scale operator's colleagues at the local elevator criticize him for not wanting to purchase that extra 160 acres, he should know why he feels hesitant. Not even the largest farm should use 100 percent of its credit capacity.

STRATEGIES TO REDUCE FINANCIAL RISK

Maintaining a credit reserve is the first strategy against financial risk in managing the farm business. The second strategy is to maintain adequate liquidity, i.e., a high ratio of current assets to current liabilities. A high current ratio protects the firm from loan default when cash flows are reduced by low prices, yields, death loss and other contributors to business risk. Adequate liquidity permits expansion of the farm firm through purchase of intermediate and long-term assets without jeopardizing repayment capacity or cash flow.

The third strategy is to use loans of adequate term or maturity. The longer the loan maturity, the lower the annual payment needed to fully amortize the loan. This strategy provides a cushion in periods of low crop or livestock prices. For example, Table 13–5 illustrates that the corn price required to pay off a loan increases dramatically with loans of short maturity, even if nothing is set aside for family living expenses.

The fourth strategy is to maintain a high proportion of self-liquidating loans. As will be expained later in this chapter, these are loans that pay for themselves out of gross, rather than net, farm income.

As noted in the preceding chapter, just distinguishing between debt and equity capital constitutes an oversimplification. Remember, owner-

TABLE 13–5.   CORN PAYOFF PRICE NEEDED TO COVER A LAND LOAN OF
$1,000 PER ACRE WHEN LOAN MATURITY VARIES

	Loan Maturity			
	10 Years	*15 Years*	*25 Years*	*30 Years*
Loan (amount per acre)	$1000	$1000	$1000	$1000
Annual principal and interest cost per acre[1]	152.41	120.43	97.72	93.06
Production costs[2]	152.46	152.46	152.46	152.46
	304.87	272.89	250.18	245.52
Payoff price — 110 bu. yield	2.77	2.48	2.27	2.23

[1]Principal and interest payments amortized over life of loan; interest rate is 13%.

[2]Includes all variable costs, labor at $4.00/hour, land taxes, and machinery fixed costs.

Source: Boehlje, M. and L. Trede. "Risk Management in Agriculture," S. James, P. Calkins, and J. Miranowski, *Selected Readings in Farm Management*, 1980.

ship of resources is not as critical as control of them. Although most capital available in agriculture comes from borrowing and savings, there is actually a whole continuum of sources of capital open to the farmer:

Equity Financing	—————— Risk ——————→		Debt Financing
savings gifts and inheritances	outside equity (partnership, corporation)	capital leasing (land, machinery)	contract sales borrowing

The modern farm uses a complex combination of these sources. In general, the items from left to right represent increasing levels of risk. Of course, farm operators would like to have a lot of savings and gifts, but they have limited control over these. In particular, they would like to receive their inheritances as soon as they begin farming, i.e., in their early twenties. Often their benefactors do not pass on until the operators are in their late thirties and forties. As to the other items on the continuum, in Chapter 9 you learned about contract sales as a way to reduce risk through marketing techniques. Contract sales often give access to production technology and advice and a more secure level of price than sales on the open market. Chapter 17 will present partnerships and corporations as ways of pooling capital, and Chapter 15 will treat land leasing and acquisition. Currently, 39 to 40 percent of the land farmed in the United States is leased. But the main source of non-equity financing is debt-financing or borrowing.

THE THREE R'S OF CREDIT

With this perspective on the importance of borrowing in agriculture, its increasing role relative to equity financing, differences by farm size, the financial risk involved and ways to manage it, let us proceed to look at how to borrow. The first concept the Potential buyer has to be aware of in borrowing is the three R's of credit: risk, returns, and repayment. Figure 13–5 gives a simplified overview of what you need to know about all three. It is drawn as a triangle because each of the three R's is related to and has interactions with the other two.

Risk

First consider risk. Chapter 8 showed that business risk can be looked at through eight analytical methods. Chapter 9 outlined some of the specific production and market strategies to achieve a reduction in business risk to the level that suits the farm manager.

Business risk, especially through its effect on current income and hence assets, influences financial risk. Four ratios are used to measure financial risk. This chapter has presented four strategies for reducing financial risk, one of which involves the repayment period shown in the bottom leg of the triangle.

There is one key farm record the farm operator must show his banker regarding risk before he can effectively talk about getting a loan. This is the net worth statement. A well-filled-out net worth statement allows the farmer, as noted in Chapter 4, to calculate all the indices used to analyze financial risk. Another important fact is that comparison of successive net worth statements shows what progress he has made over time, not only in building up equity, but also in improving his financial ratios. Thus, historical records are also critical.

Returns

In the same way that satisfactory net farm income competes against business risk, there is also a trade-off between increased equity (i.e., farm growth) and financial risk. There is also an internal conflict to be

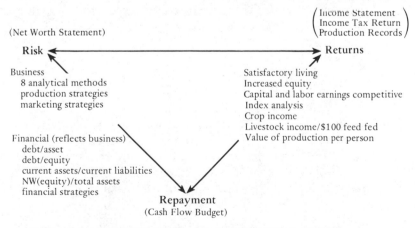

FIGURE 13–5. The Three R's of Credit.

decided in how to divide up the returns. Net farm income equals the change in net worth (i.e., the build-up in equity) plus family living expenses:

$$NFI = \text{change in net worth} + \text{family living expenses}.$$

This corresponds exactly to the macro-economic decision in the whole economy:

$$Y = S + C.$$

The farm operator would like to retain as much in net worth as possible, because the net worth itself can be used directly for investment, and indirectly as the basis for credit. Typically, larger farms not only have a larger surplus for re-investment, they also have a larger propensity to save on a proportional basis than smaller farms. This fact lends further insight into the financial reasons for the polarization of U.S. farms into two camps and the potential disappearance of viable small-scale farms.

Regardless of farm size, the farm operator would like to achieve an acceptable net farm income, including returns to capital and labor which at least match their opportunity earnings elsewhere in the economy. This explains the importance of looking at production indices to ensure that your own farm is at least as efficient as similar farms. Table 13–6 shows some representative figures from the Iowa Farm Business Association. A few of the more important of these indices are crop value/acre, livestock income/$100 feed fed, and value of production (gross profits) per person. The records the operator has to show his banker in terms of returns include the income statement for the farm (if he can show progress on historical records for more than one year, this is ideal), income tax returns (also helpful corroborative evidence), and production records on the efficiency of individual activities. If, for example, the farmer can demonstrate that he has been able to increase the number of pigs weaned per litter, the banker should be impressed.

Repayment

The level of returns is a very important factor in repayment, the third leg of the triangle. There are three other notable aspects about repayment. The first is whether the loan is self-liquidating or not. If so, it is paid out of gross farm income, and pays for itself over the term of the loan. Examples are a loan for the purchase of feeder livestock and a combine loan spread over its economic life.[1] It is financially safer to have a high proportion of self-liquidating loans. Non-self-liquidating

---

[1] *In practice the degree of self-liquidation depends upon two factors: the profitability of the investment and the term of the loan. A loan for any capital item may not be self-liquidating. Usually, the length of the loan will be shorter than the expected life of the loan purpose, except for operating items. Otherwise, the lender may have exposed himself to risk.*

TABLE 13-6. INCOME AND EXPENSES BY SIZE OF FARM, 1979

	100–179 acres	180–259 acres	260–359 acres	360–499 acres	500 acres and over
Financial Returns					
Net farm income	$20,282	$28,978	$38,603	$52,732	$93,664
Management return	–6,341	–7,043	–6,096	–782	12,654
Resources Used					
Acres per farm	153	233	321	429	792
Land value per acre	$1,462	$1,336	$1,389	$1,331	$1,227
Labor months	12.3	12.6	14.8	16.8	22.4
Livestock, feed supplies	$60,845	$73,515	$108,147	$134,373	$235,565
Machinery and equipment	$22,495	$31,117	$40,546	$48,212	$72,864
Land and buildings	$223,608	$311,270	$445,918	$570,797	$977,101
Total investment	$306,948	$415,902	$594,611	$753,382	$1,285,530
Sources of Income					
Livestock increase	$52,130	$64,741	$67,829	$82,026	$130,476
Feed fed to livestock	30,204	40,347	43,251	50,128	79,561
Livestock income over feed fed	$21,926	$24,394	$24,578	$31,898	$50,915
Crop production	32,507	51,405	69,321	90,931	156,776
Inventory value adjustment	699	1,379	2,001	4,172	8,693
Miscellaneous	3,829	4,727	5,761	6,080	11,705
Gross profits	$58,961	$81,915	$101,661	$133,081	$228,089
Expenses					
Operating	$21,948	$29,329	$35,084	$44,671	$75,758
Fixed	16,732	23,599	27,972	35,678	58,667
Efficiency					
Corn yield per acre	131	135	133	133	133
Crop value per rotated acre	235	249	245	239	241
Machine and power cost per rotated acre	109	97	84	75	67
Livestock returns per $100 feed fed	173	161	160	165	165
Gross profits per person	57,854	70,882	82,883	95,442	121,509
Gross profits per $100 expense	152	137	162	166	168
Gross profits per $100 invested	19	16	17	18	18

Source: Iowa State University Extension Service 1980 Publication, FM1789.

loans do not pay for themselves and, therefore, must be paid out of net farm income. They vie with the goal of a satisfactory living standard on the returns leg of the triangle. Land purchase is the most common example of a non-self-liquidating loan, but loans for conservation measures such as tiling, terracing and liming are others.

The second aspect of repayment is the amount of debt supportable from the annual repayment capacity. If, say, the farm operator has $1,000 which can be devoted to debt repayment, how much debt can he support? This question depends on two factors: the interest rate and the time period. As Table 13-7 shows, he should always strive for the lowest interest rate. For example, over a ten-year period, $1,000 can

TABLE 13–7. DEBT WHICH CAN BE SUPPORTED PER $1000 ANNUAL PAYMENT CAPACITY

Length of Loan in Years	*Annual Rate of Interest*					
	10%	12%	14%	16%	18%	20%
1	909	893	877	862	847	833
2	1736	1690	1647	1605	1566	1528
3	2487	2402	2322	2246	2174	2107
4	3170	3037	2914	2798	2690	2589
5	3791	3605	3433	3274	3127	2991
6	4355	4111	3889	3685	3498	3325
7	4868	4564	4288	4039	3812	3605
8	5335	4968	4639	4343	4078	3837
9	5759	5328	4946	4607	4303	4031
10	6145	5650	5216	4833	4494	4193
11	6495	5938	5453	5029	4656	4327
12	6814	6194	5660	5197	4793	4437
13	7103	6424	5842	5342	4909	4533
14	7367	6628	6002	5467	5008	4611
15	7606	6811	6143	5575	5092	4675
20	8514	7469	6623	5929	5353	4869
25	9077	7843	6873	6097	5467	4948
30	9427	8055	7002	6177	5517	4979
35	9644	8175	7070	6215	5539	4992
40	9779	8244	7105	6233	5598	4997

support $6,145 of borrowing at the ten percent interest rate but only $4,193 at the twenty-percent rate. But the question is not so clear-cut when it comes to the period of the loan. The longer the period, the greater the total amount the farm operator has to pay, but the larger the initial principal value he can support. For example, at the ten percent interest rate, his $1000 per year can support a ten-year loan of $6,145 but a 20-year loan of $8,514. This choice relates to the amount of leverage he is willing to accept and his perceptions of the level and stability of returns.

The third item under repayment is the type of loan. Credit sources and terms will be investigated at the end of the chapter.

COMPUTING CASH FLOW

Before considering credit sources it is important to be able to measure the operator's credit capacity and the very advisability of taking out a loan. As an example, let us investigate a possible purchase of land. Suppose a college graduate is considering getting into farming as a young person with no other land holdings. He looks around and finds 120 acres on sale for $1,087 per acre. This is absolutely the best prospect he can find. The land is rolling, best used primarily for forage crops; but it is cheap. The following calculations show how to work out the feasibility to this young person of buying this land:

120 acres @ $1,087	$130,440
Less down payment of $30,000 + $440 gift from uncle	− 30,440
Equals the amount to be financed	$100,000

The prospective farmer searches for credit and finds that the best terms he can get are 30 years at 14%

Checking the annual payment necessary to amortize $1,000 over 30 years (see Table 13–8), he finds:	$	142.81
The annual payment necessary to amortize a loan of $1,000	$	142.81
Times 100 equals	$	14,281
The gross returns (price times yield) from the land are estimated at	$	31,000
Less annual variable costs	$	9,000
Less annual ownership costs (DIRTI 5, incl. $14,281 principal and interest)	$	18,967
Equals remaining income	$	3,033

TABLE 13–8. ANNUAL PAYMENT NECESSARY TO AMORTIZE A LOAN OF $1000

Length of Loan in Years	*Annual Rate of Interest*					
	10%	12%	14%	16%	18%	20%
2	576.19	591.70	607.29	622.96	638.71	654.54
3	402.12	416.35	430.73	445.25	459.93	474.72
4	315.48	329.24	343.21	357.37	371.74	386.29
5	263.80	277.41	291.28	305.41	319.78	334.38
6	229.61	243.23	257.16	271.39	285.91	300.71
7	205.41	219.12	233.19	247.61	262.36	277.43
8	187.45	201.31	215.57	230.23	245.24	260.60
9	173.65	187.68	202.17	217.08	232.39	248.08
10	162.75	176.99	191.71	206.90	222.51	238.52
11	153.97	168.42	183.39	198.86	214.77	231.11
12	146.77	161.44	176.67	192.41	208.62	225.26
13	140.78	155.68	171.16	187.19	203.69	220.62
14	135.75	150.88	166.61	182.90	199.68	216.89
15	131.48	146.83	162.80	179.36	196.40	213.89
20	117.46	133.88	150.98	168.66	186.82	205.36
25	110.17	127.50	145.50	164.01	182.92	202.12
30	106.08	124.15	142.81	161.89	181.26	200.84
35	104.69	122.32	141.44	160.89	180.55	200.34
40	102.26	121.31	140.74	160.43	180.24	200.14

Is this a good purchase? There is no clearcut answer. If the prospective operator is planning to live and pay taxes on nothing but $3,000/year and expects even slight variability in his returns, then this is a very risky proposition and he might not be advised to make the land purchase.

On the other hand, if he were an established farmer in the expansion phase, he would not only have lower variable costs because of economies of size, he would also not need to live on the remaining income because other parts of the farm would already provide that. Thus, this purchase would probably be advisable for a large-scale operator. In fact, the above example illustrates seven major determinants of repayment capacity which any prospective borrower should keep in mind:

Yields	Overhead
Prices	Living expenses
Production costs	Size of farm
Flow of income & debt maturities	

USES OF CREDIT

Now that you have learned the importance and risks of credit, and the three R's of its use, what are the valid uses for credit in the farm business? There are six:

1. Create and maintain adequate size. Success in modern farming often depends upon achieving economies of size and spreading the ever-rising proportion of fixed costs over more units of output.
2. Increase the productive efficiency of individual enterprises. The farmer can do this in three ways:
   a. Adding resources to move out farther on the production function (Figure 13–6). Here the operator would be using capital to achieve

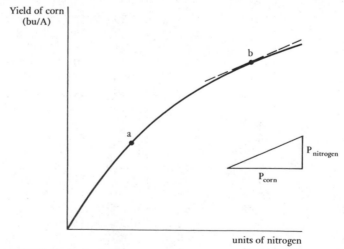

FIGURE 13–6. *Adding Resources to Increase Productive Efficiency.*

the optimum point in the factor-product relationship of economic principles. For example, he could intensify fertilizer use or install equipment for more timely livestock operations, and move from point **a** to point **b**.

b. Adopting higher-yielding technology to move the production function upward. Paying a premium price for purebred livestock is one example of such investments. However, shifting the production function upward may not always require the use of additional credit. For example, the shift to a more suitable strawberry variety may require no greater cash outlay than the previous variety.

c. Substituting resources to move along the isoquant (Figure 13–7). In this case, the operator would be using capital to acquire, say, machinery to substitute for labor, and would be optimizing the factor-factor relationship from economic principles. As you remember from Chapter 3, the decision-making rule to determine the optimum technology was:

$$MRS = \frac{\Delta\text{machinery}}{\Delta\text{labor}} = \frac{P_{\text{labor}}}{P_{\text{machinery}}}$$

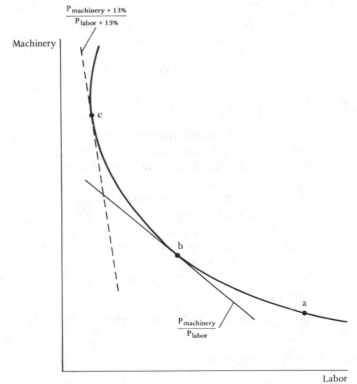

FIGURE 13–7. *Substituting Resources to Increase Productive Efficiency.*

But, once we introduce the credit aspect, we have to modify this to:

$$MRS = \frac{P_{\text{labor}}\,(1 + f_1)}{P_{\text{machinery}}\,(1 + f_2)} \, ,$$

where f_1 and f_2 are the interest rate charges on each of the two inputs. If these are the same, and both the numerator and the denominator increase by, say, 14 percent, then the slope of the price line and the optimal production point will stay the same. But suppose that the banker feels labor is a much more difficult and undependable input to manage. He may quite likely offer you a different interest rate for loans to acquire the two inputs, say 13 percent on machinery loans and 15 percent for labor hire. In this case, the price line will shift, as depicted in Figure 13–7. This will mean that instead of moving to point **b**, the producer should shift all the way up to point **c**. Thus, one's banker can influence the optimal economic position! Of course, he can also do so by limiting the amount of money the producer can borrow for each input.

3. Produce a more efficient combination of products if market conditions change or there are differential advances in production technology. This use of credit relates to the product-product relationship from economic principles. Market and technological changes will modify the price line or the production possibility frontier, respectively. As a result, the current combination of enterprises may cease to be the most profitable (Figure 13–8). Credit can help the farmer make the shift to a more profitable combination of enterprises.

4. Meet seasonal and annual fluctuations in income and expenditures. Most U.S. farms encounter the bulk of their expenses in the spring and a large proportion of their returns in the fall. Through cash flow budgeting, the farm operator can predict when and how much to borrow to match these inflows and outflows.

5. Provide continuity of the farm business. Credit allows a son or daughter to purchase the father's interest and expand and operate the farm efficiently. Alternatively, one son can purchase the interest of the farm from his non-farm siblings. Chapter 17 will deal with such intergenerational transfers.

6. Protect the business against adverse situations. In other words, the manager opts for **non-use** of part of his credit capacity. He maintains a credit reserve to tide him over periods of low farm income or poor health.

These purposes of credit can be categorized by time period as well:

Short-term (less than one year)

Operating expenses
Living expenses to tide over seasonal variations in returns
Refinance short-term obligations

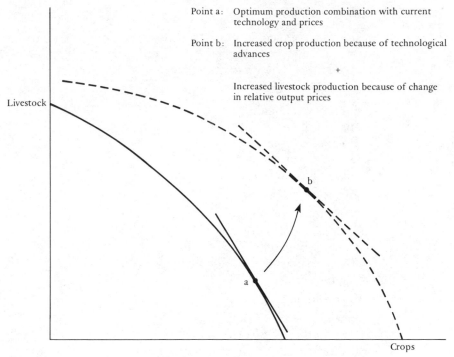

Point a: Optimum production combination with current technology and prices

Point b: Increased crop production because of technological advances

\+

Increased livestock production because of change in relative output prices

FIGURE 13–8. *The Use of Credit to Benefit from Price and Technology Changes.*

In the short run, Production Credit Associations and commercial banks are the major source of farm loans. These, if profitable, are usually self-liquidating loans.

Medium-term (1 to 7 years)

> Machinery
> Livestock expansion

Although this type of farm credit demand is increasing the most rapidly, there is a relative lack of supply of funds for these purposes. These loans tend to be at least partially self-liquidating also.

Long-term (greater than 7 years)

> Real estate
> Permanent improvements (such as tiling)
> Refinancing—short-term debts over long term to improve current
> > ratio and liquidity
> > > —existing mortgages less favorable than new mortgages

Long-term loans are often non-self-liquidating and are largely handled by Federal Banks and insurance companies.

SOURCES OF CREDIT

We have mentioned in passing some of the major sources of credit. Let us look at them in perspective and compare some of their more salient characteristics. There are three types of credit sources:

Private

Commercial banks*
Insurance companies
Finance companies
Dealers, processors
Individuals, relatives of borrower

Public

Bank for Cooperatives
Federal Land Banks
Production Credit Association*
Federal Intermediate Credit Banks
Credit Unions

Government

Farmer's Home Administration*
Commodity Credit Corporation
Rural Electrification Administration

There is quite an array of sources, and you can find out the details on each from any of the financial texts listed in the Suggested Readings at the end of the chapter. However, to give some idea of the characteristics of different credit sources, let us consider one financial source of each type (starred). The commercial banks and production credit associations are competitors for average-risk farmers, while the FmHA is set up for farmers unable to obtain credit from other sources at reasonable rates, i.e., high-risk farmers.

Commercial banks get their loan funds from demand and time deposits, retained earnings, correspondent banks and the federal reserve, and participation with PCA and FmHA. Because of their alternative opportunities for investment in government securities and other nonagricultural areas, they make available very few long-term or real estate loans. Further, their reserve requirements limit the aggregate volume of deposits available for loans and investments. Within these, the loans that can be made to one individual are limited to ten percent of a national bank's capital (25 percent on feeder cattle loans) and twenty percent of a state bank's capital (40 percent on feeder cattle loans).

Commercial banks are losing ground in both real estate markets (down from 17 to 12 percent of total lending 1950–1978) and nonreal estate markets (down from 72 to 60 percent) to Federal Land banks and Production Credit Associations, respectively, because of legal lending limitations, the seasonality of deposits and loans (both depositors and borrowers are farmers)[1], and their inability to meet the demand for intermediate-term credit.

[1] *This limitation is not so severe in branch banking states.*

Production Credit Associations were set up by Congress to finance farm production but are now publicly run. They get their funds from Federal Intermediate Credit Banks, retained earnings, and participation with local commercial banks. They give short-term and intermediate-term loans, but they generally do not offer real estate loans, especially second mortgages on Federal Land Bank loans. One problem with borrowing from Production Credit Associations is that to take out a loan one must buy nonrefundable stock in the association equal to five to ten percent of the loan value. There may also be a three percent handling charge. As you will learn, these policies incresae the effective interest rate. Still, in the period 1950 to 1978, Production Credit Associations increased their share of nonreal estate loans from 14 percent to 32 percent of the total.

The Farmers' Home Administration is a bank of last resort. It receives funds from congressional appropriations, other lenders as guaranteed loans, and emergency funds. It offers loans of all maturities, but it has two disadvantages. First, the maximum limits are $100,000 for an operating loan and $200,000 (or the value of the farm, whichever is less) for real estate loans. At today's land values, this is becoming a severe restriction. Second, as with any government organization, there are problems of supervision to make sure that the loans are obtained by truly needy people. A few years ago, it was found out that they were giving away $5,000 grants willy-nilly to anyone who asked for them and huge disaster loans to wealthy California farmers at three percent interest.

METHODS OF COMPUTING INTEREST

The method of computing interest depends upon the lending institution and the length of loan. Five common approaches are listed below:

1. Simple Interest. This is a straightforward percentage of loans of less than or equal to one year. The interest is due with the principal at the end of the period, e.g.: $1,000 for one year at 14 percent means you pay $1,140 at the end of the year.

2. Discount. Here the interest is removed before the loan is received, so the actual interest rate is higher. If the operator took out a $1,000 loan for a nominal rate of 13 percent, he would only get $870 at the beginning of the period and have to pay back the full $1,000 at the end. The formula here is:

$$\text{interest rate} = \frac{\text{amount paid back}}{\text{amount received}} - 1$$

$$= \frac{1000}{870} - 1$$

$$= 14.9\%$$

3. Add-on Interest. On a standard Production Credit Association operating loan, a total borrowing projection is made on the basis of a cash flow budget for the coming year. Interest accrues only on the outstanding principal on a weekly or daily basis throughout the year. Interest is paid off once at the end of the year to avoid having the farm operator pay interest on interest. At the same time, however, the PCA, as noted, requires purchase of what is known as B stock. In 1981, for example, a typical nominal interest rate was 16.6%. But to reflect this required purchase of stock, an extra 1.111% was added on. Thus, the total interest rate was actually 17.111%.

4. Interest on the Unpaid Balance. Figure 13–9 shows that this method can be implemented either as payments of an equal principal with declining interest and total payments (also called the Springfield method)

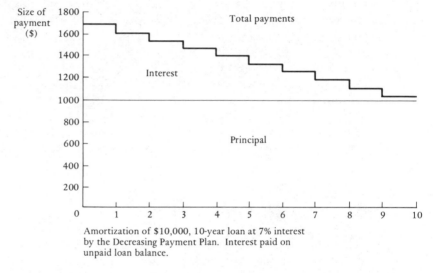

Amortization of $10,000, 10-year loan at 7% interest by the Decreasing Payment Plan. Interest paid on unpaid loan balance.

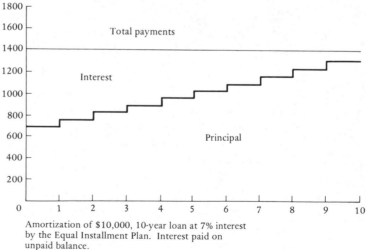

Amortization of $10,000, 10-year loan at 7% interest by the Equal Installment Plan. Interest paid on unpaid balance.

FIGURE 13–9. *The Springfield (Decreasing Payment) vs. the Standard (Equal Payment) Plan for Repayment of Long-Term Loans.*

or as equal payments (increasing principal, declining interest; also called the standard method). There is a third type, with increasing payments, often offered by the Veterans' Administration for people who expect their income to rise. Needless to say, this third type is riskier than the other two, and it might be better to opt for equal payments on a more affordable property with the intent of trading upward later.

5. *Annual Equivalent Interest Rate (AEIR).* This method helps the farm operator to compare loans with complex terms to determine the actual rate of interest. It often is used in dealer-financed purchases. The formula is as follows:

$$AEIR = \frac{2 \times \text{finance charge} \times \text{no. of payments}}{\text{original loan} \times \text{no. of years} \times (\text{no. of payments plus 1})}.$$

Now, work through two examples. First, suppose the farmer wants to buy a tractor which, after trade-in, the dealer will let him have for $24,000. The dealer says that he will give a full three years to pay, and that each of the three annual payments will be of only $11,220. What is the annual equivalent interest rate?

$$AEIR = \frac{2 \times 9660^{1} \times 3}{24,000 \times 3 \times 4} = 20.1\%.$$

The deal may sound attractive when the dealer mentions three easy payments, but it is possible that the farmer can get an intermediate-term loan elsewhere for only 13 or 15 percent. He should not be beguiled.

Second, suppose the farmer borrows $10,000 for production purposes at 12 percent add-on interest for one year with twelve equal monthly payments.

$$AEIR = \frac{2 \times 1200 \times 12}{10000 \times 1 \times 13} = 22.2\%$$

What appeared to be a 12 percent loan and quite competitive with other loan institutions, actually turns out to be 22 percent annual equivalent interest. As of 1968, when Public Law 90–321 was passed, requiring "truth in lending," a creditor is required to reveal the *AEIR*, if asked. However, it is always good to make sure the farm operator knows how to compute it himself.

SUMMARY

The growing role of borrowed capital in United States agriculture is polarizing the structure of U.S. farms into very large and very small operations. Smaller farms borrow less because of the greater financial

[1] *(3 × $11,220) – $24,000 = $9,660.*

risk which they face. Financial risk may be defined as any financial situation which jeopardizes the solvency or liquidity of the farm firm. There are four strategies which help the farm operator reduce financial risk. These include maintaining a credit reserve, maintaining adequate liquidity, using loans of adequate maturity, and maintaining a high proportion of self-liquidating loans.

Financial risk is only one of three aspects of credit decisions. The other two are returns and repayment which together with risk constitute the three R's of credit. Each aspect is related to and has interactions with the others, and there are unique records which are important to each. The net worth statement is critical for demonstrating financial risk, the income statement and production records are critical for demonstrating returns, and the cash flow budget is critical for demonstrating repayment capacity.

Valid uses for credit include creating and maintaining adequate size, increasing the efficiency of production, producing a more efficient combination of products, meeting seasonal and annual fluctuations in income and expenditures, providing continuity of the farm business, and protecting the business against adverse situations. Credit may be classified either by length of the time period (short, medium or long-term) or by the source of credit (private, public or government). For any type of credit it is important to understand how to compute interest. Five methods presented in this chapter include simple interest, the discount method, add-on interest, interest on the unpaid balance, and the annual equivalent interest rate.

TOPICS FOR DISCUSSION

1. What are the major credit institutions available to farmers in your area? Which have increased in size and importance over the past ten years? Which have decreased? Why?

2. Do small-scale farms in your area continue to be viable, or are they being absorbed into larger units? Describe the credit situation of both types of farms in view of the commodity mix produced in your state. Has credit been responsible for trends in the size structure of farms in your area? What other factors are involved?

3. Which farm records do you think are most important for obtaining access to credit? Justify your answer.

4. Are you aware of differential interest rates in your state which favor or discourage the use of certain productive assets over others? How about different loan rates for output, such as crops versus livestock? Why do you think lenders in your area have established such differential policies?

SAMPLE PROBLEMS

1. Given below is information on two farmers, A and B. Both can obtain a return on investment of 20% and must pay 15% interest on borrowed funds.

	Farmer A	Farmer B
Equity	50,000	80,000
Total assets	150,000	170,000

   a. What is each farmer's percentage return on equity?
   b. Which farmer has the higher leverage (show and explain your formula)?
   c. Which number above would you modify to show the "increasing risk principle"?

2. After trade-in, you can purchase a combine for $30,000. The dealer says, "I like young farmers: pay me $9,500 per year for four years and the combine is yours."
   a. What is the annual effective interest rate on the dealer's offer?
   b. Suppose that you could also get a PCA loan for the $30,000 for one year at 12% simple interest and five percent required purchase of stock. Assuming you get no return on the stock, what is the interest rate on the PCA loan?
   c. Which of the two loan options would you choose and for what reason(s)?

3.

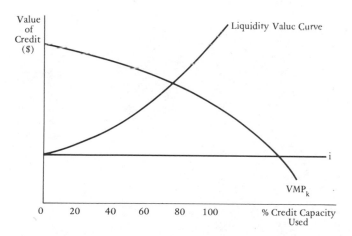

   a. If the above described your investment, borrowing and liquidity situation, what percentage of your total available credit capacity should you actually borrow?
   b. Would the credit increase ("+") or decrease ("–") if:
      1. The interest rate rose

2. Farm size expanded
3. Improved agricultural technology were developed
4. The farm passed from a 55-year-old to a 25-year-old farmer

c. Which strategy against financial risk does this diagram exemplify? Explain. What are the other three strategies to control financial risk?

SUGGESTED READINGS

Herbst, J. H. *Farm Management: Principles, Budgets, Plans*, fourth revised edition. Chapter 13. Champaign, Illinois: Stipes Publishing Company, 1976.

Hughes, D. "An Overview of Farm Sector Capital and Credit Needs." *Agricultural Finance Review: A Prospect for the Eighties.* USDA Economics and Statistics Service. Vol. 41. Washington, D.C.

Kay, R. D. *Farm Management: Planning, Control, and Implementation.* Chapter 12. New York: McGraw-Hill Book Company, 1981.

Nelson, A., W. Lee and W. Murray. *Agricultural Finance*, sixth edition. Chapters 6, 7, 9, 19–22. Ames, Iowa: Iowa State University Press, 1973.

Osburn, D., and K. Scheeberger. *Modern Agriculture Management.* Chapters 15 and 16. Reston, Virginia: Reston Publishing, 1978.

Penson, J., and D. Lins. *Agricultural Finance: An Introduction to Micro and Macro Concepts.* Englewood Cliffs, N.J.: Prentice-Hall Inc., 1980.

14

Acquiring Machinery Services

But a man who rides up on a great machine, this man
exists. He will be given messages.

Arthur Miller, A View from the Bridge

Concepts

In this chapter you will come to understand:

1. The impact of production costs upon the evolution of U.S. technology.
2. The various means to acquire farm machinery services.
3. The costs associated with acquiring machine services.
4. The importance of present value and partial budgeting techniques to making wise machinery investment decisions.
5. The integrated approach to managing farm energy requirements.

Tools

You will also gain the following skills:

1. How to evaluate ownership, joint ownership, rental, leasing, and custom hire options for acquiring machine services.
2. How to estimate the ownership costs of machinery.
3. How to estimate the operating costs of machinery.
4. How to evaluate the net present value of machinery investments.

INTRODUCTION

You should recall from Chapter 1 that United States agriculture has experienced a tremendous growth in its ability to produce food and fiber. The growth in quantity of production has been accompanied by lower per unit costs and increased quality of products. Rapid changes in available technology have been primarily responsible for the phenomenal results. The accompanying substitution of capital in the form of machinery for labor has been one of the principal hallmarks of the revolution in American agriculture. You have already studied how to use and acquire capital in Chapters 12 and 13. Because it has become the single most important type of nonreal capital, we now turn our attention to the principles of acquiring, maintaining, and properly utilizing farm machinery.

Since 1950 the costs associated with machinery have been a major portion of total farm expenditures. Table 14-1 contains data describing how machinery costs per rotated acre in the Cornbelt have increased almost four fold since 1950. Machinery cost as a percentage of total farm expenses has ranged between 40 to 50 percent over this same period. For the nation as a whole since 1950, we have seen a steady increase in machinery services on the farm. During the late 60s and early 70s there was a trend toward reduction in numbers of machines. Nevertheless, the size of machines utilized on the farm, as measured by horsepower, has been steadily increasing. The effect of the increased use of machinery services has generally been a decrease in labor requirements on the farm. At the same time, the reduction in the cost of total labor services has tended to be offset by increases in farm machinery purchase prices and the accompanying inputs necessary to operate and maintain machinery. Even though these costs have increased, the resulting increases in productivity associated with larger, more efficient machinery have caused the cost of production per unit of output to decline.

ACQUIRING MACHINE SERVICES

Extension personnel at Iowa State University have compared the various methods of acquiring machine services.[1] They suggest that in general, there are four questions to consider before deciding how to acquire farm machinery services:

1. Do you have the tools, mechanical ability and skilled labor required to operate the machine and maintain it in good working order? Modern machinery tends to be complicated both to operate and repair. Expensive tools and special training are necessary to perform proper maintenance and overhaul. Although the farm operator can seek repair services from experts, such services may not be immediately available during peak machinery use periods.
2. How much capital will you need to purchase a machine as compared to acquiring its services through a non-ownership method?

---

[1] *Ayres, George E. and James E. McGrann, "Acquiring Farm Machinery Services: Ownership, Custom Hire, Rental, Lease", Machinery Management Series, Pm-787, Iowa State University Extension Service, Ames, Iowa, July 1977.*

TABLE 14-1. FARM MACHINERY COSTS IN IOWA, 1950-1978

Year	*Machinery cost per rotated acre*[1]	*Machinery costs as a percent of Total farm expenses*	*Machinery cost per acre as a percent of gross value of corn per acre*
1950	$19	43%	26%
1955	20	48	31
1960	22	46	37
1965	25	38	27
1970	34	37	34
1975	69	40	29
1978	77	37	28

Source: *Iowa Farm Costs and Returns, 1950-1978*, Iowa Cooperative Extension Service.
[1]Machinery costs include depreciation, fuel, lubrication, repairs, and machine hire.

Factors to consider here are the level of downpayment required, the frequency and level of installment payments (if liability capital is used), and an estimate of the machinery ownership and operating costs per acre. As you learned in Chapter 3, operating capital should be allocated to activities which return the greatest marginal benefit per dollar invested. Frequently, the purchase option requires that large amounts of operating capital be tied up in the machine and therefore unavailable for other investment activities on the farm.

3. What ways are available for you to acquire machine services? The advantages and disadvantages of ownership should be compared to other acquisition schemes available in your area. This analysis should include the after-tax differences of each acquisition strategy along with expected costs and cash flow considerations.

4. How much risk is involved in purchasing the machine? The farm manager should analyze carefully how his farm production practices are likely to change in the near future. Such changes may result in limited usefulness of purchased machinery. Another factor to consider is what technological developments are likely to occur in the near future which may make a purchased machine obsolete before the farm manager is ready to sell it.

There is no single method which will be best suited to all farms for acquiring machine services. Each method should be carefully considered before committing resources to it.

Ownership

Ownership is the most popular method of acquiring long-term control of farm machinery services. Many operators gain a great deal of personal satisfaction from owning farm machinery. By owning a machine, they obtain complete control over its use. In general, the farm manager is required to provide the labor to operate the machine and is responsible for repairs and maintenance necessary to keep it in good working order. Other considerations include the risk of obsolescence and the fact that investment capital tied up in the purchase of machine services is no longer available for other farm investment activities.

When machinery is purchased from a dealer on credit (Chapter 13) the operator will generally have to pay for the machine over a shorter period of time than its useful life. This arrangement may generate short-term cash flow problems. Thus, even though machine ownership may be quite profitable for the farm business over its six to eight year economic life, a short term repayment period may result in cash flow difficulties. Other methods of acquiring machine services should be considered if serious cash-flow difficulties are anticipated. Also, if the farm business is expanding and there are high return alternatives for available capital, machinery ownership may not be the most profitable use of limited capital. If, however, the machine will be profitable over its economic life, and the investment capital necessary to purchase it cannot be more profitably used in other farm investment, ownership will probably be the most profitable means of acquiring machine services.

Joint ownership allows the operator to share responsibility for investment, repairs and labor with someone else. It may also generate enough use to make a machine profitable when it would not have been for either party alone. The two parties may be able to make payments together with neither experiencing short-term cash flow difficulty. However, cooperation is absolutely essential between parties considering the joint ownership option. Factors to consider include work habits and care of the machine; scheduling between farms; and responsibility for operating, labor, and repairs. In general, it is wise for the two operators to sign a written agreement explicitly resolving each of these details. The agreement should also include how co-ownership will be dissolved in case of disagreement, termination of farming, or death of one of the principals.

Used machinery ownership should be considered when credit or the timing of cash flows will not support the purchase of a new machine. Purchasing used farm machinery will normally require increased repair and maintenance costs. Therefore, when the farm manager purchases a used machine, he should be careful to obtain its repair and maintenance history and, if at all possible, some insight into the level of use and abuse to which the machine has been subjected. The purchase price (and therefore annual fixed ownership costs) of used machinery will tend to be lower than those of new machinery. The secret of successful used machinery ownership is to balance the higher repair and maintenance cost with lower fixed costs by reducing the purchase price. If the prospective buyer misjudges the mechanical condition of the machine and incurs higher repair costs than anticipated, or if the purchase price is too high, the total costs of owning used machinery may be just as high as or higher than the total costs of owning a new machine.

Exchange Work

Exchange work with a neighbor is probably the oldest form of short-term acquisition of farm equipment. Two or more farmers working together share labor and equipment and can thereby reduce their individual investment in machinery while still having access to a complete system. As noted in Chapter 11, exchange work involves trading labor for machinery. It may be particularly attractive to young farmers starting their operations with an older neighbor. Exchange work requires careful organization, and the parties involved must be compatible. Questions to be decided include: "Which farm will receive machinery services first when both need it?" "Who will be involved in operating the machine?" "Who pays repair costs when the machine breaks down?" and "How many hours of labor are equivalent to an hour of machine time in trade?"

Custom Hire

Custom hire is a popular method of gaining short-term control of farm machinery. Harvesting and fertilizer and pesticide application are the most popular activities undertaken by custom hire. Custom services may be available from a neighbor, a local fertilizer dealer, or a business specializing in custom farming. In general there are seven advantages to custom hiring over other methods of acquiring machine services:

1. When the manager custom hires, he is acquiring the services of both a machine and an operator. This means that the custom operator assumes the responsibility for operating and maintaining the machine. Custom hire also frees the farm manager to perform other tasks while machine operation is taking place. This is a particular advantage for young farmers without extra labor during planting and harvesting season.
2. No long term capital commitment is required. The costs of custom hiring, which are usually charged on a per unit basis, can be paid from operating capital.
3. The costs of custom hiring are tax deductible as ordinary farm expenses. However, the farm operator loses the advantages of investment tax credits and accelerated cost recovery deductions.
4. By hiring custom work the manager releases himself from all responsibility for machine repair and maintenance.
5. The farm manager has no responsibility for liquidation of the machine if he changes production practices and no longer needs it.
6. Custom rates are negotiated and fixed. The farm manager knows exactly what costs will be and can budget and project cash flow accurately.

7. The custom machine will likely be in good mechanical condition and larger and more efficient than the manager could afford on his own. By using the machine over a large number of acres (several farms), the custom operator is able to purchase larger more efficient machinery.

There are several disadvantages to custom hiring. The severity of each will depend upon the situation in one's local area. Disadvantages include:

1. Availability. There may not be a competent operator and machine for hire.
2. Quality. Because the manager will not be operating the machine himself, he will generally have little control over the quality of the job performed. However, survey results in the Midwest indicate that custom operators generally have lower field losses than owner-operators because of their greater experience in operating the machine.
3. Timeliness. The custom operator may not be able to get to the farm exactly when the manager wants him to, or during the optimal time for the crop, because of scheduling problems. During a particular stretch of bad weather the custom operator may have several farmers waiting for him. In general, it is best to work out a schedule with the custom operator before harvesting begins.

Custom hiring is particularly useful for specialized machines that are expensive to purchase and used only seasonally. This method is also attractive for beginning farm operators with limited capital resources and labor, and for other farm operators who are expanding their operations and have other uses for available capital.

Rental or Operating Lease

An operating lease or **rental** is another method of short-term machinery acquisition. The period usually extends from two to six months with charges made per acre, hour, day, week, month or season. Normally, there is a minimum charge that must be paid even if actual use is less than the specified minimum number of hours or acres in the contract. Some of the differences between rental and custom hire are:

1. The machine operator is not furnished. The farm manager must take responsibility for operating the machine and for daily care.
2. The manager will probably be required to carry liability insurance and property damage insurance on the machine.
3. The manager may be responsible for major repairs on longer

term contracts. In general, however, only the daily maintenance activities are required of the renter.

4. The manager does not have to endure the quality disadvantages of some custom hiring. Since he operates the machine, he can control the quality of the job. However, an operator with limited experience may do a worse job than an experienced custom operator. After he obtains the machine, the manager can operate it whenever he wishes during the rental period. All the same, availability may be a problem in areas where dealers are not able to supply a sufficient number of machines during peak requirement periods.

Frequently, a **rent with purchase option** program is available for farm operators. The rental contract includes a purchase option at a specified price at some future date. This provision is designed to encourage the farm operator to purchase the machine, and provides an excellent opportunity to try out a new machine before committing capital to its purchase. This type of rental option needs to be evaluated carefully from a tax management point of view. Whether or not payments on a rent with purchase option are tax deductible will depend upon the wording of the contract and the interpretation by the IRS. If the purchase option price is the original sales price or if the total of the purchase option price plus the rental payments approximates the original sales price plus interest, the contract may be interpreted to be a conditional sales contract. If it is and the operator exercises his option to purchase the equipment, the rental payments will be considered payments towards purchase. They will have to be capitalized and recovered through depreciation or ACRS. By contrast, if the rental contract states that the optional price will be fair market value for a used machine in reasonable condition on that date, and if no portion of the rental payment is designated interest or carrying charges, the contract may be interpreted as a true rental contract. In this case, rental payments may be deducted as expenses even if the operator exercises the purchase option. Of course, if he returns the machine to the dealer at the end of the rental period and does not exercise the purchase option, rental payments will be tax deductible.

Leasing as a method of acquiring farm machinery services, has not grown as rapidly in agriculture as it has in nonagricultural industries. Leasing is generally considered a long term acquisition method. Leases of four to seven years are common for most farm machinery, although longer terms may be negotiated. Just like ownership, leasing gives the farm manager complete control of the machine for the period of the lease. He is responsible for labor to operate it, for repairs and other operating expenses. At the end of the lease period, he returns the machine to the lessor. With some leasing contracts, the manager may also have the options of trading it in for a new leased machine or purchasing it.

Because payments are spread over the full lease period, they may be smaller than the payments on a short term credit-purchase contract. This capital difference becomes available for use elsewhere in the farm business. Even though lease payments may be smaller than purchase payments, they will occur over a longer period of time. Therefore, the total of all leasing payments will be larger than the purchase price. There are at least four advantages to farm machinery leasing:

1. Leasing is a hedge against inflation. Leasing payments are determined at the time the lease is signed. Thus, future payments are locked in regardless of any inflation that may occur.
2. Leasing transfers some of the risk of obsolescence to the lessor, who has to sell the used machine at the end of the lease.
3. Leasing may conserve working capital for other uses in the farm business.
4. Lease payments are tax deductible in full each year, just as rental payments or custom hire charges. However, if the operator exercises the purchase option at the end of the lease period, he should be sure the lease contract cannot be interpreted as a conditional sales contract.

Farm machinery leases are available from three major sources: commercial leasing organizations, banks, and machinery dealers. Leases from commercial leasing organizations and local banks tend to be very similar. Their leases are usually self liquidating, i.e. custom payments cover all purchase costs and interest on the investment. The customer is free to choose make, model, dealer and price. Then the leasing organization makes the actual purchase.

Most leases require the lessee to pay property or use taxes, insurance premium and repair costs. Warranty coverage is usually extended to the lessee. Leases or contracts usually require that the lessee pay a substantial penalty if the lease is terminated early. Investment credit may be retained by the leasing organization, or it may be passed on to the lessee in the form of credit against future payments. Since commercial leasing organizations and banks are not in the business of selling used farm machinery, they will usually not keep the machine at the end of the leasing period. Ordinarily, they will transfer title to the lessee under a purchase option, sell the machinery privately, or sell it at public auction.

Farm machinery leasing should be considered as a method of long-term machinery acquisition if it is available in the area. It may be more profitable than ownership in a rapidly expanding farm business with competing uses for available capital. It may also be an attractive alternative for older farmers who plan to retire in three to five years and want to use modern machinery without responsibility for liquidation. Leasing can also be advantageous for operators who rent or lease their land. If the operator loses the land, he will not be left with the machinery; if he keeps the land, he can exercise the purchase option and keep the machinery. Table 14–2 is a summary of the major characteristics of alternative methods of acquiring farm machinery services.

ESTIMATING FARM MACHINERY COSTS

The cost of machine services will vary widely according to the method of acquisition. Being able to estimate the cost of these services is a prerequisite to proper decision-making. The costs of owning and operating farm machinery can be divided into two categories—annual fixed costs which occur regardless of machine use, and variable costs which are related to the amount the machine is used. The fixed or ownership costs of machinery include depreciation, interest, taxes, insurance, and shelter (DITIS). The variable costs of machinery use include repairs, fuel, lubrication and labor (RFLL). The actual amount of cost associated with the machine will not be known until the machine has been disposed of and then only if accurate records have been kept throughout the machine's life. But these costs can be estimated if decisions regarding machine life, maintenance policies and future rate of inflation are reasonably accurate.[1]

Depreciation (D)

As you learned in Chapter 4, depreciation is a cost resulting from wear, obsolescence, and age of machinery. The degree of mechanical wear may cause the value of the machine to be slightly above or below the average value of similar machines when it is traded or sold. The introduction of new technology or major design change may make an older machine suddenly obsolete and cause a sharp decline in its remaining value. However, age is usually the most important factor in determining the remaining value of a machine. In general, the total annual depreciation cost is considered a fixed cost not affected by the number of hours of machine use. Since the cost of most machines can be fully recovered in five years using the accelerated cost recovery system, the recovery of cost will be more rapid than actual decline in value. Methods for depreciating farm machinery under the 1981 tax legislation were covered in Chapter 4.

Interest (I)

If the farmer borrows money to buy a machine, the lender will set the interest rate (Chapter 13). If the farmer uses his own capital, the interest rate charge will depend upon the opportunity cost of that capital elsewhere in the farm business. If he has unlimited capital, the opportunity cost may be the current market rate of interest. But if the farm operator has only limited capital and competition for it elsewhere in the business exists, he may need to examine alternative uses for capital and rates of

---

[1] *Sections relating to machinery cost estimates have been adapted from: Ayres, George E. and Michael Boehlje, "Estimating Farm Machinery Costs," Machinery Management Series, Pm–710, Iowa State University Extension Service, Ames, Iowa, June 1979.*

TABLE 14–2. SUMMARY OF MAJOR CHARACTERISTICS OF ALTERNATIVE METHODS OF ACQUIRING FARM MACHINERY SERVICES

Alternative acquisition methods	Tax considerations	Capital outlay for required investment	Cash flow requirement for investment	Cash flow for operation and acquiring service	Repairs and maintenance cost	Operating labor	Control over use and timeliness of operation	Risk of obsolescence
Ownership (a) Cash purchase (b) Credit purchase	(a) Full tax benefits (b) Full tax benefits plus tax deductible interest expense	(a) Full cash cost (b) Down payment	(a) High in purchase year (b) High, especially short term loans	Limited to operating costs	Full cost	Supplied by farm operator	Full control	Full risk
Custom hire	Tax deductible expense	No investment capital required	None for investment	Full custom hire cost	No cost	Comes with machinery service	Limited control over timeliness and availability can be a problem.	No risk
Renting short-term or operating lease (a) Rental (b) Conditional sales contract	(a) Deductible expense (b) Rental fee considered as payment. Investment must be capitalized.	No investment capital required	None for investment	Operating cost plus full rental fee	Limited cost cost depending on agreement	Supplied by farm operator	Limited control over timeliness and availability can be a problem.	(a) No risk (b) Full risk

Long term lease or financial lease (a) Lease with non-purchase (b) Conditional sales contract	(a) Lease payment deductible expense (b) Lease payment considered as payment. Investment must be capitalized.	No investment capital required	None for investment	Operating cost plus lease payment	Full cost	Supplied by farm operator	Full control	(a) Similar to ownership risk depending on length of the lease. (b) Full risk

Source: Ayres, George E. and James McGrann, "Acquiring Farm Machinery Services: Ownership, Custom Hire, Rental, Lease." Machinery Management Series, Pm-787, Cooperative Extension Service, Ames, Iowa, July 1977.

return. After he has determined the interest rate he must then calculate the average annual interest rate by multiplying the average investment in the machine by the interest rate:

$$\text{Interest} = \text{Rate} \times \frac{\text{original cost} + \text{salvage value}}{2}$$

Taxes, Insurance and Shelter (TIS)

Taxes, insurance, and shelter expenses are generally smaller than the sum of depreciation and interest but should be considered. Many states have phased out property taxes on farm machinery. However, if your state requires a tax on personal and business property, this amount should be estimated.

Insurance should be carried on farm machinery to allow for replacement in case of disaster such as a fire or tornado. If insurance is not carried, the risk must be assumed by the rest of the farm business. Current insurance rates for farm machinery average from six to ten dollars per thousand dollars of valuation.

There is tremendous variation in the quality of shelter provided farm machinery. Proper housing, tools, and maintenance equipment for machinery will result in better maintenance, fewer repairs in the field, and less deterioration of mechanical parts. These, in turn, should provide greater reliability in the field and a higher trade-in value. The cost of providing housing and maintenance facilities should be charged to the machinery. As a rule of thumb, a charge of two percent on the average machinery investment can be used.

The estimated cost of depreciation, interest, taxes, insurance and housing can be added together to find the total fixed cost. The total annual fixed cost of a machine does not change. But fixed cost per hour doubles when annual use is cut in half. Therefore, the more the equipment can be utilized on the farm, the lower the average power and machinery cost per unit of output.

Repairs (R)

Repairs occur because of routine wear, periodic overhaul, accidental breakage and operator carelessness and neglect. Repair costs for a particular type of machinery may vary widely from one geographic region to another because of soil type, terrain, and climate. Within a locale, repair costs vary from farm to farm because of different management policies and operator care.

The best data for estimating repair costs are one's own records of past repair expenses. Records indicate whether machines have had above or below average repair costs and when major overhauls may be needed. They also provide good information about the operator's maintenance program and mechanical ability.

Records of repair costs help estimate average repair bills. The total accumulated repair costs can be calculated as a percent of the original list price of a machine. Figures 14–1 and 14–2 demonstrate the relationship between accumulated hours of use and repair cost for several farm implements. As an example, consider a tractor costing $20,000. If the tractor is used approximately 600 hours per year it will have accumulated approximately 6,000 hours of operating life at the end of its ten-year economic life. In Figure 14–1 follow the line from the bottom axis at 6,000 hours up to the curve for two wheel drive tractors. Then follow the horizontal line to the left axis intersecting at 40 percent. Total accumulated repairs can then be calculated as:

$$0.40 \times \$20,000 = \$8,000 \text{ (for 6,000 hours)}.$$

The average repair cost per hour can then be calculated by dividing the total accumulated repair costs by the hours of life.

$$\text{Average repair cost/hour} = \frac{\$8,000}{6,000} = \$1.33/\text{hour}$$

The average repair cost per acre can also be calculated by dividing the

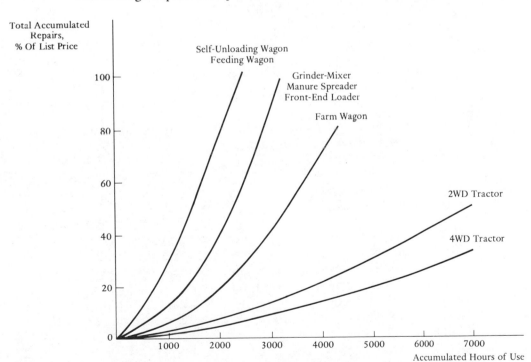

FIGURE 14–1. *The Relationship Between Accumulated Hours of Use and Total Accumulated Repairs. (Source: Ayres, G.E., and M. Boehlje, "Estimating Farm Machinery Costs," Machinery Management Series, Pm-710, Cooperative Extension Service, Iowa State University, Ames, Iowa, 1979.)*

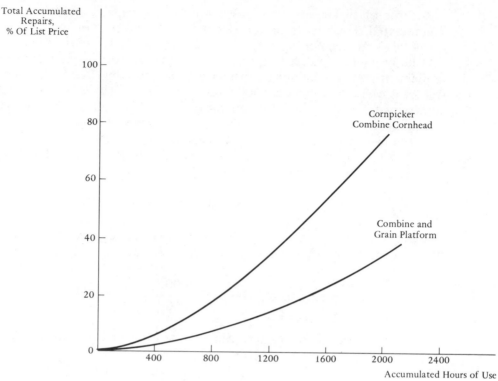

FIGURE 14-2. *The Relationship Between Accumulated Hours of Use and Total Accumulated Repairs. (Source: Ayres, G.E., and M. Boehlje, "Estimating Farm Machinery Costs," Machinery Management Series, Pm-710, Cooperative Extension Service, Iowa State University, Ames, Iowa, 1979.)*

total accumulated repairs of $8,000 by the total accumulated acres over which the tractor has been operated.

Fuel and Lubrication (FL)

Fuel costs can be estimated by obtaining average fuel use figures for various equipment in gallons per acre from extension sources. Such a listing appears in Table 14–3. These figures are then multiplied by an estimated fuel cost per gallon to calculate the average cost of fuel per acre. Fuel consumption for farm tractors used on a year-round basis can be estimated with engineering formulas based on *PTO* horsepower. The following formulas estimate average fuel consumption for three different kinds of fuel:

Average gasoline use (gallons/hour) = 0.06 × maximum *PTO* horsepower

Average diesel use (gallons/hour) = 0.044 × maximum *PTO* horsepower

Average LP gas use (gallons/hour) = 0.072 × maximum *PTO* horsepower

These formulas can be used as a rule of thumb without reference to any specific implement.

As a further rule of thumb, total lubrication costs for most farms average about fifteen percent of fuel costs. Once the fuel cost per hour or per acre has been estimated, this is simply multiplied by 0.15 to estimate total lubrication costs.

Because we live in a time of inflation, many of the estimated costs of long-term machinery operation should be adjusted for expected price increases. Table 14–4 lists inflation adjustment factors for machinery costs. By using these adjustment factors, the operator may adjust the estimated fixed costs of machinery ownership. The anticipated rate of inflation is read across the top of the table and the estimated years of useful life along the left-hand column. For example, if a 9 percent rate of inflation were anticipated and the useful life of the machine was 8 years, the fixed or ownership costs calculated in the previous formula could be adjusted by multiplying each by 1.99. Repairs and other various costs may also be adjusted by the same method.

MACHINE INVESTMENT: AN EXAMPLE

Deciding if machinery purchase is the best option will necessitate estimating the costs and benefits associated with ownership and comparing these to the costs of other available options. As you learned in Chapter 12, the value of benefits received over time must be discounted to reflect the time value of money. Costs occuring over time must also be discounted for the same reasons. Because most machinery provides an inflow of benefits and an outflow of costs over several years, it is important to evaluate these using present value techniques.

Tax regulations, especially accelerated recovery of cost and investment tax credits, must also be considered when purchase is contemplated. In general, these tax considerations will lower the effective ownership costs of machinery and are provided by the federal government to encourage investment in machinery by farm operators.

Table 14–5 contains an example of an after tax net present value analysis of purchasing a tractor. The purchase price is $32,000. The tractor is expected to generate a $15,000 inflow annually over its useful life. Column B lists the expected cash outflow necessary to purchase (year 0) and operate (years 1–10). Note that the annual operating costs increase each year, reflecting an expected price rise in inputs necessary to operate the tractor. Repair costs, which are expected to be greater toward the end of useful life are also included in this column.

Column C contains the nominal net cash flow expected each year of the tractor's useful life. This represents the net taxable income which this tractor is expected to generate before depreciation or recovery expense is deducted. Column D lists the recovery expense allowable under the accelerated cost recovery system assuming a January 1 purchase date. Subtracting this expense from net taxable income gives ad-

TABLE 14–3. FUEL REQUIRED FOR VARIOUS FIELD OPERATIONS[1]

Field Operation	Fuel Type	
	Gasoline	Diesel
Fertilization		
Spreading dry fertilizer, bulk cart	0.20	0.15
Anhydrous ammonia (30-inch spacing)	0.80	0.60
Tillage		
Shredding cornstalks	0.70	0.50
Moldboard plow	2.70	1.90
Chisel plow	1.70	1.20
Offset disk	1.35	0.95
Powered rotary tiller	2.30	1.60
Tandem disk, plowed field	1.00	0.70
Tandem disk, tilled field	0.85	0.60
Tandem disk, cornstalks	0.70	0.50
Field cultivate, plowed field	1.15	0.80
Field cultivate, tilled field	1.00	0.70
Spring-tooth harrow, plowed field	1.00	0.70
Spring-tooth harrow, tilled field	0.85	0.60
Peg-tooth harrow, tilled field	0.45	0.30
Planting (30-inch rows)		
Planter, seed only, tilled seedbed	0.65	0.45
Planter with fertilizer & pesticide attachments, tilled seedbed	0.85	0.60
Till-planter (sweep)	0.70	0.60
No-till planter (fluted coulter)	0.70	0.50
Harrow-plant combination	1.30	0.90
Rotary strip till-plant	1.50	1.05
Grain drill	0.50	0.35
Broadcast seeder	0.20	0.15
Weed Control (30-inch rows)		
Sprayer, trailer type	0.15	0.10
Rotary hoe	0.30	0.20
Sweep cultivator	0.65	0.45
Rolling cultivator	0.60	0.40
Cultivator with disk hillers	0.65	0.45
Powered rotary cultivator	1.00	0.70
Harvesting		
Cutterbar mower	0.55	0.35
Mower-conditioner, PTO	0.85	0.60
Self-propelled windrower	0.70	0.50
Rake	0.35	0.25
Baler	0.65	0.45
Stack-forming wagon	0.70	0.50
Forage harvester		
Green forage	1.35	0.95

TABLE 14–3. (continued)

Field Operation	Fuel Type	
	Gasoline	Diesel
Haylage	1.80	1.25
Corn silage	5.20	3.60
High-moisture ground ear corn	2.75	1.90
Forage blower		
Green forage	0.50	0.35
Haylage	0.35	0.25
Corn silage	2.00	1.40
High-moisture ground ear corn	0.65	0.45
Combine, soybeans	1.70	1.10
Combine, corn	2.35	1.60
Corn picker	1.75	1.15
Hauling, field plus ½ mile on graveled road	10.90	7.50
Green forage	0.55	0.35
Haylage	0.30	0.20
Corn silage	2.00	1.40
Corn grain	0.30	0.20
Soybeans	0.12	0.08
Hauling, add following values to those above for each additional mile on gravel		
Green forage	0.20	0.14
Haylage	0.30	0.20
Corn silage	1.30	0.90
Corn grain	0.20	0.15
Soybeans	0.07	0.05

[1] Figures do not include travel to and from field. Values calculated for 7-inch plowing and 4 to 5 inch operating depth for other tillage. Row crop operations calculated assuming 30 inch rows. All values calculated for central Iowa loam soil. Adjustments should be made for heavier soils, etc.

Source: Ayres, George F. "Fuel Required for Field Operations," Machinery Management Series, Pm-709, Iowa State University Extension Service, 1976.

justed taxable income (the amount of income which is subject to income tax). Assuming the operator is in a 25 percent marginal tax bracket, Column F lists the amount of the tax liability expected as a result of this purchase.

The investment tax credit (Column F) is 10 percent of purchase price. Because this is a tax credit, it is deducted directly from the total farm tax liability during the first year of ownership. Although the credit exceeds the total first year tax liability associated with the tractor, the full amount is taken under the assumption that an additional tax liability exists associated with other farm production activities not involving the use of the tractor.

Column H lists the net income expected after taxes. Because this flow of income is to be realized over a 10 year period, each year has been discounted by the appropriate factor (a 10 percent discount rate is

TABLE 14–4.   INFLATION ADJUSTMENT FACTORS FOR MACHINERY COSTS

Years	Annual Rate of Inflation (%)										
	5	*6*	*7*	*8*	*9*	*10*	*11*	*12*	*13*	*14*	*15*
1	1.05	1.06	1.07	1.08	1.09	1.10	1.11	1.12	1.13	1.14	1.15
2	1.10	1.12	1.15	1.17	1.19	1.21	1.23	1.25	1.28	1.30	1.32
3	1.16	1.19	1.23	1.26	1.30	1.33	1.37	1.40	1.44	1.48	1.52
4	1.22	1.26	1.31	1.36	1.41	1.46	1.52	1.57	1.63	1.69	1.75
5	1.28	1.34	1.40	1.47	1.54	1.61	1.69	1.76	1.84	1.93	2.01
6	1.34	1.42	1.50	1.59	1.68	1.77	1.87	1.97	2.08	2.19	2.31
7	1.41	1.50	1.61	1.71	1.83	1.95	2.08	2.21	2.35	2.50	2.66
8	1.48	1.59	1.72	1.85	1.99	2.14	2.30	2.48	2.66	2.85	3.06
9	1.55	1.69	1.84	2.00	2.17	2.36	2.56	2.77	3.00	3.25	3.52
10	1.63	1.79	1.97	2.16	2.37	2.59	2.84	3.11	3.39	3.70	4.05
11	1.71	1.90	2.11	2.33	2.58	2.85	3.15	3.48	3.84	4.22	4.65
12	1.80	2.01	2.25	2.52	2.81	3.14	3.50	3.90	4.33	4.81	5.35

assumed). The discounting results are shown in Column J, the present value of net income generated from the tractor.

Finally, Column K lists the yearly net present value of ownership after taxes. If the tractor is operated for the entire 10 year period, the net present value of ownership after taxes is $29,174 indicating a very profitable investment possibility.

OPERATING AND MAINTAINING FARM MACHINERY

The expenses associated with operating farm machinery vary widely between operators and regions of the country. Factors which influence operating costs include: operator experience, maintenance record, type of tillage system, terrain and topography over which the machine is operated and shelter provided. The operator can influence many of these costs by using good judgment and employing energy saving practices.

The experience of the operator can affect the overall use of time of machinery in performing farm tasks. Careful planning of operations will save time and fuel and result in the most efficient use of machine time. Some non-productive or overhead time will result from getting farm machinery in place. This time will vary depending on what different crops are being grown and whether the farm property is situated in one tract or widely spread over various areas.

The maintenance and adjustment of machinery and equipment can also affect operating costs. Machines should be in good repair to insure the most efficient operation. Cutting tools should be kept sharp and clean. Tillage equipment should be adjusted to the proper depth of operation so that an adequate performance is accomplished at minimum power and fuel requirements. Periodic lubrication of moving parts on

TABLE 14-5. AFTER-TAX NET PRESENT VALUE ANALYSIS OF PURCHASING A TRACTOR

Year	Estimated Cash Inflow $	Estimated Cash Outflow $	Net Cash Flow (A-B) $	Recovery $	Adjusted Taxable Income (C-D) $	Tax (25% Tax Bracket) (0.25 × E) $	Investment Credit[1] $	Net Income After Tax (C-F) $	Discount Factor[2]	Present Value (H × I) $	Sum of Net Present Value (ΣJ)
0	0	32,000	-32,000	0	—	—	—	-32,000	1.000	-32,000	-32,000
1	15,000	3,000	12,000	4,800	4,200	1,800	3,200	13,400	0.909	12,181	-19,819
2	15,000	3,100	11,900	4,040	4,860	1,215	0	10,685	0.826	8,826	-10,993
3	15,000	3,200	11,800	6,720	5,080	1,270	0	10,530	0.751	7,908	-3,085
4	15,000	3,300	11,700	6,720	4,980	1,245	0	10,455	0.683	7,141	4,056
5	15,000	3,400	11,600	6,720	4,880	1,220	0	10,380	0.621	6,446	10,502
6	15,000	3,700	11,300	0	11,300	2,825	0	8,475	0.564	4,780	15,282
7	15,000	4,100	10,900	0	10,900	2,725	0	8,175	0.513	4,194	19,476
8	15,000	4,500	10,500	0	10,500	2,625	0	7,875	0.467	3,678	23,154
9	15,000	4,900	10,100	0	10,100	2,525	0	7,575	0.424	3,212	26,366
10	15,000	5,300	9,700	0	9,700	2,425	0	7,275	0.386	2,808	29,174
Total	$150,000	$70,500	$79,500	$32,000	—	$19,875	$3,200	$62,825	—	$29,174	$29,174
	A	B	C	D	E	F	G	H	I	J	K

[1] 10% of purchase price.
[2] A discount factor of 10% is assumed.

machinery and equipment not only insures long life but helps accomplish machine work in minimum time with less energy cost.

Shelter for equipment and machinery protects it during periods of non-use. Because many farm machines are only used seasonally, it is important to protect them from weathering during the off–season.

ENERGY INVESTMENT ANALYSIS FOR FARMS

The investment decisions presented so far in this chapter have concentrated on an individual piece of machinery. These decisions therefore have been partial in nature. Similarly, the break-even examples presented in Chapter 5 also concentrated on the maximum permissible price that could be paid for an item of machinery, equipment, or a building. However, the decision as to how to acquire the optimal amount of power to operate a farm involves the whole farm and must take account of the interaction among crops and livestock production activities as well as storage and drying. Any analysis, therefore, that attempts to determine the optimal energy line-up for a farm must by its very nature be more comprehensive and more complex than an investment analysis for an individual piece of machinery or other power source.

Traditionally, farmers did not have to concern themselves with a whole farm analysis of energy use. This is because the cost of petroleum fuel, electricity and other traditional power sources used in American agriculture was quite low relative to the prices of other production factors. One of the reasons that American agriculture has become so capitalized and so machinery intensive has been the relatively cheap power sources. Because fuel was cheap, farmers accumulated an excessive average inventory of available power units to make sure they could meet the seasonal power demands of such time-inflexible operations as planting and harvest.

Since the oil shock of 1973, however, there have been dramatic increases in the cost of imported petroleum. Import supply has also become less certain. As a result, scientists at landgrant institutions and in private industry have sought alternative sources of farm energy. These include solar-powered drying facilities, the use of biomass to produce methane gas for farm fuel, and the production of alcohol from crops and crop residues either to power farm machinery directly as alcohol or to be used as a mixture with gasoline to produce gasohol. There has been further research on windmills as a power source. Natural gas and liquid petroleum gas have also been considered as alternatives to petroleum-based fuels. Researchers have even investigated the possibility of designing and using electric-powered vehicles in farm operations. As they look towards the year 2000, farm operators should become knowledgeable about these alternative power sources.

Not only are the sources changing in the energy environment, so are the options in which such power sources can be used to achieve a high level of farm output without engendering prohibitive costs. The economic principles presented in Chapter 2 provide a convenient framework for the analysis of these options. The first range of options open to farm operators is the factor-product decision. One clear example is to reduce the amount of petroleum-based fertilizers used on crops. Farmers may reduce their indirect demand for imported products by reducing the rate of nitrogen application. Thus, as energy prices increase it may be possible to maximize profit by reducing the amount of nitrogen applied. This distinction between the yield maximizing rate of application per acre and the net return maximizing rate may very well increase over time. Another example of the factor-product decision would be the use of irrigation water on crops particularly if it is supplied through a petroleum powered pump.

The second option open to farmers to reduce the amount of high cost or limited petroleum energy involves the factor-factor decision. Two important aspects of this decision regarding crop production are worth mentioning. The first is the switch from intensive tillage with high petroleum use to lower, or even zero tillage techniques which must be accompanied by a higher use of pesticides but overall lower quantities of petroleum. In other words, there is a trade-off between mechanical energy and chemical energy. A second aspect involves the choice among power units on the farm. Experiments have also been done to show the profitability of solar grain drying in contrast to traditional petroleum powered or even electric powered grain drying. Solar heating has been studied as a means to heat broiler houses in Arkansas and throughout the Southeast. Less energy can be used in confinement operations in the heating and cooling system by performing such tasks with solar facilities. Methane generators can provide an on-farm source of energy for such operations, particularly if they lie close by the livestock facility and can produce burnable gas for heating and cooling. A portion of the farm itself can be used to grow high-energy grain and residue for methane production to produce alcohol to fuel the tractors and machinery already on hand. These factor factor changes can significantly reduce the costs of energy as the prices of petroleum fuel increases.

A third avenue open to farmers involves the product-product decision. As stated in Chapter 2, this relates to the crop and livestock production patterns on the farm. Farmers may switch their production patterns from energy intensive to less energy intensive crops and livestock enterprises. Forage crops and particular legumes often require less petroleum fuel and fertilizer input than grain crops. Soybeans may be grown in narrow rows of 15 inches in order to reduce the amount of weeding which is necessary and to increase the yield per unit of energy invested.

All three of the above decision areas are affected by possibly future changes in the prices of petroleum, pesticides, fertilizers, and the alternative power sources. Unless they change their energy investments, farmers will likely continue in a price-cost squeeze that will worsen in the future. Thus, cropping patterns, management of technology, rates of fertilizer application and the disposal of waste products will become much more vital, as time progresses.

Given the increasing complexity of energy investment decisions, it is clear that an integrated approach to farm energy investment analysis is required. As mentioned, this must consider the whole farm as the unit of analysis. It would be possible to use whole-farm budgeting, as presented in Chapter 5 to analyze these decisions. However, the complexity of the decisions suggests that a linear programming format would be the easiest approach.

With linear programming it is relatively easy to include all of the options noted above, in other words to allow for varying levels of fertilizer intensity, tillage, spraying of herbicides and other pesticides, the raising of narrow-row soybeans, and so on. All these options can be included as columns within the linear programming matrix. In addition, for each activity included, alternative power sources can be included. Thus, the computer algorithm can determine not only the optimal level of technology but also the optimal power source to implement it. Thus, electric, solar, biomass, alcohol, wind, and gas power can all be included as options for many operations.

SUMMARY

In this chapter the importance of machine services to U.S. agriculture has been presented. The gradual shift from hand labor to machine labor has resulted in lower per unit costs of production. Although this shift in inputs has decreased the farm labor bill, the resulting purchases of machinery and associated operating inputs has more than offset these savings.

Acquiring machine services is fundamental to accomplishing modern farm production practices. Five methods of acquiring machine services were discussed. These included ownership, joint ownership, exchange work, custom hire, rental and lease options. The advantages and disadvantages of each were discussed.

The costs of owning and operating machinery were outlined along with the methods necessary to estimate each. Once these costs are estimated a comparison can take place which allows the farm operator to select the least cost option for acquiring machine services.

Because machinery provides a flow of benefits as well as costs over time, it is necessary to evaluate the discounted value of these costs and benefits. Federal tax regulations also affect the ownership costs of farm machinery. A comprehensive after tax net present value example was presented involving the purchase of a farm tractor.

The interaction of crop and livestock production activities necessitates a whole farm approach to acquiring and managing farm energy needs. Possible future developments and means to evaluate alternative energy and machine work sources were presented involving the economic principles presented earlier in the text.

TOPICS FOR DISCUSSION

1. What operations in your area are performed by custom hire?
   a. What are the advantages and disadvantages of performing these by custom hire?
   b. How critical is the timing of these operations to overall profits?
2. Under what conditions would machine ownership be more practical or profitable than acquiring these services by other means?
3. What factors, under management control, can reduce the annual operating costs of machinery and equipment?
4. Why is it important to consider the after-tax costs of machine ownership?
5. What are the major differences between a lease and the rental method of acquiring machine services?

SAMPLE PROBLEM

1. Call a machine dealer in your area and determine the purchase price and an estimate of annual operating costs for a particular implement. Calculate the net present value after taxes of owning this machine. You must assume an appropriate discount rate, marginal tax rate and calculate the fixed costs of ownership.

SUGGESTED READINGS

Ayres, G. E. "Estimating Farm Machinery Costs," *Machinery Management Services*, Pm–170, Cooperative Extension Service, Iowa State University, Ames, 1979.

Ayres, G. E. and M. Boehlje. "Estimating Farm Machinery Costs," *Machinery Management Series*, Pm–710, Cooperative Extension Service, Iowa State University, Ames, 1979.

Ayres, G. E. and J. M. McGrann. "Acquiring Farm Machinery Services: Ownership, Custom Hire, Rental, Lease," *Machinery Management Series*, Pm–787 Cooperative Extension Service, Iowa State University, Ames, 1977.

Edwards, W. and M. Boehlje. "Farm Machinery Selection in Iowa Under Variable Weather Conditions," *Special Report 85*, Cooperative Extension Service, Iowa State University, Ames, 1980.

Harsh, S. B., L. J. Connor and G. D. Schwab. *Managing The Farm Business*, Chapter 12, pp. 279–99, Englewood Cliffs, N.J.: Prentice Hall, Inc. 1981.

Herbst, J. J., *Farm Management: Principles, Budgets, Plans*, Chapter 9, pp. 155–74, Fourth Revised Edition, Champaign, IL: Stipes Publishing, 1980.

Luening, R. A. and W. P. Mortenson, *The Farm Management Handbook*, Chapter 22, pp 367–80, Sixth Edition, Danville, IL: The Interstate Printers and Publishers, Inc. 1979.

15

Acquiring Control of Land

Every man of discernment, while walking upon the earth. . .
is fully aware that the thing which is the source of his prosperity,
his wealth, his might, his exaltation, his advancement and power
is . . . the very earth which is trodden beneath the feet of all men.

Bahá'u'lláh, Epistle to the Son of the Wolf

Concepts

In this chapter you will come to understand:

1. How the process of entering farming has change over time.

2. Trends in land values in the twentieth century, and seven reasons which explain these trends.

3. Factors to consider in deciding whether or not to buy land and how to finance land purchases.

4. The risks involved in installment land contracts.

5. Reasons and objectives for farm leases.

6. The advantages and disadvantages of five types of farm leases.

Tools

You will also acquire the following skills:

1. How to adjust the price you should be willing to pay for land to take account of risk, appreciation, soil loss, and inflation.

2. How to determine what a farm is worth, including the value of supplies, buildings, livestock and other assets.

3. How to calculate rents for cash, flexible cash, crop-share, livestock-share, and labor-share leases.

INTRODUCTION

As with the other three factors of production (management, labor, and nonreal capital), there is no single method of acquiring land, or real capital. The first major way to obtain control of land—and remember that control is more important than ownership—is to own it. The farm operator may buy land, either individually or as part of a partnership or corporation, through cash sale, a mortgage agreement with a third party, an installment land contract, or a like-kind exchange. Or he may come to own land through gift or inheritance.

The alternative source of land control is to rent or lease real capital. There are many operations in the central states of 700 or more acres which consist entirely of rented land. Such operations make respectable profits, and because of their high percentage of variable costs, avoid business and financial risk through flexibility. As will be discussed in this chapter, leasing arrangements may take many forms, including cash, flexible cash, crop-share, livestock-share, and not necessarily the owner-ship, of the land resource. In this chapter, you will study the factors that determine how and when to obtain control of real capital.

A HISTORY OF WAYS TO ENTER FARMING

Figure 15–1 contrasts the old and the new ways of getting into farming. It used to be that almost anyone could start out as a hired man because, at the turn of the century, farm production in the United States was labor-intensive. Most farmers needed someone to help them plow by horse for the planting and harvesting of crops by hand. Thus, the de-mand for hired labor was high. In fact, most of the grandfathers and great-grandfathers of current farm operators in the United States origi-nally got into farming in this way. By working a few years, they could save their wages and build enough experience to rent land from the owner. Finally, they could buy part or all of the farmer's land or a nearby farm with similar production enterprises.

Today, however, it is much harder to enter farming unless one is lucky enough to be related to a farmer through birth[1] or marriage. The ladder has also become more complex (Figure 15–1). A young person interested in a career in agricultural production usually starts out in junior high school with a 4-H project (say raising a steer). If he does well, his father or uncle (depending upon who the operator is) lets him take over a small enterprise on the farm (say, backgrounding ten or fifteen steers), or part of a large enterprise (say, 20 acres of a 300-acre corn crop). This opportunity allows him to develop management skills without greatly affecting net farm income. Then, if he continues to be successful, his

[1] *Over 80 percent of today's farmers are children of farmers.*

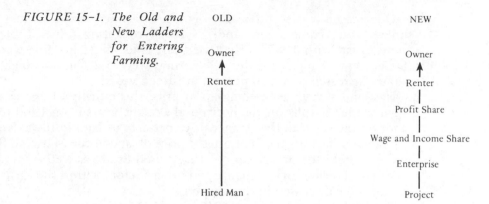

FIGURE 15–1. *The Old and New Ladders for Entering Farming.*

parents take him into a wage (fixed income of $1,500 to $2,000/year) plus income share arrangement or incentive plan (Chapter 11). This plan allows the young person to build up his equity on the one hand and challenges his skill and ingenuity on the other, because he knows that he will be getting, say, ten to fifteen percent of the net farm income. Then (and this is at the point the young person usually returns to the farm from college), he goes on to an entire profit-share arrangement with his parents, under which the wage component drops out and everyone pools labor and management. The young person has more to contribute because of his greater management skills and is willing to take more risk. Finally, after he builds up his equity, management skill, and courage, he can go on to rent and own his own farm as in the old model. Even then, the new owner often receives some financial assistance from an older operator.

Without the possibility of entry at the project level, it is difficult to get into farming at all. A story from the Midwest will illustrate this point. There was an article in the **Des Moines Register** in 1978 about a 57-year-old farmer who had acute diabetes and, therefore, had been advised by his physician long ago never to have children. Now his doctor told him that at the most he had seven or eight years to live. So he put an advertisement in the paper announcing that he was prepared to give away his farm to an enterprising man. However, there were two conditions. The first was that the young man had to go to work under the older man's tutelage for seven years to serve as a surrogate son of the kind the farmer had never had. That would be difficult enough. But the second condition was that the young man had to change his name to that of the older farmer. Now, you are probably thinking, "Nobody is ever going to accept that offer!" But if you are, you are wrong. The farmer was deluged with applications from over a thousand young people throughout the state. He selected the one he liked the best, and they are currently together on the farm working out the bargain. That someone would submerge his identity to acquire land demonstrates the lengths to which some people will go. Would you be willing to change your name to get a 480-acre farm?

One reason it is so difficult to get into farming in the United States unless you "come from land" is its skyrocketing value. Table 15-1 shows that, with 1967 as the base year, land values in 1965 were only 80 percent as high, and by 1980, they were 5.2 times as high. Land values increased over 500 percent in fifteen years!

Has land always been going up in price this quickly? In general, yes. Figure 15-2 graphs on the horizontal axis the years from 1900 to 1980 and, on the vertical, the average price per acre of land in Iowa. Note the tremendous historical increase in the price of land in the Midwest. Similar patterns hold for other parts of the United States as well. This trend is because of technological change and other factors within the agricultural sector to be discussed in this chapter.

The second conclusion from Figure 15-2 is that there are periods of depreciation as well as appreciation in land values. Particularly, if one had bought land at $255 an acre in 1920 and realized neither that there was going to be a recession in the general economy in the 1930s nor that agriculture is one of the more sensitive indicators that a recession might be coming, one would have been in a very poor position. The price of land went down continuously, so that there were many farm fore-closures. Alternatively, if one had bought in 1938, one would have been in great shape indeed. Since then, except for a small jog in 1960, there has been a steady increase in land value. The most recent recession began in 1979. At that time, there was a leveling off of the rate of increase

TABLE 15-1.   TRENDS IN THE VALUE OF IOWA FARM LAND, 1965-1980

Year	Value per acre	Dollar change	Percentage change	Index (1967 = 100)
1965	320	29	10.0	81
1966	361	41	12.5	91
1967	397	36	9.9	100
1968	409	12	3.0	103
1969	419	10	2.5	106
1970	419	0	0.0	106
1971	430	11	2.6	108
1972	482	52	12.0	121
1973	635	154	31.9	160
1974	834	199	31.3	210
1975	1095	261	31.3	276
1976	1368	273	24.9	345
1977	1450	82	6.0	365
1978	1646	196	13.5	415
1979	1958	312	19.0	493
1980	2066	108	5.5	520

Source: Harris, Duane G., et al., *Iowa Land Value Survey 1980*, Iowa State University, Ames, Iowa, 1981.

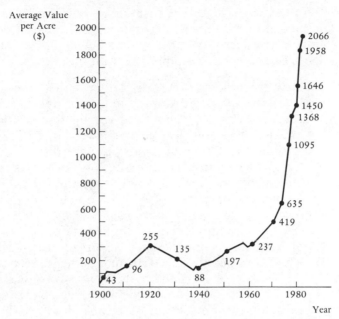

FIGURE 15-2. *Long-term Trends in the Average Value per Acre of Iowa Farmland, (Source: Harris, Duane, et al. "1980 Iowa Land Value Survey," Cooperative Extension Service, Iowa State University, Ames, Iowa, 1981.)*

in Iowa land values,[1] but there was no absolute decline. Therefore, unless one had even more lucrative investment opportunities, it continued to be profitable to buy land. In general, land is an excellent investment because its value not only increases faster than inflation but also tends to increase in noninflationary periods.

What are some of the reasons for long-term increases in land values? There are seven key factors responsible. To focus the discussion, recall the formula used to determine the present value of land, i.e., its selling price, from Chapter 13:

$$PV = \frac{E}{r}$$

where

PV = present value

E = net returns to land, i.e., net farm income per acre less returns to management and unpaid family labor

r = the discount rate adjusted for risk, inflation, and appreciation.

---

[1] *This pattern was also promoted by extremely low farm product prices and hence farmer cash flow problems which reduced effective demand for land purchase by farmers.*

So far, we have let the formula go by unquestioned, but these seven factors help to explain long-term trends in land value with which the prospective farm operator should be familiar if he ever plans to buy land. Each one has a unique effect on the present value formula.

1. New technology. New technology either increases yield and hence total revenue (e.g., through improved hybrid seed) or reduces total costs (e.g., through improved combines and other equipment). Both kinds of technological change have the effect of increasing the net returns to land and raising its present value and market price.

2. Economies of size. These reduce production costs per unit of output by pulling the farm farther out on the *LRAC* curve (Figure 15–3). Economies of size may or may not increase yield and hence total revenue at constant prices, but will definitely decrease total costs, thus increasing net returns to, and the *PV* of, land. This helps to explain why it is not foreign investors but the neighbor down the road who is buying up U.S. farmland. Some states have passed laws limiting the sale of farmland to foreigners to, say, 320 acres; even then, the land has to be converted within five years to some nonagricultural use. But the proportion of farmland owned by foreigners is only about 0.5 percent. The real increase in land values has been through bidding up by local farm operators who already have 480 acres and want to add that extra 160 acres to achieve further economies of size.

3. Commodity prices. These work in two opposite ways:
    a. They have been trending upward (though not always as fast as prices in the rest of the economy), so that we would expect a modest increase in the *PV* of land from this effect.
    b. Even with price stabilization programs (Chapter 10), commodity prices are much more variable in agriculture than nonagriculture.

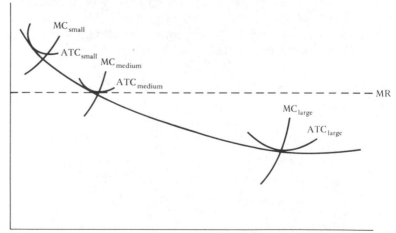

FIGURE 15–3. *The Effect of the Long-Run Average Cost Curve on the Ability to Bid for Land.*

This means there is more risk in buying land than in investing in industry. To show this price variability, the present value formula may be adjusted either by reducing the average net returns to land to reflect the probability distribution of returns, or by increasing r to account for risk. The uncertain future of price stabilization programs themselves increases this risk.

4. Interest rates and alternative investment opportunities (which establish r), must be adjusted also to reflect appreciation and inflation, as noted in Chapter 12. All of these factors are determinants of the adjusted discount rate.

5. Capital gains. Because (currently) only 40 percent of the difference between buying land, say, at $385 and selling, say, at $1,800, is taxable, and even then only at a maximum rate of 50 percent, the maximum effective tax rate is only 20 percent on capital gains income. Therefore, many people prefer to convert as much income as possible into capital gains when they realize their other "ordinary" income is taxable at the 25, 33, or even 50 percent tax level. The after-tax capital-gains value of land at the end of a planning period is discounted to be a present value basis and added to the present value of discounted after-tax future returns to land. Therefore

$$PV_{total} = PV_{capital\ gains} + PV_{net\ returns}.$$

As land appreciates during an inflationary period, the present value of capital gains becomes a larger and larger portion of total present value. Thus, for those who have the liquidity, buying farmland is a good investment.

6. Other tax regulations. Land is subject not only to income tax, but also to property and estate taxes. In general, property taxes tend to reduce the returns to land use and the price people will pay for a piece of land. However, as we shall see in comparing the corporation with the sole proprietorship in Chapter 17, there are advantages to subchapter C corporations (non-family corporations) which increase the value of land to non-family buyers of land. This drives up the value in the market place relative to a situation in which taxes are equal for all forms of business organization.

7. Government programs related to land. As with commodity prices, these have two opposing effects:
   a. Support programs (set aside, nonresource loans, and guaranteed prices) tend to increase returns from farming and thus drive up the price of land.
   b. Regulatory measures (pollution control in feedlots, soil conservation requirements, etc.) tend to increase costs and drive down land values.

The net effect depends on the relative magnitude of the two, but as the United States enters an age of limits, the federal and state governments seem to be increasing b relative to a over time.

FARM APPRAISAL AND VALUATION

All seven of the above factors are constantly at play, dynamically determining the price which the buyer should pay for land at any given time. He should work through an estimate for his own situation whenever he is thinking of buying land. There are three widely accepted approaches to farm appraisal and valuation:

1. The Income Approach. This method projects the discounted net after-tax cash flows from the farm through standard investment analysis. If there is an active rental market in the area for nonland assets such as livestock facilities, then the present value of land alone may be calculated and added to the going annual rental rates for all nonland facilities. If there is no such market, then cash flows from the land and projected use of any facilities must be discounted together.

2. The Comparable Sales Approach. Unlike the income approach, this method is used primarily to determine the market value of a farm, rather than its earning potential. The objective is to collect information on the selling price, asset inventory and valuation, dates, and locations of three or more farm sales that are as close as possible to the one you intend to buy. The ideal is to find a neighboring farm of identical size, soil type, and buildings that was sold yesterday. Obviously, this is next to impossible. But the prospective buyer can adjust other sales to approximate such an ideal by using a form such as presented in Table 15–2. If the farm was sold last year, one must increase the land value by the rate of appreciation in land. If it was sold on contract, one must adjust the method of sale to a cash equivalent basis. If the stable is four years newer, one must add some depreciation back in. And so on. Any assets that are similar, say a $50,000 homestead, do not have to be adjusted. Once the three other sales are made to resemble as closely as possible the farm you intend to buy, all you must do is average them to derive the market value.

3. The Cost Approach. This method estimates the cost of all assets as if they had to be recreated from scratch. For buildings and other nonland assets, depreciation costs for the number of years of actual use to date must be subtracted from the cost today of building comparable new facilities. For land, the easiest way to assign a cost is to borrow an estimate from the comparable sales approach for land alone. Then, merely add the estimates for land and nonland assets together to derive a value for the farm.

Your emphasis as you go about buying a farm should be on earning potential rather than market value. Therefore, the approach to be presented in the pages that follow is primarily the income approach for valuing land plus the cost or income approach for valuing nonland assets. At the same time, the comparable sales approach can provide a valuable cross-check.

As noted, the income approach is based upon the present value formula.

TABLE 15-2. COMPARABLE SALE SUMMARY

Property Characteristics	Subject	Comparable Sale 1	2	3
Seller	XXXX	_____	_____	_____
Buyer	XXXX	_____	_____	_____
Date of sale	XXXX	_____	_____	_____
Total acres	_____	_____	_____	_____
%Tillable	_____	_____	_____	_____
Corn yield/tillable acre	_____	_____	_____	_____
Soybean yield/tillable acre	_____	_____	_____	_____
Miles from market	_____	_____	_____	_____
Assessed value of buildings	_____	_____	_____	_____
Sale Price per Acre		_____	_____	_____
Adjustment for method of sale		±_____	±_____	±_____
Cash Equivalent Sale Price per Acre		_____	_____	_____
(as of date of sale) Adjustment of date of sale		±_____	±_____	±_____
Cash Equivalent Sale Price per Acre		_____	_____	_____
(As of date of appraisal)				
Other Adjustments per Acre				
Add-on sale		±_____	±_____	±_____
Farm size		±_____	±_____	±_____
Productive capacity		±_____	±_____	±_____
Improvements		±_____	±_____	±_____
Location		±_____	±_____	±_____
Other		±_____	±_____	±_____
Total other adjustments		±_____	±_____	±_____
Adjusted Sales Price per Acre		_____	_____	_____

Source: Harris, Duane G., Department of Economics, Iowa University, Ames, Iowa.

The prospective buyer should realize, however, that the present value formula has four underlying assumptions which may not always hold:

1. Future Prices and Yields Can Be Estimated with Reasonable Accuracy. As shown in Chapter 7, random, seasonal, cyclical, commodity, and trend movements influence agricultural prices. The farm operator should read farm magazines and the daily newspaper for the latest forecasts. Even then, he cannot be sure exactly what the price will be. Similarly, the yields which he can achieve on the farm may be higher or lower than those achieved by the previous farmer from whom he is buying the land. In other words, the value netted out for management returns in the present value formula may differ.

2. There is a Realistic Rate of Discount. Again, he must consider all the factors, including his after-tax opportunity rate of return and his own perceptions of risk, which affect r. This parameter differs across individuals.

3. Income Will Continue Indefinitely, at least during one's planning horizon for the land investment. Remember, this is one of the two assumptions behind this version of the present value formula. Many farmers would like to see the land kept in their family as a viable asset for generations to come. As we approach the year 2000, however, agronomists are saying that the United States' prime agricultural land is averaging ten tons of topsoil loss per acre per year of which only five tons can be replaced naturally.[1] The question arises, "Can this return continue indefinitely?"

4. Incomes Will Not Trend Up or Down. The second assumption that underlies this version of the *PV* formula is that returns are constant. Suppose, however, that because of soil loss and flagging commodity prices, the farm operator feels that his *NFI*, and hence returns to land, will trend downward by $0.50 per acre per year. Now, he may say, "That is practically nothing—why even consider it?" But there is a formula to take account of these income trends. Assume land return is $100 per acre in the present and the sale value per acre is $2,500.

$$PV = \frac{E}{r} \pm \frac{\Delta E}{r^2}, \text{ where } \Delta E = \text{annual change in net returns to land}$$

$$= \frac{\$100}{.04} - \frac{\$0.50}{.0016}$$

$$= \$2{,}188 \text{ per acre.}$$

Anyone who has not read the forecasts may blithely go ahead and be willing to pay $2,500 at the auction, but the careful land buyer should not pay above $2,188 for the land.

---

[1] *The rates of topsoil loss and replacement differ from region to region and soil type to soil type.*

Now that we have put the present value formula into perspective, we should go on to consider other factors which affect the value of the **farm** and not just the land. There are six general factors to consider in deciding what a farm is worth:

1. Size, Long-run Average Costs, Parcelization, and Distances. In other words, if the farmer is interested in taking advantage of economies of size and wishes to add 320 acres, he should check whether they are all in one place or whether they are composed of four 80-acre parcels spread ten to twelve miles apart. In the latter case, he may put in so much time, fuel, and wear-and-tear on his new large-scale machines, that the economies of size may be canceled out.

2. Soil, Topography, and Climate. These factors are extremely important in the case of dry and/or rolling land. First, the prospective farmer should go down to the Soil Conservation Service office and find the soil map for the farm in question. He should then walk over the terrain to see where terraces have been put in and other improvements made. He should also check with the state Crop and Livestock Reporting Service to determine the probability of drought and flooding in the area. Unless he knows these things, he is taking a big risk when he bids at a land auction.

3. Buildings, Fences, and Farm Layout. Are these efficient for the manager's purposes? There is a whole area of agricultural law called "fence law." If the operator buys a farm with a faulty fence, it is quite possible that the next day he may find himself in court with a case pending against him. He may have valuable buildings that are poorly situated or not suitable for his livestock raising preferences and/or machinery storage needs.

4. Water Supply. Poor water may necessitate added expense in moving the house or installing water treatment facilities. Electricity and telephone service are also critical.

5. Market Access. Suppose the prospective operator was considering two farms that were in every other respect equal. One was just off a major interstate highway. The other was far out in the hinterland of the state on an unpaved loessial road which washed out in the spring and an hour and quarter even from a surfaced state road. Of the two, he would choose the first farm because marketing costs for inputs and products would be much higher for the second farm.

6. Nearness to Relatives. Suppose again the operator was considering two farms. One of them was right across the road from his parents and the other was ten miles away. Depending upon how he feels about his parents (or his spouse's), nearness to relatives is possibly worth a positive (or negative) $1,000 to $2,000 over the years. This figure should be built into any calculations of the farm's value.

Suppose now that the young prospective farm owner is eagerly checking out the farm the day before the auction. He discovers all sorts of other assets on the property which were left when the previous operator suddenly died. How does he go about assigning a value to them? As you learned in Chapter 4, there are different rules for each of six types of assets he might find:

1. **Assets to be sold this year** include such items as hogs that are about to be marketed and grain in the bins that is about to be sold. They are definitely worth something to him, and therefore, should be built into estimates of how much the operator is willing to pay for the farm. One simply calculates their selling price net of transportation and marketing costs.

2. **Supplies** include such items as fertilizer and chemicals. They are worth something but the buyer does not want to pay too much for them. He should pay their original cost or the current market price (whichever is lower) to get a fair value.

3. **Working assets** usually refers to machinery, which should be valued at original acquisition price less depreciation. If there has been persistent inflation or deflation, market price for equivalent used assets may be used to estimate their value.

4. **Recent farm buildings** fall into the same category. If there is a fairly new hog farrowing house and it is two years old, one figures out the cost less depreciation to determine its value.

5. **Old farm buildings** are the ones that have been depreciated out. Here there is some question about whether they are useful, whether they are just occupying space which could be better used for something else or, worse yet, whether they are in the way of a combine on the way to the field. If the building is of some use, one should value it at replacement cost less depreciation for the portion of life gone. If it is not, one should subtract the cost of tearing it down from the total offer price for the farm.

6. **Raised breeding livestock**. Sows, brood cows, mares, and other breeding livestock should be valued in terms of the present value of the animal remaining to the purchases. If this is difficult to calculate, one can try to estimate the compound costs of production incurred in bringing breeding animals to that age.

The above are good methods for estimating an accounting value for each type of asset, but the total value derived from these calculations may be more than one could profitably pay. As a cross-check the prospective buyer should use the comparable sales approach to calculate the contribution of similar assets to market value in recent sales of other farm properties in the locality.

WHEN AND HOW TO PURCHASE LAND

Having taken into account all these factors in determining his maximum offer price, the prespective owner should make his decision on whether or not to buy the land and other assets of the farm. In Chapter 13 you learned that simply because the operator can squeak by with high leverage to make the payments does not mean he should but. He needs both sufficient real estate investment funds and operating capital. Otherwise, the expected outcomes of buying land with insufficient funds include:

A small, uneconomic unit (too high on the *LRAC* curve) with low net farm income potential

or

An adequate sized unit but insufficient operating capital to achieve the net farm income potential of the unit

or

More money borrowed than can be repaid out of farm income, resulting in eventual default.

Renting may be an excellent alternative in situations of capital shortage. In fact, one study of farm ownership trends for the year 2000 has predicted that the percentage of farmers who rent at least part of the land they operate will increase. The study also projects that the most successful farmers will probably be these part-renters.

If, however, capital does seem sufficient, you may then consider various methods of financing farm real estate, outlined in capsule form in Table 15-3.

A fourth alternative worth considering is to enter into a "like-kind exchange." Defined by the IRS very loosely, these exchanges do not have to be farm for farm. The farm owner could even exchange his farm for a supermarket or an apartment house. Clearly, this option is particularly attractive as one approaches retirement age, especially if one moves from a property with low cash income to one with a higher cash income. Some farm management and real estate firms handle numerous exchanges through three or more parties. The shape of the transaction may be a triangle or a polygon. One transaction in recent years involved 27 properties simultaneously! To equalize value exchanged, a small amount of

TABLE 15-3. ALTERNATIVE METHODS OF FINANCING FARM REAL ESTATE PURCHASES

A. Cash sale
  1. Entire price for deed
  2. Seller pays total capital gains tax if he does not go on to buy another property
B. Mortgage
  1. Mortgage agreement and down payment are exchanged for the deed
  2. Seller pays total capital gains tax
  3. Mortgage may be, and usually is, executed to third party lender. This is the tie-in with the sources of credit given in Chapter 13.
C. Installment land contract
  1. Buyer beneficial owner
  2. Seller retains legal title as security
  3. Seller may prorate capital gains

boot (additional cash) is also given. Only this latter is subject to capital gains taxes.

Other legal aspects of buying a farm include the following seven points:

1. Make sure you obtain a clear title to the property.
2. Check to see that there are no back taxes.
3. Obtain a full legal and physical description of the property.
4. Include the names of grantors and recipients.
5. Incorporate clear words of conveyance.
6. Agree on the time and place of signing.
7. Make sure the transaction is properly recorded with the help of competent legal counsel.

FARM LEASES

A farm lease may be defined as follows:

> An oral or written **contract** outlining how a tenant and landlord will produce and share **income**, provide for **expenses, improve** the farm, and determine the crop and livestock **program, practices**, and **compensation** for damage to the farm or termination of the lease.

The determination of each of the boldface parts of the above definition is extremely important, because—in contrast to the situation with a sole proprietor—there are two decision-makers rather than one. Unless the provisions of the lease are carefully formulated, the good of the whole may very well not equal the sum of the parts. In particular, the income, expenses, improvements, program and practices that the tenant would choose to implement in striving to achieve his rational economic interests in the short run may not coincide with those which are in the best short-run interest of the landlord and/or long-run interest of the farm.

Motivations and Objectives for Leases

There are three motives for formulating leases to acquire the control of farmland, if not its ownership:

1. Land is an expensive resource, and in most cases the single most costly production input. Unless the two parties can achieve an equitable understanding on its use through a lease, gross inefficiency in the program and practices of operating the farm, or unfairness in sharing income may result.
2. Young and beginning farmers are often unable to finance the purchase of land becasue they either lack net worth or are not in a sufficiently strong cash flow position to buy the property, as outlined earlier. In their eyes, their inability to own land is something of a

disappointment, but a lease may allow for more flexibility in the size of the operation and thus reduce risk, as you learned in Chapter 9.[1]

3. The landlord may wish to maintain ownership but not full control of the land resource. He may have one or more of three motives:

   a. He may view land as an investment opportunity. You have seen that land yields a high rate of return, especially through appreciation over time. The farmer may feel that his after-tax earnings and rate of return are higher from continuing his investment in land than from putting his money into a savings account, stocks, or bonds.

   b. The landlord may wish to hold onto the land for reasons of financial security and as a hedge against inflation. Often, land values increase faster than general prices in the economy, as noted.

   c. The landlord may wish to hold property for intergenerational transfer. He himself may be ready to retire or reduce the size of the farm he operates as he enters the downside of the farm family life cycle (Chapter 17). But his children, still young or in college, will want to have control of as much land as possible as they go through their own expansion phase of the cycle. A lease allows the retiring farmer to retain full ownership of the land while operating only a small portion or none of it.

Given the motivations of each party for entering into a lease, there are five specific objectives of every good lease. These relate directly to the boldface parts of the definition of the farm lease given earlier.

1. The fair division of **income** and **expenses**. In most cases, the two parties do not contribute similar assets to the arrangement. Typically, the landlord contributes land while the tenant contributes labor and some or all of the machinery. In this situation, how do the two parties determine the share of profits that each shall receive?

2. A profitable farming system. This relates to the term **income** in the definition and indicates that a fair division of net farm income is not sufficient; that income must be made as large as possible. This objective refers to the possible conflict in the short-run motivations of the two parties (and most leases are short-run), which may reduce total profit to be divided.

3. Assurance to the tenant that the arrangement will be continued if he abides by the conditions of the lease. The very words tenant and tenure (a guarantee that the lease will continue) are etymologically related. Any good lease should specify a timely notice of termination.

4. Assurance to the landlord that the property will be preserved. This concern has always existed in leases; however, with the use of more intensive monocropping of recent years and intensified soil loss, landlords are even more concerned that their land be preserved in this

---

[1] *At the same time, it should be noted that insecurity of tenure may also become a significant source of risk.*

age of limits. They may want to build in special compensation to the tenant for liming, soil improvement, terrace maintenance, rotations, and other non-self-liquidating **practices** that will maintain the farm as a productive asset in the long run.

5. Putting the agreement into written form. Above all, the written form helps ensure clarity; protection for the two parties, their heirs, and consigns; definite terms and provisions for continuation; and reasonable notice in the case of termination.

The written form, as with labor agreements, helps make the important practices clear in case of dispute, and itself serves as a reference in preventing disagreements. By providing an accurate description of the property; a definite term for the lease; a specific time, level and place of rent payment; the names of the landlord and tenant; and the signatures of the contracting parties, the lease makes sure that both parties know and remember all aspects of the agreement. Otherwise, the "selective recall syndrome" will mean that the landlord will forget what is least pleasant to him (e.g., that he must compensate the tenant for liming), while the tenant may forget that his payment is due on the first day of the agreed month, rather than the last.

TYPES OF FARM LEASES

There are five types of farm leases. These are listed below in order of the level of risk and returns to the tenant. The list is also in inverse order of the closeness of the working relationship between the landlord and tenant.

1. Cash lease
2. Flexible cash lease
3. Crop-share lease
4. Livestock-share lease
5. Labor-share lease

Each of these types of leases will be discussed in turn below.

Cash Leases

The cash lease simply involves a direct cash payment from the tenant to the landlord during or at the end of the crop year[1] in return for the use of a specified number of acres of land. The tenant decides exactly what he wants to grow on the land, how he will grow it, and how he will dispose of the product. The landlord waives any decision-making power (except for stipulations as to long-term soil maintenance practices) in return for the cash rent.

[1] *Often, part of the cash is paid in advance.*

The level of rent in the cash lease may be set either by consulting standards or through bargaining. One usual set of standards comes from the U.S. Department of Agriculture, which establishes suggested ratios for different types of land in different parts of the country. These ratios are then multiplied by the current market value of land to set the rental price for the land. The problem with this approach is that the ratios are for broad regions and do not fit the specific conditions of the land in question.

Setting the rent by bargaining involves careful assessment of the landlord's opportunity returns on the one hand and the amount the tenant can afford to pay out of his earnings on the other. Table 15–4 shows the calculations from the landlord's point of view for a hypothetical piece of land. The landlord wants to guarantee himself of a safe return to the value of his investment in land, and to cover his fixed (DIRTI 5) costs plus management overhead. This is the minimum value that he feels he must receive to break even in the long run. At the same time, however, he may be investing in land as a hedge against inflation or place a value on the ability to retain land in the family without working it. Therefore, it is possible to bargain the landlord down from what he will present as his "minimum" opportunity returns. For example, the prospective tenant can suggest an opportunity cost of land of three percent rather than four and reduce farm ownership costs to $23,600 for the farm and $118 per acre.

Table 15–5 shows the same problem from the point of view of the tenant. The tenant is concerned with actual, in addition to opportunity, returns. Unless he is able to earn enough net return over variable costs (and perhaps fixed machinery costs) per acre to pay himself for his own labor and management and meet the cash rent,[1] it is unwise for him to enter into the cash lease. Therefore, he must consider the yield times the price (which determine the total revenue), less the direct costs he incurs. He must also deduct interest on investment in farm machinery and operating capital he could have invested elsewhere, in addition to the opportunity earnings of his labor and management. Therefore, the

---

TABLE 15–4.   CASH RENT: THE LANDLORD'S "MINIMUM"

1. Opportunity cost of land
   200 acres × $2,500/acre × .04 . . . . $20,000
2. Land taxes
   200 acres × $1,200 assessed value/acre × .015. 3,600
3. Building ownership
   $20,000 × .12 (DIRTI) 2,400
4. Ownership and miscellaneous
   $520,000 land and building value × .005 2,600
   Total farm ownership costs (1 + 2 + 3 + 4). $28,600
   Farm ownership costs per acre 143

---

[1] *If he signs the lease, this cash rent becomes a fixed cost.*

TABLE 15-5. CASH RENT: THE TENANT'S "MAXIMUM"

	Corn	*Soybeans*
Gross Returns		
Yield	110	36
Price	3.25	7.5
Value of output	357.50	270
Costs		
Variable		
Preharvest	154	89
Harvest	42	9
Interest on operating capital	20	10
Fixed		
Own labor (valued at $5/hr.)	12	11
Overhead (4.5% of variable costs)	10	5
Management (5% of gross returns)	18	14
Net returns to land for each crop	102	132
Percentage of each crop in rotation	.67	.33
Weighted net returns to land per acre	112	
80% of net returns to reflect possibility of bad year	90	

tenant also hopes to receive an opportunity return to everything but land: i.e., capital, labor, and management. Here, too, there is some latitude. Even though each of the three factors could achieve the maximum opportunity return he cites, there is little guarantee that they could all do so at the same time. For example, if he moved to town and took a job to achieve the opportunity return to his labor, he might have to use the investment capital to pay for rent and automobile payments which would not earn him any return at all. And there is little likelihood that he could hire out as a manager in addition to working 40 hours per week at a job. The real maximum reimbursible rent for the tenant is one that results in an acceptable income to the combination of his labor, capital, and management; assures him a suitable living standard; and gives earnings that are fairly competitive, though not necessarily greater than the aggregate earnings of these three production factors in nonfarm work.

In addition, however, the tenant should adjust this maximum permissible rent downward for the worst one or two years out of ten to determine whether he will be able to meet cash flow obligations. This may drive down the maximum amount the tenant is willing to pay to a level that is beneath the landlord's minimum acceptable level, even after the adjustments in the latter noted above. Therefore, cash leases are typically found where crop yields and prices are relatively stable and/or land is a relatively small percentage of production inputs (for example, in the production of such cash crops as tobacco and vegetables).

There are at least six advantages to the tenant of entering into cash leases:

1. He can be his own boss. This is particularly important when planning changes in the production pattern or in determining whether or not to participate in government programs.
2. The tenant derives all returns to management.
3. The tenant can invest in his own machinery and livestock and use it as he sees fit.
4. The tenant can retain all the feed and byproducts derived from crop production and enjoy this complementarity between enterprises to push out his production possibility frontier.
5. The tenant reaps all the benefits of price rises, particularly if he has bargained for a fairly low floor to reflect low price periods.
6. His rate of return is higher than that from all other types of lease if he has enough capital to assume risk. But levels of both financial and business risk are higher than under any other type of lease.

There are five potential problems with cash leases:

1. In addition to cash rent, the tenant may also have to pay the landlord a security deposit that will further strap his cash-flow situation.
2. The cash rent is a fixed cost in the short-run for the tenant and may be a fairly high proportion of total revenue, especially in parts of the country where marketing outlets for cash high-valued speciality crops are not available. This narrows the margin of profitability for the tenant.
3. Unless adequate provisions for liming and rotations are included, the productivity of the farm may not be maintained over time. This is especially true if the tenant does not have a long time-horizon and does not hope, for example, to maintain this particular farm for his own use in the future. Older tenants, and young tenants anxious to move on to buy their own farms, are particularly subject to such short–sightedness.
4. Cash rents, by their very nature, do not directly reflect market prices for output. Thus, they will be too high when prices, yields, or both are low; and too low when prices and yields are more favorable than normal. In either case, one party (the tenant or the landlord,) will feel that the cash lease is unfair and seek to bring it to an early termination or to revise it down or up for next lease period. This type of situation, unique to agriculture, places an enormous amount of pressure on the very existence of cash leases.[1] Partly as a result, a variation on cash leases has arisen called the fixed product rent. This allows the tenant to deliver a

---

[1] *For this reason, cash rental rates usually average slightly lower than the value of crop share rentals in a given area.*

fixed payment in terms of bushels per acre or head of livestock to the landlord, regardless of market price.

5. The two methods noted are not necessarily accurate ways of determining cash rents. The broad averages put forward by the government may not be locally appropriate. Moreover, the landlord and tenant may lack adequate information—or intentionally misrepresent real information—and thus form an erroneous impression of the lower or upper bound from which the two parties must begin bargaining.[1]

Flexible Cash Leases

Some of these problems may be solved by opting for a hybrid of cash and crop-share leases called the flexible cash lease. In principle, this type of lease allows for the amount of cash rent to vary as either prices or yields vary, but usually not both. Its usefulness, therefore, depends on whether business risk in the area is primarily due to variability in prices or yields. If variability in prices is the main problem, then there are three variations of flexible cash lease which are commonly used:

$$1. \ \frac{\text{Index of prices received in lease period}}{\text{Index of prices received in base period}} \times \text{base rent per acre}$$

$$= \text{cash rent per acre.}$$

As an example, suppose that the prices received for crops are 20 percent higher than in the base period and the base rent per acre is $95. Then,

$$\frac{1.2}{1.0} \times 95 = \$114 \text{ cash rent per acre.}$$

The major disadvantage with this approach is that it allows for more than one crop to be considered. On the other hand, there is the disadvantage that the percentage weights used to compute the price index need to be changed over time as the relative importance of crops in the cropping system changes. It should also be noted that with this and other forms of price-oriented flexible cash leases, high prices may simply be reflecting low yields. The tenant will have less income but have to pay a higher rent to the landlord. Only if yield is locally very stable and

---

[1] *In practice, the difference between the lower and upper bounds used is not excessive. This is because bargaining usually takes place in an atmosphere where both parties are also aware of the range in current cash rental rates for similar types of property in the area. Their respective measures for breakeven rents will need to be within this range in order to develop a contract between them. Otherwise, the potential renter will rent from someone else and the landowner will rent to someone else.*

prices are set nationally without great sensitivity to local production will price-oriented flexible cash leases be advantageous to the tenant.

2. Base rent per acre + $(P_{bu} \times$ _____ *bu*.$)$ = cash rent per acre.

Suppose that the base rent is $45, the current market price for the principal crop $3, and the number of bushels specified in the agreement 25. Then,

$$\$45 + (\$3 \times 25) = \$120 \text{ cash rent per acre.}$$

The landlord and the tenant can establish the base part of the price and the number of bushels to suit local conditions. As with the previous formula, as the price of output increases, the amount of cash rent also increases. Assuming that yield is stable or that yield fluctuations are much less important than price fluctuations, then cash rent should vary as total revenue.

The two disadvantages to this method are that only one principal crop is considered and that there are very few variables to serve as the basis for amendments in the lease in future years to achieve greater equity. To meet the latter objection, there is a third formula:

3. (Base yield $\times$ base price $\times$ _____ %) +
   $[\, n \times$ (current price – base price)$]$ = cash rent per acre.

For example, if the base yield is 75 bushels per acre, the base price is $2.10, the percentage to the landlord 60 percent, the arbitrary number "n"[1] 40, and the current price $2.80, then,

$$(75 \times 2.10 \times 60\%) + [40 \times (2.80 - 2.10)] = \$123 \text{ cash rent per acre}$$

The advantage of this formula over the previous formula is that each component is disaggregated. Thus, the first expression (in parentheses) is equivalent to the base rent per acre in formula 2. However, as yields or prices show long-term trends, the separate components can be adjusted to reflect this changed situation. Similarly, the second expression (in brackets) takes account of deviations from the base price. If price should fall below the base price, then the value of this second element would be negative. Because this third formula provides more information, it is more likely that the landlord and tenant will be able to achieve agreeable amendments in the lease over time rather than cutting off the relationship entirely when external conditions change.

On the other hand, in certain parts of the country, and with commodities for which there are federal commodity stabilization programs,

---

[1] *This number has no economic identity and is simply a parameter set by the bargainers to weight the variable part of the lease.*

the variability in returns is much more a function of yield than price variability. Therefore, there are formulas such as the following:

4. Base price × current yield × % share to landlord[1] = cash rent per acre.

Assume that the base price is $2.10 and the percentage share to the landlord is 60%. If the current yield is 95 bushels per acre, then

$$\$2.10 \times 95 \times 60\% = \$120 \text{ cash rent per acre.}$$

If, however, there is a bad year and yields plummet to 60 bushels per acre, then

$$\$2.10 \times 60 \times 60\% = \$76 \text{ cash rent per acre.}$$

With this formula, the tenant is protected in a poor year. The assumption is, however, that prices are stable or relatively invariant compared with yields.

Crop-share Leases

In many agricultural settings, yields and prices are both variable and/or the tenant does not want to assume as much risk as under a cash lease or even a flexible cash lease. There are two alternative rules for establishing a crop-share lease:

1. Set up a complete farm budget, assign a target value such as 50 percent each or 60 percent and 40 percent to the two parties, and shift the cost components back and forth until the sum of the contributions of each party is equal to these target percentages. Net farm income will then also be split in the same proportions.

or

2. Determine the share of total costs (including fertilizer and other variable costs) paid by each party and divide income in this proportion. This approach will yield such percentages of breakdown for returns as 41.67% and 58.33%.

Using these methods, there are two common types of crop-share leases in use: The **fixed contribution** and the **variable plus fixed contribution**. Both lease types may be structured either using rule 1 or rule 2 above. The first type of lease is illustrated in Table 15-6. In this case, all inputs are considered fixed contributions. Thus, the landlord provides land, buildings, improvements, management and perhaps some labor, while the tenant provides power and machinery, some management and most of the labor. The tenant is entirely responsible for variable costs and pays cash rent (in accordance with rule 1 above) to the landlord. The sums of the contributions tally and are used to divide income 50–50. In fact, the cash adjustment is used to equalize the contributions.

---

[1] *This share is often determined by the proportion of total production costs the landlord contributes.*

TABLE 15-6. RENTAL SHARE AGREEMENT INCLUDING ONLY FIXED CONTRI-BUTIONS

	Whole Farm	*Owner's Share*	*Tenant's Share*
Investment Costs			
Land and buildings ($400,000 @ .03)	$12,000	$12,000	
Machinery and equipment ($60,000 @ .13)	7,800		$7,800
Total	$19,800	$12,000	$7,800
Current Farm Expenses			
Labor and Management	10,000	3,500	6,500
Repairs	2,000	400	1,600
Depreciation	9,000	3,800	5,200
Insurance	400	300	100
Taxes	3,000	2.700	300
Miscellaneous	1,500	1,365	135
Cash rent adjustment	----	-1,215	1,215
Total	$25,900	$10,850	$15,050
Grand Total of All Fixed Contributions	$45,700	$22,850	$22,850
Portion Contributed by Each Party (%)	----	50	50

The problem is that the tenant is bearing all of the variable costs, so the total farm produces less than it should. Figure 15–4 shows that in this type of lease, the tenant will equate the value of his own marginal product with the price he has to pay. If he only gets half the product from the farm buy must pay the full price for variable factor inputs

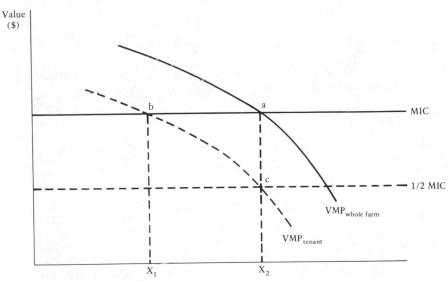

KEY

a: owner-operator optimum
b: tenant optimum if fertilizer costs not shared
c: tenant optimum if fertilizer costs shared in
    same proportion as output

FIGURE 15–4. Fertilizer Use under Two Types of Crop-Share Lease.

such as fertilizer, then these curves intersect at point b and he will apply only x_1 amount of fertilizer. The proportions used to divide income between the two parties will be equitable but the total amount of revenue to be divided will be less than the farm's full potential.

To counteract this problem, there is a second type of crop lease which takes into account the distinction between fixed and variable costs (Table 15-7). This example illustrates rule 2. As with the previous type, the division does not have to be 50-50; for our example, we show the split to be 55-45. In this case, it does not matter what the total values of the other, fixed contributions are but it does matter that such variable inputs as seen and fertilizer be split in exactly the same proportion as the overall lease (and hence fixed costs) i.e., 55-45. Only then will the tenant wish to produce at point c in Figure 15-4 and apply the optimal amount of fertilizer and other variable inputs.

There are at least five advantages of the crop-share lease to the tenant:

1. There is less risk than in a cash lease. Regardless of whether price or yield varies, or both, the landlord will be taking only a percentage of the total revenue that is actually realized.
2. Rent is paid after harvest, whereas cash rent (or a portion thereof) may be required in advance.
3. At the same time, there is a higher return to the tenant with capital and managerial skill than from a livestock-share lease.

TABLE 15-7.   RENTAL SHARE AGREEMENT INCLUDING BOTH FIXED AND VARIABLE COSTS

	Whole Farm	Owner's Share	Tenant's Share
Investment Costs			
Land and buildings ($400,000 @ .03)	$12,000	$12,000	
Machinery and equipment ($60,000 @ .13)	7,800		$7,800
Total	$19,800	$12,000	$7,800
Current Farm Expenses			
Labor (2,500 hrs. @ $4/hr.)	10,000		10,000
Repairs	2,000	400	1,600
Depreciation	9,000	3,800	5,200
Fuel and lubricants	2,200	990	1,210[1]
Machine work hired	4,000	1,800	2,200[1]
Seed and fertilizer	5,000	2,250	2,750[1]
Insurance	400	300	100
Taxes (property)	3,000	2,700	300
Miscellaneous	1,500	1,365	135
Total	$37,100	$13,605	$23,495
Grand Total of All Costs	$56,900	$25,605	$31,295
Portion Contributed by Each Party (%)	–––	45	55[1]

[1]All these items are shared 45/55.

4. For beginning tenants, a good landlord helps to manage the farm and boost common income which both parties hope to receive.
5. As noted, the owner sometimes shares variable costs to help ensure efficiency.

Livestock-share Rental Agreements

The next type of lease is the livestock-share rental agreement. Typically, the landlord provides the land and some labor while the lessee provides the power and machinery and most of the labor (Table 15–8). The two parties split management and livestock costs evenly.

The advantages to the tenant of a livestock-share lease are as follows:

1. The landlord may be experienced and help to build the tenant's managerial skill.
2. Tenure is more certain. The landlord wants to see the lease extended through the production cycle for the livestock involved. As you have seen, this cycle may be as long as 12 years in cattle.
3. Because of nutrient cycling from livestock wastes, the productivity of the farm may increase.
4. The tenant often gets free pasture and/or hay for tending the landlord's livestock.
5. The landlord often permits the tenant to raise poultry from common feed supplies.
6. The tenant furnishes a lower percentage of capital and management than in other leases.
7. Production and price risks are shared by both parties.

TABLE 15–8. LIVESTOCK-SHARE RENTAL AGREEMENT

	Whole Farm	Landlord's Share	Tenant's Share
Investment Costs			
Land and buildings ($450,000 @ .04)	$18,000	$18,000	
Machinery and equipment ($65,000 × .10)	6,500		$ 6,500
Livestock			
Interest (200 hd. × $360/hd. × .13)	9,360	4,680	4,680
Depreciation on breeding stock	4,300	2,150	2,150
Other Farm Fixed Costs			
Repairs	2,000	500	1,500
Depreciation	11,500	5,000	6,500
Management	4,000	1,000	3,000
Unpaid family labor (3,000 hr. @ $4/hr.)	12,000		12,000
Overhead	2,000	500	1,500
Total Fixed Costs	$69,660	$31,830	$37,830
Proportion Contributed by Each Party (%)[1]		45.7	54.3

[1] Used to determine the division of both income and variable operating costs such as livestock feed.

8. This type of lease constitutes one means of entry for a young farmer with limited but still moderate capital assets.

The main disadvantage of this lease is that it is unclear who has the final say about any decision. Thus, altercations between the tenant and landlord are possible.

Labor-share Lease

Last, there is the labor-share lease. The labor-share lease is as much a way for the landlord to acquire extra labor as it is for the lessee to get farming experience and build equity for an eventual down-payment on his own land. But it is often the best way for the young farmer, especially one starting off with his father to begin to climb the ladder towards eventual control of land. The lessee does have to put up with much unsolicited advice, however.

The advantages to the lessee in a labor-share lease are:

1. A minimum level of risk and investment capital are involved.
2. The lease helps him or her to develop managerial ability. This is because the lessor is usually older and more experienced.
3. There is flexibility to rewrite the lease every year and to increase the proportion of labor shared and/or convert to other types of leases.
4. The tenant profits if he manages the farm or enterprise well.

Even given the different leasing formats, there are many factors that influence the actual terms arrived at in a lease:

1. Each party's contribution
2. Alternative opportunities
3. The relative bargaining positions of the two parties
4. Custom (even if tradition leads to inefficiencies)
5. What is satisfactory to each party
6. The schedule for capital improvements and facility repairs on the farm and the present condition and capacity of such facilities
7. The perceived productivity of each party

Finally, there are always difficulties in leases. These may arise from the following eight sources:

1. Faulty knowledge or attitudes on rights and obligations.
2. Unexpectedly low income for either party. This often happens when one or both have miscalculated their benefits or costs.
3. Inequitable rental rates. This problem is related to 2 above.
4. Inadequate provision for property improvements (lime, fertilization, etc.).
5. Insufficient security for the tenant operator.

6. Economic inefficiency as a result of faulty cost sharing.
7. Scale inconsistent with risk and uncertainty in the market. This problem applies to the owner-operated farm as well.
8. Uncertain procedures for terminating the lease.

SUMMARY

Obtaining control of land is more important than the question of actual ownership. Acquiring ownership of land in the United States has increased in difficulty because of its skyrocketing price and the growing complexity of the ladder to enter farming. The price of land has increased because of new technology, economies of size, capital gains treatment of land, and other regulations. At the same time, commodity prices, interest rates, and government programs have effects which may either increase or decrease the value of land.

Three methods for appraising and valuing a farm include the income, cost, and comparable sales approaches. In addition to the present value formula for estimating the price of land, such factors as location, parcelization, water supply and farm layout must be considered. The value of nonland assets must also be assessed before one makes a bid on a farm. One may purchase land through cash sale, mortgage, installment land contract, or like-kind exchange.

If one's cash-flow position does not allow for simultaneous ownership and efficient operation of the farm, it is better to obtain control of land through a lease. Cash leases have the greatest level of risk and returns to the tenant, while labor-share leases have the greatest degree of landlord participation in the decision-making process. As a result, the optimum type of lease for one individual may be different from that for another. Whichever lease form is chosen, the lease must be in written form to avoid disputes and the "selective recall syndrome."

TOPICS FOR DISCUSSION

1. What is the current sale price of such different categories of land as cropland, pastureland, irrigated land, and unirrigated land in your part of the state? What factors determine this price? Has the price of land of these different types gone up at the same rate over time? Explain how the crops grown and the alternative uses of these different types of land affect their individual rates of increase in value.

2. Is cash purchase, mortgage sale, installment land contract, or like-kind exchange the most popular method of land acquisition in your state? Has this always been the case? Describe the advantages of the most important means of land exchange as they relate to specific conditions in your area.

3. Which is the most common sort of land lease in your area? Which of

the methods described in this chapter is the usual way to compute its terms? What percentage of farmland in the state is operated by tenants rather than owner operators? Has this percentage increased over time? Why or why not?

4. What nonland assets, such as machinery, are also leased in your state? What are the terms of some typical leases? How do these terms agree with or differ from the leasing terms for land described in this chapter and question 3 above?

SUGGESTED READINGS

Harsh, S., L. Connor, and G. Schwab. *Managing the Farm Business.* Chapter 11. Englewood Cliffs, New Jersey: Prentice Hall Inc., 1981.

Hopkin, J., P. Barry, and C. Baker. *Agricultural Financial Management*, Second Edition. Chapter 12. Danville, Ill.: Interstate Printers and Publishers, 1979.

Kay, R. D. *Farm Management: Planning, Control, Implementation.* Chapter 14. New York: McGraw-Hill Book Company, 1981.

Osburn, D. and K. Schneeberger. *Modern Agriculture Management.* Chapter 17. Reston, Virginia: Reston Publishing, 1978.

Murray, W., D. Harris, G. Miller, and N. Thompson. *Farm Appraisal and Valuation.* Sixth Edition. Ames, Iowa: Iowa State University Press, 1983.

Penson, J. and D. Lins. *Agricultural Finance.* Chapter 9. Englewood Cliffs, New Jersey: Prentice Hall Inc., 1980.

16

Strategies for Tax Management

Well, well, the world must turn upon its axis.
  And all mankind turn with it, heads or tails,
And live and die, make love and pay our taxes.
  And as the veering winds shift, shift our sails.

Byron, Don Juan

Concepts

In this chapter you will come to understand:

1. The reasons why government imposes taxes on its citizens.

2. How agriculture in the United States is given preferential treatment in incidence of taxes.

3. Taxes as both a component in and determinant of the income statement.

4. The tax aspects of incorporating the farm business.

Tools

You will also gain the following skills:

1. How to adjust whole farm budgets for taxes.

2. How to account for the effects of taxes on farm credit and financial risk.

3. How to take account of sales tax, investment tax credits, capital gains, tax shelters and tax straddles in making farm investment and purchase decisions.

4. How to develop tax sheltered plans for retirement and estate planning.

INTRODUCTION

In filling in our understanding of the components of farm business management, we have already investigated farm **objectives**, economic **principles, budgets** and their **adjustments** for risk and government programs, and acquisition and use of production **factors**. It is now time to address the last component of the definition: the tax and business organizational **structure** of the farm (Figure 16-1). This is in many ways the most complicated area of farm business management, but it is also one of the most important. Poor tax management and attempts to operate the farm under an unsuitable legal structure can negate all gains from other areas of management. In this chapter we shall address tax management. Chapter 17 will then present factors to consider in selecting an optimal business organizational structure.

REASONS FOR TAXES

Taxation is one of the major fiscal tools that governments use to control the economy and to support the provision of social services and other government activities. Thus, the general level of taxation is a fundamental

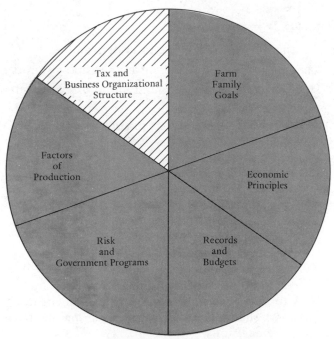

FIGURE 16-1. *The Components of Farm Business Management. Adding the tax and business organizational structure. While studied separately, each component of farm business management is essential to a full understanding of management science.*

policy question for the economy as a whole. But another policy question involves the incidence of taxation, i.e., which groups in society pay what proportion of their incomes to the government. In theory, the United States has a very progressive taxation system: those with the highest incomes pay up to 50 percent of their incomes, those with low incomes as little as 11 percent, and those least able to pay have no tax obligations.

In practice, however, other government regulations provide opportunities for the high-income populace to greatly reduce the amount of taxes they might otherwise have to pay. The record shows that the average tax percentage paid by the highest income group in the nonagricultural sector, though still progressive, is much less than 4.5 times the percentage paid by the lowest tax-paying group as the 50–11 percent spread should indicate.[1] The same study showed that the percentage of income paid in taxes by farm households in all income groups was nearly constant. It is clear that federal policies can effectively wipe out the progressivity of the tax system in U.S. agriculture. Moreover, it is the level of federal rather than state and local taxes that makes the rural tax percentage virtually constant across all income groups.

Farmers as a group enjoy lower tax burdens than nonfarmers. In addition, taxes farmers pay are largely compensated—and in some years overcompensated—by government payments from commodity support programs.[2] Farm income is highly favored, so that nonfarm capital has been attracted to the farm sector.

The rationale underlying this situation is that the federal government, in recognition of the special role of farmers in society and the particular risks they bear, has wished to give special treatment to farmers. At the same time, however, tax policies attempt to make certain that excessive gains are not realized. The result is the many rules and provisions regarding farm taxation presented in this chapter.

PREFERENTIAL TAX TREATMENT FOR FARM OPERATIONS

A few of the preferential programs that have largely helped farmers are as follows:

1. Land has been significantly under-valued for property taxes. For example, the richest Iowa farmland has a market value of $4,000 per acre, yet is only assessed at $950. The same situation exists in most other states. Moreover, as you will learn, land has been taxed for estate planning purposes at its value in use rather than its market value. This practice, which overlooks the value of land as an investment constitutes a way of converting ordinary income into capital gains.

[1] *ESCS. "U.S. Tax Policy and Agricultural Structure,"* Structure Issues of American Agriculture. *U.S.D.A./ESCS Agricultural Economic Report 438. Washington, D.C., pp. 152–160, 1979.*

[2] *USDA/ESCS. Economic Indicators of the Farm Sector: State Income and Balance Sheet Statistics, 1979. Washington, D.C., 1981.*

2. As with other businesses, farm operators who sell assets held for a long term enjoy capital gains tax treatment of the proceeds. Under current law, only 40% of the sale value of capital assets is taxable when sold, and even then at the 50 percent rate as a maximum. Therefore, anyone in a greater than 20 percent marginal tax bracket benefits when converting ordinary income into capital gains.

3. Farmers, as owners of closely-held business property, receive preferential estate tax treatment. As mentioned, farm land, as distinct from nonagricultural real property, is valued in use rather than at its market price. This policy, designed to keep family farms and other small businesses intact, greatly minimizes the loss of inheritance value in agricultural intergenerational transfers. Marital deductions, deferred payments, and other features further reduce estate taxes in agriculture.

4. There are cash, hybrid, and "crop" alternatives to accrual accounting. By reporting income under cash accounting, farmers can time the sales of outputs and purchases of inputs to drastically reduce the amount of taxes they pay (Chapter 6). Because of the progressive nature of U.S. taxation—such as it is—the more evenly distributed apparent income can be from one year to the next, the lower the overall tax bill. Only farmers are eligible for this type of preferential treatment, the original thinking being that computing their accrual income would be too sophisticated for farmers. Ironically, it is the largest farmers with the largest incomes who use their microcomputers to reduce their taxes most under this option. The progressive tax structure gives large-scale farmers much greater incentive to attempt to reduce taxes.

A farm operator may also elect to use a "hybrid" system of cash plus accrual accounting if such a system best reflects his income. There is even a "crop" method of reporting income for nontimber crops that cannot be harvested and disposed of within the tax year. The farmer has the option of assigning the cost of producing the crop to the year in which the income is realized. However, certain types of farm firms must use the accrual method. These include farm corporations with more than one million dollars of annual gross receipts (except fruit and nut farms and family-owned corporations).

5. Farmers, like other businesses, can claim accelerated depreciation or cost recovery. As noted in Chapter 4, federal law allows farmers to deduct a more than proportional share of livestock, machinery, or building expenses in the beginning years of the use of an investment asset, thus reducing the tax burden and exploiting the time value of higher after-tax earnings in early years. In a related way, the investment tax credit allows farmers to write the first six to ten percent of the purchase price of such capital assets directly off the total tax burden of the farm. Although this option is also open to other business enterprises, it still provides the farm operator a tax advantage over the ordinary rural or urban citizen.

6. Capital expenditures may be deducted as annual operating costs. The costs of raising a dairy animal to maturity are considered fully deductible when incurred. Such rules violate proper accounting practices and favor the agricultural businessman over other types of businessman.

7. Landlords may avoid social security taxes. Although the rule has not yet been passed, the IRS is considering allowing an owner to operate a farm through his agent or farm manager and still avoid the tax. This change will involve a tighter definition of material participation, under which one is required to pay the tax.

8. Investments in conservation also receive favorable tax treatment from the government. Investments in soil and water conservation practices or facilities are deductible up to 25 percent of the gross income from farming in a given year, and may be carried over to other years. If the farmer elects not to deduct the expenses when they occur, expenses are added to the basis of the land, so that they may be recovered at the time of sale. If the farmer sells the land after ten years, there is no recapture of benefits. If he sells it after between five and ten years, he must pay a prorated proportion. If he sells the land after less than five years, he must pay the entire sum of deductible expenses.

Land clearing expenses are similar to soil and water conservation expenses in that the provisions for recapture are identical to those above. However, such expenses are deducted up to $5,000 or 25% of taxable income from farming in any year. Any excess may **not** be carried over to future years and is added to the basis of the land.

9. A final area in which agriculture is well treated is the legal creation of tax shelters to distribute losses. A tax shelter is a means to remove from taxable income a certain portion of gross income which would otherwise be subject to income tax in the current year. Jones reports that the top 2.2 percent of investors claim ten percent of the agricultural losses. Often, nonfarm investors invest in agriculture specifically to offset nonfarm income through tax shelters. Given the fact that the U.S. tax system is progressive, such tax shelters are predominantly used by those in the highest income tax bracket. Jones' estimates of the break-even percentages are shown in Table 16–1. For example, the data indicate that a tax-free bond is preferrable to an investment in stock only if one's marginal tax rate is at least 39 percent. The tax shelter example to be discussed is the breeding cattle tax shelter, though investment in nut orchards and other agricultural enterprises constitutes another example.

How can the high-income farm manager or nonagricultural investor benefit from these tax shelters? Since the Tax Reform Act of 1976, limited partnerships and syndicated investments have been curtailed in their tax shelter activities, but the investor can still go through manage-

TABLE 16–1. BREAK-EVEN MARGINAL TAX RATES FOR VARIOUS FORMS OF INVESTMENT

Investment	*Compared with*	*Break-even Marginal Tax Rate*
Stock investment	Certificate of deposit	19.9%
Tax-free bond	Stock investment	39.0%
Tax shelter	Tax-free bond	60.9%

Source: Jones, John D., "Farm Tax Shelter Investments: A Financial Analysis," Unpublished Master's essay, Iowa State University, Ames, Iowa, 1979.

ment companies to contract with a rancher to raise breeding cattle. The rancher is paid a certain percentage (often five percent) of the gross profits for managing the cattle with no investment other than his management time, and the investor can have tax write-offs in three out of every five years. If he fails to earn a profit in at least the two remaining years, the IRS will consider that he is not engaging in cattle breeding for profit. If he follows these rules, he can also convert ordinary income into capital gain while operating at a tax loss. For the farm investor, there is the additional advantage that he can incorporate his tax loss from cattle breeding into the returns from other farming activities, making it difficult for the IRS to determine the effect of this tax loss strategy. Figure 16–2 shows a flowchart of the responsibilities of the various parties involved.

With these and other tax options open, it is important to understand how to use them to avoid, rather than to evade, taxes and to maximize the present value of net farm income after taxes. Society must debate on the fairness of preferential treatment for agriculture. But given the favorable current policies, it behooves every farm manager to make the best possible use of these policies.

ADJUSTING TO AFTER-TAX VALUES FOR FARM PLANNING

The common objective of the farm manager with regard to tax strategies is to maximize after-tax income, or net worth over time. The goal should be multi-period—maximizing income over a period of years may necessitate paying greater taxes this year to reduce taxes (by even more) in

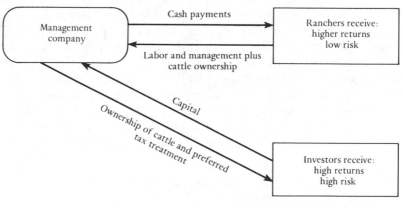

FIGURE 16–2. The Division of Responsibilities in a Breeding Cattle Tax Shelter. (Source: Adapted from Jones, John D., "Farm Shelter Investment: A Financial Analysis," Unpublished Master's essay, Iowa State University, Ames, Iowa, 1979.)

subsequent years. Expectations of future returns, costs and tax rate changes all affect income tax decisions. It goes without saying that saving or postponing taxes at the expense of the overall level and stability of farm income may be unwise.

In light of the tax concessions open to farm managers, the importance of maintaining accurate records becomes manifest. Without accurate records calculated for both accrual and cash accounting, one cannot tell which system is preferable for reporting taxes. Nor can one keep track of depreciation, investment credit, and other deductible expenses; take advantage of capital gain and loss laws; or defend items if the income tax return is audited.

Taxes pervade every area of farm management. Property taxes must be included in partial budgets: they are a key part of both DIRTI 5 and DITIS calculations. You have seen in Chapter 6 that income and other tax payments are part of the cash outflow that contributes to the net cash flow line at the top of a cash flow budget. Income and property taxes figure in the net worth statement; and also in the cash and accrual income statements, though perhaps in different amounts for the two. Chapter 15 demonstrated that property taxes are a legitimate part of the landlord's estimate of minimum cash rent that he will be able to accept from the tenant.

Indeed, the farm manager must consider taxes in almost every decision he makes in operating the farm to achieve his income and other goals. As a result, he must keep data from a wide variety of sources to make an accurate adjustment for taxes in his calculations. These data include tax tables; receipts from ordinary and capital gains sales; social security and self-employment retirement information; estimates of nonfarm income; records of investment credit and gas and oil refunds; lists of depreciation, capital purchases and other farm expenses; and a record of farm operating expenses.

Role of Taxes in the Income Statement: Component and Determinant

One of the areas in which taxes are critical is in the income statement. Obviously, taxes are a component of the income statement. But the tax advantages can allow one to change the remainder of the income statement to better advantage. There are at least eleven ways that this can be done:

1. Paying one's children for services performed, up to the value of their maximum earnings that can be earned tax free. In 1981, this was $2,300 for single persons.

2. Reporting income and losses from drought and crop failure in different years than when they occurred. Crop losses from a natural disaster may be subtracted from income reported for the previous crop year to even out reported income. The extra income from crop insurance may be reported in the year following the loss, provided the farmer can dem-

onstrate that he would have reported the income from the crop in the following year had it been successful. These concepts extend to livestock as well. Farmers reporting on the cash basis may report income from the sale of livestock forced by drought in the year after the actual sale. This option does not apply to draft, dairy, or breeding animals held for capital gains treatment, however.

3. Using deferred payments contracts. The operator may deliver the goods this year but not actually receive payment for them until early in the next tax year. To establish this type of delayed receipt of payment, it is wise to use a contract and to adhere to its terms.

4. Filing estimated tax returns in mid-January to postpone payment of the previous year's taxes from March 1 to April 15. To be eligible for this concession, two-thirds of the income from all sources must come from farming.

5. Averaging income. Income averaging, which reduces the effect of the progressive tax structure by reducing year to year income fluctuations so typical of agriculture, can help the individual operator minimize average income above the taxes. Income averaging allows a portion of uncharacteristically large years' income to be taxed at a lower marginal rate. It can be used on an irregular basis if desired. But to qualify one must provide at least 50 percent of one's own support during the previous four years. Also, five years of records are required. There are two other disadvantages: one cannot use the optional tax tables which sometimes permit one to pay less income tax, and the normal 50 percent ceiling on the tax rate does not apply.

6. Carrying back and carrying over net operating losses (NOLs). This method allows the farm operator to get the most benefit from operating losses in a poor year by spreading them over years $n - 3$, $n - 2$, etc. in order to reduce net taxable income, where n = the year of the loss. Such spreading may be taken back as many as three years and then forward as many as fifteen until the full amount of the loss is exhausted.

Table 16–2 shows an example from the 1981 Farmer's Tax Guide of carrying back and over. Suppose that the farm operator had a disaster loss in 1981 that resulted in a $42,000 NOL for the taxable year. He would distribute that loss, first back to 1978, and then forward for as many years as were necessary to use it up. In so doing, he would have to recalculate taxable income in each year. This is because not all of the original deductions were allowed. The resulting calculations result in "modified" taxable income for each year. The illustration shows that by 1989 this total NOL can be used to cancel all tax payments for the period 1978–1989. One may also elect to forgo the carryback period and use the NOL to reduce only future adjusted gross incomes. If the farmer wishes to forgo carryback, he must attach a statement to that effect in the year olf the NOL.

7. Selling inventory. An alternative strategy for a year of expected loss is to sell off large amounts of inventory so that the operator can achieve zero taxable income plus the value of tax-free personal deductions and exemptions. If a married farmer has a $15,000 loss,

TABLE 16-2. EXAMPLE OF USING A NET OPERATING LOSS (NOL) TO REDUCE TAXABLE INCOME IN OTHER YEARS

Year	Carryback or carryover	Modified taxable income	Unused carryback or carryover
1978	42,000	2,000	40,000
1979	40,000	3,000	37,000
1980	37,000	5,500	31,500
1981 (NOL Year)			
1982	31,500	7,000	24,500
1983	24,500	3,800	20,700
1984	20,700	5,700	15,000
1985	15,000	6,000	9,000
1986	9,000	2,500	6,500
1987	6,500	3,000	3,500
1988	3,500	3,300	300
1989	200	5,000	0

Source: *Farmer's Tax Guide*, Publication 225, p. 25, Internal Revenue Service, Washington, D.C., 1981.

then he can sell off as much as $18,400 and escape all income tax, due to the $3,400 floor on taxable income for joint returns.

8. Using an income tax straddle or spread. This strategy involves buying a commodity for delivery in one month and selling it in another. Before 1981 this was a legitimate investment technique, but the Internal Revenue Service has now investigated its alleged use as an intentional way of losing income to offset other earnings and reduce taxes. Since 1981, farm operators must clearly identify on their records and books on the day of a transaction that it is a hedging transaction. Otherwise, the transaction will be considered speculation. Any such speculative gain or loss will no longer be considered ordinary business gain or loss but a gain or loss on a capital investment.

9. Handling government payments wisely. Chapter 10 showed how government programs can be used to increase farm income. From the point of view of tax management, a greater proportion of the benefits from government programs can be retained. For example, the farm operator may choose to treat his CCC loan as income received in the year when the crop is finally sold rather than when he receives the money. Also, expenses of growing the crop may be used to offset income from the crop to stabilize the amount of income reported from year to year. The farmer may choose to begin this practice for any given loan but must continue to do so unless he receives special permission from the Tax Commissioner.

10. Using miscellaneous tax breaks. The farmer is eligible to deduct as a business expense the ownership costs of that part of the home regularly used for business. He may also deduct any expenses on all or parts of trips that are business related. Finally, he may take a credit of up to

$3,000 the first year and $1,500 the second year for hiring difficult-to-employ persons. These include felons, welfare recipients, the handicapped, veterans, and young people in cooperative education. You learned in Chapter 11 that, with training, such persons can develop into excellent farm workers.

Indeed, the federal government has long lists of legitimate business deductions. These include labor costs even when one hires one's own children, mileage allowances, repairs and maintenance, interest deductions, livestock supplies, real property taxes except on the nonbusiness portion of the house, fertilizer and lime costs, deposits against next year's supplies, truck and automobile licenses, farm organization dues, subscriptions to magazines and papers, travel for business purposes, accounting fees, and sales tax.

11. Increasing income in the current year in order to take advantage of cash accounting. Ways to increase income include the following:

> Perform off-farm work.
> Put off making investments and paying bills until after January 1 (or the beginning of the next year if on non-calendar year accounting.)
> Sell livestock and grain products before December 31.
> Pay bills to suppliers after January 1.
> Choose the optional straight-line method of depreciation on newly acquired machinery, breeding stock and buildings.

The converse of the above methods will lead to corresponding decreases in current income in a high-income year to avoid excessive taxation. The only exception is that one cannot switch from straight-line depreciation to another method.

The Whole Farm Budget after Taxes

In Chapter 5, you learned to use the whole farm budget grid as a convenient way to make product-product decisions. At that time, however, we did not make any adjustments for taxes. There are three areas of tax analysis that should be performed on the grid (Table 5–5) to ensure that the optimal after-tax whole-farm budget has been achieved:

1. Study the tax effects of relaxing restraints through input purchase. By buying corn and hiring labor you could pay ahead or delay payment to even out apparent income if you are on the cash system of accounting. This will favor the labor-intensive FF operations and particularly FF/CCOMM.

2. Weigh after-tax gains against increased management requirements. Even if going from FP/CCCSS to PF/CCCSS pushes you into a higher tax bracket, you will still make more money in the latter. However, because the U.S. tax system is progressive, going from, say, the 38 percent to the 42 percent tax bracket will mean that an apparent gain of $10,000 will be reduced to only $5,800! Particularly if you prefer to work with

pigs and sows rather than market hogs, this extra income may not be worth it to you.

3. Consider investment tax credit and property taxes. If you do have to invest in new finishing buildings and feeding equipment, you will gain an investment credit (on the positive side) and be able to use ACRS techniques to reduce taxable income, but (on the negative side) you will have to pay higher property taxes.

Effects of Taxes on Credit and Financial Risk

Figure 16-3 shows the effect of differing tax regulations on labor and capital on the isoquant for a typical farm. Even though, as noted, there are tax concessions for hiring certain types of labor, recovery and other concessions for capital investments are even greater. Therefore, for a

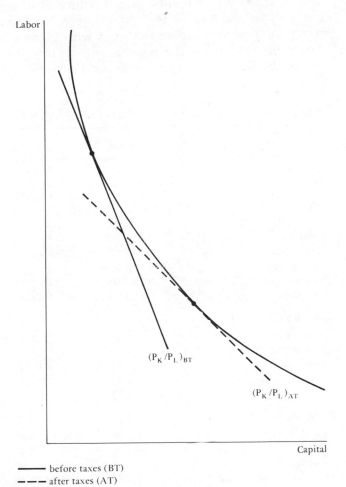

————— before taxes (BT)
– – – after taxes (AT)

FIGURE 16-3. *The Effects of Tax Regulation on the Slope of the Isocost Line.*

farmer in the 33 percent tax bracket, the effective after-tax cost of labor may be 15 percent higher than the after-tax cost of capital. The dotted line in Figure 16–3 shows how the optimal mix of production inputs differs before and after taxes.

Income taxes also have an effect on the increasing risk principle, tending to accentuate its effects, again because of the progressive tax system. Let us return to the identical twin brothers Y and Z of Chapter 13 (Table 16–3). Before taxes, Farmer Z makes $7,500 more than his brother in a better than average year, $2,500 more in a typical year, and $2,500 **less** in a poor year. In other words, before taxes, the increasing risk principle alone means that Farmer Z's income will likely be much more variable than Farmer Y's. Depending upon one's perceptions of financial risk and risk-bearing ability, this fact may already be enough to encourage one not to maintain a high debt:total asset ratio. After taxes, Farmer Z's margin of gain is reduced to $4,650 in a better-than-average year and $1,738 in a typical year. However, his margin of loss in a poor year is not reduced. Even with income averaging, for which the results tend to be the same as in a typical year, tax payments will reduce the after-tax margin of gain for Farmer Z over Farmer Y.

TABLE 16–3.   INCREASING RISK PRINCIPLE AFTER TAXES

	Farmer Y	*Farmer Z*	*Difference Z – Y*
Equity ($)	50,000	50,000	
Debt ($)	25,000	75,000	
Total assets controlled ($)	75,000	125,000	
Good year (r = 30%)			
Returns on total assets ($)	22,500	37,500	
Interest on debt capital ($)	–3,750	–11,250	
Tax bracket	17%	23%	
Net return before taxes ($)	18,750	26,250	+$7,500
Net return after taxes ($)	15,563	20,213	+$4,650
Typical year (r = 20%)[1]			
Returns on total assets ($)	15,000	25,000	
Interest on debt capital ($)	–3,750	–11,250	
Tax bracket	14%	17%	
Net return before taxes ($)	11,250	13,750	+$2,500
Net return after taxes ($)	9,675	11,413	+$1,738
Poor year (r =10%)			
Returns on total assets ($)	7,500	12,500	
Interest on debt capital ($)	–3,750	–11,250	
Tax bracket	0%	0%	
Net return before taxes ($)	3,750	1,250	–$2,500
Net return after taxes ($)	3,750	1,250	–$2,500

[1]Also yields same results if assume an equal likelihood of the three types of years occurring over the averaging period.

Effects of Taxes on the Decision Between Farming and a Nonfarm Career

Because of the above tax policies, taxation has a great effect on the decision between farming and a nonfarm career (Chapter 12). Table 16–4 shows that the progressive tax system in the United States normally has a dramatic effect on narrowing the gap between expected lifetime earnings from farm and nonfarm jobs. Before taxes, the present value of the farm career is approximately $240,000 higher, while after taxes it is less than $48,000 higher. However, previously-mentioned provisions, if exploited, could widen the gap considerably in favor of agriculture. These are:

1. More favorable estate planning provisions (we thus take the value of the investment beyond the retirement age, and even the grave).
2. Provisions for income averaging and distribution of losses.
3. Other provisions, such as spreading out apparent income by using

TABLE 16-4.   THE EFFECT OF TAXES ON THE FARM VS. NONFARM EMPLOY-
MENT DECISION

	Farm Job	*Nonfarm Job*
$PV_{cash\ flow\ income}$		
Before taxes:	$413,913	$237,365
Gross income	131,663	33,800
Terms of loan	25 yr @ 12%	24 yr @ 12%
Interest payment/year	59,063	5,250
Principal payment/year	27,000	2,400
After taxes:	$163,387	$177,765
Taxable income (gross income – interest payments)	72,600	28,550
Tax rate	38%	23$
PV_{equity}	$62,300	$5,538
$PV_{capital\ gains}$		
Before taxes	$9,230	$2,307
After taxes:	$7,384	$2,123
Tax rate	20%	8%
PV_{Total}		
Before taxes:	$485,443	$245,210
After taxes:	$233,071	$185,426
Income Superiority of farm job		
Before taxes:	$240,233	
After taxes:	$47,645	

Note: For examples on how the underlying formulas are used, see Chapter 12, where computations of after-tax present values are presented. As an exercise, the student should also test his understanding by reproducing the before-tax present values.

the cash system of accounting, paying children and the lower self-employment tax.

Tax considerations can alter considerably the choice of a career.

TAX MANAGEMENT IN PURCHASES AND INVESTMENTS

Income taxes reduce the present value of an investment by reducing the effective net income it will generate. However, investment tax credits and recovery regulations also reduce investment costs and early taxable returns, and hence increase net present value. Therefore, the net effect of tax policies on an investment must be carefully determined. If the net present value is still positive and greater than the net present value of the next investment alternative for the cash-limited farmer, then it still pays to make the investment.

Investment Tax Credits

It is possible, under certain circumstances, to claim an investment tax credit on depreciable or business–related tangible property, whether purchased used or new. The farm operator may include all livestock except horses. Specialized livestock facilities, silos, and other single-purpose structures are also eligible, in addition to facilities for pollution control.

Effective 1981, the investment tax credit is tied to the Accelerated Cost Recovery System. For property placed in service after 1980 with a three-year recovery period, the investment tax credit is 6 percent; for 5, 10, and 15 year property it is 10 percent. However, the investment tax credit may be "recaptured." This term means that investment tax credit may be taken back by the Internal Revenue Service if the asset is sold, traded, or not used for business purposes before the end of its recovery period. For every year before 3 years of use, 1/3 of the investment tax credit (i.e., 2 percent of acquisition cost) is recaptured on 3-year property. For every year before 5 full years of use, 1/5 of the investment tax credit (also 2 percent of acquisition cost) is recaptured on 5-, 10-, or 15-year property. Investment tax credit is also not allowed if the investor is not "at risk"—if he has other than a business relationship with or is related to the creditor, is protected against loss of the investment amount, or is not personally liable for repayment.

Depreciation allowances can also be recaptured in the event of sale. On real property purchased before 1981, depreciation in excess of the straight-line method is recaptured. On personal property, the portion treated as ordinary income is the lesser of the gain realized or the depreciation taken since 1961. One depreciation strategy for assets purchased before 1981 involves switching to the straight-line method as soon as the depreciation allowance for the basis (remaining book value) exceeds the regular tax depreciation allowance for the double-declining balance or sum-of-the-digits method.

Section 1231 Capital Gains

A further investment area in which farmers are given special compensation is Section 1231 assets. These are such assets as are held for more than one or two years (depending on the asset); are used in the operator's business; and are not for sale, production inventory, or copyright. Section 1231 assets are limited to land and depreciable business assets. All of any net loss in the holding of 1231 assets is tax-deductible.

There are two types of capital gains: short-term and long-term. If cattle and horses are held for at least two years, other livestock one year, futures commodities one-half year, and all other assets one year, they qualify to be considered as long-term capital assets. Gains on these assets are charged at a maximum rate of 20 percent (40 percent of value times 50 percent marginal tax rate). Capital gains losses may be used to offset up to $3,000 in ordinary income.

If an asset is held for less than the periods specified above, then it is considered a short-term capital asset, and gain or loss is reported on Schedule D of form 1040. Section 1231 assets must be lumped together to determine whether there has been a net capital gain or loss. If the net is positive, then the IRS considers that all the assets have earned a capital gain. If the net is negative, each asset is treated as producing either an ordinary gain or loss. A net loss is fully deductible from gross income. Here again, farmers and other businessmen are given flexibility to help them minimize their tax burdens. In a given year, if there is a loss in either short-term or long-term capital gains, the tax rate is 100 percent if the short-term absolute value is larger and 40 percent if the long-term is larger. If there is a loss in both, the separate rates should be used.

Tax Management in Buying or Selling a Farm

How can the farm operator best sell land and other 1231 assets so as to minimize the taxes he must pay? As presented in Chapter 15 on acquiring and managing land, there are basically four ways:

1. Cash Sale. This is the easiest way technically, but there is the danger of paying capital gains tax on the entire sale price unless new property can be purchased within 24 months.

2. Cash Sale with Unharvested Crops. The proceeds from these unharvested crops in the event of sale are treated as capital gains rather than ordinary income. Therefore, there is an advantage to planting your crop even if you are considering selling the field before it can be harvested. The only problem is that the production costs for growing the corn are considered capital investment expenses, rather than operating expenses. Hence, they increase the land basis.

3. Installment Sale. From the tax point of view, the major disadvantages of installment sales are that one can defer tax and convert it from ordinary income to capital gains, which for most operators is taxed in a lower bracket, and that one can increase the selling price and lower interest payments so as to force a higher percentage of the principal and interest received to be taxed as capital gains. Specifically, the gain reportable as income (*GRI*) in a given year is defined as follows:

$$GRI = \text{payments received} \times \frac{\text{gross profit}}{\text{contract price}}$$

$$= \text{payments received} \times \frac{\text{selling price} - \text{adjusted basis}}{\begin{array}{l}\text{cash} + \text{notes} + \text{other property} + \\ \text{any positive difference between} \\ \text{the mortgage and the basis.}\end{array}}$$

The major disadvantages of installment sales are three. First, one risks a change in tax policy during the period of the contract. If this special provision were discontinued, one could suffer a loss. Second, one is locked into a lower interest rate which could reduce the present value of a contract installment sale when compared with cash sale and reinvestment (at say 15%) of the proceeds. Third, although installment sales contracts are a way for the seller to receive income over a long period and to have it taxed as capital gains rather than ordinary income, the **unstated interest** rule can complicate matters. If the contract makes no provision for interest rate or states an excessively low interest rate (less than 9 percent between unrelated persons and less than 6 percent between relatives) the IRS has power to impute a higher interest rate. This imputation increases the buyer's interest expense (which reduces his taxable income) but increases the seller's interest (and hence taxable income). For this reason, expert legal assistance should be obtained before entering into an installment land contract. Still, installment sales contracts are popular—in recent years about 40 percent of all agricultural property sales in the cornbelt were made in this manner.

4. Exchanges of Like-kind Property. One can exchange a farm for an apartment house tax free—as long as it is an investment, all capital gains and sales taxes may be avoided. Specialty real estate companies have been known to make up to 15- or 20-way exchanges of property so that everyone involved can come out satisfied. Sometimes, an additional cash payment or "boot" is included. Taxes are based on either the gain realized or the boot received, whichever is the lesser amount. The major advantage of the like-kind exchange is that one only has to pay tax on the recognized rather than the realized gain. One can even delay the receipt of property by giving the original property to a developer in return for either credit or a partnership in the final developed use of the land. The disadvantage for many operators who use this technique to retire is that it does not give them any cash liquidity, especially in comparison with an outright sale.

TAXES IN RETIREMENT AND ESTATE PLANNING

The objectives of retirement and estate planning, as you will learn in more detail in the following chapter, are to guarantee a stable income floor for one's declining years, determine the time and form of transfer of property to one's heirs, and achieve the best strategy for asset distribution among heirs.

Retirement Planning

One way to achieve retirement goals for farm owner-operators and tenant-operators is to qualify for social security and medicare by participating in the self-employment tax plan. This plan is mandatory for all self-employment income of between $400 and $29,700 (in 1982). The standard self-employment tax is an additional 9.35 percent in 1982 over the regular income tax. There is also a farm optional method that allows operators with less than $2,400 gross or $1,600 net income to accumulate quarters (3-month periods) toward retirement benefits based upon their gross farm profit. Both these ceilings for social security self-employment taxes and the rate at which they are taxed have increased rapidly in recent years. Social security self-employment taxes are more conducive to tax management than personal and real property taxes.

Although dividend earnings from stock holdings are included in the amount on which social security tax must be paid, earnings from cash-rented land and Subchapter S corporations are exempt. Earnings from share-rented land are also exempt if the owner does not materially participate in using the land.

Still another strategy for guaranteeing constant income in retirement is the use of self-employed retirement plans. These are of three types: HR-10 or Keogh plans, individual retirement arrangements (IRAs), and simplified employee pensions (SEPs). Under such plans, one can shelter a portion of one's current income against taxes at the present, to be taxed only after retirement at the presumably lower rates of those low-income years.

A final strategy to guarantee retirement income is to invest in annuities of various kinds. These include variable, fixed, cash refund, installment-refund, and joint or survivor annuities. These can also be used as a form of estate planning, in the event that the farm operator dies before the term of such annuities is up, since annuity income automatically passes to one's heirs.

Estate Planning

One way in which the federal government helps the farm operator to pass on a larger estate to his heirs is through the use valuation of farm land held until death. This provision was introduced in the 1976 Tax Reform Act. Because land is worth more as an investment asset than as a productive asset, this provision means that for estate tax purposes, the heirs can pay much less than the market value of the land would suggest. However, there are two stipulations in the use valuation of farmland. First, the total value of the land may be reduced in this manner by not more than $750,000. Second, the heirs must continue to use the land for agriculture for at least fifteen additional years after the death of the operator. Otherwise, the estate tax savings may be recaptured.

The federal government also allows a "marital deduction" which shelters 100 percent of the estate from taxes for the surviving spouse for deaths after 1981. However, there is a unified credit on estate and gift transfers giving an equivalent deduction of $225,000 in 1982 that will increase to $600,000 for 1987 and after. Couples with estates valued at more than these amounts may wish to consider a marital deduction of less than 100 percent to relieve some of the federal estate tax burden at the death of the surviving spouse.

The federal government further allows the operator and spouse to give gifts to their heirs of $10,000 per donor per recipient per year. As will be shown in Chater 17, one advantage of forming a corporation is that exactly $10,000 worth of stock may be given away without affecting the liquidity or operation of the farm business.

Another aspect of estate planning is the cost of managing the estate itself. The farm operator will often wish to keep a certain amount of his assets liquid to cover the funeral expenses, state and federal taxes, and estate administration costs. Even here, however, the government gives the heirs a tax break. The heirs may use the remainder of the estate to secure loans to cover these expenses. Further, they may defer payment of taxes and pay them between five and fifteen years after the death of the farm operator. All they must do is keep paying interest on the amount unpaid at the rate of four percent. This tax rate is far below the market interest rate, and acts as a form of subsidized loan.

Additional ways to use tax management for efficient estate planning are to:

1. Take out medical insurance for partial dependents.
2. Create tax-sheltered education plans for children.
3. Establish lifetime trusts. This last is an especially good way to reduce costs of probate taxes.

TAX ASPECTS OF INCORPORATING THE FARM BUSINESS

As Chapter 17 will demonstrate, there are a number of advantages to farm partnerships and corporations having to do with the transfer of assets between generations and satisfying family members at different stages in the farm family life cycle. With regard to income taxes, however, it bears mention here that partnerships allow related persons of unequal resources to claim more equal incomes to each other and therefore to reduce the average total taxes that they must pay.

The tax reduction advantages from corporations are more complex. For the Subchapter S corporation, with one class of stock and up to 25 related shareholders, the advantages are similar to that of a partnership. Moreover, unlike Subchapter C corporations, the long-term capital gains of the corporation must be passed through to the shareholders, there is no double taxation of corporate income paid to shareholders as dividends, and operating losses may be used to offset personal income.

However, there are significant tax benefits from forming a Subchapter C corporation. The major benefit is that corporate taxable income is taxed at a much lower rate than personal income. The way to use this advantage to the fullest is, instead of paying dividends, pay low salaries to as many shareholders as possible.

Figure 16–4 illustrates the advantages of this approach. Suppose that there are two identical farm businesses with a net taxable farm income of $65,000. The first—and it does not matter whether you imagine it as a sole proprietorship, a partnership, or Subchapter S corporation, for they are all treated the same from the point of view of income taxes— would have to pay the federal government 48 percent of its marginal income in taxes, as shown by point **a**.

The Subchapter C corporation would not, however. Even if it paid no salaries to its shareholders, it would only have to pay a maximum of 30 percent of its marginal income in taxes, as shown by point **b**. However,

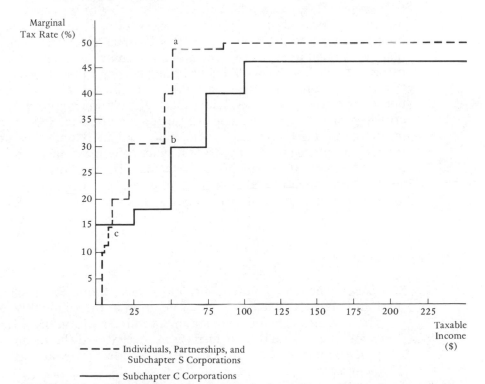

FIGURE 16–4. *Marginal Income Tax Rates for Various Types of Farm Business Organization, 1984. (Source: Adapted from U.S. Treasury, 1981.)*

if the corporation paid $13,000 salaries to each of five employees, it could reduce the tax burden dramatically to a maximum marginal rate of 14 percent on each of their salaries, paid on the personal income basis, and hence, 14 percent of the entire $50,000, as illustrated by point **c**. By paying out salaries to more people, it could reduce taxable income even further.

A related way to reduce tax liabilities of corporations is to pay rent to shareholders who lease property to the corporation and pay interest to shareholders who make loans to the corporation. In this way, only the individual pays taxes on the income, not the corporation. Thus, the astute board of trustees of a farm corporation will juggle such items back and forth until the tax burden is minimized.

SUMMARY

The government imposes taxes so that it may provide the collective services which it would be difficult or impossible for individuals to provide. Historically, agriculture in the United States has been given preferential treatment in terms of the incidence of taxes. Within the farm sector as well, the federal policies have effectively eliminated the extra taxes which higher income operators might be expected to pay.

This chapter has shown how to adjust a number of the types of analysis presented previously in this text for taxes. For example, you have seen how to adjust to after-tax values the income statement, whole farm plan, credit and financial risk decisions, the choice of a farm vs. nonfarm career, and decisions on buying or selling a farm. In most cases the relative merits of one investment or course of action change as one compares before and after tax values. One aspect of taxation which is gaining increasing importance in U.S. agriculture is the effect of federal policies on incorporating the farm business. The tax benefits are greatest from forming a Subchapter C corporation where the maximum rate of taxation is 46 percent, versus 50 percent for all other forms of business entity. Through paying salaries to employees, the marginal tax rate paid by Subchapter C corporations can be further reduced.

TOPICS FOR DISCUSSION

1. Discuss whether or not you think farmers should be given concessions in terms of the incidence of taxation in the United States. Consider the incidence of taxes among producers within the agricultural sector, the unique role of farmers in society, and the advantage that some nonfarm investors take of tax advantages to agricultural operations.
2. Do you feel that there are tax-loss farming operations in your state? Which commodities do they produce, who invests in them, and what

effect do they have on agricultural production, marketing, and income distribution in your state (and the nation)?

3. It has been said that farmers should continue to be able to use the cash method of accounting because the accrual method of accounting is too sophisticated and time-consuming for the typical operator. Discuss this assertion in the light of today's typical operator in your state.

4. Why has the federal government felt it necessary to grant special estate planning concessions to agricultural operators? Do you feel this is correct and equitable given the needs of society as a whole and the role of farmers in it? Relate your answer to how property is owned, acquired, and managed in the agricultural versus the non-agricultural sectors. Discuss the economies of add-ons and the question of whether farming should be limited to those whose relatives are already farm owners.

SUGGESTED READINGS

Harsh, S. L. Connor, and J. Schwab. *Managing the Farm Business.* Chapter 13. Englewood Cliffs, New Jersey: Prentice-Hall Inc., 1981.

Jones, John D. *Farm Tax Shelter Investments: A Financial Analysis.* Unpublished master's paper. Ames, Iowa: Iowa State University, 1979.

Kay, R. D. *Farm Management: Planning, Control, and Implementation.* Chapter 17. New York: McGraw-Hill Book Company, 1981.

Harl, Neil. *Farm Estate and Business Planning.* Skokie, Illinois: Agri Business Publications, 1978.

Nelson, A. W. Lee, and W. Murray. *Agricultural Finance: Sixth Edition.* Chapter 17. Ames, Iowa: Iowa State University Press, 1973.

Osburn, D. and K. Schneeberger. *Modern Agriculture Management.* Chapter 21. Reston, Virginia: Reston Publishing, 1978.

Penson, J. and D. Lins. *Agricultural Finance.* Chapter 11. Englewood Cliffs, N.J.: Prentice-Hall, Inc., 1980.

Farmer's Tax Guide: Income and Self-employment Tax. U.S. Department of the Treasury, Internal Revenue Service. Publication 225. Washington, D.C., 1980.

Weston, J. F. W. Brigham. *Essentials of Managerial Finance.* Fifth Edition. Hinsdale, Illinois: The Dryden Press, 1979.

17

Selecting the Best Farm Business Organizational Structure

The labor unions shall have a square deal,
and the corporations shall have a square deal,
and in addition, all private citizens shall have a square deal.

Roosevelt, Address.

Concepts

In this chapter you will come to understand:

1. The relative importance of sole proprietorships, partnerships, and corporations in the current structure of U.S. agriculture.
2. The farm family life cycle.
3. The conflicting goals of parents, off-farm heirs, and on-farm heirs.
4. The characteristics, advantages and disadvantages of sole proprietorships, partnerships, and corporations.

Tools

You will also gain the following skills:

1. How to discuss the merits of changing the farm business organizational structure with the members of a farm family.

INTRODUCTION

Up till now in this text, you have been learning about farm business decision making from the point of view of the sole proprietorship. True, Chapter 11 explored employer-employee relations in managing farm labor. Chapter 15 confronted the problems of landlords taking on tenants. But even these were modified forms of sole proprietorship. Since most farms fall into this category, the approach so far has certainly been justified. This chapter will proceed to complete the last topic of the farm management pie: farm business organizational structure.

There are many types of farm business operating arrangements. These include trusts; leasing arrangements, some of which you have already studied; and the relationships between employer and employee. The two latter types keep managerial decisions—or the primary weight of them—in the sole proprietor. However, by far the most important forms of farm business operating arrangements are the three types of farm business structure called sole proprietorship, partnership, and corporation.

Table 17–1 shows the percentages of U.S. farms which are organized under each type of structure. Of the U.S. sample corporations, 92 percent were those with fewer than ten shareholders, i.e., family or subchapter S corporations.[1] Indeed, it is useful to divide farm corporations into two types:

1. Subchapter C or "regular" corporations which are taxed and treated exactly like a large, industrial corporation; and
2. Subchapter S corporations, also called "tax-option" corporations, which have the main advantage of minimizing costs of intergenerational transfer (Figure 17–1).

There are also two types of partnerships: those with and without limited partners. Limited partnership regulations were established in different states in different years.

Since Chapter 7 of this text, you have seen that what is right or wrong for a farm operator depends on his/her particular situation. For example, the amount of risk suitable for one farmer may not be for another. One farmer may feel comfortable with a flexible cash lease while another

TABLE 17–1. PROPORTION OF U.S. FARMS WITH VARIOUS TYPES OF FARM BUSINESS ORGANIZATIONAL STRUCTURE

	Sole Partnership	Partnership	Corporations	Hired manager and other
	(%)	(%)	(%)	(%)
Iowa, 1976[1]	88.5	9.4	1.7	0.2
U.S., 1974[2]	89.5	8.6	1.7	0.2
U.S., 1969[3]	85.4	12.8	1.2	0.6

[1] E. Hoiberg and W. Huffman. 1978. Profile of Iowa Farms and Farm Families, 1976. Iowa Agriculture and Home Economics Experiment Stations and Cooperative Extension Service Bulletin P-141. Iowa State University, Ames.

[2] U.S. 1974 Census of Agriculture, Vol. IV, part 5.

[3] U.S. 1969 Census of Agriculture.

[1] *As of 1981, family corporations could include up to 25 related persons.*

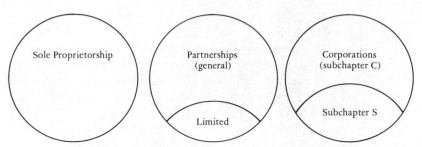

FIGURE 17-1. Types of Farm Business Organizational Structure.

needs a crop-share lease. Similarly, it is difficult to say which of the five types of farm business structure shown in Figure 17-1 will be best for a given farm family. What we can do is outline the characteristics, advantages and disadvantages of each, so that when it comes time for the farm operator to decide, he will be able to make an informed decision.

The Farm Family Life Cycle

Before moving on to look at these organizational options in detail, an introduction to the farm family life cycle can paint the backdrop for our comparison. Typically, a farmer starts out in agriculture as a young person, and, as described in the discussion of leverage in Chapter 13, wants to see his farm grow as quickly as possible (Figure 17-2). Then his desire for expansion begins to taper off. At age 55 or 60 he wants to begin to slow down, get more security and coast into retirement. He prefers to take less chance with income stability because of the rising

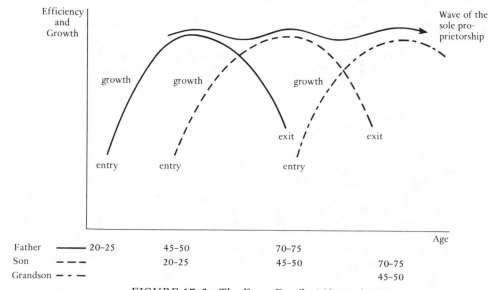

FIGURE 17-2. The Farm Family Life Cycle.

probability of poor health. If he has no offspring, he may very well reduce the size of his operation and even sell it, toward the bottom of the curve. Someone else will have to start at the entry stage and go through the whole extreme cycle.

If he does have offspring, he can hand the farm over to them. No matter how well they get along, there is still a dip at the transition period, which makes a wave pattern of the life cycle of the farm firm. This is because the son wants to expand the operation as quickly as possible while the father wants to contract it. The son may have better management ideas from a university education, but he also lacks his father's long years' experience with the particular soil of the farm. This type of wave motion can slow down the rate of growth of the farm by reducing leverage and even rate of return. Thus, the sole proprietorship may lose ground and even perish in comparison with larger partnerships and corporations. Minimizing the lag in intergenerational transfer is therefore of critical concern in deciding on the optimal business structure of the farm firm.

Against this backdrop, individual actors within the family at different stages in their lives have different goals at the critical period of transition represented by the dips in Figure 17-2. These are the parents, the off-farm heirs, and the on-farm heirs.

Parents

The parents have four distinct objectives. First, they would like to maintain reasonable security of income and capital funds for retirement. Even if they want to show their generosity to their children, they do not want to forfeit all their cash income and the equity they have built up. They probably want to travel, perhaps abroad, or move to Miami. Therefore, they would like to choose a form of farm business organization which will allow them some money during this transition stage.

Second, they want an equitable disposition of family wealth among their heirs. As sensitive human beings, they do not want to see either the children who have moved off the farm (the off-farm heirs) or those who have stayed on the farm (on-farm heirs) treated unfairly. Each child should get a roughly equal share of the estate at their death.

Third, they would like to minimize death taxes and estate settlement costs. It is not enough just to make sure that each child gets an equal share of the estate; the parents would like to make sure that the estate is as big as possible. Everyone needs a will or an estate plan; if you are imprudent enough not to have one ready, then the government will be sure to have one for you which treats the government very generously.

Fourth, the parents would like to reduce the management responsibilities for the surviving spouse. In 1950, there were nine men over the age of 65 for every ten women. Now, that number has been reduced to seven men for every ten women. This means that there is a growing likelihood that the surviving spouse will be a woman. The farm organizational structure chosen should guarantee her a good income while shifting much of the management decisions to the children.

Off-farm Heirs

Off-farm heirs, such as the daughter who becomes a lawyer and moves to another state or the son who goes to work as a salesman for an automobile dealership in the capital city, have three major objectives. First, they would like certainty of income. They see the farm as a source of extra money, but they would like it to come to them in even amounts from one year to the next. However, from the discussion of **business** risk in Chapter 8 you know that this is not the case in agriculture. They would probably be willing to sell their share of the farm and put it into savings bonds.

Second, the off-farm heirs want stability of assets. This goal relates to the **financial** risk described in Chapter 13. They want the farm assets to grow (as nonfarm assets will likely not) but they do not want to risk going into cattle at the wrong time and the possibility of bankruptcy.

Therefore, as a third goal, they also desire some say in the management of the farm after the death of the parents. If their capital is going to be tied up in the business, they want to participate in decisions about how it is to be used.

On-farm Heirs

On-farm heirs are the one or two children who really enjoy farming and, after working through the net present value of farming compared with nonfarm work (see Chapter 12), elect to remain. They have three goals. First, they desire a very clear title to the farm property on the death of their parents. They want it understood that it is they who will farm and that they will be allowed to keep the farming unit intact.

Second, they feel they have a right to a fair annual income based upon their greater management contribution to the farm business. They feel that since they are often dependent on agriculture for their entire livelihood, they should be entitled to most of the income in a bad year. Similarly, in a good year, they feel that they should have a proportionally greater share of the income to compensate the management stresses they have gone through.

Third, they want a major voice in farm management decision making. In case of conflict of opinion regarding the destiny of the farm, they wish to have the deciding vote.

The objectives of the above **dramatis personae** may be and often are in conflict. The resolution and minimization of such conflict in the entry-growth-exit fluctuation of the farm family life cycle depends upon an optimal farm business structure.

ADVANTAGES AND DISADVANTAGES OF DIFFERENT BUSINESS STRUCTURES

With this background on the stage and the actors, it is time to consider the major characteristics of each farm business structure and to weigh its advantages and disadvantages. It will be helpful to consider the sole proprietorship first, because it is probably most familiar and then use it

TABLE 17-2. CHARACTERISTICS, ADVANTAGES AND DISADVANTAGES OF THREE FARM BUSINESS ORGANIZATIONAL STRUCTURES

	Sole Proprietorship	Partnership	Corporation
Nature of entity	Single individual, though may hire others or lease production factors to or from others	Defined as "two or more individuals who pool their assets (limited) and management (general) to operate a farm firm." May be between parents and children, but children cannot make commitments on the part of partnership unless they are deemed "by a reasonable and prudent person to be acting as responsible." Your 12-year-old could never sell the farm for $400/acre at the local elevator, but your 17 ½ year-old might. Must be cautious.	Legal person separate from its shareholder owners. Subchapter C corporations are just like large nonagricultural corporations. Subchapter S are formed by 25 or fewer related individuals who, in some states, together farm no more than 5000 acres. Definitions differ from one state to the next.
Life of business	Terminates at death, and linked directly to the life cycle of the operator. The wave motion due to biology is greatest in sole proprietorship. Even when one hands on to one's children, the likelihood that the farm will continue is least secure. Also, the amount handed down to heirs is the smallest under the sole proprietorship because of tax liability.	Agreed term (e.g., 6 weeks or 60 years), terminates at the death of a general partner but not a limited one. Also not affected if limited partner withdraws. General partnership may be oral, but it is best to have it in writing.	Perpetual or fixed term of years as expressed in articles of incorporation. The shareholders may vote liquidation at any time. It is wise not to get into a corporation as soon as you leave college to return to the farm; should generally try leases and partnerships first. The reason is you may get trapped into putting in most of the skilled management but have a minority stock, and never be able to dissolve or get out without selling your entire interest in the farm and causing a family rupture.

TABLE 17-20 (continued)

	Sole Proprietorship	Partnership	Corporation
Source of capital	Personal from retained earnings diverted out of NFI from family living (lower living standard) or based upon the current equity of the firm. Both bases of capital are likely to be smaller than under other business organizations and put a crimp on living standards.	Loans, earnings, and partner equity (see sources of capital, Chapter 13). The very purpose of limited partnerships is to attract capital from partners without management responsibility.	Contributions of the shareholders for stock and sale of additional stock (in the case of Subchapter S) to related parties (e.g. distant maiden aunt). Bonds may be issued to nonvoting members, an ideal way to treat off-farm heirs equitably without giving them management responsibility.
Management decisions	No conflicts but have to be a jack-of-all-trades. You may be the best mechanic and hog raiser but weak on managing row crops and forages. Thus, decisions will be quick and decisive, but the implementation function of management may be lacking.	General partners share the decisions, therefore, can form a partnership with someone who knows all about row and forage crops to complement your own skills. But may have conflicts of opinion and decision delays.	As in any corporation, the shareholders elect a board of directors who elect officers to manage the business. In Subchapter S, this may become inbred, and all these may be the same people: the husband and wife! More extreme version of the good and bad points of a partnership.
Limits on business activity	Proprietor's discretion can invest in feeder cattle or stock market if wants.	Partnership agreement, can specifically decide not to raise feeder cattle or invest in stock market.	Same as in partnership except more rigidly enforced through the articles of incorporation and the state incorporation law.
Organizational cost	None. No minimum records except income tax (including employee withholdings and workman's compensation, if you hire help). Just say to yourself in the mirror one day, "I'm going to form a sole proprietorship!"	Must keep separate bank account and accurate records. Even people of trustworthy character can have misunderstandings. General may be oral, limited must have written agreement. Reports must also be made to limited partners.	Organization, legal, and filing fees costly. Franchise tax varies by state. Federal stamp tax on stock transfers. Annual meetings and reports. Subchapter S must file tax report quarterly.

	(Sole Proprietorship)	Partnership	Corporation
Income taxes	All net farm income is taxable progressively, including the returns to labor and management (your "salary"). There is a 60% deduction for long-term capital gains.	Essentially same as sole proprietorship. Partnership pays no taxes, just file a 1065 form. Each partner fills out a 1040 form, as in sole proprietorship. Even salaries paid to general partners are taxable to recipients. But partnership ends if tax records show change of 50% or more in capital assets or profits during the past 12 months. Even death does not end partnership until after the last tax payment.	Shareholders pay taxes on the dividends paid to them and on salaries paid to them as employees of the corporation. These salaries are then deducted from the taxable income of the corporation, which files a separate tax return. Unlike the partnership and sole proprietorship, the corporation has no capital gains exemption but can offset capital gains with capital losses. There is a more favorable tax rate for corporations (see Chapter 16); can achieve optimal point by salaries to your children. The above applies to Subchapter C only; Subchapter S is taxed just like a partnership, except if NFI over $1 million, must use accrual accounting.
Liability	Total personal and private assets for the obligations of the firm. If you go bankrupt, all you get to keep is your house and 40 acres. Everything else, including your car and snowmobile (or bird dog), is taken.	Limited partner just liable to the extent of the money he has invested in the firm. But general partners are liable to the extent of first their partnership and then their private assets in the case of the partnership obligations (such as being sued for what the hired man did). But outside creditors of one partner cannot take the others' partnership shares. Limit for partnership obligations is all but house and 40 acres.	Advantage is that the shareholders are not liable for corporate obligations. The maximum liability of each equals his own investment in stock. If hired man kills someone, shareholders never run the danger of losing personal assets.

TABLE 17-20 (continued)

	Sole Proprietorship	Partnership	Corporation
Transfer of interest	Terminates proprietorship. Obviously, if you sell the farm, you terminate the farm firm life cycle.	If one partner sells his farm partnership to someone else he automatically dissolves the partnership; however, a new one may be formed if all the other partners agree.	Can transfer stocks or bonds without any effect on the business. If you are also one of the directors or officers, the corporation will simply elect someone else.
Intergenerational transfer	All resources and title must be transferred on the death of the proprietor. You may have joint tenancy or tenancy in common with your spouse, but sooner or later, all the property will be subject to probate and hence estate taxes.	Difficult to plan for continuity beyond the first generation. Can the survivors to continue. Still, each partner's property titles must be transferred and are subject to probate on death. Uniform Gifts to Minors Act ($10,000 tax-free gift from each parent to each child per year) cannot be used to hold partnership interests.	Only the deceased's stock is subject to probate, not the underlying assets. Fractionalized ownership makes possible easier transfer by passing stocks tax-free under the Uniform Gifts to Minors Act. Parents can give away up to 49% of the stock and still retain majority decision power. They can also pay themselves a salary, say $25,000/year, thus satisfying their retirement goals. Regular corporations have two classes of stock, which give further advantages in estate planning.

as a basis of comparison with the other forms with regard to the following points:

1. The nature of the entity
2. The life of the business
3. Sources of capital
4. Who makes management decisions
5. The limits on business activity
6. Organizational costs
7. Income tax considerations
8. Liability
9. The means of transfer of interest to new participants
10. Intergenerational transfer of interest from parents to children

Table 17-2 gives the major characteristics of sole proprietorships, partnerships, and corporations with respect to these points.

SUMMARY

There are five types of farm business organization: sole proprietorship, general and limited partnerships, and Subchapter C and Subchapter S corporations. As with risk management and the acquisition of farm resources, it is impossible to say which of these forms of farm business organization is best for all individuals. The point on the farm family life cycle, the goals and aspirations of parents, off-farm heirs, and on-farm heirs, and the relative forcefulness of the personalities of the individuals involved all contribute to the decision as to the optimal form for the farm business. Parents are concerned with retirement, a fair division of their wealth among their children, minimal estate settlement costs, and reducing burdens for the surviving spouse. Off-farm heirs are concerned with certainty of income, stability of assets, and some role in the management process. Finally, on-farm heirs are concerned with a clear title to the property, a fair annual income, and a major voice in management.

Farm business organizations may be compared with respect to ten different characteristics: their nature, life, liability, capital sources, managers, business limits, means of transfer of interest, intergenerational transfers, income tax considerations and organizational costs. Chapter 16 presented some information on income tax considerations. This chapter has been devoted to outlining how each of these factors differs from one type of farm business organization to the next.

TOPICS FOR DISCUSSION

1. What is the percentage of sole proprietorships, general and limited partnerships, Subchapter S and Subchapter C corporations, and professionally managed farms in your state? How do these figures differ from the national averages and why?

2. At what stage in the farm family life cycle is the farm with which you have the most experience? What goal conflicts, if any, do you see among the members of the farm family? Is the farm currently operated as a sole proprietorship, partnership, or corporation? Do you think its farm business organizational structure should be changed? If so, to what and why? If not, why?

3. What trends do you predict in the relative proportions of different types of farm business and organizational structure in the U.S.? Why do you predict such trends? Justify your answer in terms of the environmental, credit, commodity-support, and other current policies of federal and state governments. Do economies of size also figure in, and how?

SUGGESTED READINGS

Harl, Neil *Farm Estate and Business Planning.* Skokie, Illinois: Agri Business Publications, 1978.

Harl, Neil et al. *The Farm Corporation.* North Central Regional Extension Publication No. 11, 1974.

Harsh, S., L. Connor, and G. Schwab. *Managing the Farm Business.* Chapter 15. Englewood Cliffs, New Jersey: Prentice-Hall Inc., 1981.

Kay, R. D. *Farm Management: Planning, Control, and Implementation.* Chapter 11. New York: McGraw-Hill Book Company, 1981.

Osburn, D. and K. Schneeberger. *Modern Agriculture Management.* Chapter 14. Reston, Virginia: Reston Publishing, 1978.

Penson, J. and D. Lins. *Agricultural Finance.* Englewood Cliffs, New Jersey: Prentice-Hall Inc., 1980.

Thomas, K. and M. Boehlje. *Farm Business Arrangements: Which One For You?* North Central Regional Publication No. 50, 1976.

Index